PORTUGUESE BRAZIL
The King's Plantation

This is a volume in

STUDIES IN SOCIAL DISCONTINUITY

A complete list of titles in this series appears at the end of this volume.

PORTUGUESE BRAZIL

The King's Plantation

James Lang

Department of Sociology
and Center for Latin American Studies
Vanderbilt University
Nashville, Tennessee

ACADEMIC PRESS

A Subsidiary of Harcourt Brace Jovanovich, Publishers

New York   London   Toronto   Sydney   San Francisco

ACADEMIC PRESS, INC.
111 Fifth Avenue, New York, New York 10003

United Kingdom Edition published by
ACADEMIC PRESS, INC. (LONDON) LTD.
24/28 Oval Road, London NW1 7DX

Library of Congress Cataloging in Publication Data

Lang, James.
  Portuguese Brazil.

  (Studies in social discontinuity)
  Bibliography: p.
  Includes index.
    1. Brazil--Economic conditions.   2. Brazil--
Commerce--History.   3. Brazil--Politics and government.
4. Portugal--Colonies--America--Administration.
I. Title. II. Series.
HC187.L3355   380.1'0981   79–21005
ISBN 0–12–436480–2

PRINTED IN THE UNITED STATES OF AMERICA

79 80 81 82   9 8 7 6 5 4 3 2 1

Contents

III Empire by Trade: The Seventeenth Century

IV Brazil: The Golden Age, 1690–1750

V The Luso-Brazilian Empire, 1750–1821

VI Imperial Reorganization after 1750: The Spanish Indies, English America, Brazil

Preface

Do the Americas have a common history? When Herbert Eugene Bolton raised this question in his presidential address to the American Historical Society in 1933, he emphasized similar events that had shaped the "epic of greater America." European colonists, for example, had to adapt their parent cultures to the American environment; they found ways to exploit indigenous peoples and each region's natural resources. As the competition for empire intensified, each metropolis tried to monopolize colonial trade and consolidate its political control overseas. Between 1776 and 1826, revolts transformed most of Europe's colonies into independent states. We need not agree with Bolton's selection of events to be sympathetic to the task he defined: to view the history of the Americas in a comparative context that reaches beyond the boundaries of regions and states.[1]

One justification for such an approach is that it allows us to pursue a

---

[1] See Herbert Eugene Bolton, "The Epic of Greater America," *American Historical Review* 38 (1933), pp. 448–474. Reprinted in Lewis Hanke, ed., *Do the Americas Have a Common History? A Critique of the Bolton Theory* (New York, 1964), pp. 67–100.

particular problem through a greater range of variation. As Durkheim observed in his *Rules of Sociological Method*, "One cannot explain a social fact of any complexity except by following its complete development through all social species."[2] The social unit this study analyzes is a colonial system: Portugal's American empire. In a previous work I compared basic features of the colonial regimes that Spain and England established in the New World.[3] Both studies have a similar focus: how to explain the shifting commercial and political arrangements that linked American colonial empires to their respective mother countries.

Colonial status implied a dependent relationship between the parent states and their overseas American territories. The nature of this dependence, and the effect it had on the way colonists organized their economic activities, political institutions, and religious practices, varied significantly. For example, Wallerstein has stressed the common peripheral status that Brazil and the Spanish Indies shared with respect to Europe's world-economy.[4] But compared to Brazil's export economy, seventeenth-century Spanish America had a greater degree of self-sufficiency. By the time Spain's transatlantic trade collapsed in the 1630s, colonial dependence in Hispanic America was primarily political and spiritual, not economic. By contrast, Brazil supplied Portugal with agricultural exports on a scale Spanish America never duplicated—at least, not until the Bourbon reforms.[5]

Spain and Portugal shared a common Iberian heritage, and from 1580 to 1640, even the same king; thus, many studies focus on the similarities between Brazil and Spanish America. Approached piecemeal, such a perspective has validity. The town councils, the organization of the bureaucracy, the way taxes were collected, how the crown structured the religious hierarchy—all these aspects of Iberian colonization in the New World bear a generic resemblance and provide a sharp contrast to what happened in English America. But when Brazil is analyzed as part of a distinct colonial system, basic structural differences displace surface similarities.

---

[2] Emile Durkheim, *The Rules of Sociological Method*, edited and translated by Sarah A. Solovay, John H. Mueller, and George E. G. Gatlin (1938: New York, 1966), p. 139.

[3] James Lang, *Conquest and Commerce: Spain and England in the Americas* (New York, 1975).

[4] Immanuel Wallerstein, *The Modern World-System: Capitalist Agriculture and the Origins of the European World-Economy in the Sixteenth Century* (New York, 1974), pp. 67–129.

[5] In the nineteenth century, British capitalists consolidated Spanish America's underdevelopment; see also Celso Furtado, *Economic Development of Latin America*, translated by Suzette Macedo (Cambridge, Eng., 1976), pp. 14–41.

Viewed as an export economy that depended on slave labor, Brazil had more in common with English Virginia and Barbados than it ever did with Spanish Mexico and Peru. England, however, became significant to Europe's world-economy; it opened new markets for the Chesapeake's expanding tobacco crop. Portugal became a weak client-state and a poor salesman for Brazil's sugar; by the 1670s, competition from English Barbados had cut into Brazil's traditional sugar markets. Although significant parallels can be drawn between the export zones in Brazil and English America, the similarities should also be assessed within the context of each colonial regime. In Brazil, office-holding was an enterprise the king shared with Brazil's planters, merchants, and ranchers. Tax collection often solidified Luso-Brazilian interests. [6] In English America, strong assemblies controlled taxation and thus curbed the crown's patronage powers.

Portuguese Brazil: The King's Plantation examines the development of Brazil from initial settlement to independence. Brazil's early colonization is analyzed within the context of Portuguese expansion in the Atlantic islands, Africa, and Asia. The study argues that the way the Portuguese crown siphoned off the profits from the empire's trade retarded the growth of a strong merchant class. The most important role of the royal bureaucracy set up in Lisbon was to organize and tax trade. Brazil's early reliance on sugar exports fit neatly into this fiscal scheme; the bureaucracy collected taxes on the colony's sugar when it was unloaded in Lisbon. Consequently, the crown was able to profit from Brazil's development without establishing an elaborate overseas bureaucracy. Until the eighteenth century, when gold strikes drew the crown's officials into Brazil's interior, the bureaucracy was concentrated in a few colonial ports; even then, only Salvador, the colonial capital, had a strong royal government. By contrast, the Spanish colonies had the most comprehensive bureaucracy in the New World.

The Portuguese crown profited by taxing Brazil's trades in sugar, slaves, gold, and tobacco. Luso-Brazilian merchants, however, depended on foreign capital. The study shows how the Dutch in the seventeenth century, and the English in the eighteenth, gained more from Brazil's export economy than the Portuguese.

In 1750, Portugal's colonial problem had little to do with Brazil. The fleets were richer than ever; Luso-Brazilian trade was booming. But at the core of that prosperity was a simple exchange of Brazil's gold for England's textiles. The Portuguese were reduced to commission agents for British

---

[6] The Lusitanians were pre-Roman inhabitants of Portugal; hence, the prefix *Luso*.

merchants. The profits from Portugal's empire ended up in Lisbon. The problem was not how to change Brazil, but how to change Portugal. Pombal's reforms (1750–1777) challenged the old order in the metropolis, not Brazil's planters. By subsidizing a small group of Lisbon businessmen, Pombal created wealthy entrepreneurs with enough capital to finance important sectors of Luso-Brazilian trade.

The point of departure for analyzing Brazil's colonial history is the export economy. As long as Brazil did not produce its own version of import substitution, as long as Brazil could find new exports to pay its bills, then dependency paid dividends on both sides of the Atlantic. The way Pombal and his disciples diagnosed Portugal's situation counseled accommodation with Brazil's planters, not a collision course.

Between 1750 and 1780 Spain, England, and Portugal reorganized their American empires. The strategy that each state adopted suggests how different their empires were. The Spanish Bourbons reasserted Madrid's control over a bureaucracy that local interests had subverted. Parliament tried to impose new taxes in English America, despite the opposition of strong colonial assemblies. And Portugal wanted to dislodge the English from the dominant role they played in Luso-Brazilian trade. Chapter VI analyzes differences between Spanish, English, and Portuguese colonization. The thesis is that the significant variation between colonial systems can be explained by tracing the social implications behind the Spanish-American bureaucracy, English America's assemblies, and Brazil's export economy.

For Spain and England, the New World provided the first great stage for conquest and colonization. This was not true in the case of Portugal; between 1480 and 1580, overseas expansion focused on the Atlantic islands, Africa, and Asia—not America. How this previous experience shaped the kind of regime the Portuguese established in Brazil is the subject of Chapter I.

Acknowledgments

In helping me edit this and a previous manuscript, William Christian taught me that a pair of scissors is a writer's friend.

Alexandrino Severino guided me through my first shaky months of Portuguese. With a summer grant from the Center for Latin American Studies at Vanderbilt University (1975), I studied Portuguese in Bahia and visited Brazil's colonial cities.

When the research began, Eul-Soo Pang brought sources to my attention that I might otherwise have overlooked.

I completed the manuscript in 1977–1978, while a fellow at the Woodrow Wilson International Center for Scholars, and received concurrent support from the American Council of Learned Societies. I wish to thank Charles Tilly, Charles Gibson, Eric Wolf, Peter Marzahl, Ronald Spores, and Mayer Zald, who wrote letters on my behalf.

I presented the final chapter as a colloquium paper at the Wilson Center; the commentators on that occasion, Marcus Cunliffe and Emília Viotti da Costa, provided helpful suggestions. Charles Tilly, William Christian, and Emilio Willems read an earlier version of the manuscript, pointed out errors, and convinced me to make revisions.

This book relies on a wide range of secondary sources; my greatest debt is to other scholars. Consequently, I felt a special obligation to take footnotes seriously; I hope the reader will follow them carefully and give credit where credit is due.

I dedicate this book to Eliot Rosewater, Sissy Hankshaw, José Arcadio Buendía, and Riobaldo.

PORTUGUESE BRAZIL
The King's Plantation

I

Portuguese Expansion

The Portuguese reached Brazil on the way to India. To pick up favorable winds, Pedro Alvares Cabral sailed west from the Cape Verde Islands and reached the eastern shore of South America in 1500.[1] He dispatched a vessel to Portugal with the news and then continued the voyage to India. Later a few trading posts were set up on islands off the coast to barter with the inhabitants for *pau brasil* (brazilwood), a hardwood whose heavy logs yield a red dye. The area known as Brazil was so designated because of the initial importance of brazilwood.

Brazil had fallen to the Portuguese by the terms of the Treaty of Tordesillas (1494), which recognized the separate spheres of Portuguese and Spanish imperialism. According to the terms of the treaty, Spain was permitted to sail westward to regions 370 leagues (1184 miles) west of the

---

[1] The Portuguese may have reached Brazil earlier, as any India-bound ship sailing west from Cape Verde Islands can reach the Brazilian coast. See A. Da Silva Rego, *Portuguese Colonization in the Sixteenth Century: A Study of the Royal Ordinances* (Johannesburg, 1965), p. 31; and A. H. de Oliveira Marques, *History of Portugal*, 2 vols. (New York, 1972), vol. 1, p. 223.

Map 1 Portugal.

Cape Verde Islands and Portugal secured its claims to the African coast and to regions east of the Tordesillas line. Since the South American continent extends 40 degrees east of the Isthmus of Panama, a large portion of the South American landmass fell within the Portuguese sphere.

The rapid expansion of the Spanish empire depended upon silver and upon the control of an indigenous labor force reorganized by the Spaniards to meet the requirements of a European-style economy. While the Spaniards were taking over a skilled American peasantry, the Portuguese, in contrast, were setting up a string of trading stations that stretched from the African coast to India and the Far East. During most of the sixteenth century, Brazil was the backstage of the Portuguese empire, a pale reflection of Asian accomplishments.

Eventually, the king of Portugal promoted Brazilian colonization. In the 1530s he granted large tracts of land along the coast to several proprietors who agreed to set up towns and plantations at their own expense, but most of these ventures failed. In the end, state funds provided the capital for successful colonies. In 1549 the king financed the expedition of Tomé de Sousa, first governor-general of Brazil; Sousa founded the colony of Bahia on the Bay of All Saints, and Bahia's royal capital—Salvador.[2]

In 1560 Spanish Mexico City was a thriving inland metropolis of 100,000 inhabitants; it contained impressive government buildings, a university, monasteries, churches, and a flourishing printing press.[3] Portuguese Salvador, however, was still a struggling coastal settlement vulnerable to Indian raids and attacks from the French, who disputed Portugal's claim to Brazil. For while the Spanish government concentrated its imperial energies in America, the Portuguese crown was organizing its monopoly on the Asian spice trade. Brazil was only a small part of a larger commercial enterprise that encompassed Portugal, Africa, and India.

ROYAL GOVERNMENT IN PORTUGAL

Feudalism in Portugal diverged sharply from patterns in Western Europe, but dispersed political authority was still one of its essential characteristics. Many of the king's vassals administered justice and col-

---

[2] Contemporaries referred to both the captaincy and to its capital as Bahia. To avoid confusion, I have used the city's official name, Salvador.

[3] Stuart B. Schwartz, "Cities of Empire: Mexico and Bahia in the Sixteenth Century," *Journal of Inter-American Studies* 11 (1969), pp. 616–637.

lected local taxes; they received labor services from the peasantry and a portion of surplus production. Wealth was essentially a corollary of land-holding. The large estates and jurisdictional authority of the king's vassals checked, even challenged, royal sovereignty.

During the High Middle Ages the strength of the Portuguese monarchy depended on the extent and productivity of crown lands. But the royal patrimony was always in danger of depletion. The king granted lands in feudal form to reward his favorite vassals. Land parceled out by the crown supported the Church, the military orders, and princes of the royal blood. Second and third sons, generously endowed with lands by their royal father, created rival dynasties that jeopardized the basis of the crown's authority. The concentration and dispersal of crown lands thus created a cycle of strong kings alternating with weak ones.[4]

Overseas expansion gave the king a chance to reshape domestic politics to his own advantage. The creation of a commercial empire under the king's aegis strengthened his position with the nobility and the *Cortes*, an assembly that represented the towns. Since the king monopolized trade with the lands newly discovered by royal navigators, he had sources of income and patronage to use against his rivals. Afonso V (1438–1481), always in need of funds, convened the Cortes semiannually to request tax increases; between 1502 and 1544, when trade had increased, his wealthy successors summoned it only three times.[5] Backed by windfall profits, the crown extended its control over domestic administration. The lands formerly parceled out to the military orders were added to the royal patrimony. The king curtailed municipal autonomy and feudal jurisdictions. The *juiz de fóra* (outside judge), appointed and paid by the crown, gradually replaced the *juiz ordinário* (local judge) elected by the town councils; by 1580 the king's men had replaced local judges in 50 of Portugal's urban centers. To further bolster the crown's authority, Portugal was divided into six provinces and 26 districts, each called a *correção*. The king's district official, the *corregidor*, enforced the crown's laws, rendered justice, supervised public works, and reviewed municipal elections. Although the correção predated the sixteenth century, it was not until the Manueline Code (1512–1521) provided a uniform set of laws to apply to towns and cities that the corregidor played an important role in local administration.[6]

---

[4] Oliveira Marques, *History of Portugal*, vol. 1, pp. 86–89, 118–132; also see António Sérgio, *Breve interpretação da história de Portugal* (Lisbon, 1972), pp. 13–35.

[5] Oliveira Marques, *History of Portugal*, vol. 1, p. 189.

[6] On royal centralization, see Stuart B. Schwartz, *Sovereignty and Society in Colonial Brazil: The High Court of Bahia and Its Judges, 1609–1751* (Berkeley, 1973), pp. 5–9, 11; Oliveira Marques, *History of Portugal*, vol. 1, pp. 181, 187–189; and Stanley G. Payne, *A History of Spain and Portugal*, 2 vols. (Madison, Wisconsin, 1973), vol. 1, pp. 225–227.

Much as the state imposed common weights and measures on the standards of individual communities, a more centralized royal government displaced local authorities. The degree of consolidation achieved was striking: comprehensive political subdivisions and a fairly uniform set of offices replaced the intricate mosaic of earlier periods. Still, the corporate structure of medieval society remained strong, since craft guilds, towns, the Church, and the nobility retained many of their ancient rights. Corporate groups continued to control local resources, and they provided an ordered context for everyday life. Although significantly strengthened, royal government was strongest in the towns and cities, especially the great ports; for while the king was Portugal's greatest landlord, he was also the realm's greatest merchant.

To increase their incomes, fifteenth-century kings had to find new ways to tax domestic production; in this they faced the opposition of powerful corporate groups that jealously guarded their privileges and purses. But in Portugal, where the king played a major role in organizing overseas trade, commercial expansion provided revenue unencumbered by the traditional arrangements that structured agricultural production and local industries. Financially, the greatest payoff came from creating new procedures to tax and license trade; the profits helped pay for the state's enlarged domestic bureaucracy. Running a trading system was easier and less dangerous than attacking the rights of the Church, the nobility, and the towns. This new situation is reflected in the radically different postures João II (1481–1495) and Manuel I (1495–1521) assumed toward the great feudal nobility.[7]

Afonso V had kept the nobility satisfied by generously distributing crown lands. To recover his shattered inheritance, João II reversed his father's policies; he attacked feudal rights and reduced royal grants. In retaliation, the upper nobility schemed against the throne, but the king managed to thwart the plot hatched by the rival Braganza dynasty. Within a few years, João II had killed or exiled most of the conspirators and taken over their estates.[8] At the same time, the king reinforced his position by expanding the bureaucracy; for once, the crown's increased authority endured, although not because the upper nobility was destroyed. Manuel I restored the estates and privileges of the Braganzas and other noble families banished by his predecessor. And he could afford to

---

[7] On the general crisis the state faced during the High Middle Ages, see Immanuel Wallerstein, *The Modern World-System* (New York, 1974), pp. 15–54. That Portugal's kings had engaged in trade for centuries is stressed in Bailey W. Diffie and George D. Winius, *Foundations of the Portuguese Empire, 1415–1580* (Minneapolis, Minnesota, 1977), pp. 16–17, 21–22, 37–41.

[8] See Oliveira Marques, *History of Portugal*, vol. 1, pp. 209–212; and Christopher Bell, *Portugal and the Quest for the Indies* (New York, 1974), pp. 135–140.

do so. In 1515 the crown drew 68% of its revenues from overseas trade.[9] Following the example of the king, who was a merchant and monopolist, the nobles invested in the empire's trade and shipping, thereby earning a share of the profits.[10] The ruinous warfare between the crown and the nobility over a fixed resource—land—had ended. A chastened nobility, interested in trade and patronage, found itself more dependent on the crown than ever before.

Portugal's nobles participated in commercial expansion to a greater extent than was characteristic of other European states.[11] This development was consistent with the comparatively peaceful relationship that had existed between the king and his vassals since the consolidation of the House of Aviz under John I (1383–1433). Viewed relative to the War of the Roses in England, the Hundred Years War in France, or the warfare that plagued Castile before the reign of Ferdinand and Isabella, Portugal enjoyed considerable political stability during the fifteenth century. Freed from civil strife at home, Portuguese merchants and navigators supported by powerful patrons such as Prince Henry the Navigator (1394–1460) or the king, entered the trades with Africa and the Far East before any of their European rivals.

PORTUGAL'S SEABORNE EMPIRE

In 1433 King Duarte (1433–1438) granted the Madeira archipelago to his brother, Prince Henry the Navigator. A century later, João III (1521–1557) granted tracts of land in America to 12 proprietors. Brazil provided the last arena for Portuguese expansion. For Spain, America formed the core of a land-based empire, whereas for Portugal, Brazil was a junior partner in a commercial system organized around the spice fleets. The Portuguese were not conquerors so much as they were traders. They did not really establish an empire anywhere in Africa or Asia, if by an empire we mean a political system consisting of wide, relatively centralized territories.[12] The traffic in gold, slaves, and spices, and the way these trades were organized, held the Portuguese "empire" together, not bu-

---

[9] Vitorino Magalhâes Godinho, "Finanças públicas e estrutura do estado," *Dicionário*, vol. 3, p. 33.

[10] Oliveira Marques, *History of Portugal*, vol. 1, pp. 180–181; and Vitorino Magalhães Godinho, "Complexo histórico-geográfico," in Dicionário de história do Portugal, ed. Joel Serrão, 6 vols. (Lisbon, 1975), vol. 2, p. 133.

[11] See Payne, *History of Spain and Portugal*, vol. 1, p. 224.

[12] See S. N. Eisenstadt, "Empires," in ed. David L. Sills *International Encyclopedia of the Social Sciences*, 17 vols. (New York, 1968), vol. 5, pp. 41–49.

reaucratic institutions. Thus, when the colonization of Brazil began in the 1530s, it occurred within a larger trading system whose features were already well defined.

THE ATLANTIC ISLANDS

Due south of Portugal, the Moroccan coast stretches south and west toward the Canary Islands. Madeira and the Azores are located to the north and west of the Canaries. Together these lands form the perimeter of a vast southern sea whose limits were well-known to Portuguese and Castilian navigators in the 1430s.[13] The only inhabited islands, the Canaries, were a source of rivalry between Castile and Portugal for over half a century. The Treaty of Alcáçovas (1479) recognized Castilian claims to the Canaries and Portuguese sovereignty in Madeira and the Azores. Expansion south of the Canaries was acknowledged to be a Portuguese monopoly.

Madeira

Madeira, the first archipelago settled by the Portuguese, was granted to Prince Henry as a life-time fief. As proprietor, Prince Henry divided the islands into a series of captaincies, ceding to each captain extensive control over the administration of justice and the distribution of land to settlers.[14] Each captain held a monopoly over the sale of salt and the construction of mills and communal ovens. Although uninhabited, the islands were rich in wood, dyes, and fish. Settlement was underway by the 1440s, and wheat was exported. But sugar cane, brought to Madeira from the Algarve in southern Portugal, soon became the most important export.[15] Eventually, the concentration on sugar meant that textiles, hardware, meat, salt, and even wheat had to be imported. Production reached 20,000 *arrobas* by 1470 (1 arroba = 32 lbs.) and 80,000 by the 1490s. Small and medium-sized farms, whose yields rarely exceeded 500 arrobas annually, predominated. By 1500, slaves made up a significant part of the labor force: they numbered about 2000 in a population of

---

[13] See Bailey W. Diffie, *Prelude to Empire: Portugal's Overseas Expansion before Henry the Navigator* (Lincoln, Nebraska, 1960).

[14] On the establishment of the captaincies, see Charles Verlinden, *The Beginnings of Modern Colonization* (Ithaca, New York, 1970). The text of a typical grant is reprinted in Diffie and Winius, *Portuguese Empire*, pp. 303–304.

[15] Virgínia Rau and Jorge de Macedo, *O açúcar da Madeira nos fins do século XV* (Funchal, 1962), p. 11. The sugar industry branched out from the Eastern Mediterranean to Sicily, Spain, Portugal, and the Atlantic Islands: see Verlinden, *Modern Colonization*, pp. 20–24.

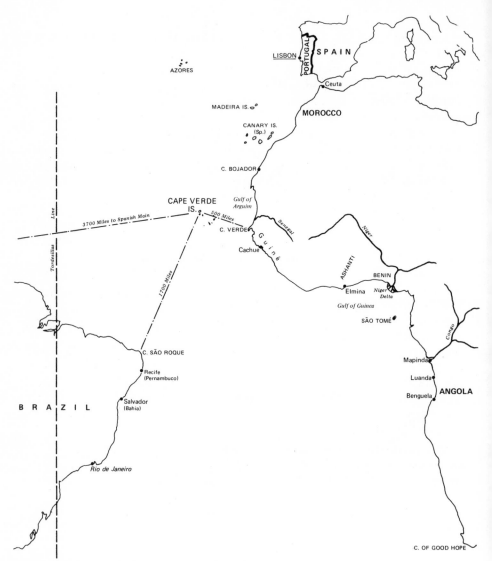

Map 2 Portuguese expansion: the Atlantic, 1580.

15,000 to 18,000.[16] Peak harvests during the early sixteenth century produced between 120,000 and 200,000 arrobas, refined by 100 small sugar mills.[17] After 1550 soil exhaustion and competition from São Tomé and Brazil undermined the industry. Gradually vine cultivation was introduced, and during the seventeenth century wine became the chief export.[18]

Madeira was a huge commercial center for its day. Sugar was packed and shipped to markets in Portugal, the Mediterranean, and northern Europe by way of the royal factory (feitoria) at Antwerp. Aristocratic proprietors and the king, after he resumed sovereignty over the islands, were the greatest sugar merchants. A certain percentage of production, varying from one-tenth to one-fifth, was an integral part of the crown's regalia. Including customs duties and sales taxes, the king's share was one-fourth to one-third of each sugar crop.[19] As the industry prospered, the crown took a greater interest in organizing sales.

The Madeira sugar trade with Portugal was the preserve of the realm's smaller merchants. Exporting sugar abroad, however, required a special license that had to be purchased from the king. Only wealthy merchants had enough capital to buy these contracts, which at times the king sold to Italian traders rather than to his own subjects. At first all sugar had to pass through Lisbon, but when production began to outpace domestic consumption, the king allowed sugar exports from Madeira directly to foreign markets. To dispose of its own sugar, the crown worked out special contracts. In 1498 the king had some 40,000 arrobas of sugar to market: he sent 20,000 to the royal factory at Antwerp; 3000 to England; 15,000 to Venice; and 2000 to Rome.[20]

The contract business supervised by the treasury was an important addition to the crown's patronage system. Since nobles and bureaucrats often invested in trade, doling out contracts was a way for the king to reward faithful vassals and officials. Contracts could even be used to cancel out the king's debts. In 1524 João III sold 3000 arrobas of sugar to a nobleman whose father-in-law, a merchant, had loaned money to the crown. Of the amount due, a portion was discounted to pay off the loan.[21]

[16] Joel Serrão, "Madeira," Dictionário, vol. 4, p. 129.

[17] Vitorino Magalhães Godinho, Os descobrimentos e a economia mundial, 2 vols. (Lisbon, 1963–1965), vol. 2, pp. 427–431; Rau and Macedo, Açúcar da Madeira, pp. 12–22.

[18] Serrão, "Madeira," pp. 124–130; and Oliveira Marques, History of Portugal, vol. 1, pp. 151–154, 369–370.

[19] Godinho, Descobrimentos, vol. 2, p. 442.

[20] Ibid., pp. 444, 437–450. On the role of Italian merchants in Portugal's trade, see also Verlinden, Modern Colonization, pp. 98–112.

[21] Godinho, Descobrimentos, vol. 2, p. 446.

As Portugal's overseas trade branched out, so did the king's network of factories and employees. A factory was a commercial establishment where merchandise was purchased, sold, and stored under the watchful eye of the factor (*feitor*), an official appointed and paid by the king. At an important center like Antwerp, the factor was a consul of sorts, who looked after Portugal's commercial interests; in particular, he supervised the king's financial transactions, making purchases and selling commodities on his patron's behalf. Where trade was less developed, as in Brazil, the factories were simple trading stations where a few goods were bartered. In Brazil, the merchants who leased the brazilwood concession from the crown ran the factories.[22]

The Azores

Like Madeira, the Azores were granted to Prince Henry.[23] Settlement did not begin until the 1460s, however. The major exports were wheat and woad, a plant of the mustard family whose leaves yield a blue dye. Wheat was the primary export during the fifteenth century, but by the 1570s woad predominated: over 3000 tons by the 1590s.[24] Unlike Madeira, in the Azores sugar production was never very significant, and slave labor did not make up a significant portion of the labor force. Even in Madeira, slaves supplemented but did not replace Portuguese workers. One reason for this was that the islands had drawn their labor force from Portugal before the slave trade became well-established. When Madeira turned to sugar production during the 1470s, there were already enough workers available. Besides, if Madeira's planters wanted to buy slaves, they had to compete with Lisbon, the principal slave market.

The Cape Verde Islands and São Tomé

The colonization of the uninhabited Cape Verde Islands (due west of Senegal) and São Tomé (in the Gulf of Guinea) was directly related to the slave trade, however. The Cape Verde Islands were granted to the king's brother, Prince Fernando, who introduced the captaincy system soon thereafter. But settlement was difficult since the new lands were not suited to commercial agriculture. Significantly, one of the privileges granted to settlers in 1466 was the right to trade freely in African slaves.

---

[22] See Virgínia Rau, "Feitores e feitorias: instrumentos do comércio internacional Português no século XVI," *Broteria* 81 (1965), pp. 458–478; and Diffie and Winius, *Portuguese Empire*, pp. 313–317.

[23] On the early history of the Azores, see Francisco Carriero da Costa "Açores," *Dicionário*, vol. 1, pp. 18–20; Verlinden, *Modern Colonization*, pp. 220–240; and Oliveira Marques, *History of Portugal*, vol. 1, pp. 239–240, 370–372.

[24] Oliveira Marques, *History of Portugal*, vol. 1, p. 371.

The islands served as a port of call for Portuguese expeditions along the African coast, but mainly they developed as a center for the slave trade.[25]

In São Tomé, colonization began in the 1490s under the direction of captains appointed by the king.[26] Sugar, cultivated by slaves that the Portuguese brought from their African trading stations, quickly became the chief export. The king had anticipated such a development; an executive order issued in 1485 stipulated that one-fourth the island's sugar crop belonged to the crown. In 1517 this share was 25,000 arrobas, so total production was probably around 100,000. The king was an active partner in the sugar business; he constructed mills with his own capital and leased them for 5000 arrobas annually. In 1528 the king's factor on the island was shipping his master's sugar directly to the royal factory at Antwerp. At mid-century the island of São Tomé had 60 mills producing a total of 150,000 arrobas of sugar.[27] São Tomé also benefitted from its proximity to the slave region of the Guinea coast; it served as a port of call for the slave trade in the South Atlantic. Slaves accounted for one-half the population in 1500 and 75% by the end of the century. Some planters had as many as 200 slaves.[28]

The proprietors and captains who organized the settlement of the Atlantic Islands did so at their own expense, and held seignorial jurisdiction over the lands they received. The crown, however, was cautious. Prince Henry's lordship terminated at his death, although the captaincies he established in Madeira and the Azores were hereditary. By the 1480s the crown was a more jealous guardian of its prerogatives. João II, for example, appointed his own captains to undertake the settlement of São Tomé. In 1520 the crown was sending its corregedores to most of the islands to supervise the captains and the town councils.[29] As the scope and frequency of Portuguese voyages in the South Atlantic increased, so did the degree of royal supervision. This trend, evident in the Atlantic Islands, can be seen in the development of the African trades.

AFRICA

Portuguese navigation along the African coast coincided with the constant warfare between Portuguese Christians and the Moors in North Africa. In 1415 the Portuguese established a military base in Morocco at

---

[25] Ibid., pp. 240–242, 372–373; and Verlinden, *Modern Colonization*, pp. 161–180.

[26] Oliveira Marques, *History of Portugal*, vol. 1, pp. 242–243, 374–376.

[27] Godinho, *Descobrimentos*, vol. 2, pp. 452–454.

[28] Ibid., pp. 543, 455.

[29] Schwartz, *Sovereignty and Society*, pp. 18–19.

Ceuta. From Ceuta and ports in the Algarve, such as Lagos and Faro, the Portuguese launched their attacks along the coast.[30] Contacts ranged from peaceful trade to piracy. The Portuguese raided Moroccan towns, seized merchandise, and sold captives into slavery. The king exercised a kind of monopoly over warfare in the region that the papacy officially recognized.[31] During the first half of the fifteenth century, trade, voyages of discovery, and warfare against Islam were complementary activities. This is evident in the career of Prince Henry the Navigator. Although he sponsored the early voyages of discovery, he was equally a crusader. He was governor of the Algarve and the military stronghold at Ceuta; his mastership of the Order of Christ placed a permanent military force at his command. There was hardly a more persistent advocate of the conquest of Morocco than Prince Henry. Only gradually did the Portuguese realize that in trying to outflank Islam in Morocco they had discovered new lands. In the early 1440s when the Portuguese first reached the Gulf of Arguim (Mauritania), they applied the same standards to Saharan Africans that they did to Moroccan Infidels: they raided villages and took prisoners to be sold as slaves. But the Portuguese soon decided regular trade was better for the slave business than sporadic raids, and in 1450 they set up a trading station on the island of Arguim off the coast.[32]

The Slave Trade

Initially, African trade and privateering were open to all Portuguese subjects. But in 1443 the newly recognized potential of African trade led to tighter control. The regent, Prince Pedro, granted a monopoly on the African trade south of Cape Bojador to Prince Henry. Trade now required a special license, and a percentage of the profits went to the crown's favorite monopolist. Later, Prince Henry leased the business to a commercial company for 10 years. After Prince Henry's death in 1460, the crown reassumed control. King Afonso V completed the construction of a fortress on Arguim and granted the trading concession to his son and heir Prince Dom João (1469). The prince, in turn, rented out his monopoly to a wealthy Lisbon merchant, Fernão Gomes. By then the

---

[30] The Algarve is the southernmost province of Portugal, skirting both the Mediterranean and the Atlantic.

[31] Silva Rego, *Portuguese Colonization*, pp. 16–18.

[32] Basil Davidson, *The African Slave Trade* (Boston, 1961), pp. 33–40. On the relationship between the war against Islam, expansion, and slavery, see A. J. R. Russell-Wood, "Iberian Expansion and the Issue of Black Slavery: Changing Portuguese Attitudes, 1440–1770," *American Historical Review* 83 (1978), pp. 22–33. On Prince Henry, see Diffie and Winius, *Portuguese Empire*, pp. 113–122; Oliveira Marques, *History of Portugal*, pp. 142–145.

Portuguese had explored the African coastline from the Gulf of Arguim to Sierra Leone, a region they called Guiné. After assuming the throne in 1481, João II farmed out the new branches of the African trade, granting licenses on an individual basis and on varying terms.[33]

Between 1450 and 1505, the Portuguese established at least 14 major trading stations in Guiné and purchased an estimated 140,000 to 170,000 slaves.[34] Exactly who had the right to participate in the trade was a confusing affair because the crown approved so many different arrangements. Trade along each river, for example, was often rented out jointly or as a separate concession. Besides the contractors, who paid the crown a percentage, the king sometimes invested his own capital in ships and merchandise to rake in more of the profits.

Slaves from Guiné were carried to the Cape Verde Islands and then reexported to Portugal. The Cape Verdeans lobbied to maintain the island of Santiago as an entrepôt for the trade. For the islanders, the slave trade was a major source of employment. Familiar with the coast and African languages, they often served as intermediaries, even for unlicensed traders. These freelance activities of the Cape Verdeans, however, threatened the king's monopoly. In 1518 the crown reduced Santiago's role in the slave traffic, but the islanders continued to infest the Guinean coast, selling slaves to all comers.[35]

The Portuguese traded a wide variety of goods in exchange for slaves: wheat and horses (especially along the Saharan littoral), brass rings and bowls, trinkets, beads, blankets, cloaks, tunics, scarves, red and blue cloth, and embroideries.[36] Until Brazil's sugar planters switched from Indian to slave labor, most slaves were shipped to Portugal—at least 300,000 during the sixteenth century. In Lisbon and the Algarve, slaves made up 10% of the population. Slaves were also reexported to Castille, especially Seville, the entrepôt for Spain's American trade. The king defended Lisbon's trade with Seville because it kept prices and profits high by preventing an oversupply of slaves in Portugal.[37]

Trading Slaves for Gold

As the Portuguese advanced down the African coast, they expanded their operations. The fortress of São Jorge da Mina (Elmina), built at the king's expense in 1482, dominated the region between present-day Liberia

---

[33] Godinho, *Descobrimentos*, vol. 2, pp. 522–524.

[34] Ibid., pp. 527–530. These and other figures on the slave trade should be treated as rough estimates.

[35] See Walter Rodney, A *History of the Upper Guinea Coast 1545–1800* (Oxford, 1970), pp. 71–94.

[36] Godinho, *Descobrimentos*, p. 527.

[37] Ibid., pp. 539–543, 548–549; also Russell-Wood, "Iberian Expansion," pp. 16–20.

and Ghana. Gold rather than slaves made trade with the Mina coast attractive. The crown did not lease the gold trade to private individuals or companies. Instead the king's agents supervised the gold business and administered the fortress and its environs. As part of their salary, they had the right to purchase gold up to an amount specified in their orders. From 1504 to 1521, some 410 kilos of gold valued at more than 100,000 *cruzados* reached Lisbon each year.[38]

The Portuguese dealt with intermediaries; they did not control the source of gold, which was the Kingdom of Ashanti. During the 1490s the Portuguese opened new branches in the slave business. In the Niger Delta (Gulf of Guinea), where the Kingdom of Benin was consolidating its power over neighboring chiefdoms, the Portuguese purchased prisoners of war and sent them as slaves to São Jorge da Mina. The captives were purchased in turn by the king's factors at Mina and then resold for gold to the Ashanti, who used slaves as miners and carriers. In addition, the Portuguese exchanged woolens, linen cloth, and artifacts of brass and copper for gold. Much of the merchandise used in African trade, especially textiles and hardware, was of English, French, Flemish, and Castilian origin.[39]

Bartering slaves and merchandise for Ashanti gold did not originate with the Portuguese. Regular caravans already linked West African kingdoms to the Islamic world of North Africa. But the Portuguese provided a greater abundance of desirable goods than did other kingdoms. Gradually trade was rerouted from the interior, creating a new role in the slave trade for African societies nearer the coast.[40]

How the slave trade altered the social organization of African kingdoms has yet to be thoroughly studied.[41] The Portuguese, however, did not control their African trading partners. Factories were established by agreement, and the Portuguese were prevented from trading directly with the interior.[42] There was a balance of power between Europeans and the

---

[38] Godinho, *Descobrimentos*, vol. 1, pp. 192–193, 186–193. Gold imports fell considerably over the next decade, revived in the 1530s, and declined again after 1544. The cruzado was Portugal's monetary unit; its value was fixed (1517) at 400 *réis*.

[39] Ibid., p. 187; also Charles R. Boxer, *The Portuguese Seaborne Empire: 1415–1825* (New York, 1969), p. 29.

[40] Godinho, *Descobrimentos*, vol. 1, p. 193.

[41] For a later period see Philip D. Curtin, *Economic Change in Pre-colonial Africa: Senegambia in the Era of the Slave Trade* (Madison, Wisconsin, 1975).

[42] E. E. Rich, "Colonial Settlement and Its Labor Problems." In *The Economy of Expanding Europe in the Sixteenth and Seventeenth Centuries*, Cambridge Economic History of Europe, vol. 4 eds. E. E. Rich and C. H. Wilson (Cambridge, Eng., 1967), pp. 308–311.

densely populated, agrarian kingdoms of West African that precluded systematic colonization.[43]

Growth of the Slave Trade

Portugal established its most important slave-trading ports along the Congolese–Angolan coast. The region was divided into a series of small tributary states that made up a loosely organized kingdom. When the Congolese king, Afonso I (1506–1543), converted to Christianity and introduced the new religion into his realm. The Portuguese crown, in recognition of the kingdom's special religious status, restricted the trade to a single factory set up at Mapinda. But São Tomé's sugar industry created a lucrative market for slaves, and planters and governors carried on a flourishing contraband traffic that bypassed Mapinda's customs house. After Afonso's death, the Portuguese intervened in struggles between the new king and his vassal states. As Portugal's influence spread, so did the Angolan slave trade. For subsequently, from their bases at Luanda and Benguela, the Portuguese sent slaves to Brazil and the Spanish Indies.[44]

The slave trades were divided into contract zones such as Arguim, the Guinea rivers, the Niger Delta, and São Tomé–Angola. Each region was ceded to a single contractor who usually subleased his monopoly to a host of smaller traders. Contracts did not go exclusively to the Portuguese. The Florentine merchant Bartholomew Marchione, for example, held the contract for the Niger Delta (mid-1480s) and later for the Guinea rivers (1490–1492) at an annual rent of 40,000 cruzados. The slave trade was not just a business for merchants, however. The king was a slave trader and so were high dignitaries of the state. Judges, governors, royal councilors, the crown's factors, and the ecclesiastical hierarchy all participated, either by backing merchant contractors, or by obtaining permission from the crown to buy and sell a specified number of slaves.[45]

New state institutions were formed to watch over the king's interests in trade. In the 1460s the crown set up an agency in Lisbon, the House of Guiné (*Casa da Guiné*), to organize and supervise the crown's African

---

[43] The Dutch who settled along the Cape of Good Hope are an exception. However, the region was sparsely settled by the Hottentots, who lived in small, nomadic groups, and combined hunting and gathering with cattle herding. The Dutch displaced them with little difficulty.

[44] Godinho, *Descobrimentos*, vol. 2, p. 535. For the kingdom of the Congo, see Davidson, *African Slave Trade*, pp. 117–162; also Boxer, *Portuguese Seaborne Empire*, pp. 97–103.

[45] Godinho, *Descobrimentos*, vol. 2, pp. 240, 573–576. Throughout the study, conversions from réis to cruzados are made at the rate of 400 réis = 1 cruzado.

trades. The House of Guiné served as a royal warehouse, collecting the crown's share of slaves as stipulated in the various contracts and settling disputes over commerce and navigation.[46] With the opening of the Mina gold trade in the 1480s, the functions of the House of Guiné expanded: it received the gold sent from São Jorge and stored the assorted European goods used in the trade.[47] By then the slave trade was so important that a distinct agency, the House of Slaves (*Casa dos Escravos*), received the captives brought to Lisbon on the king's account and those handed over by private merchants in fulfillment of their contracts.[48]

The crown's network of factors and royal officials followed Portuguese merchants to the Atlantic Islands and the African coast. But overall administration followed no single pattern since Portuguese settlements ranged from small trading posts to agricultural colonies. The crown had to organize both a commercial system, whose diverse trades it exploited directly or through contracts, and a series of permanent settlements run by Portuguese captains and proprietors.

BUREAUCRACY VERSUS TRADE: ASIAN SPICES

Cortés built Mexico City on the site of the once-great Aztec capital Tenochtitlán, where razed Aztec temples became foundations for the cathedral and the massive government buildings that dominated the plaza. The construction of Mexico City, the capital of Spain's first American viceroyalty, heralded the victory of the conquistadors over the densely populated, agrarian society of the Aztecs. The pantheon of Catholic Spain replaced the profane deities of Aztec ritual.

The conquest of Mexico redefined the relationship between Spain and America. To tap America's wealth, Spain set up the most comprehensive bureaucracy in the New World. How else could it prevent the presumptuous conquistadors from becoming too powerful? How else could it protect the Indians, supervise a diverse agricultural economy, and tax silver production? While Spain faced the task of consolidating a territorial empire, Portugal ran a trading system. Between 1498 and 1515 the Portuguese seized a major share in the Asian spice trade. The sale of spices in Europe, the organization of factories and warehouses, the provisioning of

---

[46] Maria Emília Cordeiro Ferreira, "Mina, Casa da," *Dicionário*, vol. 4, pp. 300–302.

[47] Its name was changed to the Mine House (*Casa da Mina*).

[48] Godinho, *Descobrimentos*, vol. 2, p. 541.

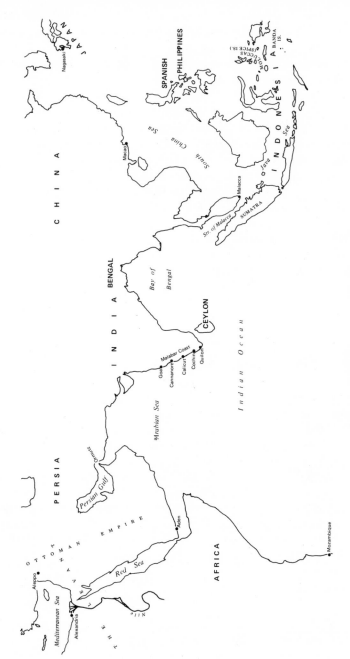

Map 3 Portuguese expansion: Asia, 1550.

the India fleet, and the enforcement of commercial monopolies—such were the concerns of the Portuguese king in his Asian empire. To control the spice trade, the king's commander in Asia, Alfonso de Albuquerque (1509–1515), built fortresses, fought naval battles, and conquered key commercial cities. The center of Portugal's sixteenth-century empire was the splendid Indian port of Goa: the Portuguese prevailed upon the sea, not upon the land.

Bringing spices to Lisbon was the ultimate justification for the factories and fortresses maintained in Asia at the king's expense. Profits were unprecedented. Spices accounted for 27% of all royal revenues in 1506. By 1518 the spice trade made up 39% of total state revenues—more than the combined total of all other overseas trades, and more than the value of the domestic revenues collected in Portugal.[49] Success in Asia was dramatically and rapidly achieved. By combining force and diplomacy, the Portuguese became new intermediaries in an on-going system of production and distribution.

A flourishing monsoon trading system had already existed before Vasco da Gama's voyage of 1498. Pepper, ginger, clove, cinnamon, mace, and nutmeg were the principal spices traded.[50] Of these, only pepper was an item of mass consumption. The rest were luxury products. Pepper was produced chiefly along India's Malabar coast and supplied to markets in the Levant. Arab merchants brought Malabar pepper to the great spice markets at Ormuts (by the entrance to the Persian Gulf) and Aden (at the mouth of the Red Sea). From these centers, pepper reached Mediterranean markets at Aleppo, Syria and Alexandria, Egypt, where, in turn, Venetian merchants purchased pepper for distribution in Europe. Ceylon produced the best grades of cinnamon. Ginger grew in many regions, but that of Malabar and Bengala, India was especially valued. Several small islands in the Indonesian archipelago produced almost all the mace, nutmegs, and cloves: mace and nutmeg came from the Banda Islands, while the Moluccas (Ambonia, Ternate, and Tidore) produced cloves. The crossroads for this extensive east–west seaborne spice trade was the port of Malacca, which stood at the gateway between the Indian

---

[49] Godinho, "Finanças públicas," p. 33. These estimates are derived by computations from the table.

[50] The discussion of the spice trade is based on the following sources: Fernand Braudel, *The Mediterranean and the Mediterranean World in the Age of Philip II*, trans. Siân Reynolds. 2 vols. (New York, 1972–1973), vol. 1, pp. 543–570; Boxer, *Portuguese Seaborne Empire*, pp. 39–64; Diffie and Winius, *Portuguese Empire*, pp. 220–271; Godinho, *Descobrimentos*, vol. 1, pp. 471–534, vol. 2, pp. 33–100; idem, "Especiarias," *Dicionário*, vol. 2, pp. 443–448; E. L. J. Coornaert, "Economic Institutions and the New World (The State Institutions)," and G. B. Masefield, "Crops and Livestock (The Spice Trade)." In *The Economy of Expanding Europe*, pp. 229–240, 288–289; and Maria Emília Cordeiro Ferreira, "India, Casa da," *Dicionário*, vol. 3, pp. 281–289.

Ocean and the Java Sea. Indian merchants carried pepper, cinnamon, ginger, and cotton textiles to Malacca and loaded nutmegs, cloves, and mace for the return voyage. The spice trade in Malacca even attracted Chinese merchants.

Initially, the Portuguese participated in the spice trade on equal terms with Asian merchants. But Manuel I devised a more ambitious geopolitical strategy; its objective was to control the Indian Ocean and Asian trade. Alfonso de Albuquerque, captain-general of the fleet, seized Goa (1510), a magnificent port from which the Portuguese could dominate the Malabar pepper trade; Malacca (1511); and Ormuts (1515). All were key points in the distribution system. The Portuguese thus cut off overland traffic from its sources of supply in an attempt to reroute the European spice trade around the Cape of Good Hope.

Spices sold by the Portuguese quickly captured the Antwerp market, the major distribution point for northern Europe. Even the Venetians offered to buy their spices in Lisbon.[51] The success of the Portuguese can be partly attributed to the decline of Meditarranean competition as a result of the Portuguese military offensive. But the key to Portugal's success was not simply the seizure of Ormuts or the blockade of Aden. Portuguese trading stations along the Malabar coast at important ports like Cannanore, Calicut, Cochin, and Quilon allowed the Portuguese to purchase spices directly from producers, thus undercutting their competitors.

During the first one-third of the sixteenth century, spice cargoes averaged between 40,000 and 50,000 *quintals* (1 quintal = 130 lbs.); in the 1540s and 1550s, they averaged from 60,000 to 75,000 quintals. Pepper was by far the most important and profitable commodity, accounting for between 20,000 and 45,000 quintals of the total.[52] Despite their access to Asian markets, the Portuguese never completely monopolized the spice trade and, after mid-century, Levantine competition revived. Between 1505 and 1550, however, most of Europe's pepper came via the Cape of Good Hope.

Arab and Indian ships continued to ply the Indian Ocean, participating in the interportal trades much as before the days of Vasco da Gama. But now, Asian merchants had to take out licenses and pay customs duties to the Portuguese crown. The Portuguese channeled much of this Asian trade through their factories and key ports such as Goa and Malacca. East of the Strait of Malacca, the attempt to license trade and confine shipping to Portuguese factories failed. The Portuguese loaded their cargoes of mace, nutmeg, and cloves unmolested, but they were merely one group

[51] Braudel, *The Mediterranean*, vol. 1, p. 544.
[52] Godinho, "Especiarias," p. 447.

of traders among many. Chinese and Malay merchants, for example, were able to sail the Java Sea without Portuguese interference. In fact, a Portuguese squadron that tried to force its way into the Chinese trade was defeated by the Chinese Coast Guard in 1522. Eventually, a factory was established at Macao, but on Chinese terms.

The Portuguese were really involved in two separate categories of trade. There was the direct trade between Lisbon, Goa, and the Malabar coast. But there were also innumerable inter-Asian trades involving Portuguese ships whose cargoes were not necessarily destined for Lisbon. Most of the cloves, nutmeg, and mace collected in Indonesia were sold by the Portuguese in Malacca, Goa, and Ormuts; relatively small amounts reached Lisbon. The Portuguese in Macao carried trade between China and Japan (Nagasaki). Each year, a huge carrack loaded with European merchandise went from Goa to Macao via Malacca to buy Chinese silks and porcelain. For the most part, Portuguese interportal shipping was manned by Asian seamen, working under a few white or Eurasian officers.[53] These ancillary trades allowed the Portuguese to buy some of their spices with other Asian commodities, rather than with expensive imports from Lisbon. Much of the gold that was exchanged for pepper came from southeast Africa, Sumatra, and China; Indian textiles helped pay for the spices obtained in Indonesia.[54]

The India House

Albuquerque's strategic victories in Asia were as momentous for Portugal as the conquest of Mexico was for Spain. It committed the Portuguese to a vast commercial empire in which trading centers rather than agricultural settlements predominated. The Portuguese neither produced spices nor did they reorganize local production to control it more effectively. The Portuguese were shippers and traders, and from the king's point of view, all efforts were directed to a single end: the provisioning of the India fleet with European merchandise and the loading of spices in Asia. How was such a vast enterprise run?

Asian trade depended on annual fleets that left Lisbon in late March to reach destinations on the Indian coast in September or October. The return fleet departed from India in late December, arriving in Lisbon by mid-summer. The round trip voyage, under favorable conditions, took about a year and a half. During the first quarter of the sixteenth century,

---

[53] Boxer, *Portuguese Seaborne Empire*, p. 57.
[54] Charles R. Boxer, "Portugal's *Drang nach Osten*," *American Historical Review* 75 (1970), p. 1689.

the fleets included an average of 7 to 14 400-ton vessels. By mid-century there were only about 5 vessels to a fleet, but the ships were larger, averaging between 600 and 1000 tons.[55]

At first, trade with India was open to any merchant with the means to arm and provision a ship. Cargoes were sold in Lisbon subject only to customs duties of five cruzados for each quintal of spices. In 1506, however, the spice trade became a royal concession directly exploited by the crown until 1570.[56] Only the king could import and market spices or export the major items used in the spice trade; copper, for example, was the single most important export exchanged for pepper. Copper could be purchased only by the king, who obtained his supply in Antwerp from Italian and German suppliers.[57] Alongside the crown's spice monopoly there were free trades in Portuguese goods such as wine, olive oil, cheese, dried fruit and fish; and in reexported hardware and textiles obtained in northern Europe.

That the king cornered the empire's spice trade was not surprising; he already was an experienced monopolist. The crown directly financed the Mina gold trade, and the African slave business and brazilwood concessions were monopolies leased by the crown. For half a century royal factors had outfitted the king's ships for use in the sugar, slave, and gold trades. The House of Guiné, the crown's African trade agency, provided a model that could be applied to the spice business. In 1503 the crown established a separate agency for Asian trade, the India House (*Casa da Índia*).

As the spice trade grew in importance, the India House became the chief commercial establishment in Portugal. Although the spice business was a royal enterprise, a series of concessions legitimized other forms of participation—especially for the crown's favorite entrepreneurs. For example, the king did not pay his employees a fixed salary. Instead, they were allowed to import varying quantities of duty-free spices in direct relationship to their ranks: soldiers and sailors, 3 quintals; the pilot, 80 quintals; the captain, 180 quintals. In addition, the king permitted an assortment of crown officials, nobles, and churchmen to invest in his import–export business. Contracts stated the quantity of spices involved, the amount of money to be invested, and the king's share, which was

---

[55] Boxer, *Portuguese Seaborne Empire*, p. 207; Godinho, *Descobrimentos*, vol. 2, pp. 77, 71–82.

[56] See Godinho, *Descobrimentos*, vol. 2, pp. 82–100.

[57] On the importance of copper in the pepper trade, see Godinho, *Descobrimentos*, vol. 2, pp. 31–42. In addition, the crown exported specie, silver, coral, lead, and mercury. After 1580 copper exports declined whereas increasing quantities of Spanish silver went to India and China.

anywhere from 25 to 50% of the profits. Those who had the right to participate but lacked the capital to take advantage of it, could sell their concessions and the space reserved for their merchandise. The buying and selling of spices was not usually permitted on an individual basis. Purchases were made in bulk at the royal factories in India. Return cargoes went to the India House in Lisbon, which made all sales and paid each participant his share of the profits, as specified in the contracts. This cumbersome arrangement could tie up an investor's capital for years at a time; obligations from the fleets of 1508 and 1510 were only discharged by the India House in 1516.[58]

What was the crown's share of the total traffic? Of the cargoes loaded in Lisbon for the India fleet of 1506, 25% belonged to the crown. In 1543 the king's share of the returning fleet, valued at 600,000 cruzados, was 60%.[59] The exact proportions in other years can only be surmised. But one thing is clear: the merchant-king held the single largest share of the trade. Even when the crown doled out contracts, it still controlled the purchase of spices in India and the marketing of them in Lisbon; in addition, the crown monopolized crucial exports such as copper.

Until about 1550 the India House sent the largest consignment of spices to Antwerp: between 20,000 and 40,000 quintals, largely of pepper. Antwerp was the commercial center of the North Atlantic. The city had sugar refineries where merchandise could be processed for reexport. At Antwerp spices were sold to German and Italian merchants who in turn supplied the Portuguese with copper and silver from central and eastern Europe; these metals were indispensible for buying spices in Asia.

All the spices, of course, did not go to Antwerp. The India House sold quantities in Lisbon to both Portuguese and foreign merchants. Spices were shipped to England and sent to the great fair at Medina del Campo in Spain. Eventually the crown's participation in the spice trade declined. Spice contracts were sold to foreign merchants who set up shop in Lisbon instead of Antwerp.[60]

The India Houses, an enormous warehouse that stood near the royal palace in Lisbon, was the "hinge on which everything turned," for the agency coordinated imperial trade.[61] Here oriental goods were unloaded,

---

[58] Ibid., pp. 88–91; Cordeiro Ferreira, "India, Casa da," p. 282.

[59] Godinho, *Descobrimentos*, vol. 2, pp. 91–92.

[60] Ibid., pp. 226–234; see also Braudel, *The Mediterranean*, vol. 1, pp. 543–570; and S. T. Bindoff, "The Greatness of Antwerp," in *The Reformation 1520–1559*, New Cambridge Modern History, vol. 2 ed. G. R. Elton (London, 1958), pp. 50–69.

[61] Braudel, *The Mediterranean*, vol. 1, p. 561; see also Cordeira Ferreira, "India, Casa da," pp. 281–289.

stored, and distributed. The king's chief factor supervised agency affairs. He was responsible for assembling fleets, selling spices, buying exports, and discharging contracts. The officials of the India House ran the crown's scattered factories, enforced commercial regulations, levied fines, and made minor appointments. Most major factories along the Malabar coast had substantial warehouses in which to store spices and the wares imported from Portugal. A chief factor was in charge, and was supervised by a general administrator stationed in Goa.

How much authority the Portuguese actually had in any region depended on how they acquired the right to set up factories in the first place. In cities they conquered (Goa, Malacca, Ormuts), the crown controlled trade and collected customs duties. At factories set up in states under Portuguese protection, such as Cochin and Quilon, the crown ran the pepper trade, whereas other trades remained under native control. Throughout most of the Indonesian archipelago the Portuguese simply traded according to local laws and customs.[62]

A BREAK IN THE PATTERN: BRAZILIAN COLONIZATION

Although Spain did not neglect overseas trade, it also established a powerful bureaucracy in its new dominions and created a special agency, the Council of the Indies, to oversee American administration. A distinctive feature of Portuguese expansion, by contrast, was the energy the crown devoted to organizing trade, as opposed to territorial administration. For in 1530 Portugal's overseas territory was limited to the Atlantic Islands, to coastal fortresses and factories, and to mercantile settlements like those at Goa, Malacca, and Macao. Portugal established colonies only in the sense that its nationals resided overseas in distinct Portuguese communities. Such communities often existed at the sufferance of local rulers. The common pattern was the trading colony, which followed the practices of medieval city-states such as Venice and Genoa, from which "colonies" of Venetian merchants scattered across Europe and the Mediterranean. Such colonies were instruments of trade rather than settlement. Around 1530 more Portuguese resided in the Atlantic Islands than in all the trading stations that stretched from Cacheu on the Guinean coast to Macao.[63] Only in Brazil did Portugal initiate a true settle-

---

[62] Godinho, *Descobrimentos*, vol. 2, pp. 64–70.

[63] Boxer estimates the maximum number of Portuguese in Asia at about 10,000; see *Portuguese Seaborne Empire*, p. 53.

ment policy, meaning one that implied the development of large-scale commercial agriculture, the control of extensive territory, and the wholesale subjugation of a foreign population. In the sixteenth century the Portuguese empire was a vast warehouse; in the next century it was to become a plantation.

PORTUGUESE BRAZIL, 1500–1580

We have taken a considerable detour before reaching our destination: Brazilian colonization. But our discussion follows the path that brought the Portuguese to America and reduces the early history of Brazil to its proper dimensions. For many years Brazil represented simply another trade area. Even after occupation began in the 1530s, Brazil's importance was offset by the special role spices played in the financial operations of the Portuguese state. A policy of settlement did not replace coastal factories until three decades after Cabral reached the Brazilian littoral in 1500. The first cargo of brazilwood arrived the following year, and the dyewood trade soon became a royal monopoly. The crown farmed out the brazilwood concession much as it did the African trades. Contractors agreed to establish trading stations, explore the coast, and pay the stipulated duties on brazilwood. In 1506 Fernão de Loronha purchased a concession for an annual rent of 4000 cruzados,[64] and other merchants also received licenses.[65] From 1505 to 1515 some 20,000 quintals (1200 tons) of brazilwood reached Lisbon, where most of it was reshipped to Antwerp.[66] To facilitate trade, contractors maintained a series of coastal factories. They bartered knives, tools, textiles, metal objects, and glass beads for brazilwood and food supplies. Indigenous workers cut, prepared, and delivered the trees to the factories. Thus, in return for their goods, the Portuguese received both brazilwood and Indian labor.[67]

The dyewood business was profitable and easy to manage. The direct voyage from Lisbon to the northeast of Brazil could be made in about 8 weeks, and the commodities used in the trade were inexpensive. Until

---

[64] Roberto C. Simonsen, *História econômica do Brasil: 1500–1820* (1937: São Paulo, 1962), p. 54.

[65] Apparently Loronho was not the only contract holder. See John Leonard Vogt, Jr., "Portuguese Exploration in Brazil and the Feitoria System, 1500–1530: The First Economic Cycle of Brazilian History" (doctoral thesis, University of Virginia, 1967), pp. 89–94.

[66] Frédéric Mauro, "Comércio cum O Brasil," *Dicionário*, vol. 2, p. 108.

[67] Alexander Marchant, *From Barter to Slavery* (Baltimore, 1942), pp. 46–47, 28–47.

about 1515 the trade was almost entirely in Portuguese hands. Three major factories were in operation at São Vicente, Cabo Frio, and Itamaracá. But a few factories strung out along Brazil's immense coastline could not prevent the French from intruding on the dyewood trade. They attacked the factories, seized Portuguese ships, made contact with the Indians, and flooded the Flanders market with brazilwood.[68] In 1516 and 1526 the king sent squadrons to clear the French from Brazilian waters; but compared to Africa, where they settled strategic islands and maintained fortresses to protect their factories, the Portuguese held only a tenuous grip on Brazil. Until the 1540s Brazil belonged as much to the French as to the Portuguese. In 1531 the French captured the Portuguese factory in Itamaracá and left a garrison of 60 men behind for its defense. Although retaken a year later, the episode underscored the seriousness of the French threat.

If Portugal was to protect its claims to Brazil, it either had to maintain a fleet in Brazilian waters or set up permanent colonies capable of self-defense. Even before the French seized Itamaracá, the king endorsed a settlement strategy. The purpose of Martim Afonso's expedition in 1530 was not just to attack the French. His squadron of four vessels brought soldiers, royal officials, priests, mechanics, laborers, and a sizeable contingent of settlers to Brazil.[69] A new colony was set up on the island of São Vicente, the site of a once flourishing dyewood factory; sugar cultivation and cattle raising were introduced almost immediately. The king granted São Vicente to Martim Afonso; similarly, he divided the rest of Brazil into a series of captaincies whose proprietors agreed to assume the financial liabilities of settlement. Of the twelve captaincies, only eight (Itamaracá, Pernambuco, Bahia, Ilhéos, Pôrto Seguro, Espírito Santo, Parahýba do Sul, and São Vicente) were actually settled, and only two of these flourished: São Vicente and Pernambuco.

Although colonizing the Atlantic Islands provided a precedent for the proprietary regime in Brazil, the decision to replace dyewood factories with agricultural colonies departed from the commercial pattern that predominated in Africa and Asia. Why did the crown return to an older strategy? The French presented a direct threat to Portuguese claims in America, and settlement was a defensive policy. By settling Brazil, the Portuguese crown hoped to pre-empt French colonization. Colonization was also a question of resources. Profits from the African slave trade and Asian spices covered the cost of local trading stations and fortresses.

---

[68] Vogt, "Portuguese Exploration in Brazil," pp. 159–178.
[69] Marchant, *From Barter to Slavery*, p. 50.

However, Brazil, with the exception of dyewood, yielded little. The crown's share of the brazilwood business could not pay for defending the coast. In America defense implied settlement, and profitable settlements implied commercial agriculture—in particular, sugar. Sugar cane had turned Portuguese Madeira and São Tomé into flourishing colonies, and sugar was already being successfully produced in America by the Spaniards.[70] Agriculture required a considerable labor force: slaves worked on the plantations of São Tomé, and Indian labor made the early sugar industry in Hispañola and Mexico possible. In Brazil the Indians cut and loaded dyewood; the Portuguese also expected them to work on Portuguese sugar plantations. The colonists could make the land productive—if the Indians did the work.

In Africa and Asia, densely populated, agrarian kingdoms could not be displaced or easily conquered. Although they had built a strong fortress at São Jorge da Mina, the Portuguese could not expand their commercial activities into the interior. During the 1570s African resistance blocked attempts to set up a captaincy in Angola, and although the Portuguese remained as slave traders, they were confined to their fortresses at Luanda and Benguela.[71] Brazil's coast, however, was sparsely populated by warring tribes organized into relatively small kinship groups. The coastal Tupinambá supplemented the cultivation of manioc, their principal staple, with hunting and gathering. Their large villages were only semipermanent, since the exhaustion of fields and game required periodic relocation. Constant intertribal warfare was limited by well-defined rules; the total and sustained warfare practiced by the Portuguese had been unknown. The loosely organized tribal structure and the communal, subsistence character of the Indian economy made it difficult for the tribes to assemble large numbers of warriors for any length of time. Although Brazilian Indians could mount swift, destructive attacks, burning sugar mills and forcing the Portuguese into their forts, their way of life made it impossible to sustain long-term warfare against their adversaries.[72] Unlike the Africans, they were unable to resist Portuguese intrusion.

---

[70] See Mervyn Ratekin, "The Early Sugar Industry in Española," *Hispanic American Historical Review* 34 (1954), pp. 1–19.

[71] See Silva Rego, *Portuguese Colonization*, pp. 97–116.

[72] See Stuart B. Schwartz, "Indian Labor and New World Plantations: European Demands and Indian Responses in Northeastern Brazil," *American Historical Review* 83 (1978), pp. 44–50; also Florestan Fernandes, "Antecedentes indígenas: organização social das tribos tupis," in A *época colonial. Do descobrimento à expansão territorial*, História geral da civilização brassileira, vol. 1(1) ed. Sérgio Buarque de Holanda (São Paulo, 1960), pp. 72–86.

THE CAPTAINCIES

The proprietary system, slavery, and sugar cultivation—patterns already present in the Atlantic Islands—shaped the colonization of Brazil. The charters granted to Brazil's proprietors stipulated the privileges they could enjoy within their captaincies. They controlled land distribution, dispensed justice, granted town charters, and licensed mills. These hereditary grants even exempted the captaincies from the visits of corregedores. But proprietors did not run the dyewood business; this the king kept as a monopoly. The crown also levied royal taxes on Brazil's trade—treasury officials accompanied the proprietors.[73]

During the early years most of the captaincies produced sugar, but warfare with the Indians soon destroyed many of the sugar mills and ruined the settlements. The conflict was over Indian labor, and by the 1540s, the Portuguese had resolved this conflict successfully only in Pernambuco and São Vicente. In most captaincies the Portuguese relied on barter to obtain Indian workers. But the barter system was inadequate because it failed to produce a dependable work force and created competition that increased the price of labor. In Pernambuco, for example, both brazilwood traders and settlers needed Indian workers. They glutted the local market with more goods than could possibly be used, and thereafter the Indians worked reluctantly or withheld their labor altogether. Since labor was indispensable to the cultivation of sugar and manioc, the settlers began to enslave Indians. Retaliatory wars followed, financially ruining several proprietors. Only Pernambuco's captain, Duarte de Albuquerque Coelho, had the capital to hire mercenaries and the military experience to lead expeditions against the Indians. In São Vicente, Alfonso's captaincy, the Portuguese and their Indian allies raided neighboring tribes. Backed by Flemish capital, São Vicente had six sugar mills and 3000 Indian slaves in 1548.[74]

Hostile Indians, lack of capital, proprietor–settler conflicts, and continued French harrassment reduced many colonies to weak seafront enclaves. Even the most promising captaincies were still vulnerable to attack by Indians, and could not mobilize against French intruders in other regions of Brazil. The system of autonomous captaincies made

[73] See Marchant, *From Barter to Slavery*, pp. 57–60; idem, "Feudal and Capitalistic Elements in the Portuguese Settlement of Brazil," *Hispanic American Historical Review* 22 (1942), pp. 493–512; H. B. Johnson, Jr., "The Donatary Captaincy in Perspective: Portuguese Backgrounds to the Settlement of Brazil," *Hispanic American Historical Review* 52 (1972), pp. 203–214; and Silva Rego, *Portuguese Colonization*, pp. 68–77.

[74] Marchant, *From Barter to Slavery*, pp. 48–80; also Godinho, *Descobrimentos*, vol. 2, p. 459.

collective defense impossible. To defeat the Indians and drive out the French required the crown's assistance.

In 1549 the king imposed a general government on the scattered captaincies and appointed Tomé de Sousa governor-general of Brazil (1549–1553) with power to curb the proprietors. Sousa's instructions ordered him to build a royal capital (Salvador) for Bahia—a captaincy the crown purchased after the proprietor's death—pacify the Indians, inspect the remaining captaincies, and expel the French. How important the crown considered this project is indicated by its investment: 300,000 cruzados to equip Sousa's fleet and provision struggling Bahia.[75] To assert its judicial powers, the crown appointed an *ouvidor-geral* (general judge) to supervise local judges elected by the town councils. In addition, a *provedor-mór*, or king's factor, was to inspect the way customs officials collected royal taxes.[76]

The influence of the royal government was sporadic and disjointed. Although Tomé de Sousa made brief visits to the southern captaincies, his successor, Duarte da Costa (1553–1557), never ventured beyond Bahia.[77] It was Mem de Sá, governor-general for 15 years (1558–1572), who established respect for the king's authority and expelled the French. He defeated the coastal tribes, prepared a law code for the entire colony, and supported the Jesuit missions. In the south, where the French and their Indian allies menaced São Vicente, he destroyed the enemy base on Guanabara Bay (Fort Coligny) and founded Rio de Janeiro (1567) as a defensive position against further incursions.[78]

By the 1570s a pattern had emerged that would permanently shape the character of Brazil. Royal authority, although legitimized throughout Brazil in theory, in practice was constant and effective only in Bahia. In other provinces the proprietor or his delegates continued to serve as captains. Only when the governor-general, the ouvidor-geral, or the provedor-mór inspected a captaincy was the principle of royal control actually implemented. During the entire sixteenth century royal officials never visited prosperous Pernambuco, which was owned by one of the king's favorite vassals.

Within Bahia, the crown concentrated on promoting the sugar industry. It built a sugar mill at royal expense to aid smaller landowners. As

---

[75] Ruth Lapham Butler, "Thomé de Sousa, First Governor-General of Brazil, 1549–1553," *Mid-America* **24** (1942), pp. 229–251.

[76] See Schwartz, *Sovereignty and Society*, pp. 22–41.

[77] See Ruth Lapham Butler, "Duarte da Costa, Second Governor-General of Brazil," *Mid-America* **25** (1943), pp. 163–179.

[78] See Ruth Lapham Butler, "Mem de Sá, Third Governor-General of Brazil, 1557–1572," *Mid-America* **26** (1944), pp. 111–137.

early as 1552 the king sent African slaves to Salvador to be sold, on his behalf, as labor for the sugar plantations. A few years later, to encourage large-scale production, planters were permitted to import up to 120 slaves from Angola at one-third the usual customs duties.[79] Brazil was becoming a sugar plantation, the first region in the New World in which export agriculture predominated.

Brazil's sugar production soon rivaled that of São Tomé and Madeira, and the basis was established for phenomenal growth. In 1570 Brazil had 60 mills producing about 180,000 arrobas of sugar annually. Production centered in two captaincies: Pernambuco with 23 mills, and Bahia with 18. The remaining mills were distributed as follows: Itamarcá, 1; Ilhéos, 8; Pôrto Seguro, 5; Espírito Santo, 1; São Vicente, 4.[80] Rio de Janeiro, a crown colony only lately founded, had none. This concentration of productive capacity in the two great northern captaincies continued for over a century, balanced only by the subsequent growth of Rio de Janeiro.

Although small landowners predominated, Pernambuco and Bahia also had large plantations that employed from 200 to 300 slaves.[81] Almost all the slaves in Brazil were Indians seized in defensive wars, licensed expeditions, or illegal raids into the interior. During the 1570s, however, plantation owners began to replace Indian labor with African slaves. One reason for the shift was the decline in the indigenous population: during the 1560s smallpox and measle epidemics reduced Bahia's labor force by half. In addition, to facilitate conversion and assimilation, the king allowed the Jesuits to concentrate the Indians in separate villages and planters had to negotiate with the Jesuits to obtain an adequate work force.

High mortality rates and new regulations were not the only reasons planters found high-priced African slaves more attractive than cheap Indian labor. African slaves were more productive and skilled than native workers; the systematic, continuous effort sugar production required had no precedent in the leisure-centered Indian cultures. Between 1570 and 1600 Angola alone supplied Brazil with over 50,000 slaves.[82] In the mid-1580s one-third of Pernambuco's labor force was African. By the 1620s Brazil's sugar zone was a land of blacks and mulattos rather than Indians and mestizos.[83]

---

[79] Godinho, Descobrimentos, vol. 2, p. 544; also Butler, "Mem de Sá," p. 120.

[80] These frequently cited figures are compiled from the contemporary account of Pero de Magalhães de Gandavo, The Histories of Brazil, trans. John B. Stetson (1922: Boston, 1972), pp. 131–151; see also Godinho, Descobrimentos, vol. 2, p. 461.

[81] Magalhães de Gondavo, Histories of Brazil, p. 41.

[82] Godinho, Descobrimentos, vol. 2, pp. 544–545.

[83] This section is based on Schwartz, "Indian Labor," pp. 50–79. Also see Marchant,

ROYAL GOVERNMENT

Royal government in sixteenth-century Brazil had little in common with Spanish America. A governor-general and a crew of itinerant officials does not constitute a bureaucracy; in addition, Brazil had only one bishop and no convents or monasteries. The crown's officials stayed in the sugar ports, ignoring the interior and the less productive captaincies. Whereas the Spanish crown needed a bureaucracy to tax silver and collect sales taxes in Hispanic America's great interior cities, such a strategy was largely irrelevant to Brazil's less diversified export economy. The king did not need to invest in a large contingent of bureaucrats because, one way or another, Brazil's wealth ended up in Portugal. Sugar went to metropolitan ports where it could be taxed, and slave traders had to buy a license from the king. Such was the logic of Portuguese expansion everywhere. Portugal's merchant-king organized the state to tax overseas trade and run crown monopolies. Sixteenth-century Spain extracted its largest revenues from Castilian taxpayers, but in Portugal 65% of the state's income was derived from the empire's trade.[84]

The bulk of Portuguese trade was with Asia, not Brazil. Even in the 1580s Brazil's sugar industry could not compete with the profits the king made on Asian spices. The factor of the India House, not the governor-general in Bahia, held center stage. The state looked to its ships more than it did to the administration of Portugal itself. In its preoccupation with provisioning the India fleets, parceling out the slave trade, and organizing spice contracts, the crown's thrust toward domestic centralization, which had reached its climax with the Manueline Code (1521), gradually subsided. The profits from trade could pay for a stronger bureaucracy, but they also made such an investment superfluous. Rather than improve provincial administration at home, the crown chose to organize overseas trade and reap the dividends. Thus the crown created ways to skim off imperial profits at the ports, but neglected the territorial bureaucracy. By the time Tomé de Sousa had arrived in Brazil, the India House was the most important state agency in Portugal. Whereas Castile's bureaucracy provided a coherent model for colonial administration in Spanish America, royal government in Portugal was decentralized and segmented—a consequence of the regime's commercial success.

From Barter to Slavery, pp. 102–122; and Dauril Alden, "Black Robes Versus White Settlers: The Struggle for 'Freedom of the Indians' in Colonial Brazil," in Attitudes of the Colonial Powers Toward the American Indian, eds. Howard Peckham and Charles Gibson, (Salt Lake City, 1969), pp. 19–45.

[84] See John Lynch, Spain under the Hapsburgs, 2 vols. (Oxford, 1964–1969), vol. 1, pp. 128–129; and Godinho, "Finanças públicas," pp. 33–34, 37–38.

Portugal's pattern of strength in the ports and weakness in the interior was to be repeated in Brazil.

THE COMMERCIAL STATE: END OF AN ERA

The Portuguese state's income came primarily from profits related to overseas trade. Trade and expansion were enterprises capitalized by the crown, the nobility, the clergy, and great merchants—foreign as well as Portuguese.[85] State capitalism had provided the initial advantage of permitting Portugal to concentrate its resources upon a single enterprise, the expansion of Portuguese commerce. The short-term results were spectacular: in 1550 branches of Portuguese trade reached to four continents. In the long run, however, Portugal's commercial system could not withstand foreign competition. In 1600 Portugal occupied a relatively weak position within Europe's world economy. What happened?

For Portugal, expansion created new sources of wealth for the king and the nobility to exploit. Because the king restricted participation in the trading system to himself and his favored nobles, expansion enriched the aristocratic leisure class, rather than creating a strong merchant class that would have recycled profits back into trade or created banks to provide capital. Consequently, Portugal's feudal structure, far from being challenged, was reinforced.[86] Diverting profits from trade into estates was not peculiar to Portugal, but the scale on which capital drained from the commercial sector was.[87]

The king's direct participation in the pepper trade and his monopoly on exports such as copper cut off the realm's merchants from lucrative sources of investment.[88] Even when the crown allowed individuals to share in these enterprises, the privilege often went to royal officials and members of the nobility. Although Brazil's sugar trade was open to all metropolitan merchants, as were the trades in wine, olive oil, dried fish, and textiles, they did not yield the spectacular returns of the spice trade.

---

[85] The nobility's role in trade is a major theme in the literature on Portuguese expansion. Besides specific instances previously noted, see Godinho, "Complexo histórico-geográfico," pp. 133–134; Jorge Borges de Macedo, "Burguesia: na época moderna," *Dicionário*, vol. 1, pp. 397–402; idem, "Comércio externo," *Dicionário*, vol. 2, p. 116. On the role foreigners played in Portugal's trade, see Godinho, *Descobrimentos*, vol. 2, pp. 234–260, and Virgínia Rau, *Estudos de história económica* (Lisbon, 1961), pp. 35–62; idem, *Estudos de história* (Lisbon, 1968), pp. 75–158.

[86] Oliveira Marques, *History of Portugal*, vol. 1, p. 265.

[87] See Braudel, *The Mediterranean*, vol. 1, pp. 525–527.

[88] Godinho, "Finanças públicas," p. 40.

Monopolies that the king did not typically exploit with his own funds, such as the slave trades, went to great merchants, both Portuguese and foreigners, who had enough capital to buy the contracts. The realm's wealthiest merchants, often backed by the capital the nobility supplied, were not about to challenge the state that granted them their lucrative concessions. Thus, the way trade was organized prevented merchants from developing into a strong, coherent class that could force the state to protect its interests.

The Consolidation of the Merchant Class:
A Comparison

When expansion began, Portugal had a small merchant class that traded in traditional agricultural commodities. The risk capital that sustained expansion and paid for Portuguese factories came from the king and great merchant-nobles. From the start, the crown controlled the dynamic sector of the economy. Merchants had to negotiate with the state to participate in the most profitable trades. In Portugal the merchants became a dependent class tied to state monopolies. But what might have happened had the realm's merchants financed expansion without the king's help? The king, outmaneuvered and short of income, would have remained more dependent on taxes approved by the Cortes. In such a situation a class of prosperous, independent merchants could have played a decisive role. As it was, the king could finance the state with the income derived from his trading monopolies; the bargaining power of the Cortes was thus reduced.

In seventeenth-century England and the Netherlands the relationship of merchants to the state was quite different. By the time overseas expansion began, a century later than in Portugal and Spain, regional trades and industries had provided merchants with independent sources of capital. In neither England or the Netherlands did trade evolve as a royal concession nor the king as the realm's chief merchant. Instead of royal factories, in these countries merchants formed companies to capitalize trade and colonization. Dutch and English entrepreneurs proved jealous guardians of their wealth. Their sovereigns had to bargain hard with strong assemblies for more revenue. In both England and the Netherlands, the long-run result was a state tied to the fortunes of its merchants.[89]

---

[89] On this theme see Charles H. Wilson, *England's Apprenticeship 1603–1763* (London, 1965); idem, "Trade, Society and the State." In *The Economy of Expanding Europe*, pp. 487–550; Violet Barbour, *Capitalism in Amsterdam in the Seventeenth Century* (1950: Ann Arbor, 1966).

In Portugal and Spain, however, merchants could not prevent the state from pursuing policies ruinous to trade. Spanish kings seized shipments of privately registered silver consigned to the merchants of Seville, and issued interest-bearing notes to them instead. In 1566 the Portuguese crown nullified its spice contracts and appropriated all the goods on the India fleet, granting paper notes in recompense, "to the discredit of the king, the scandal of the country, and with grave prejudice to the merchants."[90] It is difficult to imagine the king of England seizing tobacco shipments, or the Stadholder confiscating the goods of the Dutch East India Company.

The Decline of the Portuguese Monopoly

Since the king was the greatest merchant and drew the largest share of his revenue from trade, state expenditures directly affected the capitalization of trade. Between 1522 and 1543 the crown's expenditures for royal marriages and dowries exceeded the cost of the garrisons in Morocco and the fleets sent to the Indian Ocean, Africa, and Brazil.[91] The king was the realm's greatest merchant but also its most extravagant spender. If the crown devoured the profits, how was trade to be financed? By midcentury the state's financial position was precarious. The crown borrowed money and issued interest-bearing letters of exchange, using the spice trade as collateral. The interest alone rose from 80,000 cruzados in 1522 to 390,000 in 1543. By then the total debt in letters of exchange stood at almost 3 million cruzados—750,000 cruzados more than the value of the India fleet that year.[92] Short of capital and overburdened with a far-flung empire that was difficult and expensive to defend, the crown had less to invest in the trades that linked Goa to Lisbon and Antwerp. In 1548 the king closed the royal factory at Antwerp and withdrew from the carrying trade. Northern merchants now bought their pepper direct from the India House in Lisbon. Although the king sold spices in Antwerp, German and Italian merchants whose trading networks branched throughout central Europe handled the distribution. The so-called Portuguese monopoly stopped at Antwerp. By then the consolidation of Turkish power in the Levant had reopened the overland spice trade with the Mediterranean and entered direct competition against Portugal. In 1560 half of Europe's pepper came from the Levant.

A further blow to the Portuguese monopoly was due to a structural

---

[90] Godinho, *Descobrimentos*, vol. 2, p. 259.

[91] Godinho, "Finanças públicas," p. 36.

[92] Ibid., pp. 34–35. See also Diffie and Winius, *Portuguese Empire*, pp. 406–422.

defect of the trading system: Portugal did not produce the items exchanged for spices and slaves. Copper, silver, textiles, and hardware were purchased at Antwerp. When the debt-ridden crown forfeited the northern carrying trade the Portuguese were pushed out of Antwerp and back to Lisbon. To insure a steady supply of essential exports and high prices for spices, the king signed contracts in Lisbon with competing groups of German and Italian merchants. As never before, the pepper trade now relied on foreign capital and produced profits for outsiders. Foreign merchants had taken over additional links in the trading chain.[93]

The trade between Lisbon and Goa continued as the special preserve of the crown until 1570, when the crown terminated its Asian monopolies. With profits shrinking and expenses mounting, the king abandoned direct exploitation of Goa's spice trade; he now acted less as a merchant and more as a concessionaire. But by then the damage had been done.[94]

Although open trading for Portuguese merchants prevailed for a few years after the monopoly ended, a contract system for trading particular spices soon appeared. In 1586 the king leased the right to purchase pepper in India to the Welsers, a German trading house. This did not mean that the Welsers could bypass the India House or the factories along the Malabar coast. The state still made its profits, and Portuguese ships still carried merchandise. But foreign capital now financed the prized pepper trade.[95] Portuguese merchants could not afford to lease contracts on the crown's terms. The India House operated at the crown's expense, but produced profits for the rest of Europe.

In 1600, pushed to the periphery of the European economy, Portugal was a clearinghouse for others. This function was not essential, and commercially stronger states like the Netherlands expelled the Portuguese from many of their factories in Africa, India, and the Far East. By 1650 the great bulk of the trade between Europe and Asia bypassed Portugal altogether. The Portuguese empire became primarily an American empire. Brazil found itself linked to a weak state unable to extend and protect the markets for colonial products.

---

[93] The king's reliance on foreign businessmen for funds is discussed in Rau, *Estudos de história*, pp. 150–158.

[94] See J. B. Harrison, "Colonial Development and International Rivalries Outside Europe: Asia and Africa," in *The Counter Reformation and the Price Revolution 1559–1610*, New Cambridge Modern History, vol. 3, ed. R. B. Wernham, (Cambridge, Eng., 1968), pp. 533–536, and Braudel, *The Mediterranean*, vol. 1, pp. 543–556.

[95] Godinho, *Descobrimentos*, vol. 2, pp. 84–86, 93–97.

II

Brazil's Royal Government: The Seventeenth Century

BRAZIL AND THE SPANISH INDIES: A COMPARISON

Portugal turned Brazil into a sugar plantation; Spain took over an Indian empire. As colonial regimes Portuguese and Spanish America diverged from the beginning, and those differences were never bridged by a common Iberian heritage. Commercial agriculture linked to European and African markets was a dominant factor in Brazil's economic development, whereas the growth of Spanish-American agriculture was tied to the demands of local and regional markets, and had less to do with the world economy.[1]

---

[1] Although this study emphasizes the divergent organization of each empire, Iberians shared common cultural traits. See Emilio Willems, *Latin American Culture: An Anthropological Synthesis* (New York, 1975). For examples of the domestic orientation of Spanish-American agriculture, see Ward J. Barrett and Stuart B. Schwartz, "Comparación entre dos economías azucareras coloniales: Morelos, México y Bahía, Brasil," in *Haciendas, latifundias y plantaciones en América Latina*, ed. Enrique Florescano, (Mexico City, 1975), pp. 532–572; Robert G. Keith, *Conquest and Agrarian Change: The Emergence of the*

Spanish America was an empire of towns. As the focus of economic, political, and religious life, the town stood at the center of Hispanic culture in the New World. Indian labor, a diversified domestic economy, mining, and a fluorishing system of overland trade created an economic base for towns. Urban life, in turn, supported the extension of Hispanic institutions to America on a grand scale. Although Brazil, too, had urban centers, it was above all an empire of sugar mills. Everything depended on sugar production, and the industry monopolized the land and the colony's labor force. As surrogate towns, however, Brazil's plantations provided too narrow a base for replicating the social order of the metropolis. Urban life in Brazil developed slowly, confined as it was to a few coastal ports. As a consequence, royal government, ecclesiastical organization, and cultural institutions such as the university made their appearance on a reduced scale, if at all. Although settlements sprang up, they often lacked the formal coherence municipal councils provided in Spanish America.[2]

By the end of the sixteenth century 300,000 Spaniards had emigrated to the New World, where they lived in hundreds of towns with diverse economic functions.[3] There were almost as many bureaucrats in the Indies as in Spain itself. Spanish America's two viceroyalties were divided into 10 Audiencias (High Courts) and a bewildering collection of smaller political units. During the 1570s, for example, the viceroyalty of New Spain was broken up into 70 alcadías mayores and over 200 corregimientos.[4] The alcaldes and corregidores, or their lieutenants, presided over the municipal councils (cabildos) established in the principal towns of each district. In 1630 Spanish America had 5 archdioceses, 29 dioceses, and 10 universities. There were 334 monasteries, 74 convents, 94 hospitals, and 23 colleges (colegios).[5]

Hacienda System on the Peruvian Coast (Cambridge, Mass., 1976); and eds. Ida Altman and James Lockhart, Provinces of Early Mexico: Variants of Spanish American Regional Evolution (Los Angeles, 1976).

[2] How the export economy retarded the growth of towns is discussed in Richard M. Morse, "Brazil's Urban Development: Colony and Empire," in From Colony to Nation: Essays on the Independence of Brazil, ed. A. J. R. Russell-Wood, (Baltimore, 1975), pp. 155–181; and Stuart B. Schwartz, "Free Labor in a Slave Economy," in Colonial Roots of Modern Brazil, ed. Dauril Alden, (Berkeley, 1973), pp. 164–167.

[3] Woodrow Borah, "The Mixing of Populations," in First Images of America: The Impact of the New World on the Old, ed. Fredi Chiappelli, 2 vols. (Berkeley, 1976), vol. 2, p. 708.

[4] Peter Gerhard, A Guide to the Historical Geography of New Spain (Cambridge, Eng., 1972), p. 14.

[5] Jorge E. Hardoy and Carmen Aranovich, "Urban Scales and Functions in Spanish America Towards the Year 1600: First Results," Latin American Research Review 5 (1970), pp. 81–86.

Brazil's sugar economy impeded the spread of institutions that would have depended on a city for support.[6] In 1600 there were only 30,000 Portuguese in Brazil's 14 captaincies, and about 20 towns.[7] Throughout the colonial period Brazil never had a university. Until 1676 Salvador was the seat of the colony's only diocese, and it was often without its bishop.[8] Between 1609 and 1751 Brazil had only one High Court (*Relação*). Salvador boasted the colony's first convent, but not until 1677. During the eighteenth century, however, the gold strikes in Minas Gerais provided a new focus for urban life as bureaucrats and clergymen followed the miners into the interior. Even then the social, economic, and political realities the export economy imposed on Brazil diverged sharply from conditions in Spanish Mexico and Peru.

BRAZIL: THE KING'S REALM

During the seventeenth century Brazilian colonization took three distinct political forms. The fertile, rain-soaked coast supported the sugar plantations of Pernambuco, Bahia, and Rio de Janeiro. In the ports of these captaincies the presence of royal officials was a fact of daily political life. On the other hand, the king's men rarely ventured to the Paulista settlements, located across the coastal mountains on the southern plateau. In the semiarid interior (*sertão*) of the northeast, where ranching predominated, powerful families managed local affairs. How effectively each region—fertile coast, plateau, and sertão—was linked to the king's bureaucracy and Portugal's trading system varied considerably.

THE UNION OF PORTUGAL AND SPAIN

Sebastião, the childless, young king of Portugal, died in a disastrous campaign against Islamic Morocco (1578). The king of Spain, Philip II (1556–1598), was the son of the Portuguese princess, Isabella, and had a strong claim to the Portuguese throne and the military strength of Spain to back him up. From 1580 to 1640 Portugal and its empire were part of the dynastic inheritance of the Spanish kings. Portugal, however, was

---

[6] See Robert Richard, "Comparison of Evangelization in Portuguese and Spanish America," *The Americas* 14 (1958), pp. 444–453.

[7] Roberto C. Simonsen, *História econômica do Brasil* (São Paulo, 1967), p. 121. On the number of towns, see Morse, "Urban Development," p. 164.

[8] Francis A. Dutra, "The Brazilian Hierarchy in the Seventeenth Century," *Records of the American Catholic Historical Society* 83 (1972), pp. 171–172.

neither absorbed by Spain nor governed by Spanish officials, and Brazil did not become a Spanish viceroyalty administered by the Council of the Indies. By the terms of the Cortes held at Tomar (1581), Philip II agreed to respect the constitutional integrity of Portugal and its possessions: he promised not to convoke the Cortes outside the kingdom, and never to legislate on the realm's affairs in a foreign assembly; bureaucratic and ecclesiastical patronage remained a Portuguese affair, as did colonial trade. The king retained advisors and officials, all of Portuguese birth, who formed a Council of Portugal. Portugal remained a separate kingdom, and Brazilian affairs were managed by Portuguese councils and judicial tribunals. Thus, despite the union with Spain, Brazil was still treated as a Portuguese colony. When Portugal reasserted its independence in 1640 there were few Spanish partisans on hand to contest Brazil's loyalty.[9]

By sixteenth-century standards Castile was Europe's strongest bureaucratic state: Castilian taxes provided the singe largest contribution to the Spanish imperium.[10] Given the strong institutional presence that Spain maintained in her American colonies and the weakness of royal government in Brazil, why didn't the new king bring Brazilian administration into line with practices in Spanish America? The Spanish monarchy was obligated to respect the rights of its Portuguese subjects; it did not have a free hand in Brazil, and Philip II was careful not to alienate his new subjects. The status of Portugal was part of a general pattern of regional decentralization that also recognized the special rights of Catalonia and Aragon. Furthermore, the crown's share of sugar production was not profitable enough to pay for a major reorganization of the bureaucracy. Sugar chests could not compete with American silver as the keystone for royal government. Spanish interest in Brazil was primarily strategic. As long as the Portuguese held the region, the overland routes from São Paulo to Potosí, the great mining center of Upper Peru, could be protected. Recife or Salvador in Dutch hands could pose a serious threat to Spanish America and the silver fleets. Thus, by and large, Spain was content to leave Brazil to the Portuguese. As was true of the Portuguese House of Aviz, the Spanish Hapsburgs were mainly interested in the great commercial monopolies that belonged to the crown. Although the sugar trade was open to all Portuguese merchants and ports, the Spanish crown organized the spice trade and sold the slave contracts

---

[9] John Lynch, *Spain under the Hapsburgs*, 2 vols. (Oxford, 1964–1969), vol. 1, pp. 309–311; A. H. de Oliveira Marques, *History of Portugal*, 2 vols. (New York, 1972), vol. 1, pp. 312–318.

[10] Lynch, *Spain under the Hapsburgs*, vol. 1, pp. 128–134, 180–197.

(*asientos*). It was the contract for pepper purchases in India that Philip II was soon "hawking around Europe, hoping to deprive the Dutch and English of the peppers and spices they were in the habit of buying in Lisbon."[11] To the Portuguese crown Brazil had been of small though growing importance. To Spain it was still the tail end of an empire, a third level priority after Spanish America's silver and Asia's spices.[12]

ADJUSTMENTS IN THE
JUDICIAL BUREAUCRACY

Dispensing justice is a fundamental aspect of kingship. In Portugal towns had once appointed their own local judges (juizes ordinários). During the sixteenth century, however, crown-appointed magistrates (juizes de fóra) with law degrees from Coimbra University took over in the realm's towns and cities. Overseas, the proprietors and captains who colonized the Atlantic Islands and Brazil received broad judicial mandates. By the 1570s, however, the crown reduced these powers, and experienced royal magistrates (ouvidores) were sent to supervise local judges in Madeira, the Azores, São Tomé, Cabo Verde, Angola, and Brazil. Their decisions could be appealed to the High Court in Portugal (*Casa da Suplicação*). Supervision of the judicial bureaucracy fell to the *Desembargo do Paço*, a royal council that advised the king on legal matters. In the 1580s and 1590s Philip II established a special commission of prominent Portuguese lawyers to revise the kingdom's law code. The Philippine Ordinances were completed in 1595 and issued in 1603. An additional High Court, which supplemented the Casa da Suplicação, was set up in Oporto. The crown reviewed the performance of magistrates in Portugal, and weeded out the negligent and incompetent, and strengthened the judiciary in Africa and Asia.[13]

In Brazil a single superior magistrate (ouvidor-geral) for all the captaincies could hardly provide routine supervision, and he was further burdened by nonjudicial responsibilities. Those who held the post also served as military commanders, or had to assume the duties of the superinten-

---

[11] Fernand Braudel, *The Mediterranean and the Mediterranean World in the Age of Philip II*, trans. Siân Reynolds, 2 vols. (New York, 1972–1973), vol. 1, p. 561.

[12] Stuart B. Schwartz, "Luso-Spanish Relations in Hapsburg Brazil, 1580–1640," *The Americas* 25 (1968), p. 35.

[13] Stuart B. Schwartz, *Sovereignty and Society in Colonial Brazil: The High Court of Bahia and Its Judges, 1609–1751* (Berkeley, 1973), pp. 3–21, 42–52; Bailey W. Diffie and George D. Winius, *Foundations of the Portuguese Empire, 1415–1580* (Minneapolis, 1977), pp. 310–311.

dent of the treasury (provedor-mór). Until the seventeenth century judicial administration was directed by individuals rather than a distinct governmental agency. Philip II instructed the Desembargo do Paço to draw up suggestions for judicial reform in Brazil. In 1588, following the recommendations of the Desembargo do Paço, the king approved the establishment of a Brazilian High Court. Most of the judges appointed to the tribunal, however, never reached Brazil. Not until 1609, after a delay of 2 decades, was a Brazilian High Court finally installed in the city of Salvador. At the same time, the crown appointed a special magistrate for the southern captaincies (*ouvidor do sul*).[14]

The High Court

The magistrates who served on the Relação, or High Court, were professional lawyers with degrees from Coimbra. Appointment to Bahia's High Court was an important step in a judicial career. Those selected were usually seasoned bureaucrats who had served both as juizes de fóra in provincial towns and as circuit judges (ouvidores). The magistrates chosen for the Brazilian tribunal had an average of 15 years previous experience in the judiciary, both in Portugal and overseas. The king selected judges from lists drawn up by the Desembargo do Paço. Promotions were based on several criteria: seniority, merit, precedent, and personal ties influenced decisions. It is difficult to weigh these principles precisely, but personal connections alone rarely sufficed.[15]

The bureaucracy embodied the king's authority, and the magistracy depended on the crown's patronage. Unlike the nobles, whose independent status rested on lineage and entailed estates, a judge's prestige depended on his rank in the bureaucracy. A sample of 100 High Court justices who served in Bahia between 1609 and 1759 shows that only 8 were the descendants of *fidalgos* (noblemen). The largest group, 22, were the sons of magistrates. Most of the remainder were sons of merchants, 9; minor officeholders, 11; military officers, 9; artisan-shopkeepers, 6; modest landowners, 11; and "honorable" men qualified to serve on municipal councils, 17. Although the humble origins of many judges reinforced their dependence on the crown, it also meant that the king had to buttress their authority in a society acutely conscious of social ranking. They received high salaries, were exempt from certain taxes, and their persons were inviolate; they also were often rewarded with membership in the prestigious military orders such as the Orders of Christ and Santiago.[16]

---

[14] See Stuart B. Schwartz, *Sovereignty and Society*, pp. 56–64, 126.

[15] Ibid., pp. 294, 308–313.

[16] Ibid., pp. 173, 290, 302–305; between 1609 and 1759, 168 magistrates served on Bahia's High Court. On the military orders, see Francis A. Dutra, "Membership in the Order of

Map 4 Colonial Brazil, 1660.

Legal training could be obtained only at Coimbra, and magistrates, whether born in Portugal or the colonies, absorbed standards of conduct from the professional socialization acquired in the course of their university education. The ideal magistrate was a man "who separated himself fully from the influence of others, and who lived his life guided only by the regulations of his profession and the desires of the crown."[17] To protect professional standards, royal ordinances sought to isolate the magistrates from situations that might compromise their impartiality. Judges, for example, were forbidden to conduct business or own land within their jurisdictions; they were not to marry Brazilian women or to serve as godparents and marriage sponsors. Such prohibitions, however, had more the character of general guidelines than strictly enforced rules of conduct. The crown tolerated, indeed, practically institutionalized, exceptions to the rule. Still, blatant disregard for at least the spirit of prescribed standards could end a judicial career.[18]

The Brazilian tribunal was composed of 10 judges. The governor-general presided over the Relação, although he could not vote on judicial matters. When the governor-general left the captaincy (between 1609 and 1625 the governors spent most of their time in Pernambuco) the chancellor, who was also chief justice of the Relação, assumed responsibility for administration in Bahia. The judges sometimes met as a corporate body: for example, to approve appeals to the Casa da Suplicação in Portugal, to ajudicate charges brought against the governor-general, or to make formal recommendations to the crown. But the High Court's daily business was conducted by the judges according to their separate functions. The magistrate who served as ouvidor-geral held court three times a week, exercised original jurisdiction over civil and criminal cases arising in Bahia, and held appellate jurisdiction over criminal cases for the rest of Brazil. Appeals from his decisions or those of subordinate judges, such as the ouvidores in various captaincies, could be made to a special panel of High Court magistrates. The crown judge heard cases that involved the treasury: he held jurisdiction of the first instance in Bahia and heard appeals from the decisions of the treasury officers (provedores) in each captaincy. The chief treasury official in Brazil, the provedor-mór, although not a judge, could hear cases that did not exceed 50 cruzados. The crown's attorney prosecuted criminal cases and represented the crown in suits brought against the treasury.[19]

Christ in the Seventeenth Century: Its Rights and Obligations," *The Americas* 27 (1970), pp. 3–25.
    [17] Schwartz, *Sovereignty and Society*, p. 173.
    [18] Ibid., pp. 172–175, 292–295.
    [19] This description is based on Schwartz, *Sovereignty and Society*, pp. 62–67. My under-

One of the High Court's methods of expediting the judicial process was by reducing the number of cases appealed to Portugal. In this respect the tribunal provided a service to colonists involved in legal disputes. As servants of the king, however, judges were expected to enforce the crown's directives. Consequently, the tribunal was also a potential threat to Brazil's merchants and planters. Attempts to clamp down on contraband trade or to enforce legislation that restricted the use of Indian labor jeopardized long-standing arrangements.

In 1612 the crown set up a special *junta* (tribunal) to investigate tax evasion, fraud in the treasury, and contraband trade. Although the investigation was headed by the secretary of Lisbon's customs house, two High Court judges served on the commission, as did the newly appointed provedor-mór of the treasury. The junta checked the treasury's accounts, collected back taxes, and heard testimony on illegal commercial practices. Violators were usually given several years to pay their fines or reimburse the treasury, as the purpose of the junta was to increase revenues, not to send guilty colonists back to Portugal.[20]

The High Court and the
Indian Labor Dispute

The most serious dispute handled by the High Court concerned the means by which the colonists obtained and used Indian labor. In the early seventeenth century Bahia's sugar planters still needed native workers. Labor was secured either by slave-raiding expeditions into the interior (*entradas*) or by drawing workers from the Jesuit-run villages (*aldeias*). The Society of Jesus consistently opposed enslavement, and the aldeias were a kind of controlled substitute. The Hapsburgs had aggressively pursued the "freedom of the Indians" in Spanish America. The attempt to restrict the use of Indian labor in Brazil was quite consistent with policies applied elsewhere in America.[21]

---

standing of the High Court and its relationship to society is also shaped by John Phelan, *The Kingdom of Quito* (Madison, 1967); and Mark A. Burkholder and D. S. Chandler, *From Impotence to Authority: The Spanish Crown and the American Audiencias, 1687–1808* (Columbia, Mo., 1977).

[20] Schwartz, *Sovereignty and Society*, pp. 159–162.

[21] On the role of Indian labor in Brazil, see Stuart B. Schwartz, "Indian Labor and New World Plantations: European Demands and Indian Responses in Northeast Brazil," *American Historical Review* 83 (1978), pp. 43–79; Charles R. Boxer, *Salvador de Sá and the Struggle for Angola and Brazil* (London, 1952), pp. 124–125. Generally, see John Hemming, *Red Gold: The Conquest of the Brazilian Indians, 1500–1760* (Cambridge, Mass., 1978), pp. 97–118, 139–160; and Dauril Alden, "Black Robes Versus White Settlers: The Struggle for the 'Freedom of the Indians' in Colonial Brazil," in *Attitudes of the Colonial Powers Toward the American Indians*, eds. Howard Peckham and Charles Gibson, (Salt Lake City, 1969),

In 1609 the crown prohibited enslavement under any circumstances and ordered that all Indian captives be freed. Furthermore, colonists were to pay wages for any labor drawn from the aldeias. Only the Jesuits were allowed to bring Indians from the interior, and then the Indians were to be gathered into villages under the Order's control. So that the full weight of its authority could be applied, the crown issued the ordinances only after the judges arrived in Salvador. Such strict regulations had few precedents in Portuguese America.

The reaction in Salvador was swift and decisive. The town council (*câmara*) met and sent an official protest to the governor-general and the chancellor of the High Court; the câmara even threatened to expel the Jesuits from the city. Faced with a rebellion that endangered the entire mission effort, the Jesuits accepted the enslavement of Indians already captured. In his correspondence with the king, Governor-general Diogo de Meneses (1608–1612) supported the planters. He noted that "expeditions to bring Indians to the coast were beneficial and their prevention would lead to a shrinking of the labor force."[22] Faced with such opposition, and concerned that sugar production would be disrupted, the crown backed down. Although the freedom of the Indians was asserted again in 1611, enslavement and expeditions were permitted under certain conditions and the aldeias continued to provide a cheap source of labor.[23]

The role the High Court played in this dispute is uncertain. But it was quite clear the tribunal provided a new and more powerful base for royal government. Although the king's initiative on the question of Indian labor was muted, the Relação created a potential for enforcement that had not existed previously. Over the next decade the actions of the High Court were to provoke a steady stream of complaints from the Salvador câmara, the proprietor of Pernambuco, and officials of the southern captaincies.

Judicial Review and the Problem of Intermarriage

The High Court provided a cadre of trained officials who could assume diverse responsibilities. Special investigations and ad hoc committees or juntas sometimes required the judges to leave Bahia. For example, High Court judges selected by the governor-general usually conducted reviews

---

pp. 19–45. How Spain intervened to protect Indian workers in Spanish America is described in Charles Gibson, *Spain in America* (New York, 1966), pp. 136–159.

[22] Schwartz, *Sovereignty and Society*, p. 137.

[23] Schwartz, *Sovereignty and Society*, pp. 122–139, 191; Hemming, *Red Gold*, pp. 314–316.

(*residências*) of officials in each captaincy—the governors (capitães-mores), local treasury officers (provedores), and judges (ouvidores)—at the end of their terms. In extraordinary cases, the king responded to complaints by commissioning a special inquiry, or *devassa*. Such general investigations, often linked to conducting residências, went beyond simple judicial review. Judges inspected the treasury records, reviewed the procedures of the câmaras, and inquired into the performance of local officials. They not only made reports but suggested and implemented remedies under the governor-general's authority.[24]

Although they were in theory triennial, reviews occurred infrequently, especially outside Bahia. Between 1652 and 1676, for example, judges made no outside tours of inspection, even to villages in Bahia.[25] When such inquiries did take place, local officials were hostile to what they saw as outside interference: the magistrates who reviewed the terms of Rio de Janeiro's governors (1612, 1619, 1624) encountered considerable opposition.[26] In Spanish America, if the residência did not provide an effective check on the crown's officials, at least the reviews were frequent and routine.[27] When it received serious complaints from the colonies, the Council of the Indies frequently appointed a special visitor-general from Spain armed with extensive powers. In such cases colonial governors and judges crossed the visitor-general at their peril.[28] During the seventeenth century such comprehensive reviews rarely occurred in Brazil.

Although the High Court was a judicial tribunal, it was directly involved in administration both as a corporate body and with respect to the tasks assigned its judges. How captains, treasury officials, and municipal councils lived up to their job descriptions determined how royal legislation was applied; therefore, reviewing these officials was as essential to legal administration as hearing appeals in court. The distinction was not so much between justice and administration as it was between policy making and enforcement of statutes. The king, assisted by councils in Portugal, made decisions and drew up the appropriate orders. The governor-general, provincial captains, and treasury officials implemented the crown's directives; the Relação reviewed performance and dealt with litigation. At least, this was the official scheme, although not the daily reality. To what extent was the bureaucracy actually the king's disin-

---

[24] Schwartz, *Sovereignty and Society*, pp. 154–170.

[25] A. J. R. Russell-Wood, *Fidalgos and Philanthropists: The Santa Casa da Misericórdia of Bahia, 1550–1755* (Berkeley, 1968), p. 244.

[26] Schwartz, *Sovereignty and Society*, pp. 163–170.

[27] See Peter Marzahl, "Imperial Control," in *Town in the Empire: Government, Politics, and Society in Seventeenth-Century Popayán* (Austin, 1978), pp. 123–136.

[28] See Phelan, *Kingdom of Quito*, pp. 243–264.

terested and trustworthy servant? It is, after all, one thing to establish bureaucratic posts, and quite another to maintain surveillance over the incumbents—even in the twentieth century.

A system of recruitment and promotion provided some check on officeholders. By rotating officials—High Court judges, for example, were limited to 6-year terms—the crown prevented the highest offices from becoming the sinecures of their incumbents. Nevertheless, some judges served for extended periods. The problem was not simply length of service, but whether or not judges remained aloof from entanglements that compromised their role. By and large they did not. Judges married Brazilian women, especially from the Recôncavo;[29] they served as godparents and marriage sponsors; and they obtained membership in the *Misericórdia*, a prestigious society in Salvador dedicated to charitable works. The Misericórdia was a kind of elite social club whose members included the best families in the captaincy. During the seventeenth century, five High Court judges and five governors-general were also presidents of the Misericórdia. In 1716, after judges had held the presidency 5 years in succession, the king prohibited the practice. He distrusted the kind of influence multiple officeholding created, especially when the positions were prestigious and were held within a small society such as Bahia, where all the important families were interrelated.[30]

Although the High Court represented metropolitan authority, it was also an extension of Brazilian kinship structures. Between 1609 and 1751 about 20% of the judges who served on the tribunal petitioned and received approval to marry Brazilian women.[31] Although this practice did not have a direct influence on the formation of colonial policy, marriage and other ritualized social ties (e.g., godparentage and marriage sponsorship) created obligations that elite families could enlist to protect themselves.[32] Well-placed relatives, both in Brazil and Portugal, provided the first lines of defense. The marriage market exchanged planter wealth for the political connections of judges, governors, and treasury officials. Judges who acquired property and relatives in Brazil were often reluctant to leave the captaincy after their terms. Some even turned down promotions to superior tribunals in Portugal. Such was the case of Judge

---

[29] The Recôncavo was the rich sugar producing region around the Bay of All Saints where the colonial capital, Salvador, was situated.

[30] Russell-Wood, *Fidalgos and Philanthropists*, pp. 111, 372–373.

[31] Schwartz, *Sovereignty and Society*, p. 177. For a discussion of how kinship structures affected the Relação, see pp. 177–182, 338–356.

[32] This is a general aspect of Latin America culture. See Sidney W. Mintz and Eric R. Wolf, "An Analysis of Ritual Co-Parenthood (compadrazgo)," *Southwest Journal of Anthropology* 6 (1950), pp. 341–368.

Bernardo de Sousa Estrela, who resigned the royal service at 60 years of age. He spent the next 30 years of his life in Salvador, living on his estates and acquiring a reputation for piety.[33]

Ties to local families were even stronger when men born in Brazil held colonial posts. Ten Brazilian-born magistrates occupied seats on the Relação between 1653 and 1752, a practice that drew a mixed response from Salvador's câmara. While upholding the rights of the Brazilian-born, the câmara cautioned against their appointment to the tribunal, "where ties of family and friendship would pervert the impartiality they should possess."[34]

Business interests also linked officials to colonial society. Judges purchased land, invested in sugar mills, loaned and borrowed money, and sponsored commercial ventures. Cristovão de Burgos, a Brazilian-born magistrate who served on the High Court for 26 years (1654–1680), owned extensive tracts of land, numerous slaves, and three sugar mills in the Recôncavo. Judging from notarial records, the acquisition of sugar plantations was the primary economic goal of most magistrates, whether Brazilian-born or Portuguese; this was accomplished through purchase, inheritance, or dowry.[35] Although salaries were substantial, only the most frugal magistrate could move his household to Bahia, rent lodgings, and maintain an appropriate life style within the limits of his official income. Most judges looked for ways to supplement their salaries. Pero de Cascais, one of the original members of the Relação, invested in whaling. Caetano Brito de Figueiredo borrowed money to purchase a sugar mill and cane fields. In the 1720s two judges were dismissed for òpenly engaging in the slave trade. Magistrates were often in debt, and some used their judicial posts to thwart their creditors. Magistrate Azevedo Monteiro rented cane fields during the 1660s and then refused to pay the owner his rent.[36]

Such examples are not isolated occurrences; they reflect persistent patterns. Joined in multiple fashion to colonial society, royal officials were seldom impartial, and they often acquired a distinctly Brazilian perspective.[37] The bureaucracy was really a shared organization. It represented the interests of the crown, but the routine operations of judges, governors, and treasury officials were subject to considerable local influence, if not outright subversion. The crown knew that its officials were also businessmen. Land sales and loan transactions were all duly

---

[33] Schwartz, *Sovereignty and Society*, p. 307.

[34] Charles R. Boxer, *Portuguese Society in the Tropics: The Municipal Councils of Goa, Macao, Bahia, and Luanda, 1510–1800* (Madison, 1965), p. 88.

[35] Schwartz, *Sovereignty and Society*, p. 333.

[36] Ibid., pp. 328–334.

[37] Ibid., pp. 314–326.

notarized and registered. These practices did not usually challenge the lines of authority that royal government implied, and so they were tolerated as long as the king and his councils were not flooded with complaints about particular officials. Although planters could use their friends and relatives to influence judicial proceedings, they had to seek redress within the king's bureaucracy. Thus disputes between officials, litigation over property rights, jurisdictional conflicts, accusations of fraud and favoritism in the treasury, charges brought against officeholders—all of these issues were resolved by the crown's agents or passed on to Portugal for a final ruling.

ROYAL GOVERNMENT IN ENGLISH AMERICA AND BRAZIL: A COMPARISON

Unlike the Portuguese in Brazil, English Americans organized local politics around the threat they thought royal government posed to local institutions. During the 1640s, while the king and Parliament fought a civil war at home, colonial assemblies gained authority at the crown's expense. In Massachusetts, dissident Puritans established a godly commonwealth safe from the king's surveillance. Until the 1660s only Virginia had a royal governor, and even then, the assembly assumed responsibility for the colony's ecclesiastical organization.[38] Following the precedent set by the House of Commons, colonial leaders adopted an opposition ideology, a notion of rights and privileges that the colonies possessed with respect to the crown's claims.[39] Conflict often arrayed the royal governor and his council against the assembly, whose membership was determined independently by colonists. The assembly successfully defended its control over local taxation and restricted the crown's executive power. Ambitious men courted the votes of their planter neighbors and fellow townsmen because the assembly's patronage tended to outdistance that available to royal governors.[40]

In Brazil, colonists defended their interests not by controlling separate institutions but by infiltrating the bureaucracy. Disputes were not resolved by colonial courts and juries; câmaras did not establish laws for the various captaincies, nor did they decide on the nature and level of

---

[38] William H. Seiler, "The Anglican Parish in Virginia," in Seventeenth-Century America, ed. James Morton Smith (Chapel Hill, 1959), pp. 119–142.

[39] How developed this position was, even in the seventeenth century, is stressed by David S. Lovejoy, The Glorious Revolution in America (New York, 1972).

[40] See Bernard Bailyn, The Origins of American Politics (New York, 1967).

Brazilian taxation. These issues were resolved in Portugal and litigated by the bureaucracy in Brazil. Royal government, despite its limitations, maintained this hierarchical structure intact. The clash between the metropolis and its colonists in Brazil rarely assumed a sharp focus, although on occasion the municipal councils made a judicious compromise necessary. In these situations, most notably on questions of Indian labor, the câmaras drew up lengthy memorials and sent them to Portugal; the king and his councilors reviewed matters and reached a decision. Brazil's royal government, with its overlapping jurisdictions, unending litigation, and complex system of appeals, tended to diffuse conflict. Conversely, in English America the assembly's institutionalized role in politics created a legitimate base for the governor's opponents. The gap between the English crown's exaggerated claims and the assembly's actual powers generated serious and persistent conflict that was difficult to deflect.

BUREAUCRATIC CONTROL

The Portuguese crown kept the Brazilian bureaucracy in line in part by controlling appointments, but the most effective check was that different branches of the bureaucracy kept tabs on each other. The High Court's authority countered that of the governor-general, who needed the tribunal to staff special committees, draw up reports, and undertake residências. Furthermore, the governor-general's orders were subject to the legal review of the High Court's chancellor, and the tribunal supervised the governor-general's residência. The governor-general, in turn, exercised important controls over the magistrates. He could suspend judges, and his evaluation of their performance could hinder or further careers. The crown monitored those officials far removed from the king's presence by institutionalizing a system of mutual surveillance.[41] Let us illustrate this point with an example.

The treasury, the Relação, and the governor-general exercised distinct fiscal, judicial, and administrative functions, but the extent to which specific acts fell within the province of each was a matter of dispute. The magistrates, for example, kept a watchful eye on the treasury, since its decisions often affected their business ventures and those of their associates. Such was the case in 1614 when treasury superintendent (provedor-mór) Sabastião Borges introduced the monopoly contract system for whaling. The first contract was purchased for a suspiciously low price, provoking the High Court's intervention. The tribunal ordered

---

[41] Schwartz, *Sovereignty and Society*, pp. 192–198.

Borges to surrender all documents pertinent to the contract's sale. The superintendent refused, arguing that the Relação had no authority to judge him in treasury matters. Judge Pero de Cascais, who invested in the local whale fisheries and was hardly a disinterested party, countered this protest in a position paper addressed to the crown. He argued that the contract system represented an innovation without prior authorization and was therefore subject to judicial review. The Treasury Council in Lisbon upheld the Relação. Subsequently, the crown instructed the superintendent to either auction the contract to the highest bidder or to impose a tax on whale hunters.[42]

This is an interesting example for several reasons. First of all, it shows how different segments of the bureaucracy kept a jealous eye on one another, if only because the actions of any one branch cut into the patrimony of other bureaucrats and their friends. Second, it illustrates how conflict was diffused. Several different disputes were being fought simultaneously: there was the institutional rivalry between the High Court and the treasury, both defending their jurisdictional turf; the investments of Pero de Cascais were at stake; and local interests were also involved—not only the interests of those who had already invested in whale fishing, but also of those who stood behind the contract signed with the treasury. The resolution was in terms of judicial procedure. The struggle over the control of whaling remained sub rosa. This was a persistent pattern. The economic interests involved in disputes were often lost in a tangle of bureaucratic infighting and family rivalries. Unraveling these Gordian knots is a problem in genealogy, family history, personal antagonisms, and bureaucratic jealousies that makes tracing "colonial opposition" to the crown extremely difficult. Not that such considerations did not bear upon the proceedings of English assemblies. But debate and voting in assemblies, self-interested as it was, identified adversaries in a way that closed judicial proceedings did not permit.

Although the Portuguese crown possessed different means of varying effectiveness to restrain the most important officials, there were positions scattered throughout the bureaucracy that the crown sold to incumbents. The creation and sale of offices was common practice, not only in the Portuguese empire but also in France and the Spanish Indies.[43] Although the organization and extent of such sales in Brazil is uncertain, clerking

---

[42] Ibid., pp. 212–214.

[43] See Wolfram Fisher and Peter Lundgreen, "The Recruitment and Training of Administrative and Technical Personnel," in *The Formation of National States in Western Europe*, ed. Charles Tilly (Princeton, 1975), pp. 495–496; John H. Parry, *The Sale of Public Offices in the Spanish Indies*, (Berkeley, 1953) (Ibero-Americana 54); and Koenraad W. Swart, *Sale of Offices in the Seventeenth Century* (Amsterdam, 1975), pp. 1–81.

positions in the judiciary were sold—even passed on in dowries. During the 1680s a Brazilian-born High Court judge owned the chief treasury post in Pernambuco. Some officeholders entitled to collect fees for their services, such as notaries, paid 10% of the position's estimated annual yield to the treasury. The governor-general and provincial captains exercised considerable control over local patronage. Indeed, they were accused of creating salaried posts for their friends and relatives at the treasury's expense. Whether the positions were sold directly by the crown or doled out locally, the recipients were frequently colonial-born. As bureaucratic posts continued to multiply, especially during the eighteenth century, sugar planters, merchants, and lawyers enjoyed the spoils of royal government. At its lower echelons, the bureaucracy was essentially the property of the colonial elite. They had a stake in royal government that bound their interests to the crown.[44] Whereas in English America ambitious colonists got elected to the assembly, in Brazil they purchased offices.

The Church and the Towns

The Church

At the highest level, competing jurisdictions limited the arbitrary exercise of authority by judges, governors, and treasury officials; in addition, the church and the municipal councils provided countervailing sources of influence. The church was a distinct organization whose members were subject to ecclesiastical courts and not the Relação. By the terms of the *Padronado Real*, the king had the right to make appointments to all ecclesiastical posts in Brazil. Evangelization was a royal monopoly; the missionary activities of religious orders such as the Jesuits required the king's mandate. During the 1670s Brazil's only episcopal see, Bahia, became an archdiocese and new bishoprics were created in Pernambuco, Rio de Janeiro, and Maranhão. Although bishops were invariably Portuguese-born, Brazilian-born clergymen were entrenched in the cathedral chapters. The ambitions of the clergy, especially the missionaries, frequently collided with those of the civil bureaucracy, creating disputes that had to be resolved in Portugal. The church, however, never acquired the economic and social significance in Brazil that it did in Spanish America.[45]

---

[44] See Dauril Alden, *Royal Government in Colonial Brazil: With Special Reference to the Administration of the Marquis of Lavradio, Viceroy, 1769–1779* (Berkeley, 1968), pp. 22–24, 294–298; Schwartz, *Sovereignty and Society*, pp. 143–144, 194–195; A. J. R. Russell-Wood, "Women and Society in Colonial Brazil," *Journal of Latin American Studies* 9 (1977), p. 15.

[45] See Dutra, "Brazilian Hierarchy," pp. 171–186; and Charles R. Boxer, *The Portuguese*

The Town Councils

The town councils were the only formal institutions run by Brazilians. The câmara's composition varied, but it usually included two justices of the peace (*juizes ordinários*), three aldermen, and a town attorney. The council appointed a secretary, a town crier, and employees to supervise municipal services. As in Spanish America, the town council kept a list of prominent citizens eligible to participate in municipal elections. These citizens assembled in the câmara's chambers and selected six men to serve as electors. The electors could not be related to the candidates or to each other. After dividing into pairs, the electors drew up separate lists of the candidates they considered most qualified. From these lists, the provincial magistrate (ouvidor) or the governor (capitão-mór) selected three candidates for each office. The names were sealed in wax balls and placed in a sack. On New Year's Day the balls were shuffled and drawn at random. The citizens thus selected held office for the year. Every 3 years, after all the names had been drawn, a new list of candidates was compiled.[46]

In Spanish America, the crown sold seats on the *cabildo*; municipal offices often passed from father to son. But in Brazil membership changed annually, since service was normally restricted to one term every 3 years; thus, a larger pool of citizens shared municipal offices. Nevertheless, the câmara's overall composition, like that of the cabildo, reflected the dominant interests of the community: in Salvador, for example, sugar planters predominated.[47]

To what extent did the town councils control their affairs without interference from proprietors or royal officials? Salvador's câmara labored under the shadow of the governor-general, the High Court, and the bishop. In Rio de Janeiro and Pernambuco, governors and proprietors could manipulate elections. The ouvidor, for example, had the right to

Seaborne Empire 1415–1825 (New York, 1969), pp. 228–248. How important the Spanish-American church was in the daily life of a colonial town is discussed in Marzahl, *Town in the Empire*, pp. 137–158. On the church's economic role, see François Chevalier, *Land and Society in Colonial Mexico: The Great Hacienda*, trans., Alvin Eustis (Berkeley, 1963), pp. 229–262. Controlling the wealthy religious orders and their Creole friars posed a serious problem to the Council of the Indies. See Antonine Tibesar, "The Alternativa: A Study in Spanish-Creole Relations in Seventeenth-Century Peru," *The Americas* 11 (1955), pp. 229–283.
  [46] Boxer, *Salvador de Sá*, pp. 30–34.
  [47] Boxer, *Portuguese Society*, p. 104; Alden, *Royal Government*, p. 296. Although based on the late colonial period, see Caio Prado, *The Colonial Background of Modern Brazil*, trans. Suzette Macedo (Berkeley, 1967), pp. 366–373. On the Spanish cabildo, see John P. Moore, *The Cabildo in Peru under the Hapsburgs* (Durham, 1954), and Marzahl, *Town in the Empire*, pp. 57–73.

review the triennial lists in secret. Although the ouvidor was the crown's representative, the king often let the proprietor or governor make the appointment subject to subsequent royal approval. Thus, the ouvidor was in a position to promote the governor's supporters. Nevertheless, the town council played a major role in determining its own membership: it bestowed citizenship, and these citizens designated the electors.

The câmara's opposition sometimes modified or reversed the crown's decisions, as occurred with the Indian legislation of 1609. New prohibitions against slave raiding in 1639 created strong resistance in the southern captaincies, where Indian labor was still essential to the economy. These laws simply could not be enforced; in São Paulo and Santos, the câmaras even expelled the Jesuits. In 1644 the town councils in Salvador and Rio de Janiero refused to pay a new export tax whose purpose was to provide escorts for the sugar fleet; the convoy's captain, Salvador de Sá, had to negotiate directly with the indignant câmaras.[48]

There were 10 High Courts in Spanish America that could mediate between local elites and the metropolis; they often suspended controversial laws while appeals were made to Spain. Brazil, however, had only one High Court, and it was suspended between 1626 and 1652 with the result that royal officials had to deal directly with the town councils. Still, the câmara's powers had serious limitations. Whereas it could appeal decisions and delay enforcement of legislation, it lacked the ability to initiate or to enact laws, or to define and defend colonial interests in any consistent and institutionalized fashion. The câmaras simply did not have the powers of English assemblies.

As a basic unit of colonial administration, the câmara performed services for the crown; in particular, it became a tax collector. In Salvador the town council paid the garrison, and after the Dutch wars (1621–1654) the municipality was burdened with a war indemnity that amounted to 90,000 cruzados per annum in 1688. To defray these costs, the king allowed the council to levy duties on rum, wines, and sugar; collection was leased to professional tax farmers. The town also had an independent source of income that came from taxing foodstuffs and from renting municipal property set aside as the town's patrimony. These revenues helped to pay for local services. For example, the câmara set prices for staples such as meat, manioc, wine, and fish; licensed shopkeepers and traders; verified weights and measures; and was responsible for sanitation and public works. It also played an active role in the export economy. Salvador's council, in consultation with exporters and producers, annually fixed the price of sugar and set freight rates. Because they were tied to

---

[48] Boxer, *Salvador de Sá*, pp. 131–140, 189–190.

the dominant interests of the community, the câmaras were at once the king's willing allies and troublesome sources of opposition; in their correspondence with the king they rarely hesitated to criticize officials or to complain about new taxes and policies.[49]

In Portugal the juiz de fóra had replaced many of the realm's local judges. But during most of the seventeenth century Brazil's town councils continued to elect a juiz ordinário, although his decisions could be appealed to the ouvidor. Still, the juiz ordinário held original jurisdiction in many civil and criminal cases. In Spanish America royal officials presided over the town councils, but in Brazil an elected councilman presided, and the position rotated.

As Brazil's royal government expanded, it interfered more in town affairs. In 1696 the crown appointed a juiz de fóra to preside over Salvador's câmara, and abolished the post of juiz ordinário. The Relação now reviewed the list of citizens eligible for seats, and the governor-general appointed councilmen directly from the High Court's amended tally. Still, for most of the seventeenth century Brazil's town councils were subject to less bureaucratic supervision than were the Spanish American cabildos.[50]

The Treasury

The crown-appointed superintendent (provedor-mór) in Bahia had final jurisdiction over all exchequer affairs in Brazil; he worked under the governor-general's direction and that of the treasury council. The council, which was established in 1652, included four High Court judges. Elsewhere, the local governor and the provedor supervised provincial treasuries.

As Brazil's economy expanded, the crown began to cover its expenses and make a profit. The most important internal tax was the tithe, a 10% levy on all sources of production. In theory an ecclesiastical tax administered by the crown to support the secular clergy, tithe revenues were also used to defray the cost of the High Court, pay salaries, finance special commissions, and reimburse the judges who undertook residências. Since sugar production was the dominant economic activity in Brazil, it provided the base for taxation.

Although they were responsible for tithe revenues, treasury officials

---

[49] Boxer, *Portuguese Society*, pp. 79–80, 107–108. For an analysis of eighteenth-century town government (Vila Rica, Minas Gerais) and its various functions, see A. J. R. Russell-Wood, "Local Government in Portuguese America: A Study in Cultural Divergence," *Comparative Studies in Society and History* 16 (1974), pp. 187–231.

[50] Boxer, *Portuguese Society*, pp. 74–75; Schwartz, *Sovereignty and Society*, pp. 268–269; Alden, *Royal Government*, p. 423.

were not tax collectors. The exchequer awarded collection contracts to businessmen for fixed periods, supposedly on the basis of competitive bidding. Contracts stated the sum to be received by the treasury and the profit margins of collectors; that is, the amount in excess of the contract price they could retain. Since specie was scarce in Brazil, taxes were often collected in kind. Contractors had to provide some security against their bids, but default was not uncommon, especially if harvests were poor. Because of draught, for example, the 2-year tithe contract for 1613–1614, purchased for 54,000 cruzados, had to be readjusted. In the contract business, jurisdictional disputes between the High Court and the treasury were constant, as were charges of fraud and racketeering.[51]

Taxes on trade, whether levied in America or Portugal, made Brazil profitable to the mother country. Sugar exports were subject to a 10% ad valorem tax collected in Brazil and a 20% duty in Portugal.[52] As with the tithe, the collection of Brazilian export duties was leased by contract. In 1612 the tax revenues from Bahia were worth 125,000 cruzados.[53] Foreign merchandise destined for Brazil paid export duties in Portugal. In addition, the crown leased its monopolies on brazilwood, salt (1658–1801), whale fishing (1603–1798), and tobacco sales (1642–1820). Between 1602 and 1612 the brazilwood contracts were worth a total of 90,000 cruzados;[54] in 1659 the tobacco monopoly sold for 64,700 cruzados.[55]

This description of Brazil's royal government, focused on the colony's only High Court, exaggerates the significance of the bureaucracy. Compared to Hispanic America, Brazil's bureaucracy was less extensive; it lacked the depth and symmetry of the Spanish scheme. True, Brazil's High Court had much in common with the Spanish-American Audiencia. Appeals to the crown, jurisdictional conflicts, the erosion of bureaucratic standards, the way kinship and business ties linked judges to colonial families—these are familiar themes in the bureaucratic history of both empires.[56] Such an emphasis, however, has greater justification in the Spanish case, as there were 10 High Courts strategically placed throughout the Spanish Indies. Consequently, observations based on a

---

[51] Schwartz, *Sovereignty and Society*, pp. 210–215. On Brazilian taxation, see Dorival Teixeira Vieira, "Política financiera," in *História geral da civilização brasileira*, ed. Sérgio Buarque de Holanda, vol. 1 (2), *A epoca colonial: Aministação, economia, sociedade* (São Paulo, 1960), pp. 340–351; and Prado, *Colonial Background*, pp. 375–378.

[52] Vitorino Magalhães Godinho, *Os descobrimentos e a economia mundial*, 2 vols. (Lisbon, 1963–1965), vol. 2, p. 471.

[53] Engel Sluiter, "Report on the State of Brazil, 1612 (Rezão do Estado do Brasil)," *Hispanic American Historical Review* **29** (1949), p. 526.

[54] Simonsen, *História econômica*, p. 63.

[55] Boxer, *Salvador de Sá*, p. 384.

[56] For example, see Peter J. Bakewell, *Silver Mining and Society in Colonial Mexico:*

case study of a particular Audiencia can be stated as generalizations that apply to a larger population. This is simply not true with respect to Brazil's Relação. In Spanish America the king's officeholders and the clergy played essential roles in the town's daily life. Although the local bureaucracy did not always conform to the Spanish crown's mandate, even a provincial capital like Popayán, Colombia still had a full-fledged ecclesiastical establishment, to judge from the records of the many synods held there.[57] Of course, the great central valleys of Mexico and Peru had hundreds of towns in 1600; by contrast, Brazil was still a series of coastal enclaves. Not until the 1690s, after gold was discovered in Minas Gerais, did the crown try to impose its authority in the backlands.

THE SUGAR CAPTAINCIES

The resources of Brazil passed through its major ports: Salvador, Olinda-Recife,[58] and Rio de Janeiro. Rainfall, soil conditions, and the lack of natural harbors limited sugar cultivation to a narrow, coastal strip that rarely exceeded 30 to 50 miles in depth. Numerous small rivers and a protected coastline made the Pernambucan littoral an ideal place for settlement. The great Bay of All Saints with its many inlets provided a natural transportation system for the plantations in the fertile Recôncavo that surrounded Salvador. The lands bordering Guanabara Bay, wedged between the mountains and the sea, supported the sugar industry of Rio de Janeiro. Aside from these major settlements, there remained only secondary clusters scattered along the coast.[59] As the productive capacity of Brazil was overwhelmingly concentrated around a few urban centers, so was royal government concentrated. The king's officials stayed in the principal cities when they were not on special assignment elsewhere.

In 1614 Brazil had about 50,000 Portuguese colonists. Seventy percent settled in Bahia and Pernambuco: 15,000 in Bahia and 20,000 in Pernambuco.[60] During the 1620s Rio de Janiero also became an important sugar

---

Zacatecas, 1546–1700 (Cambridge, Eng., 1971); Phelan, *Kingdom of Quito*; Burkholder and Chandler, *Impotence to Authority*.

[57] Marzahl, *Town in the Empire*, pp. 137–158.

[58] Olinda, located on a steep bluff overlooking the sea, was the capital of Pernambuco. Recife, a few miles to the south, was the captaincy's port. An ill-built and overcrowded shanty town, Recife did not have its own câmara until 1709. The tendency was for planters to reside in Olinda, merchants in Recife. Since both towns were so close together and economically integrated, they are treated in the text as a single entity. See Charles R. Boxer, *The Golden Age of Brazil*, 1695–1750 (Berkeley, 1962), pp. 109–111.

[59] Prado, *Colonial Background*, pp. 33–35.

[60] Boxer, *Salvador de Sá*, p. 17. The figures for Bahia and Pernambuco are from Sluiter, "Rezão do Estado," pp. 534–548. The number of households listed (*moradores brancos*) are multiplied by 5.

producer. In 1627 almost 80% of Brazil's sugar mills were in three captaincies: Pernambuco, 100; Bahia, 50; and Rio de Janeiro, 40.[61] This concentration of wealth and population continued throughout most of the
century. There was only one captaincy where the crown maintained the
full weight of its bureaucratic arsenal, however—Bahia. Or perhaps more
accurately, there was only one city with such an arsenal—Salvador.

BAHIA: A PROFESSIONAL BUREAUCRACY

Salvador was Bahia's commercial and cultural center as well as Brazil's
capital. The planters' social life moved between the city and the plantation. The mills and sugar farms made up rural communities free from the
interference of either the crown or the Church. Planters, however, did
not lead an isolated existence on their estates. Since sugar was an export
crop, planters had to deal with the merchants of Salvador, and they could
not afford to ignore the political life of the capital. If officials did not come
to the plantations, it was because such visits were unnecessary. Sugar,
slaves, textiles, equipment for the mills, and provisions all passed through
Salvador. To protect their interests against treasury officials, governors,
and judges, planters had to be active participants in the social life of the
capital. The great planter families of the Recôncavo maintained separate
houses in town, held municipal posts, served on the Misericórdia's board
of directors, joined religious brotherhoods in the city, sought marriages
for their daughters with high officials, and obtained offices for themselves
and their sons. Royal institutions, although confined to Salvador, were
essential reference points for Bahian planters, who had to come to terms
with authorities in the capital. The same relationship between the cities
and the countryside could also be found in Pernambuco and Rio de
Janeiro. In these captaincies, however, powerful extended families,
rather than the crown, controlled political patronage.

FAMILY CONTROL

Pernambuco

During the sixteenth century Pernambuco's powerful proprietors prevented the crown from restricting their privileges.[62] Although the king

---

[61] Godinho, *Descobrimentos*, vol. 2, p. 463.

[62] The discussion of Pernambuco is based on Francis A. Dutra, "Centralization vs.
Donatarial Privilege: Pernambuco, 1602–1630" in *Colonial Roots of Modern Brazil*, ed.
Dauril Alden, (Berkeley, 1973), pp. 19–60; idem, "Matias de Albuquerque: A Seventeenth-

filled treasury posts at his pleasure, the Albuquerque Coelho family appointed the circuit judge (ouvidor) and the provincial captain-governor (capitão-mór). The proprietor's cronies monopolized seats on Olinda's town council and organized expansion. The conquest of the northeastern littoral was designed to thwart French and Dutch occupation; it was also a profitable enterprise. The merchants of Olinda-Recife, clients of the proprietor, became wealthy supplying the settlers who left Pernambuco for the new lands of the north. Jerónimo de Albuquerque and Jerónimo Fragoso de Albuquerque, relatives of the proprietor, became captains in Maranhão and Pará, respectively.[63]

After 1572 the proprietors resided in Portugal and named substitutes as captains, mostly relatives. A broad coalition of merchants and planters, along with the capitão-mór and his lieutenants, ran the captaincy. In 1601, when the third proprietor died leaving his 10-year-old son, Duarte, as heir, the king curbed proprietary authority in the captaincy. Duarte was not permitted to select his own capitão-mór, as had been customary. Although Duarte continued to appoint the ouvidor, the governor-general's superior authority more than offset what powers remained to the Albuquerque Coelho family. Between 1602 and 1617 four governors-general spent a total of 8 years in Pernambuco. Until 1621, when the king appointed Duarte's brother, Matias de Albuquerque, as capitão-mór, the governor-general's business activities undercut the interests allied to the proprietor's family. The result was a battle over positions in the local bureaucracy that pitted the defenders of proprietary privilege against the new factions tied to the governor-general.

The king had ordered his governors to stop in Pernambuco on the way to Bahia; however, they stayed longer than the crown had intended, taking over the supply business to the north and entangling themselves in local politics. In fact, it took special orders from the king to prod his governors from Pernambuco to assume their duties in Bahia. As the wealthiest province in Brazil, Pernambuco provided attractive business opportunities. Governor-general Diogo Botelho (1603–1607), for example, was accused of "illicit activities in Pernambucan commerce from the slave trade to the sale of wine."[64] Gaspar de Sousa (1613–1617) personally led an expedition against the French in Maranhão; he so controlled the

---

Century Capitão-Mór of Pernambuco and Governor-General of Brazil," (doctoral thesis, New York University, 1968). The royal grant to Duarte Coelho is reprinted in A Documentary History of Brazil, ed. E. Bradford Burns, (New York, 1966), pp. 33–50.

[63] Dutra, "Centralization vs. Donatarial Privilege," pp. 51–52.

[64] Francis A. Dutra, "A New Look into Diogo Botelho's Stay in Pernambuco, 1602–1603," Luso-Brazilian Review 4 (1967), p. 30.

affairs of the captaincy that the capitão-mór asked for a new assignment because "the governor-general did everything."[65] His enemies accused Gaspar de Sousa of "conspiring with the sugar planters to defraud the royal treasury of great sums of money annually."[66] Luís de Sousa (1617–1621) stirred up the most controversy. He not only took over the business of conquering Maranhão, but he also appointed his friends to sensitive bureaucratic posts. When the office of capitão-mór fell vacant, he named his crony, João Pais Barreto, a wealthy Pernambucan planter, to the post. Barreto, in turn, named his own man to serve as ship inspector in Recife, a post usually filled by the proprietor. These maneuvers provoked a storm of protest from the Albuquerque Coelho faction that culminated with the imprisonment of the proprietor's uncle, Cristovão de Albuquerque.[67]

A decade of accusations against the governor-general's profiteering brought decisive action from the king. He appointed Matias de Albuquerque capitão-mór and prohibited the governor-general from residing in the captaincy, thus strengthening local authority at Bahia's expense. That the power of the governor-general needed to be checked was amply demonstrated by Matias de Albuquerque, who uncovered flagrant abuses in the treasury. The customs officials, for example, unlawfully taxed slaves that passed through Recife and distributed the profits among themselves. Matias alleged that Luís de Sousa sent "goods to Maranhão at excessive prices, often close to twice their value, . . . and that many supplies for which he received payment never arrived."[68] The governor-general protested his innocence, but the king revoked Sousa's jurisdiction over the supply business and placed it in the hands of Matias de Albuquerque. In fact, the capitão-mór reassumed his role as superintendent of the northeast. Finally, the crown upheld the capitão-mór's right to fill minor posts, thus curbing the appointive powers of the governor-general. When Matias left Pernambuco in 1627, the capitão-mor's powers vis-a-vis the central government were firmly established. But these gains did not fall to the proprietor. The king appointed his own nominee to replace Matias. Then the Dutch captured Recife in 1630 and soon dominated the entire northeast coast. When the Portuguese reestablished control in 1654, Pernambuco became a royal colony. Even then, the governors of Pernambuco steadfastly resisted interference from Bahia.[69]

---

[65] Dutra, "Centralization vs. Donatarial Privilege," p. 30.
[66] Dutra, "Matias de Albuquerque," p. 207.
[67] Dutra, "Centralization vs. Donatarial Privilege," pp. 30–31.
[68] Ibid., pp. 47, 54–60.
[69] Alden, *Royal Government*, pp. 36–39.

Rio de Janeiro

Although in theory a royal colony, Rio de Janeiro was virtually the possession of the Correia de Sá family. Rio was founded in 1567 by governor-general Mem de Sá, and its governorship became almost the birthright of the de Sá clan. After Mem de Sá's first term as governor (1568–1571), his son, followed, in turn, by his grandson, held the post periodically for 50 of the next 90 years. Using the governorship as a political base, the de Sá's built up extensive holdings of land, sugar plantations, and slaves. Salvador Correia de Sá, grandson of the dynasty's patriarch, employed 700 slaves on his plantations and cattle ranches; he was the captaincy's largest landowner, and perhaps the greatest estate owner in Brazil.[70] The Correias and their supporters dominated the municipal council and held most of the minor posts in the captaincy. Just how profitable such influence was can be seen in the case of the warehouse Salvador de Sá constructed in 1636 for weighing and storing sugar. Such a facility was badly needed and Salvador de Sá offered to build it at his own expense provided that he was given monopoly on weighing all the sugar exported from the captaincy. The câmara agreed to these conditions, allowing de Sá to collect a fee of 40 réis (400 réis = 1 cruzado) on each chest stored in the warehouse. The contract was later renewed by the câmara in perpetuity. The Correia family kept its monopoly until 1850![71]

From his first term as governor (1637–1643) until he left Brazil permanently in 1662, Salvador de Sá dominated the affairs of Rio de Janeiro and even those of neighboring captaincies. The crown extended his commission to the captaincy of São Vicente, which included the Paulista settlements across the mountains on the southern plateau. Authorities in Bahia resented the semiindependent status of Rio de Janeiro and, in particular, the special role the Correia de Sá family played in the southern captaincies.

Portugal revolted against Spanish rule in 1640, and the Duke of Braganza assumed the throne. Although Salvador declared allegiance to the new Portuguese royal house, the king distrusted the governor's connections with the Spanish nobility and revoked his jurisdiction over São Vicente. In 1643 de Sá resigned his post and left for Portugal so that he could defend his family's interests directly. Over the next 15 years Salvador distinguished himself in the Dutch wars. As a reward the king detached the southern captaincies from the authority of Bahia (1658) and

---

[70] Boxer, *Salvador de Sá*, pp. 139–140.
[71] Ibid., pp. 114–115.

appointed de Sá captain-general of the south. The patronage kingdom of the Correia clan had reached its height. Salvador's cousin was already serving as governor of Rio de Janeiro. In addition, his relatives held the posts of administrator of the mines, provedor of the treasury, president of the câmara, and commander of the Rio garrison.[72]

The concentration of offices in the hands of a single family naturally provoked opposition from those exluded. One of Salvador's first acts as captain-general was to ask Rio's citizens for new taxes to support the garrison. His proposals were rejected at an open meeting. Undaunted, he turned to his friends and relatives on the câmara. He persuaded them to impose a stiff poll tax on the community, to be adjusted to the rank and wealth of each individual, but assessed and collected by his cronies. His objectives accomplished, Salvador went on a tour of inspection to São Vicente. In his absence, the city revolted.[73]

In a formal declaration dated 2 November 1660, the insurgents repudiated their allegiance to the governor "because of the many taxes, imposts, and tyrannies with which he terrorizes this exhausted people."[74] They demanded abolition of the poll tax and an investigation of the treasury, and called for new elections to the câmara, "uninfluenced by the threats and bribes of Salvador and his representatives."[75] The rebels drew up new electoral lists purging the town council of de Sá's adherents. The newly formed câmara, under the leadership of Jerónimo Barbalho, deposed the acting governor and assumed control of the city. The Corriea clan was stripped of its offices. The garrison, its salaries substantially in arrears, supported the rebels. Although mob action was an important aspect of the revolt—the homes of Salvador and his friends were sacked—the rebels included some of the captaincy's leading citizens and members of the clergy. The victory, however, was short lived. Several months later, entering the city at night, Salvador staged a countercoup; the rebel ringleader was executed and his head displayed in the town square. Although Salvador had crushed the uprising, the discontent it represented alarmed the crown, which acted with uncharacteristic decisiveness to break the Correia oligarchy. Salvador and his son were recalled to Portugal, their property was temporarily seized by the crown, and the family never held the governorship again. The southern captaincies returned to the jurisdiction of Bahia's governor-general.[76]

---

72 Ibid., pp. 303–304.
73 Ibid., pp. 311–329.
74 Ibid., p. 113.
75 Ibid., p. 113.
76 Ibid., pp. 311–329.

GOVERNMENT AMONG CAPTAINCIES:
DID THEY SHARE A COMMON PATTERN?

To what extent do these sketches of royal government modify conclusions we reached with respect to Bahia? One revision is certainly in order: neither the Relação nor the governor-general exercised routine supervision over officials in other captaincies. In Pernambuco, the capitão-mór and the governor-general fought over the right to fill vacant offices. Only when a governor-general or a High Court magistrate actually visited a captaincy could superior authority be asserted effectively, and even then local hostility to such interference produced charges and countercharges that had to be resolved in Portugal. True, appeals from the decisions of local judges did reach the Relação; but royal government was centralized only in a very limited way. Far from being an intermediary between the metropolis and the captaincies, Bahia's officials were constantly at loggerheads with their nominal subordinates; in the end, Lisbon had to ajudicate disputes. Brazil's royal government is best seen as a series of decentralized, semiindependent captaincies whose governors, treasury officials, and câmaras dealt directly with Lisbon. The temporary detachment of the southern captaincies from Bahia's nominal authority simply recognized a division that had already existed. In the north, Maranhão and Pará were completely independent of Brazil's capital.

In Bahia the High Court provided a pool of professional bureaucrats dependent on the crown; each sector of the bureaucracy kept a watchful eye on its rivals. In Pernambuco and Rio de Janeiro offices became the patrimony of powerful extended families. By contrast, the Spanish crown rarely granted its institutional authority to colonial families. After the conquest, the authority of Spanish viceroys, Audiencias, and crown-appointed corregidores reduced the initial significance of the town councils and the broad mandates bestowed on the first conquistadors. Not that colonial families in the Spanish Indies failed to amass wealth, status, and power. They purchased local offices, and their sons became lawyers and judges, even serving on the Audiencias. In Brazil the crown chose to exercise its authority through particular families rather than through its own professional staff. That this occurred in a captaincy as important as Rio de Janeiro was without precedent in Spanish America.

Eventually the crown restricted the powers of the Albuquerque-Coelhos and the Correias. But the creation of a professional bureaucracy on the Bahian model was a slow and sporadic affair. Only toward the end of the seventeenth century did the crown bolster the ranks of the magistracy by appointing more royal judges (ouvidores) to newly created judicial districts (ouvidorias), and sending juizes de fóra to preside over the principal towns. Still, the independence of local governors from Salvador continued, since each new governor was in a position to erect his own patronage system—in alliance, of course, with local families.

In other ways, however, colonial government in Pernambuco and Rio de Janeiro duplicated the situation in Bahia. As the examples suggest, the governorship, the treasury, and numerous minor posts were in some respects business enterprises. While he was governor-general, António Teles da Silva (1642–1647) moonlighted as a sugar merchant and made a fortune.[77] Because they were involved in an export economy that filtered sugar, slaves, and equipment through major ports, planters could not ignore the city. The basic relationship between town and countryside was the same in all the great sugar captaincies. In Bahia planters welcomed professional bureaucrats into their social circles, in Pernambuco and Rio de Janeiro they allied themselves to the Albuquerque Coelhos or the Correias. In both situations colonial administration was a business whose profits were shared with local merchants and the planter aristocracy. Colonists had a stake in officeholding, although exactly who had access to the spoils constantly shifted.

As in Bahia, conflict rarely arrayed the crown against its colonists. The dispute between the Albuquerques and Luís de Sousa and the Rio revolt of 1660 were domestic quarrels over local patronage. The adversary was not Lisbon but other colonists. The role of the crown was to dole out rewards and punishments once the dust had settled. Regardless of who the incumbents were or how they were selected, bureaucratic positions represented independent sources of authority that came from the metropolis and were not derived from the colonial social order. When local rivalries could not be kept within bounds, matters were resolved in Portugal by the king and his councilors—the ultimate sources of authority. In the sugar captaincies officialdom was an accepted aspect of routine social life, but it had the greatest impact in the coastal cities as it was the planters and ranchers, not the bureaucrats, who ran the countryside.

BEYOND THE COAST: SÃO PAULO

The Serra do Mar, a rugged mountain range that rises abruptly from sea level to heights of 4000 feet, forms a natural barrier between the interior and the coast. This escarpment, which at some points juts out into the sea, begins in Espírito Santo and stretches as far south as Rio

---

[77] Virgínia Rau, "Fortunas ultramarinas e a nobreza portuguesa no seculo XVII," *Revista Portuguesa de História* 8 (1959), pp. 1–25.

Grande do Sul. The range leaves a narrow coastal strip of land hemmed in between the mountains and the sea. There are no navigable rivers opening Minas Gerais or the Paulista plateau to the coast: mule train was the chief means of transportation along the steep, narrow trail between the port of Santos and São Paulo.

São Paulo is situated on the edge of a vast plateau near the river Tietê and has access to a river network that flows west and south to the Paraná and the Paraguay. Unlike the sugar captaincies, which looked to Portugal, São Paulo faces the interior. Agricultural production was largely for local needs, although salted meat and hides reached Santos in modest quantities. The most important business was slave hunting. The organization of such expeditions (*bandeiras*) was a community effort that involved the principal Paulista families, their clientele, who were often *mamelucos*,[78] and Indian allies. During the 1620s the life of the *bandeirantes*,[79] was described in a report to the king as a constant "going and coming, buying and selling of Indians."[80] The fusion of Indian and European cultures in the backlands of São Paulo created a distinct culture whose lingua franca was Tupí-Guaraní, and whose customs and cosmology had indigenous roots. Unlike the sugar captaincies, where officeholding conferred authority and created abundant business opportunities, in São Paulo authority was defined by a person's standing in powerful patriarchal families and by the qualities of leadership and endurance displayed on the bandeiras. Although they were nominally linked to the captaincy of São Vicente, the Paulista settlements were in fact autonomous.[81]

Paulista autonomy is amply demonstrated by their defiance of royal prohibitions against slave hunting. The dispute over Indian labor was one conflict that clearly arrayed colonial interests against the crown, as we discussed with regard to the dissent new Indian legislation caused in Bahia in 1609. In Bahia, however, entradas were allowed only in cases in which a "just war" was approved by royal authorities. In São Paulo the

---

[78] The mamelucos were the offspring of Indian and European parents; in the context of São Paulo, Mörner defines them as "half-breed Brazilian slave-hunters." See Magnus Mörner, *The Political and Economic Activities of the Jesuits in the La Plata Region* (Stockholm, 1953), p. 243.

[79] A bandeirante was someone who participated in a bandeira; by extension, the Paulistas of the seventeenth century are collectively called bandeirantes, although the term was not so applied by contemporaries.

[80] Justo Mansilla and Simon Maceta, "Atrocities of the Paulista," in *The Bandeirantes: The Historical Role of the Brazilian Pathfinders*, ed. Richard M. Morse (New York, 1965), p. 88.

[81] Richard M. Morse, "Introduction," in *The Bandeirantes*, pp. 3–36; and Boxer, *Salvador de Sá*, pp. 22–28.

bandierantes continued their slave hunting in blatant disregard of the king's law.

It was the responsibility of the ouvidor appointed to the southern captaincies to make routine visits to São Paulo, but most kept their distance. When he did venture to the plateau, the cautious ouvidor restricted himself to ordering the affairs of the câmara; he avoided the explosive issue of Indian slavery. The same pattern was evident in the first devassas sent from Bahia to the southern captaincies. Antão de Misquita, the High Court judge who visited São Paulo in 1619, standardized municipal elections and ordered the câmara to keep the Santos road in good repair; he did not raise the question of the crown's Indian policy. Indeed, his stubborn predecessor, Manoel Bravo, had insisted on investigating "matters of the sertão." Not only did Bravo confront the opposition of the câmara, but his life was threatened: angry Paulistas shot arrows into his house at night.[82]

The Jesuits, who maintained several Indian aldeias in the vicinity of São Paulo, opposed the bandeiras. But the São Paulo clergy did not form a united front. The Carmelites, for example, invested in slave raiding to secure labor for their monastery.[83] Some clergymen, under their guise as chaplains, were active participants.[84] Despite Jesuit criticism, slave hunting remained the backbone of the Paulista economy. Besides supplying the local market, the bandeirantes sold slaves in Santos, from whence the captives were shipped to Rio de Janeiro and even Salvador.[85]

As the bandieras ventured further into the interior, they clashed with the Spanish mission settlements in Guairá and Tape.[86] Between 1626 and 1640 the Paulistas devastated the missions, and took thousands of captives.[87] Provoked by these attacks, the king issued a series of strong decrees (1639) that prohibited bandeiras, liberated all captive Indians, and demanded the imprisonment of the leading Paulista slavers. The São Paulo câmara, far from complying, defiantly expelled the Jesuits from the plateau. The governor of Rio de Janeiro, Salvador de Sá, tried to reach São Paulo to negotiate the Order's reinstatement. But the câmara refused to recognize his authority and blocked the mountain trails. The events

---

[82] Schwartz, *Sovereignty and Society*, pp. 162–170.

[83] José de Alcantara Machedo, "Life and Death of a Bandeirante," in *Bandeirantes*, p. 70.

[84] Boxer, *Salvador de Sá*, p. 130.

[85] Ibid., pp. 25–26; and Schwartz, *Sovereignty and Society*, p. 115.

[86] Guairá was located between the Paranápanema and Iguaçú rivers in the present-day states of Paraná and São Paulo. Tape, between the Ibicuí and Jacuí, was in the state of Rio Grande do Sul.

[87] Magnus Mörner, *The Political and Economic Activities of the Jesuits in the La Plata Region* (Stockholm, 1953), p. 91. Also see pp. 87–102.

that took place in São Paulo stand in sharp contrast to those in Rio de Janeiro. As an important market for Indian slaves the Rio captaincy was directly affected by the king's decree. In Rio, however, Governor de Sá intervened between the angry colonists and the Jesuits, preventing expulsion of the order. In São Paulo there were no royal officials who could negotiate with the Paulistas, nor were the bandeirantes swayed by the king's hostility to slave hunting. Almost immediately, they laid plans to attack the Guaraní missions located in the present-day Argentine province of Missiones.[88]

The bandeiras had an important geopolitical dimension. As the Paulistas destroyed the Spanish missions, they advanced beyond the Tordesillas line, encroaching upon supposedly Spanish territory. This was not a crucial consideration during the period of Iberian Union. After 1640, however, the Paulista incursions posed a major threat to Spanish claims. The destruction of mission settlements in Guairá and Tape eliminated key Spanish bases bordering the southern captaincies. To prevent further deterioration of Spanish influence in the region, Madrid encouraged the Jesuits to arm the strategic Guaraní missions. The defensive measures taken by the Jesuits proved both successful and necessary. In 1641 the Guaraní defeated a bandeira of some 400 Paulistas and 2000 Tupí allies.[89]

The new Portuguese royal house did not aggressively dispute the Indian question with the Paulistas. Faced with Spanish hostility in Europe, the Dutch occupation of Pernambuco, and renewed Dutch attacks on Portuguese possessions in Africa and Asia, the new king was hardly in a position to stamp out slave hunting. Instead, the Paulistas, who mixed slave hunting with settlement and exploration, became the crown's major ally against the Spanish in the borderlands. Special bandeiras founded satellite communities around São Paulo, for example. Such settlements were not confined to the hinterland of São Paulo. A bandeira led by Domingos de Brito Peixoto established the town of Laguna in Santa Catarina in 1684.[90]

The Paulistas also began to enter the crown's service. They fought against the Dutch and sent expeditions against the Indians impeding settlement in Bahia, Rio Grande do Norte, and Ceará. It was a Paulista bandeira that destroyed the greal *quilombo* (settlement of escaped slaves) of Palmares in the 1690s.[91] The crown also promoted exploratory expedi-

---

[88] Boxer, *Salvador de Sá*, pp. 152–153, 121–140. Also see Hemming, *Red Gold*, pp. 238–282.

[89] Mörner, *Activities of the Jesuits*, p. 97.

[90] Morse, "Introduction," in *Bandeirantes*, pp. 25–28.

[91] Ernesto Ennes, "The Conquest of Palmares," in *Bandeirantes*, pp. 114–126; Hemming, *Red Gold*, pp. 359–363.

tions. The great bandeira of António Raposo Tavares (1648–1651) "circumnavigated" Brazil by following the course of interior rivers all the way from São Paulo to Belem at the mouth of the Amazon.[92] But prospecting became the major service the bandeirantes performed. The crown offered royal prizes and honors to those who formed bandeiras to search for gold. Such was the case of Fernão Dias Pais and other leading Paulistas. They organized expeditions at their own expense in return for future profits guaranteed by the crown.[93] In the 1670s the frantic search for gold rivaled slave hunting. The crown now enlisted the Paulistas to support imperial schemes, but the region's de facto autonomy continued. It was the gold rush rather than the business of commissioning bandeiras that finally brought a royal governor to the plateau.

THE BACKLANDS

Royal officials such as the capitão-mór of Pernambuco played an active role in establishing coastal settlements in Ceará, Maranhão, and Pará. But the coast had to be protected lest the French and Dutch create rival colonies that could threaten Iberian control of Brazil. Expansion into the interior, beyond the coastal sugar captaincies, was not, however, a strategic necessity. Just as the Paulistas organized their bandeiras with but sporadic interference, so too, the occupation of the backlands was not a royal enterprise. The routine authority of the crown was confined to the forts and coastal cities. How urban-centered and export-oriented colonial administration actually was can be illustrated not only in terms of the distant Brazilian backlands but even in the immediate vicinity of Salvador, the colonial capital. After the Relação was reestablished in 1652, it was a quarter-century before the judges inspected the villages of the Recôncavo. It was not until the eighteenth century that professional magistrates were introduced at the local level. Great planter families really controlled the countryside, or at least the agricultural zone serving the mills.

The desultory character of the king's regime in rural areas is also evident with respect to the quilombos, renegade settlements that were scattered throughout Bahia in direct opposition to plantation society. Formed by escaped slaves, Indian half-breeds, and mulattos, quilombos

---

[92] Jaime Cortesão, "The Greatest Bandeira of the Greatest Bandeirante" in Bandeirantes, pp. 100–113.

[93] Manoel Cardozo, "The Last Adventure of Fernão Dias Pais (1674–1681)," Hispanic American Historical Review 26 (1946), pp. 467–479; idem, "Dom Roderigo de Castel-Blanco and the Brazilian El Dorado, 1673–1682," The Americas 1 (1944), pp. 131–159.

were located near towns and plantations in areas made inaccessible by the marshes and protected inlets of the Recôncavo. Typically, they were not self-sufficient communities. They lived off neighboring settlements, combining subsistence agriculture with highway theft, cattle rustling, and extortion.[94] This was not true of Palmares, the most famous of all the Brazilian quilombos.

Palmares was a self-sufficient African kingdom located in the interior of Alagoas at some distance from the centers of European settlement. In 1677 Palmares had several thousand inhabitants who lived in 10 villages spread over a 90-mile territory.[95] Paulista mercenaries finally destroyed the kingdom in 1694, but only after a 2-year siege. Both in terms of its size and the length of time it survived (1603–1694), Palmares was exceptional. In Bahia colonial authorities periodically licensed expeditions against the quilombos. The number of quilombos formed, and the extent of their geographical distribution, however, indicates that they presented a serious and persistent problem. For ridding the captaincy of its troublesome quilombos, especially those around Salvador, was still an issue in 1760.[96] In Spanish America quilombos menaced regions further from the empire's great urban centers, because plantation slavery flourished in the tropical, coastal lowlands rather than in the more densely populated Indian sierra.[97]

The Cattle Ranchers

The growth of sugar production necessitated a corresponding increase in the quantity of livestock. The plantations needed oxen to pull carts of cane from the fields to the mills, to clear the land, plant, cultivate, and harvest. A typical water mill had 14 pairs of oxen on hand to transport cane and fuel at harvest time. An ox-powered mill needed, in addition, several teams of six to eight oxen to turn the mill. As the supply of cattle grew, salted dried-beef (charque) became a dietary staple, and hides filled a variety of local needs: ropes, waterbags, sacks of all sizes, feed-bags for

---

[94] Stuart B. Schwartz, "The Mocambo: Slave Resistance in Colonial Bahia," *Journal of Social History* 3 (1970), pp. 319–322.

[95] R. K. Kent, "Palmares: An African State in Brazil," *Journal of African History* 6 (1965), p. 198. The largest town had 1500 houses, the second largest settlement, 800.

[96] Schwartz, "Mocambo," pp. 319–328. Also, see the documents reprinted in Pedro Tomás Pedreira, "Os quilombos baianos," *Revista Brasileira de Geografia* 24 (1962), pp. 79–93.

[97] See Richard Price, Ed., *Maroon Societies: Rebel Slave Communities in the Americas* (New York, 1973), pp. 31–103; and Kenneth R. Andrews, *The Spanish Caribbean. Trade and Plunder, 1530–1630* (New Haven, 1978), pp. 34–35, 136–145.

horses and mules, clothing—all were made from different grades of leather. As tobacco production increased, leather was used to wrap cured tobacco for export. Although some hides were exported, the market for cattle, dried beef, and leather products was primarily a domestic one.[98]

Initially, stockraising and sugar production were joint activities. Planters kept their own herds, which grazed around the sugar farms. Gradually, however, grazing was confined to marginal lands at ever greater distances from the plantations. Stockraising became a distinct economic activity. Cattlemen moving north from Bahia and south from Pernambuco began to occupy the São Francisco valley in the 1620s. Thereafter, stockraising spread rapidly into the valley. In 1711, according to the contemporary chronicler, Antonil, there were 1 million head of cattle in the valley.[99]

The São Francisco river rises in the mountains of Minas Gerais about 150 miles from São Paulo; it flows north–northeast paralleling the Brazilian littoral for almost 2000 miles and then bends south and west, emptying into the Atlantic midway between Recife and Salvador. Unlike many rivers in the semiarid Northeast, the São Francisco is perennial. The cyclical flooding of the river creates rich pasture lands dotted with salt licks. In addition to providing a suitable ecology for stockraising, the São Francisco also provides a natural corridor into the interior, linking Minas Gerais to the northern captaincies. The Paulista bandeiras enlisted against the quilombos and hostile Indians reached the Northeast by following the São Francisco.

The disinherited peoples of the coast, displaced Indians, mulattos, escaped slaves, and destitute Portuguese, were the first squatters in the backlands. They did not duplicate cultural traits of the sugar zone such as formal religion, marriage, and municipal councils. From the perspective of coastal society, the semiarid interior, or sertão, was a zone of lawlessness and banditry where there was no legitimate authority. Armed bands "infested the trails, attacked the ranches, stole cattle, and kept the population in a state of unrest."[100] It was the ranchers with their private armies who conquered these outcasts and incorporated them into the local economy as herdsmen and retainers. Still, the pacification of the Brazilian sertão was a gradual and always incomplete process, even to the twentieth century. Isolated settlements combined different forms of ban-

---

[98] Rollie E. Poppino, "Cattle Industry in Colonial Brazil," Mid-America 20 (1949), pp. 223–224, 140–243.

[99] Ibid., pp. 225–227; and Andre João Antonil, Cultura e opulencia do Brasil por suas drogas e minas, trans. into French by Andrée Mansuy (1711: Paris, 1968), p. 474.

[100] Poppino, "Cattle Industry," p. 229.

ditry with subsistence agriculture and clustered around water holes in regions too arid for stockraising.[101]

The crown accepted the cattle ranchers' fait accompli in the backlands, granting them title to the lands they occupied and even making them military commanders of the regions they dominated. Battles between rival landowners and their mercenaries were a routine aspect of life in the sertão. Colonial authorities were distant and passive bystanders. In fact, the crown had surrendered the sertão to powerful families who ordered society in their own way. The interior of Bahia, for example, was owned mainly by two clans: the Guedes de Brito of the House of Ponte and the Dias d'Avila of the House of Torre. The Brito family owned 160 leagues (about 480 miles) along the São Francisco.[102] In the interior of Ceará, which was settled by ranchers in the 1690s, the powerful Feitosa clan dominated local politics for more than two centuries.[103]

In 1700 the ranchers of the Northeast and the Paulistas had penetrated a vast new territory that dwarfed the coastal sugar captaincies. The pattern of relatively compact settlements devoted to sugar and tobacco production was now but one characteristic of colonial Brazil. Bandeirantes and *nordestinos* (inhabitants of the Northeast) were dispersed over a vast hinterland. The folkways of the *sertanejos* (inhabitants of the sertão) and the Paulistas, the rules of the bandeira, family networks, the ties between the *patrão* (rancher) and his *vaqueiros* (cowboys) defined social life. Officeholders and clergymen, merchants and municipal councils did not structure this society as they did in the cities and coastal captaincies. Bandeirantes and ranchers did not have to ally themselves with royal officials; there was no rural bureaucracy to co-opt. The institutional forms that embodied the authority of the metropolis were tied to the coastal, export economy. The result was that in the backlands authority gravitated to powerful extended families. In Brazil the family proved to be an enduring adversary of the state.[104] The role of bureaucracy as an essential link between the crown and colonial society, a fact of life in the sugar captaincies, did not apply to the backlands. The reconquest of the interior was never accomplished by the colonial regime, as Euclides da Cunha's description of the siege of Canudos (1890s) testifies.[105]

---

[101] Prado, *Colonial Background*, pp. 61–64.

[102] Poppino, "Cattle Industry," p. 233. Also, see Russell-Wood, *Fidalgos and Philanthropists*, p. 62.

[103] See Billy Jaynes Chandler, *The Feitosas and the Sertão dos Inhamuns* (Gainesville, 1972). The political significance of powerful Brazilian clans is also emphasized in Gilberto Freyre, *The Masters and the Slaves*, trans. Samuel Putnam (New York, 1964), pp. 30–31.

[104] See Luis Aguiar de Costa Pinto, *Lutas de famílias no Brasil* (São Paulo, 1949).

[105] Euclides Da Cunha, *Rebellion in the Backlands (Os Sertões)*, trans. Samuel Putnam

BRAZIL'S BUREAUCRACY: CONCLUSION

The crown's plan called for a professionally trained corps of magistrates who dispensed justice impartially and implemented the king's law. The competing jurisdictions of the governor-general, the High Court, and the treasury created a system of mutual surveillance. Superior authorities in Salvador, supplemented by periodic visits from higher-ups, kept tabs on officials in subordinate captaincies. This model, of course, was mostly a fiction. Business activities and kinship ties undercut the official scheme, permitting the colonial elite to share in the profits of royal government. Even in Bahia, where the crown filled the most important offices, the lower echelons became the property of their incumbents. Nonetheless, whether patronage was distributed by the crown, by provincial governors, or by entrenched families as in Pernambuco and Rio de Janeiro, bureaucratic posts still derived their authority from the king. In the backlands, where there were few posts to fill, social authority did not depend on the definitions of the metropolis.

Not until the 1670s did the crown manage to link the ambitions of the bandeirantes to its own geopolitical and economic ends; even then, judges, governors, bishops, and treasury officials stayed in Rio de Janeiro. The São Francisco valley and the northeastern sertão, with its great ranches and small, widely dispersed population, produced an authority structure unrelated to the crown's intentions. Granted, every region of the Americas had its "backlands"; there were no equivalents in Spanish America to São Paulo, a city that expelled Jesuits on its own authority and barred the plateau to the king's governors. Despite the towering Andes that separated Spanish settlements such as Asunción and Buenos Aires from the distant Audiencia of Charcas both these towns had their bishops, governors, and military commanders; and they were not exempt from special investigations commissioned by the Council of the Indies.[106] In English America, as the frontier expanded the assemblies created new townships and counties. In Massachusetts, towns with at least 40 voters had to send representatives to the assembly. Increasing the delegation tied new regions to the established political order.[107] Of course, nowhere was institutional authority, whether of assemblies or Audiencias, uni-

---

(1897: Chicago, 1944). Also, see Peter Singelmann, "Political Structure and Social Banditry in Northeast Brazil," *Journal of Latin American Studies* 7 (1975), pp. 59–83; Ralph della Cava, "Brazilian Messianism and National Institutions: A Reappraisal of Canudos and Joaseiro," *Hispanic American Historical Review* 48 (1968), pp. 402–420; idem, *Miracle at Joaseiro* (New York, 1970).

[106] See Mörner, *Activities of the Jesuits*, pp. 87–101, 112–133.
[107] Bailyn, *Origins of American Politics*, pp. 80–83.

formly applied or respected. But only in Brazil did the backlands escape the supervision of colonial authorities so completely and for so long that time can be reckoned not in decades but in centuries. Only in Brazil did the sertão so dwarf the territory linked to the bureaucracy.

As the tool of the state, the bureaucracy's effectiveness depends on the degree of routine control exercised over officeholders. The bureaucracy is the state's servant to the extent that the state builds up a professional staff, sets standards for performance, and enforces compliance with defined expectations. The state, in short, needs a system of recruitment, training, promotion, surveillance, and payment. The more the status of officials depends exclusively on their positions within the bureaucratic hierarchy, the greater the state's control over incumbents. In Brazil royal government was but a remote reflection of such ideal conditions.

Only the High Court magistrates were actually part of a professional staff. Later, as the crown appointed a juiz de fóra to preside over important town councils and created new districts for more circuit judges (ouvidores), the ranks of the magistracy expanded. However, as judges acquired wealth, wives, and business partners in Brazil, the threat of withholding promotions became a relatively weak sanction. Routine surveillance over incumbents was never achieved. Only in Bahia, where competing institutions jealously guarded their jurisdictions, was there an operative system of mutual checks and restraints. In Pernambuco and Rio de Janeiro the privileges enjoyed by the proprietary family and the monopoly over offices extended to the Correias directly violated the principle of royal control. Devassas and residências were far from routine, and offices were sold to incumbents, even those in the treasury. Although the crown eventually appointed its own governors and treasury officials to these captaincies, local administration was to remain a joint enterprise. Governors and treasury officials allied to local families ran the captaincies. Governors were not really part of a professional bureaucracy; they were chosen from the ranks of the nobility, often as a reward for past services. Officeholding was essentially a business, almost exclusively so at the lowest ranks. For governors and treasury officials, service to the crown was but one aspect of their jobs. Salaries did not really cover expenses, nor were they intended to do so. Consequently, officials were also businessmen on the side, investing in trade, borrowing money, and purchasing real estate—nor were such activities necessarily prohibited. But in the absence of strong institutional checks, the capitão-mór, using the broad powers of the governorship as a base, could erect his own patronage system by drawing influential colonial families into his orbit. Or, perhaps, the colonial elite co-opted the governor.

In the seventeenth century no European state had yet managed to construct a professional bureaucracy that directly collected local taxes or controlled provincial administration. Even in the eighteenth century French *intendants* depended on local lieutenants who purchased their posts.[108] In Spanish America the crown sold offices on a grand scale and farmed out the collection of sales taxes to the town councils.[109] At the level of the Audiencia, however, a class of professional judges orchestrated royal government; and the Audiencia, as opposed to the Relação, was a widespread and fundamental institution. Below the Audiencia, governors, bishops, alcaldes majores, and corregidores took up residence in hundreds of towns throughout the Spanish Indies. Colonial administration in Brazil was but a shadow of its Spanish neighbor.

Lisbon did not take stronger measures to bolster its bureaucratic base because in many respects the wealth of Brazil could be tapped without an extensive bureaucracy. The Portuguese empire was a trading system. Taxes on trade yielded the bulk of the crown's revenues. As long as Portugal remained the clearinghouse for colonial trade, Brazil's productive capacity could be taxed as it passed through Lisbon, Oporto, or Vianna. If royal government ignored the countryside, it was because everything of value in Brazil ultimately came to Recife, Salvador, or Rio de Janeiro. The resources of the interior, cattle ranching and subsistence agriculture, hardly justified establishing bureaucratic posts in the backlands. The planter could not survive without exporting his sugar and importing his materials and equipment. Trade was Brazil's lifeline. By organizing and taxing trade, Portugal lived off its American colony without investing the profits in bureaucrats.

---

[108] Wolfram Fischer and Peter Lundgreen, "Recruitment and Training," in *Formation of National States*, p. 502.

[109] For example, see Robert Sidney Smith, "Sales Taxes in New Spain, 1575–1770," *Hispanic American Historical Review* 28 (1948), pp. 2–37.

III

Empire by Trade:
The Seventeenth Century

IBERIAN RETRENCHMENT

The Asian spice trade was still Portugal's most valuable overseas enterprise in 1580, but the spectacular growth of the sugar industry soon made Brazil a vital link in the empire's economy. Between 1610 and 1620 Brazil exported over 700,000 arrobas of sugar a year just to Lisbon.[1] According to Matias de Albuquerque, Brazil's governor-general (1624–1625), hundreds of small ships made regular voyages between Portuguese and Brazilian ports; the sugar trade's value he estimated at 4 million cruzados a year.[2] Portugal's empire was shifting toward the Atlantic and its flourishing trades in sugar, African slaves, and supplies for Brazil's mills and settlers.

The Decline of Asian Trade

Although Brazil prospered, Asian trade was slipping from Lisbon's grasp. Pepper cargoes had averaged around 20,000 quintals in the 1580s,

---

[1] Vitorino Magalhães Godinho, "Portugal, as frotas do açúcar e as frotas do ouro (1670–1770)," *Revista de História* 15 (1953), p. 73.

[2] Vitorino Magalhães Godinho, *Os descobrimentos e a economia mundial*, 2 vols. (Lisbon, 1963–1965), vol. 2, p. 471.

but from 1611 to 1626 cargoes fell to about 10,000 a year—less than a third
of the volume carried in the 1540s.[3] Five or six overloaded and often
unseaworthy vessels tenuously linked Lisbon and Goa; all the merchandise and personnel destined for Asia in a given year had to be crammed
aboard these ships. Between 1570 and 1599 only 9 Asia-bound ships
perished, but during the years 1600 to 1629 the number jumped to 31.
From 1591 to 1600 16 of 39 homeward-bound ships were lost.[4] In addition,
the inter-Asian trades managed by the Portuguese in partnership with
Asian merchants prospered more than Lisbon's spice business; and since
customs duties collected in Asian trade went to local administration and
defense, there was little left to be sent back to Portugal.[5]

Portugal's reduced Asian trade reflected the difficulty of marketing the
empire's pepper in Europe. The spices Venice obtained in the Levant
provided an alternative supply, but until the 1580s the Dutch were good
customers of Portugal as they supplied Baltic markets with spices purchased in Lisbon. The Protestant Dutch, however, were Spain's mortal
enemies; after Philip II seized the Portuguese throne Dutch traders were
no longer welcome in Lusitanian ports: ipso facto they became Portugal's
enemies too. The pepper trade was soon caught up in Spain's foreign
policy. To weaken his Dutch adversaries, Philip II tried to reroute the
spice trade through different middlemen.[6] The strategy failed because
Spain was struggling to protect its own shipping in the North Atlantic—a
battle that was ultimately lost. The period of Iberian Union (1580–1640)
was decisive for Spain's decline as an Atlantic power and for Dutch
ascendancy. The revolt of the Dutch Netherlands destroyed the old
commercial order. Portugal, already a client state in the Atlantic's commercial system, was followed into dependency by its Spanish overlords.[7]

Spain and the Netherlands had been part of the dynastic holdings of
the same royal family. Charles V, the young Burgundian ruler of the Low

[3] Ibid., 103–106.

[4] Ibid., pp. 77–82. In the 1620s departures from Lisbon averaged around six ships a year;
see Charles R. Boxer, The Portuguese Seaborne Empire: 1415–1822 (New York, 1969), pp.
381–382; and Godinho, Descobrimentos, p. 77.

[5] See J. B. Harrison, "Colonial Development and International Rivalries Outside Europe:
(2) Asia and Africa, in New Cambridge Modern History, ed. R. B. Wernham, vols. (London,
1968), vol. 3, The Counter Reformation and the Price Revolution, pp. 532–558; and Boxer,
Portuguese Seaborne Empire, pp. 514–518.

[6] See Fernand Braudel, The Mediterranean and the Mediterranean World in the Age of
Phillip II, trans. Siân Reynolds, 2 vols. (2nd ed. New York, 1972–1973), vol. 1, pp. 556–562.

[7] On Spain's decline, see I. A. A. Thompson, War and Government in Hapsburg Spain
1560–1620 (London, 1976); Peter Pierson, Philip II of Spain (London, 1975); J. H. Elliott,
Imperial Spain 1469–1716 (New York, 1963); idem, The Revolt of the Catalans: A Study in
the Decline of Spain 1598–1640) (Cambridge, Eng., 1963).

Countries, inherited the Spanish empire from his grandparents, Ferdinand and Isabella. During his long reign (1516–1556), imperial trade expanded rapidly, creating an economic network that included Antwerp, Seville, and the New World. Dutch, Flemish, and Spanish merchants shared in the profitable seaborne trades between Northern Europe and the Peninsula. Antwerp, the commercial capital of the Netherlands, had over 100 Spanish merchants in 1560, forming the city's largest foreign colony. Spain imported fine textiles, naval stores, Baltic grain, armaments, and metallurgical products essential to agriculture and industry from Antwerp, both for domestic use and for reexport to the colonies. To pay for these products, Spanish merchants sent about 60% of Castile's wool to the Netherlands, along with salt, olive oil, wine, and dried fruit, plus small quantities of colonial imports like cochineal (a red dye) and hides. Spain's modest exports could not compensate for the growing volume of expensive, imported manufactured goods, but colonial trade helped to balance the deficit. The Spanish fleets that left Seville for the Indies returned with silver from Mexico and Peru. To cover their debts with northern suppliers, Seville's merchants, in turn, remitted bullion to Antwerp. The exchange produced a deficit on Spain's account, but it mattered little from an imperial perspective. The wealthy Low Countries paid taxes and made loans that bolstered the crown's credit; in one 5-year period, Charles V exacted new grants from the provincial estates (assemblies) worth 8 million ducats. With respect to the crown's income and the empire's trade, the Netherlands were pivotal possessions.[8]

The Revolt of the Netherlands

Philip II (1556–1598) took over his father's Spanish and Burgundian kingdoms, but his aggressive fiscal policies, coupled with an all-out attack on Dutch Calvinism, provoked bitter opposition led by the provincial estates.[9] In 1568 the Netherlands revolted openly, beginning an 80-year struggle that would exhaust Spain, devastate Antwerp, and drive Spanish shipping from the North Atlantic. Spain lacked the naval strength to protect simultaneously both its American commerce and the Atlantic route to the embattled Netherlands. Although England and Spain were

---

[8] See John Lynch, *Spain under the Hapsburgs*, 2 vols. (Oxford, 1964–1969), vol. 1, pp. 140–147, 273; S. T. Bindoff, "The Greatness of Antwerp," in New Cambrdidge Modern History, ed. G. R. Elton, (London, 1958), vol. 2, *The Reformation 1520–1559* pp. 50–69; and H. G. Koenigsberger, "The Empire of Charles V in Europe," in *Reformation*, p. 318.

[9] See Peter Geyl, *The Revolt of the Netherlands (1555–1609)* (London, 1932); and Gordon Griffiths, "The Revolutionary Character of the Revolt in the Netherlands," *Comparative Studies in Society and History* 2 (1960), pp. 452–472.

nominally at peace from 1568 to 1585, English privateers joined with the Dutch to harass Spanish shipping. The war ruined the carrying trades that Biscayan ports such as Bilbao, Laredo, and Santander had enjoyed with the Netherlands. In 1582 there were only three Spanish firms left in Antwerp. So dangerous had the North Atlantic become that Santander's merchants refused to risk their ships by transporting the king's silver to the Low Countries. To pay Spanish troops in the Netherlands, American silver had to be carried overland to Antwerp from Genoa. Genoese bankers, who handled the steady flow of bullion northwards, became the Spanish crown's financiers.[10]

One objective of the great Spanish Armada of 1588 was to break the Dutch monopoly on Peninsular trade, thus reopening the North Atlantic to Spanish shipping. However, the Armada failed. Spain and its colonies still provided markets for northern exports; Iberia remained an important source of raw materials; and American silver still covered the deficit. But now the imperial treasury no longer profited from Dutch prosperity, and Spanish merchants, deprived of their northern carrying trades, made less on the exchange. Dutch traders carried off 25% of the silver the fleets brought back to Seville.[11] Spain could not stem the traffic; it desperately needed the Baltic grain, naval stores, and industrial goods rebel shipping supplied. The Dutch, well-armed with merchandise, capital, and ships, reduced their Spanish counterparts to commission agents.[12] In 1595 and 1598, when the Spanish government temporarily halted Dutch trade, some 500 rebel vessels were caught in Iberian ports.[13]

After being ousted from the North Atlantic, Spain's commerce fell back on Seville and the fleets that supplied America. But foreign capital infiltrated colonial trade, too. Dutch firms, enriched by their trades with the Peninsula, advanced goods on credit to Seville's merchants, to be paid for when the silver fleets arrived. Dutch merchandise was entered in account books as Castilian or Portuguese. The trade was clandestine, since the Dutch, as enemies of Spain, could not establish a resident colony in Seville. Seville's merchants became middlemen who "saw goods pass through and took their percentage, but were reluctant to risk their own capital."[14] Instead of channeling their profits back into trade, Spanish

---

[10] Braudel, *Mediterranean*, vol. 1, p. 483, 500–517.

[11] Violet Barbour, *Capitalism in Amsterdam in the 17th Century* (1950: Ann Arbor, 1966), pp. 49–52.

[12] Lynch, *Spain under the Hapsburgs*, vol. 2, p. 141.

[13] Engel Sluiter, "Dutch-Spanish Rivalry in the Caribbean Area, 1594–1609," *Hispanic American Historical Review* 28 (1948), p. 170.

[14] Braudel, *Mediterranean*, vol. 1, p. 368.

merchants invested in government bonds or entailed estates. Thus, in the 1590s, Seville's trade had come to depend on Dutch capital.[15]

In 1609 Spain and the Dutch United Provinces signed a 12-year truce. Spain maintained control over Antwerp and Belgium, and the rebellious northern provinces formed a separate state whose commercial capital was Amsterdam. By then Antwerp's industry and trade had declined; Amsterdam had become the North Atlantic's new entrepôt. Antwerp had been an international city where merchants from different countries shared in trade, shipping, and banking. In Amsterdam, however, the Dutch monopolized the city's commercial life. Dutch ships went everywhere— to the Baltic, Iberia, the Mediterranean, and the Far East—gathering in world trade. Dutch capital and Dutch merchants, not colonies of foreigners, sustained the nation's trade. Amsterdam's ascendancy symbolized the new age of mercantilism in the North Atlantic. The Dutch took over trade, not European territory. The first truly commercial state took shape in the Netherlands, where merchants, rather than the king, controlled the government.[16]

THE SHIFT OF POWER

Let us now return to the question of Portuguese spices. The reason it was so difficult to carry on the trade between Goa and Lisbon was because Portugal's Atlantic shipping became less secure after the defeat of the Armada.[17] By the end of the century Dutch merchants had entered the Mediterranean and were themselves buying spices in the Levant. Dutch–Spanish hostilities precluded an obvious solution to the ailing India fleets: Dutch firms could have handled the pepper contracts, both for purchases in India and sales in Europe. But this path was closed since Dutch firms were illegal in the Spanish king's domain. Furthermore, the contract system for spices was more resistant to Dutch capital than was the Seville trade. The crown leased the business to German and Italian firms, sometimes in association with the wealthiest Iberian merchants—

---

[15] Ibid., pp. 629–640. Government bonds proved to be poor investments: see Alvaro Castillo Pintado, "Los juros de Castilla: Apogeo y fin de un instrumento de crédito," *Hispania, Revista Española de Historia* **23** (1963), pp. 42–70.

[16] See D. J. Rooda, "The Ruling Classes in Amsterdam in the Seventeenth Century," in *Britain and the Netherlands*, eds. J. S. Bromley and E. H. Kossmann, 2 vols. (London, 1960–1964), vol. 2, pp. 109–132; Charles R. Boxer, *The Dutch Seaborne Empire 1600–1800* (New York, 1970), pp. 31–53; and Barbour, *Capitalism in Amsterdam*.

[17] Braudel, *Mediterranean*, vol. 1, pp. 560–570.

and the spice contracts were expensive. In 1606 contractors had to pay the crown 75,000 cruzados for each ship dispatched—60,000 in advance.[18] The United Provinces resolved the spice problem in 1602. To dislodge the Portuguese in Asia, they established the East India Company with a capital of 6.5 million florins.[19]

Spain was in no position to strengthen Portugal's Asian empire. Despite its role in American trade, Seville had never become a financial center; Spanish merchants lacked enough capital to take over the spice contracts. In 1600 Seville was primarily a transit point that had colonies of foreign merchants but no supporting industries. During the first 30 years of the seventeenth century more than 130 foreigners—Flemings, Portuguese, Italians, and Frenchmen—obtained naturalization rights to trade directly with the Spanish Indies. Seville alone had 12,000 foreign residents in 1640. Trade with America, once reserved for Spanish merchants and vessels, had assumed the character of an international venture. Not only did trade depend on foreign capital, but the Spaniards had to hire foreign ships. During the years 1579 to 1587, foreign vessels made up only about 6% of the fleets. This rose to 21% between 1579 and 1587, and increased substantially thereafter. In the 1640s the crown's policy was simply to give preference to Spanish ships when they were available.[20] By then, Portugal had successfully achieved independence. But it could not reverse the shift in commercial dominance to northern Europe. Lisbon became a trading post for the Dutch and the English.

Although Spanish merchants profited less than previously from the Indies trade, taxes on American silver production continued to provide the crown with a crucial source of revenue; between 1596 and 1615 the fleets returned with over 33 million pesos worth of silver for the king.[21] Additional sums went to fortify American ports and defend the fleets.[22] So while Spain lost the battle for the Netherlands, it jealously defended the Indies and Brazil. Spain managed to keep foreign merchants out of Hispanic America; they had to trade through Seville and the fleets. Iberian trade and colonization in the New World was not seriously challenged until the 1620s.

The Portuguese, although they were still considered foreigners, had the right to travel and settle in the Spanish empire. Carrying slaves from

---

[18] Godinho, *Descobrimentos*, vol. 2, pp. 92–100.

[19] Boxer, *Dutch Seaborne Empire*, p. 24.

[20] These figures are from Lynch, *Spain under the Hapsburgs*, vol. 1, p. 166; vol. 2, pp. 141, 170–171.

[21] Earl J. Hamilton, *American Treasure and the Price Revolution in Spain, 1501–1650* (Cambridge, Mass., 1934), p. 34.

[22] Lynch, *Spain under the Hapsburgs*, vol. 2, pp. 173–193.

Africa to the Spanish and using Brazil as a base for shipping goods to Buenos Aires, Portuguese merchants gained more from the Iberian alliance than the Spaniards. It is not surprising that many Portuguese merchants preferred the Spanish empire. Silver-rich Mexico and Peru offered more opportunities than Brazil's sugar economy. Seville's merchants, however, preferred the Indies trade; they stayed out of Brazil.

THE SUGAR TRADE

The Goa trade could yield great profits to a few wealthy merchants, provided that the ships returned safely to Lisbon. Luxury goods such as furniture, precious stones, Indian calicoes, Chinese silks and porcelains became important items of trade.[23] Brazil's sugar trade, on the other hand, required only modest investments and produced modest profits. It involved hundreds of swift, small caravels of 90 to 150 tons, and was open to all merchants and all ports of Portugal and Brazil.[24] Lisbon was the main sugar port, although smaller coastal towns like Oporto, Vianna, Lagos, and Faro also participated. The passage to Brazil was a matter of weeks, as opposed to the six to eight months journey from Portugal to Goa, so smaller ships carrying fewer supplies and fewer arms could be used. The cargo of a single Indiaman could easily be worth 500,000 cruzados, whereas 100 tons of sugar carried on an average-size caravel was probably only worth about 20,000 cruzados.[25] In the 1620s Recife loaded 130 ships annually; Bahia, about 75; and Rio de Janeiro, 30. Even small Portuguese ports such as Vianna had large merchant marines.[26] The sugar trade, the preserve of smaller merchants, kept the secondary ports and the provincial bourgeois prosperous.[27]

---

[23] A. H. de Oliveira Marques, *History of Portugal*, 2 vols. (New York, 1972), vol. 1, pp. 344–345; Godinho, *Descobrimentos*, pp. 102, 107–108. This was a gradual shift that became more pronounced once the Dutch ousted the Portuguese from their spice factories; see Charles R. Boxer, "The Principal Ports of Call in the *Carreira da India*," *Luso-Brazilian Review* 8 (1971), pp. 18–20.

[24] Boxer, *Portuguese Seaborne Empire*, p. 220. On ship construction and tonnage see Frédéric Mauro, *Le Portugal et l'Atlantique au XVII\u1d49 siècle (1570–1670)* (Paris, 1960), pp. 29–49.

[25] This estimate is based on a cargo of 7000 *arrobas* (100 tons), evenly divided between white and brown sugar selling at 2000 réis and 1000 réis respectively. On prices, see Mauro, *Le Portugal*, pp. 246–247.

[26] Charles R. Boxer, "Padre António Vieira, S. J., and the Institution of the Brazil Company in 1649," *Hispanic American Historical Review* 28 (1948), p. 477.

[27] Godinho, *Descobrimentos*, vol. 2, p. 472.

Brazil was the first region in the Americas to specialize in export agriculture. In 1570 60 mills produced 180,000 arrobas of sugar; in 1612, some 190 mills yielded over 800,000 arrobas. Fifteen years later, in 1627, exports exceeded 1 million arrobas (about 32 million lbs) manufactured by about 230 mills.[28] Contemporaries estimated the value of Brazil's sugar crop at about 1 million cruzados in 1590 and 4 million in 1627.[29] The sugar industry was concentrated geographically, and Pernambuco and Bahia had 65% of all the mills in Brazil: of the 230 mills in operation in 1627, 100 were in Pernambuco, 50 in Bahia. Rio de Janeiro was also an important and growing producer. With no more than a couple of mills in 1612, the Rio captaincy had 40 mills by 1627 and the number steadily increased. The large water-powered mills could turn out 10,000 arrobas of raw sugar yearly. The smaller mills used oxen, and yielded 3000 to 5000 arrobas. Perhaps 20% of Brazil's mills had a capacity in excess of 5000 arrobas.[30]

The mill, or *engenho*, was much more than simply a grinding stone or press. It was actually a processing plant composed of distinct installations—the press, the boiler vats, and the purgery—and skilled laborers were needed to oversee the various steps of production. The tall, cylindrical stalk of the sugar cane is filled with a sweet liquid. Once cut, the cane will resprout, producing successive, though poorer crops, without replanting. To obtain optimum yields, harvested sugar cane has to be processed almost immediately. The liquid was drained from the stalk by crushing the cane between heavy, iron-plated millstones turned by water power or oxen. Wooden troughs conducted the extract to huge copper vats, where it was boiled and then transferred to a second vat, boiled afresh, scummed, and then strained. From the great vats in the boiler house, the hot, amber liquid ran into large kettles where it was purged, i.e., boiled and constantly stirred until it partly congealed. This thick semiliquid, slightly cooled, was poured into hundreds of large earthen jars, each with a small hole at the base. As it cooled, it crystallized into sugar mixed with molasses. The jars, containing about an arroba of sugar, were then covered with soft, wet clay. As the water filtered through, it removed the molasses and whitened the sugar. Brown sugar, still mixed with molasses, adhered to the inside of the jar. The two grades of sugar—white (*blanco*) and brown (*muscavado*)—were heaped in the sun

---

[28] Ibid., pp. 461–464. Also see Mauro, *Le Portugal*, pp. 192–196.

[29] Godinho, *Descobrimentos*, vol. 2, pp. 462, 471.

[30] Ibid., pp. 464–465.

to dry, and then packed in huge chests for export.[31] The price of white sugar usually exceeded that of muscavado by 50 to 60%.[32]

The mill was an agroindustrial unit; its operation required skilled craftsmen and able administrators in addition to slaves. The largest employed 10 to 20 salaried workers and about 100 slaves; with their quarters and workshops, the mills resembled small villages.[33] The sugar master, who managed refining, received room and board plus a salary of 400 cruzados. He was assisted by boilers, purgers, potters, and crators—all salaried—who resembled foremen in different parts of the mill.[34] Besides those directly responsible for production, the mill employed coopers, blacksmiths, cattle drivers, boatmen, fishermen, carpenters, and mechanics. Portuguese workers, apparently, held many of the top positions, while freedmen and slaves were usually to be found doing semiskilled and unskilled tasks. During the eighteenth century slaves moved into skilled jobs, some even serving as sugar masters.[35] At the great mill of Sergipe do Conde in the Bahian Recôncavo, records show that from 1622 to 1635 salaries accounted for 19% of total expenditures; although the mill had from 60 to 100 slaves, their purchase accounted for only 12% of operating costs.[36]

A medium-sized mill with 50 slaves represented a capital investment of about 40,000 cruzados and required continuous outlays: overhead at the large mill of Sergipe, for example, was 11,500 cruzados annually.[37] Besides labor costs there was the investment in capital goods, fuelwood, oxen, and foodstuffs. Manioc and vegetables were grown locally, but many staples were imported: olive oil, flour, codfish, and salt, for example.

---

[31] This description draws upon the following sources: Charles R. Boxer, *The Dutch in Brazil 1624–1654* (1957: Hamden, Conn., 1973), pp. 141–142; John Ogilby, "America, being the latest and most accurate description of the New World containing the Original of the Inhabitants, and the Remarkable Voyages thither" (London, 1671), pp. 503–505, quoted in A. J. R. Russell-Wood, *Fidalgos and Philanthropists: The Santa Casa da Misericórdia of Bahia* (Berkeley, 1968), pp. 53–54; Richard Flecknoe, "A True and Faithful Account of Ten Years Travells in Europe, Asia, Affrique and America" (London, 1665), pp. 79–80, quoted in Charles R. Boxer, *Salvador de Sá and the Struggle for Brazil and Angola 1602–1686* (London, 1952), p. 234.

[32] Mauro, *Le Portugal*, pp. 241–246.

[33] Boxer, *Dutch in Brazil*, p. 32.

[34] Godinho, *Descobrimentos*, vol. 2, p. 468.

[35] Stuart B. Schwartz, "Free Labor in a Slave Economy: the *Lavradores de Cana* of Colonial Bahia," in *The Colonial Roots of Modern Brazil*, ed. Dauril Alden (Berkeley, 1973), pp. 152, 180.

[36] Frédéric Mauro, *Nova história e nôvo mundo* (São Paulo, 1969), p. 143.

[37] Godinho, *Descobrimentos*, vol. 2, p. 469, and Mauro, *Nova história*, p. 143. This figure is derived from the table as follows: 55,195,393 réis ÷ 12 years = 4,599,612 réis per year ÷ 400 réis = 11,499 cruzados.

Sugar production created a rising demand for cattle. An ox-driven mill needed 15 to 20 teams just to keep the mill operating, and the oxen had to be replaced every 3 years.[38] Even a water-powered mill like Sergipe kept a herd of oxen to transport cane and sugar.

The mill owner did not necessarily work the plantation's land on his own account, nor did the cane brought to the mill come exclusively from his estates. In Bahia many cane growers owned land but did not have the capital to set up mills. They could process their cane where they chose, but one-half the yield went to the mill owner. The majority of the growers, however, were sharecroppers, and many of them quite prosperous. They leased their lands from the mill owners for relatively long contract periods: 6, 9 and sometimes 18 years, usually as a *partido de terço:* one-third to the grower, two-thirds to the mill.[39] There were 800 to 1000 growers furnishing cane for the mills of Bahia in 1629.[40] Until the 1660s the Sergipe mill leased all of its land to cane growers. Agriculture was intensive since plots were a relatively small 3 to 6 hectares in size. A typical grower had between 7 and 15 slaves, 12 to 24 teams of oxen, and several carts. In the 1620s, a good farm represented an investment of about 3000 cruzados.[41] Besides cane, the growers supplied mills with fuelwood. A contemporary noted that one mill burnt 40 fathoms of wood daily;[42] 21% of Sergipe's expenses went to fuel.[43] Cutting and transporting firewood, hewing boards, and making crates provided extra funds for the cane growers.[44] Although they varied considerably in wealth and social standing, a prosperous cane grower occupied a respected social position and was eligible for election to the câmara, a privilege denied artisans and shopkeepers.[45]

Colonial Brazil's reputation as a land of slaves and great sugar plantations must be balanced by the many cane growers who owned or leased small farms, making modest investments in equipment and slaves; furthermore, wage labor played an essential role in the economy. Moreover, sugar was not Brazil's only export. Bahian tobacco, when laced with molasses, was a prized commodity and was exchanged for slaves. The purchase of tobacco for export was a monopoly that the crown leased to contractors. Although the quantity exported is difficult to estimate, the

---

[38] Godinho, *Descobrimentos*, vol. 2, p. 466; and Celso Furtado, The Economic Growth of Brazil, trans. Ricardo de Aguiar and Eric Charles Drysdale (Berkeley, 1963), p. 47.

[39] Schwartz, "Free Labor in a Slave Economy," pp. 154–159.

[40] Ibid., p. 181.

[41] Ibid., pp. 173–176.

[42] Ogilby, "America, being the latest," p. 54.

[43] Mauro, *Nova história*, p. 143.

[44] Schwartz, "Free Labor in a Slave Economy," pp. 170–171.

[45] Ibid., pp. 176–177.

tobacco contract sold for 15,500 cruzados in 1638, 32,000 cruzados in 1642, and redoubled in value by 1659.[46] When the sugar industry declined during the 1680s, many cane growers converted to tobacco, the small man's crop. In 1720 Bahia tobacco was almost as important an export as sugar.

The colony's revenues came primarily from taxes on sugar. A portion of the sugar crop, theoretically one-tenth, belonged to the crown, but the amount collected added up to considerably less. Abreu de Brito wrote to the king in 1591, claiming that the treasury was being cheated on the Pernambucan tithe contracts. The contractors purchased the concession for 28,500 cruzados, a price that suggested a harvest of 142,500 arrobas, since an arroba of sugar was then selling for around two cruzados.[47] Brito estimated that actual production was 378,000 arrobas, however, and that the tithe contract was really worth 75,600 cruzados.[48] In 1613, although production had doubled, the tithe farm brought only 43,400 cruzados.[49] Brito failed to mention that the tithe business was expensive to operate. The tax was difficult to assess, and it was collected in kind. In the 1590s contractors had to ship their sugar to Portugal and sell it before they could pay off the king.[50] Matias de Albuquerque estimated that the tax farmers who bid 150,000 cruzados for the Brazilian tithe contract in 1627 had to collect 200,000 cruzados just to cover their expenses.[51] Although collection costs certainly reduced the value of tithe contracts, the crown reduced them further by creating tax loopholes to stimulate production. For example, water-driven mills were exempt from the tithe for the first 10 years of operation. To keep their tax-free status, owners renovated or relocated their mills and then claimed exemptions, or they registered ox-driven mills as water-powered ones.[52] This fraud, of course, required the collusion of mill owners, tax farmers, and royal officials.

The taxes collected in Brazil could not pay for the fortification of the coastal cities, but they did cover the on-going cost of colonial adminis-

---

[46] Roberto C. Simonsen, *História econômica do Brasil: 1500–1820* (1937: São Paulo, 1962), p. 368; and Vitorino Magalhães Godinho, "Portugal and Her Empire (1640–1670)," in New Cambridge Modern History, ed. F. L. Carsten. (London, 1961), vol. 5, *The Ascendancy of France 1648–1688*, p. 385. The Crown abandoned the monopoly system between 1642 and 1659, but doubled import duties.

[47] 142,500 arrobas × 10% = 14,250 arrobas × 2 cruzados = 28,500 cruzados (contract price).

[48] 378,000 arrobas × 10% = 37,800 arrobas × 2 cruzados = 75,600 cruzados (contract price).

[49] Mauro, *Le Portugal*, p. 219.

[50] Engel Sluiter, "Os Holandeses no Brasil antes de 1621," *Revista do Instituto Arqueológico Histórica e Geográfico Pernambucano* 46 (1961), p. 201.

[51] Mauro, *Le Portugal*, p. 220.

[52] Mauro, *Nova história*, p. 197, and Godinho, *Descobrimentos*, vol. 2, p. 471.

tration. And, if sugar partially escaped the colonial tithe, it was not so easy to avoid duties paid at metropolitan ports like Lisbon. A 20% ad valorem tax was levied on all sugar brought to Portugal, on top of the sales tax levied on all transactions. During the 1620s taxes accounted for about 30% of the price of sugar.[53] Lisbon prices stood at about 4 cruzados for an arroba of white sugar and 3 cruzados for muscavado—double the Brazilian prices. Since sugar exports were about 1 million arrobas in 1627, the total value of Brazil's sugar was at least 3.5 million cruzados. If 30% of this amount represented taxation, sugar taxes yielded over 1 million cruzados—40% of the state's revenue.[54] To safeguard Brazil's sugar industry and its own income, the state protected the mill owners and growers from foreclosure. Slaves, oxen, and equipment could not be seized for nonpayment of debts, only sugar.[55]

Brazil's loaf sugar was remelted and recrystalized in Europe before it was put on the market. In 1556 Antwerp had 19 refineries;[56] at that time, most sugar came from the Atlantic Islands on Portuguese ships. The war in the Netherlands, however, ruined Antwerp's sugar business and reduced Portugal's carrying trade. During the 1590s the Dutch carried the bulk of Brazil's sugar to Amsterdam, northern Europe's new center for refining and distribution. While the truce was in effect (1609-1621), 100 Dutch ships imported 40,000 to 50,000 chests of sugar a year, each containing about 20 arrobas of sugar; they supplied Holland's 29 refineries.[57]

Dutch merchants did not limit their activities to the European end of the sugar trade. Carrying textiles, equipment, and provisions, they made direct voyages between Portugal and Brazil, and they didn't always return to Lisbon to pay the sugar tax.[58] In 1594 Philip II prohibited this traffic, but Portuguese sugar merchants, since they needed Dutch shipping, registered rebel vessels under their own names. Portuguese officials stationed in the ports protected local merchants and their Dutch partners against Spanish reprisals. In 1621 Dutch vessels flying the Portuguese flag

---

[53] Mauro, Nova história, pp. 197–199; and Godinho, Descobrimentos, vol. 2, p. 471.

[54] This figure is simply a rough estimate. In 1628 Portugal's revenues were about 2.5 million cruzados: see Oliveira Marques, History of Portugal, vol. 1, p. 278.

[55] David Grant Smith, "The Mercantile Class of Portugal and Brazil in the Seventeenth Century: A Socio-Economic Study," (doctoral dissertation, University of Texas, 1975), p. 392.

[56] Noel Deerr, The History of Sugar, 2 vols. (London, 1949–1950), vol. 2, p. 453.

[57] Engel Sluiter, "Dutch Maritime Power and the Colonial Status Quo, 1585–1641," Pacific Historical Review 2 (1942), p. 35. On the number of arrobas in a chest of sugar, see Boxer, Salvador de Sá, p. 180 n. 48.

[58] Sluiter, "Holandeses," pp. 202, 196–206. Also see Mário Neme, "A Bahia e o atlântico," Anais do Museo Paulista 17 (1963), pp. 173–178.

accounted for at least one-half the shipping in Luso-Brazilian trade.[59] Although the sugar trade was a joint Portuguese–Dutch enterprise, the Dutch were, in fact, the senior partners; they made profits on every phase of the business from shipping and credit operations to refining and distribution. The sugar trade was an essential component in Dutch commerce; it accounted for more than one-fourth the state's tonnage receipts.[60] It was the Dutch entrepreneurs, not the Portuguese, who expanded the market for Brazil's sugar. The Dutch promoted sales and extended credit to Brazil's mill owners and planters, ususally through Portuguese merchants.[61] In general, consumption grew as rapidly as production, so that between 1580 and 1620, prices remained relatively stable despite vast increases in sugar exports.[62] When the truce with Spain ended, the Dutch tried to take over Brazil's sugar plantations so they could control both distribution and production.

THE SLAVE TRADE

The sugar industry was dependent upon slave labor. Slaves planted, tended, cut, and transported the cane crop; they kept the mills running. When disease and the rigor of agricultural labor had reduced the Indian population, the planters imported African workers. In 1600 there were 60,000 African slaves, which accounted for one-half the total slave population in Brazil, and about 30,000 Portuguese colonists.[63] Only the sugar trade itself engaged more Portuguese ships than the slave traffic. During the 18 months between December, 1624 and August, 1626 75 ships carried 17,708 *peças* of slaves from Luanda, Angola, to Brazil and the Spanish Indies.[64,65]

The king farmed out the slave trade to private businessmen. Until the 1590s Genoese merchants often held the contracts for the Spanish Indies; thereafter, the Portuguese took over.[66] Thus, union with Spain created

---

[59] Boxer, *Dutch in Brazil*, pp. 20–21.

[60] Matthew Edel, "The Brazilian Sugar Cycle of the Seventeenth Century and the Rise of West Indian Competition," *Caribbean Studies* 9 (1969), p. 27.

[61] See Furtado, *Economic Growth of Brazil*, pp. 8–9.

[62] For a list of prices and sugar exports, see Mauro, *Le Portugal*, pp. 236–247.

[63] Godinho, *Descobrimentos*, vol. 2, pp. 544–545.

[64] A slave from 15 to 25 years of age was designated a peça. Three slaves aged 8 to 14, or 26 to 35 made up two peças; slaves less than 8 years old or over 36 were counted as one-half a peça. See Carlos Frederico Montenegro de Sousa Miguel, "Escravatura," in *Diciónario de história de Portugal*, Joel Serrão, ed., 6 vols. (Lisbon, 1975–1978), vol. 2, p. 422.

[65] Mauro, *Le Portugal*, p. 175.

[66] Godinho, *Descobrimentos*, vol. 2, pp. 552–554.

new markets for Portuguese slave traders. Between 1580 and 1640 the most important contracts were for Guiné via Cape Verde, which supplied the Spanish Indies, and Angola, which supplied Brazil. Contractors were actually tax farmers who rented the right to collect duties on the slave trade; it was a profitable enterprise. Those who held the Angolan contract (1587–1591), paid an annual fee of 11 *contos* (1 conto = 1,000,000 réis = 2500 cruzados). The established levy of 3000 réis on each slave carried to Brazil and 6000 réis on those sent to the Spanish Indies, yielded profits of almost 100%.[67] To participate, slavers had to obtain a license from the concessionaires and register with the India House before departure from Portugal. This license or subcontract stated where the slaves were to be obtained, the cargo's destination, the number of slaves the captain could load, and the tax on each peça of slaves.[68] To prevent fraud, factors in Angola certified the cargo, making sure that captains did not load more slaves than their contracts permitted, and confiscated unlicensed vessels. Once in Brazil, the captain presented his Angolan registration to port officials, who took an inventory and collected the duties.

Despite these precautions, contraband trade was always a serious problem. The actual slave traffic with Spanish America, for example, may have exceeded the registered trade by as much as 40%.[69] Duties had to be paid on all slaves loaded in Guiné or Angola, even if they died in transit.[70] The sale price of the Angolan contract had doubled, becoming 24 contos annually by 1600, and taxes rose by one-third.[71] In Brazil factors collected a duty of 4000 réis for each peça, or about 30% of the profits.[72] To escape taxes, which were twice higher for Spanish America, slave traders either avoided the factories altogether and sold slaves in America clandestinely, or they bribed the factors to undercount the cargoes.

In the seventeenth century slave ships rarely exceeded 300 tons. They were unsanitary and overcrowded, transporting about 500 slaves each. Mortality on the shorter voyage, Angola–Brazil, was at least 20%; mortality reached 40% on the longer passage to the Spanish Indies.[73] During the

---

[67] Ibid., pp. 535–536. On the role the Cape Verde Islands played in the slave trade from Guiné see T. Bentley Duncan, *Atlantic Islands:Madeira, the Azores and the Cape Verdes in Seventeenth-Century Commerce and Navigation* (Chicago, 1972), pp. 195–238.

[68] For a discussion of the slave contracts see Mauro, *Le Portugal*, pp. 157–169. On the slave trade, also see Neme, "A Bahia e o atlântico," pp. 208–246.

[69] Godinho, *Descobrimentos*, vol. 2, p. 554.

[70] Sometimes the contracts allowed a mortality rate of 10%; see Mauro, *Le Portugal*, p. 163.

[71] Ibid., p. 158.

[72] Ibid., pp. 172–173; and *Nova história*, p. 197.

[73] Godinho, *Descobrimentos*, vol. 2, pp. 570–571.

60 years of dynastic union Portuguese traders carried 400,000 slaves to Spanish America;[74] from 1575 to 1650 Angola alone sent 385,000 peças to Brazil. The growth of the Brazilian slave trade paralleled that of sugar production. Yearly averages rose from 4000 peças in the 1570s and 1580s to 7500 in the 1590s and 10,500 during the next half century.[75]

An exchange of commodities and capital sustained the slave trade. Ships leaving Portugal for Angola and Guiné carried Brazilian tobacco and sugar-cane brandy, as well as textiles, iron tools, and utensils. After selling their slaves in Brazil, traders took on sugar, tobacco, hides, and whale oil for the return journey. Ships bound directly for the colony freighted Dutch textiles, hardware, equipment for the mills, luxury items such as silks and Chinese porcelain, and provisions of dried fish, flour, olive oil, and wine. The vitality of these trades depended on Brazil's expanding sugar industry, which was linked in turn to Dutch marketing and capital. Amsterdam, Lisbon, Luanda, and Bahia all participated in a South Atlantic trading system linked together by hundreds of ships and their assorted cargoes.[76]

COMMERCIAL PENETRATION:
THE PORTUGUESE IN SPANISH AMERICA

Unlike the Brazilian sugar trade, Spain's American trade was restricted to large annual fleets assembled in Seville under the watchful eye of the House of Trade. In 1608, a record year, 200 ships carried 54,000 tons of merchandise to Spanish America.[77] Compared to the Brazil trade, total tonnage was greater, ships larger, and the cargoes of more spectacular value. Spanish America had a more developed economy, a larger population, and silver to pay for the floating warehouses sent from Spain. Between 1581 and 1630 merchants sent back over 200 million pesos worth of silver to Spain.[78] Until the 1570s Mexico's mines produced most of America's bullion, and Mexico purchased the largest share of the imports. Thereafter, Upper Peru (Bolivia) and its mining center, Potosí, boomed. From 1586 to 1625 64% of all registered silver sent to Spain came

---

[74] Ibid., p. 555.

[75] Ibid., p. 545. These are the total sums of the estimates of yearly averages, correcting for slaves sent to the Spanish Indies and São Tomé. They do not include an estimate of slaves brought to Brazil from Guiné do Cabo Verde, nor take contraband into account. Mauro's estimate for the years 1570 to 1670 is 400,000; see Le Portugal, pp. 179–180.

[76] See Neme, "A Bahia e o atlântico," pp. 292–302.

[77] Lynch, Spain under the Hapsburgs, vol. 2, p. 187.

[78] Hamilton, American Treasure, p. 34.

from Peru—79% by 1630.[79] Consequently, Peru became Spain's best customer, and the mines of Potosí the crown's prized possession. Taxes on silver production furnished 80% of Lima's treasury receipts, and came to over 3 million pesos yearly from 1615 to 1621.[80] Potosí was one of the great urban centers of Spanish America; in 1600 it had a population of over 120,000.[81] It also provided an insatiable market. As a source of income for the state and as a privileged zone for Spanish traders, Potosí's security was a top priority.

Spanish and Peruvian merchants controlled the mining zone's trade. That part of the Spanish fleet with goods destined for Peru unloaded their cargoes in Portobello, Panama. The merchandise was carted across the isthmus, reloaded on colonial ships destined for Callao—Lima's port— and Africa, which supplied Potosí. Thousands of mules and llamas traversed the 400 miles of mountainous terrain that separated coastal Africa from the mines; they carried in merchandise and returned with silver. Provisioning Potosí and its satellites with food was likewise a major undertaking. Due to the region's high elevation, cold climate, and poor soil, supplies had to be carted in over great distances. The Argentine province of Tucumán, which bordered Upper Peru, prospered by sending mules, wheat, fruit, hides, and tallow to the mining zone;[82,83] it also provided a depôt for contraband goods from Brazil. Thus, although Brazil kept the Atlantic coast free of enemy settlements, it also created an alternative to the overtaxed, high priced fleet system that filtered everything through Portobello.

Spanish officials did not supervise the Brazil trade, nor was it subject to or as heavily taxed as the fleet system. Portuguese caravels set sail for Brazil at will, and they brought more merchandise than the colony needed. Brazil's surplus imports were destined for Spanish colonies in the Plata estuary, and finally for Potosí.[84] The contraband traffic exchanged slaves, textiles, hardware, and sugar for Spanish salted beef and wheat, but above all for Potosí's silver.[85] To make their purchases, Peruvian merchants sometimes brought their silver to Buenos Aires and even to Brazilian ports since merchandise in Peru, when it came from Brazil via

---

[79] Lynch, *Spain under the Hapsburgs*, vol. 2, pp. 188–189.

[80] Ibid., p. 222.

[81] Lewis Hanke, *The Imperial City of Potosí* (The Hague, 1956), p. 1.

[82] Colonial Tucumán was a vast province that included seven of the modern Argentine provinces and part of Paraguay.

[83] Lynch, *Spain under the Hapsburgs*, vol. 2, p. 219.

[84] Boxer, *Salvador de Sá*, pp. 73–81.

[85] See Alice Canabrava, *O comércio português no Rio da Plata, 1580–1640* (São Paulo, 1944), pp. 116–125.

Buenos Aires, cost one-third less than competing goods imported from Seville via Portobello, Callao, and Arica. Licensed traders found their markets glutted with similar, cheaper commodities.[86] The Portuguese directed a traffic that claimed at its height (1600–1625) as much as 25% of Potosí's total silver production.[87]

The slave trade provided a convenient cover for illegal operations.[88] The crown authorized contractors to supply Buenos Aires with 600 slaves annually. Besides slaves, the permission ships loaded merchandise in Angola and Brazil. Factors in Buenos Aires ran the contraband organization in collusion with Spanish officials. Although officially suspended in 1609, the slave trade continued unabated, averaging 1500 slaves a year—most destined for Peru as domestic servants.[89] When the governor of Buenos Aires tried to investigate, he found the contraband organization so formidable and its lobbyists so effective that witnesses refused to testify.[90] The trade flourished because of the proximity of Brazil and the weak Spanish supervision caused by the region's distance from the Audiencia of Charcas in Upper Peru. The key to the operation, however, was the unregistered silver that escaped the mining district. Once smelted, silver bullion was supposed to be sent to the nearest treasury office to be taxed, assayed, and stamped. After subtracting the king's share, a fifth, the treasury purchased the silver from miners at a fixed rate. But fraudulent practices followed the path of silver from the mine to the smelting house and into the treasury; perhaps one-half Peru's silver escaped registration and the king, much of it ending up in Buenos Aires.[91] Smugglers at the port managed a thriving illegal trade in silver ingots worth 1 million pesos annually.[92]

Inconsistency marked Spain's policy in the Plata estuary. Although it was sanctioned in 1592, trade with Brazil was prohibited four years later. Between 1602 and 1618, however, the crown permitted local authorities

---

[86] Boxer, *Salvador de Sá*, pp. 74–79.

[87] Lynch, *Spain under the Hapsburgs*, vol. 2, p. 179. Cross sets the minimum quantity of silver smuggled out of Buenos Aires at 750,000 pesos a year, or 15% of Potosí's total production. See Harry E. Cross, "Commerce and Orthodoxy: A Spanish Response to Portuguese Commercial Penetration in the Viceroyalty of Peru, 1580–1640," *The Americas* 35 (1978), p. 154.

[88] See Mario Rodríguez, "The Genesis of Economic Attitudes in the Rio de La Plata," *Hispanic American Historical Review* 36 (1956), pp. 171–189.

[89] Canabrava, *O comércio*, p. 83, and Marie Helmer, "Comércio e contrabando entre Bahia e Potosí no século XVI," *Revista de História*, (1953), p. 207.

[90] Rodríguez, "Genesis of Economic Attitudes," p. 177.

[91] Such contemporary estimates are difficult to verify, but the traffic in unregistered silver was certainly large. See Helmer, "Comércio e contrabando," pp. 204–205.

[92] Boxer, *Salvador de Sá*, p. 78.

Map 5 Iberian America, 1620.

to license a limited exchange of Spanish wheat, jerked beef, and tallow for clothing and household goods imported from Brazil. Such concessions simply provided a pretext for smuggling. Whereas Spanish authorities defended the fleet system, the strategic Platine settlements needed markets for their products. In principle, the solution was simple—an annual fleet between Seville and Buenos Aires. But direct trade was bound to draw greater quantities of silver to the Plata estuary, and Spain lacked the shipping and naval support this implied. Such a strategy meant diverting naval strength from the Caribbean, where Dutch and English privateers proved a constant menace, and it meant dislodging the powerful commercial interests tied to the Portobello–Lima route. Consequently, contraband operations continued, aided by the legal pretexts Spanish policy created, but without improving the market situation for the ranches and towns along the Paraná-Paraguay river. The region's cattlemen, especially the Paraguayans, were cut off from trade by their rivals: the dried beef and grain exported to Brazil came from Tucumán, not the Plata estuary. Because Tucumán and its market centers, like Córdoba, were depôts for Potosí's illegal silver exports, the region's merchants had strong allies in Buenos Aires, including the Portuguese and the port's treasury officials. Excluded from the silver trade, Platine ranchers were caught between inflated prices at Buenos Aires and a depressed market for their own products; they became fierce adversaries of the Portuguese contraband trade. When Portugal revolted in 1640 Platine settlers staunchly adhered to Spain and resisted Brazilian penetration of the borderlands.[93]

Spain's defeat in the Netherlands and the North Atlantic was serious and permanent. But the defeat of the Armada and reverses in Europe did not dislodge the Spaniards from their American empire, nor did it disrupt the fleet system. Dutch merchants siphoned off Spanish silver in Seville rather than in America. It was not Spain's enemies but her Portuguese neighbors who mounted the greatest attack on the Seville–Cadiz monopoly. Between 1580 and 1640, with their bases in Brazil, their control of the slave trade, and their cover as allies, the Portuguese entered Spanish America on a scale impossible for other foreigners. Since the 1580s they had obtained naturalization rights to trade with the Indies from Seville; a half-century later they made up 25% of the city's population.[94] From Seville, Portuguese merchants soon branched out to Spanish America's most important commercial centers. They became members of Mexico City's powerful merchant guild; they were entrenched in Cartagena, Potosí, and Buenos Aires; and they dominated Lima's retail trade.[95] In 1619 the Portuguese owned or were masters of 18 ships in the Peruvian merchant marine.[96] The licensed slave trade with

---

[93] Rodríguez, "Genesis of Economic Attitudes," pp. 176–189.

[94] Vitorina Magalhães Godinho, "1580 e a Restauração," in *Dicionário de história de Portugal*, ed. Joel Serrão, 6 vols. (Lisbon, 1975), vol. 5, p. 311.

[95] See Lewis Hanke, "The Portuguese in Spanish America with Special Reference to the Villa Imperial de Potosí," *Revista de Historia de America* **51** (1961), pp. 12–15; Lynch, *Spain under the Hapsburgs*, vol. 2, pp. 169–171; Louisa Schell Hoberman, "Merchants in Seventeenth-Century Mexico City: A Preliminary Portrait," *Hispanic American Historical Review* **57** (1977), pp. 495–499; Seymour B. Liebman, "The Great Conspiracy in New Spain," *The Americas* **30** (1973), pp. 18–31; Godinho, "Restauração," p. 311; and Cross, "Commerce and Orthodoxy," pp. 151–158.

[96] Lynch, *Spain under the Hapsburgs*, vol. 2, p. 170.

Mexico and Tierra Firme—6000 to 7000 slaves were traded annually—provided additional opportunities for contraband and another gateway to the Spanish Indies. For Portuguese businessmen held most of the contracts;[97] and they brought far more slaves than was permitted, and plenty of merchandise.[98] Critics complained that the slave ships were "full of Portuguese who pose as sailors, and all of them remain in the Indies, trading."[99] Having discharged their cargoes, slave ships did not return empty to Portugal. In 1621, for example, Trinidad and Cumuná, Venezuela produced 20,000 arrobas of tobacco; the Portuguese took it back to Europe illegally. They probably carried Mexico's cochineal exports too, for although Spanish imports of cochineal dropped drastically, large quantities still left Mexico.[100] Protected by their semilegitimate status, Portuguese merchants provided an alternative to the overtaxed fleet system—and not just at Buenos Aires. When the Spanish fleets arrived in Portobello and Cartagena, they found both ports well stocked with similar, cheaper goods imported through Brazil.[101]

So, although union with Spain damaged the spice trade, the Portuguese recouped their fortunes in Spanish America. The licensed slave trade, linked to contraband operations, tapped American silver at its source, providing badly needed specie for the Portuguese economy. But these advantages suffered serious blows in the 1630s, not so much because of Spanish opposition, but because of the Dutch attack on the Portuguese Empire.

THE GLOBAL STRUGGLE WITH THE DUTCH

In 1590 the Spanish and Portuguese still organized the seaborne trades with America, Asia, and Africa. But Iberia's role as a global collector was precarious. The Peninsula provided neither the major markets for pepper, sugar, and dyes, nor did it produce the bulk of the exports exchanged for slaves, sugar, and spices. Spanish America's more diversified agricul-

---

[97] Tierra Firme refers to that part of continental South America bordering the Caribbean; roughly coastal Venezuela, Colombia, and Panama.

[98] Godinho, Descobrimentos, vol. 2, p. 554; Boxer, Portuguese Seaborne Empire, pp. 336–337; and Cross, "Commerce and Orthodoxy," pp. 154–155.

[99] Frederick P. Bowser, The African Slave in Colonial Peru, 1524–1650 (Stanford, 1974), pp. 55–62.

[100] Lynch, Spain under the Hapsburgs, vol. 2, pp. 164, 195. The Portuguese had traded in the Caribbean since the 1550s. See Kenneth R. Andrews, The Spanish Caribbean:Trade and Plunder, 1530–1630 (New Haven, 1978), pp. 72–79.

[101] Boxer, Salvador de Sá, p. 78. Boxer assumes these goods came via Buenos Aires, but more likely they came on the slave ships.

ture reduced its dependence on imported grain, olive oil, and wine. After 1590, imports from northern Europe rather than Spain's exports dominated American trade.[102] Spain retained less of America's silver because she produced a shrinking share of what America consumed. In Brazil, where monoculture predominated, the colonial sugar economy still provided an important market for Portugal's agricultural exports. Still, Portugal was primarily a transit point for reexports, whether from Brazil, the Far East, or northern Europe.

Iberia blocked direct foreign access to colonial markets, but the Dutch took over the Peninsula's trade with northern Europe. During the 1590s, however, the Spanish goverment twice closed its ports to the Dutch. Although temporary, these measures accelerated Dutch attempts to open direct trade with America. Initial contacts focused on the Caribbean, especially coastal Venezuela, a region poorly supplied by the fleet system. The great salt pans lying along the Araya lagoon near Cumuná afforded a cheaper supply than that available in Portugal, and salt was essential to the Dutch herring industry. By 1600 the Dutch had developed a thriving trade in the region, selling merchandise and returning with salt and tobacco. During the next 5 years more than 600 Dutch salt ships and 55 smuggling vessels came to the Araya-Cumuná area.[103] A Spanish counterattack (1605–1606) involving 14 galleons and 2500 men drove out the Dutch and temporarily halted the trade. During the truce years (1609–1621) forays in the Americas abated; Dutch merchants could enter Iberian ports and they had indirect but effective ways to penetrate the Seville trade. In the South Atlantic, Portugal's sugar and slave trades flourished. For the moment, Dutch expansion concentrated on Asia, not America.

The Twelve Years' Truce had tacitly recognized America as an Iberian preserve, but it intensified the struggle for commercial supremacy in the Far East. Although sugar was readily obtainable in Portugal, the contract system delivered shrinking pepper cargoes and kept spices out of Dutch hands. Portugal's Asian empire was an assortment of loosely connected factories, quite vulnerable to Dutch incursions. The Dutch were better financed, and had more ships and able seamen when they invaded Portugal's empire. Avoiding India, the center of Portuguese strength, the Dutch obtained spices in the Indonesian archipelago—a region tenuously linked to the Portuguese stronghold at Malacca. Squadrons sent out by the East India Company protected Dutch bases. By 1605 fleets regularly

---

[102] On the changing character of Spain's American trade see Lynch, *Spain under the Hapsburgs*, vol. 2, pp. 184–193; and Pierre and Huguette Chaunu, "The Atlantic Economy and the World Economy," in *Essays in European Economic History 1500–1800*, ed. Peter Earle, (Oxford, 1974), pp. 113–124.

[103] Sluiter, "Dutch-Spanish Rivalry," p. 178, also see pp. 165–196.

left Amsterdam for the company's factories on Java, Borneo, and the
Spice Islands; they returned with cargoes of spices, porcelains, and
silks.[104] Despite persistent Luso-Spanish counterattacks launched from
Manila and Malacca, the East India Company steadily expanded its
operations. Between 1611 and 1621 the Dutch sent out twice as many
ships as the Portuguese, and they brought back more spices.[105] When war
with Spain resumed in Europe, the East India Company mounted a
prolonged and successful campaign; its naval power provided the margin
of victory. Dutch blockades of Goa (1638–1644) and the Malacca Strait
(1634–1640) hemmed in the Portuguese and ruined their trade. After a
5-month siege during 1641, Malacca, Portugal's last important base in the
Far East, fell. As the company gained control over clove, mace, and
nutmeg production in the Malaccas, the cinnamon of coastal Ceylon,
and Malabar's pepper, it destroyed the once flourishing Portuguese spice
trade. Portugal still occupied Goa and kept a foothold in Macao, and the
India fleet still sailed, but the cargoes were merely a trickle compared to
the merchandise the Dutch carried.[106]

Portugal rather than Spain bore the brunt of the Dutch global attack,
for the Lusitanian empire embraced three continents and posed enormous defense problems. In Asia and Africa, for example, the Portuguese
had small trading colonies, not territorial settlements. The Dutch took
over the factories and made their own arrangements with spice producers
and native slave traders. Brazil's export economy, so dependent on a few
great ports, was susceptible to the same strategy. If the Dutch captured
Recife and Salvador, they could control sugar production. Spanish
America, by contrast, was a more tightly knit empire occupied by hundreds of towns, and was therefore less vulnerable to Dutch conquest. The
Dutch harassed Spanish shipping, attacked ports, and even captured an
entire silver fleet, but such maneuvers had little impact on the Spanish-
American economies. With its silver mines, diversified agriculture, textile
industries, and flourishing regional trades, Spanish America had a degree
of self-sufficiency Dutch seapower could not challenge. A successful
strike against Cartagena, Veracruz, or Callao might disrupt overseas
trade. But the economic heartland of the Spanish Indies lay beyond the

---

[104] Sluiter, "Dutch Maritime Power," p. 32.

[105] See Niels Steensgaard, "European Shipping to Asia 1497–1700," *Scandinavian Economic History Review* 18 (1970), p. 9, and Kristof Glamann, *Dutch–Asiatic Trade 1620–
1740* (The Hague, 1958), pp. 12–49.

[106] On the collapse of Portugal's Asian empire see Boxer, *Portuguese Seaborne Empire*, pp.
106–127; how the Dutch reorganized Asian trade is discussed in Glamann, *Dutch–Asiatic
Trade*, pp. 73–284.

coastal zone in the rugged sierra. To capture the great prize—the silver mines—required an invasion of the interior, a strategy beyond Dutch capabilities. In 1620 major Atlantic and Pacific ports had massive fortifications paid for by American silver.[107] Spain successfully concentrated its naval strength on fleet defense, preventing the Dutch from severing the seaborne links with America. Only twice during the seventeenth century did Spain's enemies inflict a major blow against the fleets. Dutch objectives in Spanish America were primarily trade and plunder, not territory. When Spanish–Dutch hostilities ended in 1648, the most important Dutch acquisition was the island of Curaçao, a small contraband base off the coast of Venezuela.

Dutch expansion zeroed in on Portugal's empire much more than on Spain's. The East India Company, which was backed by stockholders throughout the Netherlands and protected from competition by the States-General, held a monopoly on all Dutch trade with the Far East. The company proved both a successful business enterprise and a highly adaptable war-machine. To consolidate and pay for the Atlantic war, the States-General chartered a companion corporation in 1621, the West India Company (WIC). As the Pope had divided the world between Spain and Portugal, so the Dutch parceled it out to their companies.

A board of directors, the Heeren Nineteen, ran the WIC. The company was granted a monopoly on all Atlantic trade beyond Europe. On its own authority, it could make alliances with West African kingdoms, build fortresses, appoint governors, and maintain troops.[108] The States-General provided a 1 million florin subsidy. Although its stock subscriptions did not sell as quickly as those for the East India Company (two years versus one month), by the end of 1623 the WIC had a working capital of over 7 million florins.[109]

The Heeren Nineteen and the States-General designed a strategy to control Europe's sugar supply.[110] The Dutch already refined and distributed most of Brazil's sugar; if in addition they seized Recife, Salvador, and Luanda, they could control production and the industry's labor supply. In 1624 a Dutch fleet captured Brazil's capital city; the following year, the Dutch unsuccessfully attacked Rio de Janeiro and the African fortress, São Jorge da Mina. The Dutch onslaught provoked immediate coun-

---

[107] Lynch, *Spain under the Hapsburgs*, vol. 2, pp. 173–184.

[108] Boxer, *Dutch in Brazil*, p. 8.

[109] Boxer, *Dutch Seaborne Empire*, pp. 24–25.

[110] This was hardly a new scheme. The Dutch attempted the feat in 1599, but they never got beyond São Tomé. See Sluiter, "Holandeses," pp. 203–204.

termeasures. Brazil was Portugal's prized possession, and Salvador's capitulation endangered Spanish fleets and the Platine route to Potosí as well. Within months a combined Luso-Spanish armada composed of 52 ships and 12,000 men retook the city before the arrival of Dutch reinforcements. Portugal, however, lacked the naval strength to protect the sugar trade. In 1627 and 1628 the WIC's ships seized over 4500 chests of sugar (90,000 arrobas) from Portuguese vessels, some in Salvador's harbor. Stockholders, whose confidence had dwindled after the company lost Salvador, were buoyant when Piet Heyn captured the entire Spanish silver fleet in 1628; the booty brought 12 million guilders into the coffers. The company paid off its outstanding debt and returned a dividend of 75%. These profitable forays against Iberia's Atlantic commerce bolstered the WIC's credit. In 1629 the company outfitted a squadron of 67 ships and 7000 men that would capture Recife; the Dutch would remain in Brazil for the next quarter-century (1620–1654). The loss of Recife was but one episode in a series of Iberian disasters. While the Dutch quickly dispatched reinforcements to hold Recife, men, ships, and money were slowly and reluctantly assembled in Lisbon. Financially exhausted, Lisbon and Madrid haggled over how to meet the costs of the expedition. It was well over a year before a relief fleet, primarily of Spanish warships, left Portugal. By then the Dutch were entrenched in Pernambuco and could not be dislodged.[111]

The Dutch seized Recife to control sugar production. The company expected that duties on sugar exports and a monopoly on slaves and dyewoods would more than cover expenses. The Dutch were simply replacing Portuguese traders, as they had in Africa and Asia. New agreements could be made with mill owners, much as the Dutch had struck new bargains with slavers and spice growers. Asian suppliers might have viewed a transfer of trading posts from Portuguese to Dutch hands with indifference. But Recife was not an Asian factory. In Pernambuco, Portuguese settlers controlled the countryside, and they fought a long and destructive war against Dutch occupation. The pacification of the várzea, the sugar growing region around Recife-Olinda, was only accomplished in 1636; by then, many mills were in ruins and sugar production had sharply declined. Even though the WIC still preyed on Iberian shipping, its debts in 1636 amounted to 18 million florins.[112] Sugar exports increased subsequently, but the cost of defense and provisioning ate away the profits.

---

[111] See Boxer, *Dutch in Brazil*, pp. 21–31.
[112] Ibid., pp. 32–66.

PORTUGUESE INDEPENDENCE:
THE STRUGGLE FOR BRAZIL

Until the 1620s union with Spain was beneficial to Portugal's Atlantic empire. But the loss of Pernambuco and Spain's failure to expel the Dutch altered the character of the alliance. The Dutch war was a consequence of Spain's foreign policy, a policy that now threatened vital Portuguese interests tied to transatlantic trade. In Peru, where Spanish merchants resented Protuguese competition, the Inquisition, backed by Lima's merchant guild, viciously attacked Portuguese businessmen. To the Holy Office, Portuguese merchants and Jews were indistinguishable. During the purge of 1635–1639, two-thirds of those convicted were Portuguese with business connections.[113] Reverses in the Atlantic and the Far East, Spanish violations of the terms of union, and Madrid's demands for extraordinary grants and loans—1 million cruzados between 1619 and 1630—alienated the Portuguese aristocracy.[114] The revolt was also a popular reaction against an intensified Castilian nationalism that threatened the autonomy of both Portugal and Catalonia.[115] The Catalans, in fact, revolted first. When the Spanish king tried to mobilize the Portuguese to fight in Catalonia, the nobility organized its own coup d'état. The 1640 revolt produced a change of kings and of foreign policy; it provoked virtually no resistance at home or in Brazil, where the bureaucracy remained under Portuguese control. The duke of Braganza was proclaimed King João IV (1640–1656); a few months later, peace negotiations opened at the Hague. Portugal hoped to conclude an immediate truce with the Dutch, and perhaps even strike a bargain for Pernambuco's return.

In 1640 Dutch ascendancy was irreversible in the Far East. The viability of Portuguese independence from Spain depended on Brazil, since sugar taxes propped up the state's declining commercial revenues. Spain intended to recover Portugal, but the war in Catalonia diverted Spanish arms for over a decade. The defense of Brazil, not a struggle with Spain, was Portugal's immediate priority. For the Dutch, Portuguese independence promised greater security in Pernambuco; without Spanish backing, the Portuguese empire was more vulnerable than ever. The value of

---

[113] Cross, "Commerce and Orthodoxy," pp. 159–167.

[114] See Lynch, *Spain under the Hapsburgs*, vol. 2, pp. 108–115; and Godinho, "Restauração," pp. 307–326.

[115] J. H. Elliott, "The Spanish Peninsula, 1598–1648," in New Cambridge Modern History, ed. J. P. Cooper. (London, 1970), vol. 4, *The Decline of Spain and the Thirty Years' War, 1609–1648/59* pp. 460–468.

WIC stock rose 21%, from 105 to 128 florins.[116] The East and West India Companies initially opposed a truce, as they hoped to expand their conquests at Portugal's expense. But there were strong commercial interests supporting accommodation. Many Dutch merchants, particularly those in Amsterdam, had a brisk trade with Portugal. They carried textiles and northern manufactures to Lisbon, and returned laden with sugar and salt. Although the Dutch rejected Portugal's offer to buy back Pernambuco, they agreed to a 10-year truce. The States-General, however, delayed ratification for several months. During the interim, the WIC strengthened its position in Brazil by capturing São Luís do Maranhão, and launched a successful attack on Angola, seizing Luanda, Benguela, and São Tomé. The Dutch Atlantic empire now threatened to engulf Portuguese Brazil.

With Angola's slave trade in hand and Maranhão subdued, a Netherlands Brazil finally seemed viable. Sugar exports recovered, mounting to 600,000 arrobas in 1639.[117] Still, the Dutch hardly monopolized the industry: Bahia and Rio de Janeiro out-produced Pernambuco, and the truce, at least, reduced attacks on Portuguese shipping. Moreover, the costs of provisioning Dutch Brazil were particularly high because the conquest had disrupted old channels of supply. Although Dutch merchants provided capital to renovate the mills, it was Brazilian mill owners who bore the debt: 2 million florins in 1644.[118] Netherlands Brazil remained an occupied colony. The Dutch, who were primarily merchants and money-lenders, did not become cane growers or mill owners. Hostility between the debt-ridden planters and their Dutch creditors kept resistance alive. As a Dutch contemporary ominously observed, "the Portuguese scheme night and day to escape our rule and avoid paying what they owe us."[119] An alien minority that clung to urban life in Recife-Olinda, the Dutch did not control the countryside. Skirmishes in the várzea plagued company rule, ceasing but for a brief three years (1642–1645). Although the WIC had been strengthened by the acquisition of Angola, its weakness in Pernambuco's countryside proved to be the company's undoing. In 1645 the colonists of the várzea revolted and defeated the Dutch in a pitched battle at Tabocas. Within a few months the company lost everything outside its fortified coastal towns. In Maranhão Brazilians retook São Luís before the Dutch could send reinforcements. It was the guerrilla war in the countryside, not the crown's

---

[116] Boxer, *Dutch in Brazil*, p. 102, also see pp. 102–111.
[117] Godinho, *Descobrimentos*, vol. 2, p. 464.
[118] Boxer, *Dutch in Brazil*, p. 157.
[119] Ibid., p. 164.

initiative, that paralyzed Dutch Brazil. The king even refused to aid loyal Pernambuco, considering its revolt doomed to failure. To avoid another Atlantic war, the Portuguese crown offered to restore Pernambuco to the Dutch in exchange for the restitution of Angola. But the WIC was determined to recover control of the sugar industry and retain its hold on the indispensable slave trade.[120]

The WIC renewed hostilities in 1647, sending an armada to Salvador that seized the strategic island of Itaparica in the port's harbor, thus imperiling the sugar trade. This move broke the impasse. The king dispatched the Royal Fleet, which normally guarded Lisbon, to Salvador. A smaller squadron commanded by Salvador de Sá was sent to Rio de Janeiro under orders to retake Angola. The WIC, for its part, lobbied for additional support from the States-General. After considerable delay, a powerful fleet finally set sail, but by then the Dutch had already evacuated Itaparica. With Salvador secure, the Portuguese Royal Fleet stayed in the harbor, unwilling to risk everything in a naval battle. Unopposed, the Dutch sent reinforcments to Recife and attacked the várzea, but were soundly defeated. At the end of 1648 the Portuguese still controlled the countryside while the Dutch dominated the sea.

Although the Royal Fleet refused battle, five warships did join de Sá's squadron at Rio, which was then preparing to attack Luanda. Rio's câmara raised a loan of 60,000 cruzados to finance the expedition, and with good reason—sugar-cane brandy traded for slaves was a regional specialty.[121] The funds raised at Rio helped pay for the squadron's ships, men, and munitions. This fleet of 15 ships and 1400 men retook Luanda in 1648 and eventually restored Portuguese control in Benguela and São Tomé.[122] The Dutch admiral at Recife knew of the impending attack on Angola, but with the Royal Fleet waiting in Salvador's harbor he could not abandon Recife to pursue de Sá's fleet; still, the Dutch inflicted serious damage on the sugar trade by taking more than 200 Portuguese ships in two years (1647–1648).[123]

Such losses forced Portugal to abandon its longstanding policy of free trade with Brazil. The crown created a private corporation, the Brazil Company, to protect sugar exports. All trade with Brazil was confined to annual fleets convoyed by the company's warships. To attract investors, the company received extensive commercial privileges: a monopoly on es-

---

[120] Ibid., p. 178, also see pp. 159–190.

[121] Boxer, *Salvador de Sá*, p. 255; and Godinho, "Portugal and Her Empire (1640–1670)," p. 385.

[122] For a more detailed account see Boxer, *Salvador de Sá*, pp. 256–271.

[123] Boxer, "Padre António Vieira," p. 477.

sential colonial imports—wine, cereals, olive oil, and codfish—sold at company prices; the right to levy a fixed tax on all sugar, tobacco, and hide exports; and a monopoly on brazilwood.[124] Rio's sugar was shipped to Salvador to await the convoys. The company's first armada, comprised of 48 merchantmen and 18 warships, reached Bahia in 1650, reinforcing the Royal Fleet. By then the Dutch fleet had abandoned Recife, leaving the port exposed to a Portuguese seaborne attack. Although Brazil's governor-general surreptitiously aided the rebels, the crown strictly limited the fleet to defensive action. Portugal's objectives were to protect the sugar trade, strengthen Bahia, and recover Angola—meanwhile provoking the Dutch as little as possible, lest they divert the Baltic or East India fleets to blockade Lisbon. But the Dutch never concentrated their naval strength on a determined counteroffensive. The deadlock in Brazil continued until the first of three Anglo–Dutch commercial wars (1652–1654). With the Dutch tied down in the North Atlantic and unable to retaliate, the Brazil Company's armada besieged Recife and the Dutch capitulated (1654).[125]

Portugal had a respectable merchant marine in 1640, but it could not match the Dutch fleets that plied the Baltic, supplied the Peninsula, and carried the spice trade. How, then, did Portugal manage to defeat the WIC? The very diversity of Dutch trade hurt the company, since it had to fight for support against rival commercial interests. Holland, the richest province, was dominated by the powerful city of Amsterdam, which had a greater stake in the Portuguese salt trade than in Dutch Brazil. In fact, the Hollanders sold the Portuguese the naval stores and equipment that helped them to outfit the Brazil fleet.[126] The East India Company had its strongest chamber in Amsterdam, and it viewed the WIC as a competitor for stockholders and state support. Amsterdam's wealthy merchants preferred an empire of trade to the unpredictable returns of colonization.[127] Compared to Dutch trades in the Baltic, the spice trade, and Iberian commerce, Netherlands Brazil was far from the first priority. The war in Brazil drained the company's resources; by 1645, shares purchased at 100 florins had fallen to 46, and dividends were rarely paid. In contrast, the

[124] Gustavo de Freitas, "A Companhia Geral do Comércio do Brasil (1649–1720), II: A instituição da companhia," *Revista de História*, (1951), pp. 85–92. Also consult Boxer, "Padre António Vieira," pp. 474–497; David Grant Smith, "Old Christian Merchants and the Foundation of the Brazil Company, 1649," *Hispanic American Historical Review* 54 (1974), pp. 233–259, idem., "Mercantile Class," pp. 168–176.

[125] This summary of events is based on Boxer, *Dutch in Brazil*, pp. 161–245.

[126] Ibid., pp. 189–190. Dutch merchants also supplied their Spanish adversaries with war materials. See Barbour, *Capitalism in Amsterdam*, pp. 39–40.

[127] Barbour, *Capitalism in Amsterdam* pp. 139–140.

East India Company's shares were quoted at 460 florins. [128] Aid to the WIC was but grudgingly approved and provincial contributions were often in arrears; while the States-General granted subsidies, the provincial assemblies paid the bills, and no province considered itself under obligation unless it had individually consented to the subsidy. [129] In 1651 the WIC lobbied fiercely for additional funds to relieve Recife. But Holland refused to contribute until the other provinces paid their shares and their arrears too. Internal provincial rivalries, insolvency, and the prolonged guerrilla war in Brazil rather than Portugal's hard-pressed fleets undermined the WIC's viability as a corporate enterprise. [130]

ENGLAND'S BRAZIL TRADE

The English, not the Dutch, broke Iberia's monopoly on American colonization. Although Spain could still protect the territory her colonists occupied, she could no longer police the New World. Unlike the Dutch, who had staged a frontal assault on Brazil, the English concentrated on continental North America, beyond the range of Iberian resistance; by 1650 England had established a series of viable coastal settlements. The Caribbean was also open to foreign penetration, since Spanish settlers, attracted by Mexico's silver and its skilled Indian labor, left all but the largest islands sparsely settled. Spain followed a policy of strategic withdrawal from the Lesser Antilles that stressed fleet defense, security for the mainland, and protection of Spanish settlements in Cuba, Hispañola, and Puerto Rico. [131] By midcentury the English had colonized Barbados and neighboring islands, and by 1654 they occupied previously neglected Jamaica. From 1620 to 1642, while the WIC exhausted its resources in Brazil, some 58,000 Englishmen, mostly Puritans, migrated to America. [132] England was now an Atlantic and American power in its own right—a major Dutch rival. English woolen products, especially the

---

[128] Boxer, *Dutch in Brazil*, p. 149.

[129] Ibid., p. 175.

[130] Ibid., pp. 216–220, 255–258; and W. J. Van Hoboken, "The Dutch West India Company: The Political Background of its Rise and Decline," in *Britain and the Netherlands*, vol. 1, pp. 41–61.

[131] See Roland D. Hussey, "Spanish Reaction to Foreign Aggression in the Caribbean to About 1680," *Hispanic American Historical Review* 9 (1929), pp. 286–302; Andrews, *Spanish Caribbean*, pp. 198–255.

[132] Carl Bridenbaugh, *Vexed and Troubled Englishmen, 1590–1642* (New York, 1968), pp. 394–395.

lighter, colorful new draperies, competed with Dutch cloth throughout Europe, and the English East India Company challenged the Dutch in the Far East.[133] The Navigation Act of 1651 was directed squarely against Amsterdam's reexport trade; it required that merchandise brought to England had to be carried on English ships directly from the country that produced it.[134]

English merchants, already active in Mediterranean textile markets, forged new ties with Portugal and Brazil.[135] In 1648 at least 20 English ships fought in Brazil; Salvador de Sá hired several for his attack on Luanda, and once established, the Brazil Company regularly chartered English carriers. In addition, English merchants purchased special licenses to trade directly with Brazil apart from the fleets.[136] In the late 1650s England's share of the sugar and textile trade was of sufficient importance to give it a stake in Portugal's independence, and Luso–Anglo commercial ties began to complicate Dutch foreign policy. To attack the Brazil fleet meant risking hostilities with the English, whose ships sailed with the convoys. The Hollanders and the English competed for Portuguese markets and Brazilian sugar. If the Dutch were to blockade Lisbon, it would only divert more of the carrying trade to the English. Ultimately, England's support helped to guarantee Portugal's survival. As of 1660 no foreign ambassador resided in the court at Lisbon; the Papacy even refused to approve bishops appointed by the Portuguese king! But the following year, a treaty with England ended Portugal's diplomatic isolation. The king of England, Charles II (1660–1685), took the Portuguese infanta as his bride in exchange for a dowry of 2 million cruzados and extensive commercial privileges. England, in turn, agreed to defend Portugal's maritime trade, and maintained a fleet off the Lusitanian coast to protect the returning Brazil fleets. During Spain's last desperate attempt to crush Portugal (1661–1663), English warships prevented an Hispanic attack on Lisbon.[137] Such assistance was hardly disinterested. Between 1665 and 1670, 60 English ships carried Newfoundland cod to Portugal, and some 80 ships from London and West Country ports brought textiles and hardware. All told, from 150 to 200 English ships a

---

[133] See Charles Wilson, "Cloth Production and International Competition in the Seventeenth Century," *Economic History Review* **13** (1960), pp. 209–221.

[134] Charles Wilson, *England's Apprenticeship 1603–1763* (New York, 1965), p. 62.

[135] See Richard T. Rapp, "The Unmaking of the Mediterranean Trade Hegemony: International Trade Rivalry and the Commercial Revolution," *Journal of Economic History* **35** (1975), pp. 499–525.

[136] Boxer, "English Shipping in the Brazil Trade, 1640–1665," *Mariner's Mirror* **37** (1951), pp. 204, 213, 215.

[137] Boxer, *Salvador de Sá*, pp. 337–339.

year carried merchandise to Portugal or accompanied the fleets to Brazil.[138]

The Portuguese negotiated a Dutch treaty in 1662, and in 1668 English mediation finally secured Spain's reluctant acceptance of Portuguese sovereignty. The Atlantic world now recognized Portugal's independence, and the Dutch accepted the loss of Pernambuco. Portugal paid dearly for the privilege, however: it owed the United Provinces a 4 million cruzado indemnity it secured, in part, by granting tax rebates from the Setubal salt trade.[139] England also obtained commercial concessions. English merchants were exempt from Portuguese courts and police; they could set up their own trading firms in Portugal, practice their Protestant religion, and send ships with the Brazil fleets. Portuguese customs duties on English goods could not exceed 23% of their declared value. Subsequent Portuguese attempts to develop domestic industries suffered from English competition that the Portuguese could neither exclude nor sufficiently tax.[140]

An independent Portugal had reentered the Atlantic world, but that world was less Iberian and more mercantilistic than in 1580. In America, England and France busily carved out rival empires. At home, Portugal could not dislodge the Dutch and the English, whose merchants carried Portugal's exports abroad and flooded Portugal's markets with foreign wares. Portuguese trade now focused on that corner of the Atlantic it had managed to retain—Angola and Brazil.

PORTUGAL'S MERCHANTS

In the sixteenth century the king's role in the empire's trade protected the monarchy against possible challenges from the nobility or the realm's merchants. In 1640, however, Far Eastern trade was in a shambles. Whether the Braganza king would end up as the founder of a new royal house or on the scaffold was an open question. Foreigners were reluctant to invest in a state with an uncertain future. To finance his precarious realm, the king had to rely on Portuguese merchants and taxes from the sugar trade. Lisbon's businessmen supplied capital to the Brazil Company and its fleets; their loans paid for the troops defending the border with

---

[138] Boxer, "English Shipping," p. 230 n. 2.

[139] Boxer, *Dutch in Brazil*, pp. 254–255.

[140] Richard Lodge, "The English Factory at Lisbon," *Transactions of the Royal Historical Society* 16 (1933), pp. 213–216. The effects of the treaties on Portugal's economy are discussed in Sandro Sideri, *Trade and Power, Informal Colonialism in Anglo-Portuguese Relations* (Rotterdam, 1970), pp. 19–39.

Spain. In return the king granted them liens on state revenues; the crown's merchant-bankers became the realm's tax farmers. What made the difference between the great merchant and the humble sugar trader was the acquisition of state contracts.[141] Despite the king's reliance on Lisbon's merchants,. however, they did not become powerful enough to displace the nobility; merchants were a passive group politically. During the 1530s and 1540s the main obstacle came from the way the crown had organized trade; in 1640 very different circumstances were to impede the state's businessmen.

New Christians in the Mercantile Community

Expelled from Spain in the 1490s, thousands of Jews fled to Portugal. For their own protection they had to become Christians, but their orthodoxy was always suspect. Many of these New Christians became merchants in Lisbon, especially in the sugar and slave trades.[142] They were, however, considered dangerous deviants within the body politic. By the 1640s New Christians accounted for about 60% of Lisbon's mercantile community. While Old Christians were merchants too—in fact, they constituted a majority in cities like Salvador and Oporto—the profession carried the stigma of the crypto-Jew. Those identified as New Christians were denied entrance to the universities and could not hold public office. Since these merchants were barred from the bureaucracy, they advanced their careers and their family's status by becoming landowners. The successful merchant proved his worth by abandoning trade.[143]

In England and France the nobility also opposed ambitious merchants; but there was no Inquisition to institutionalize this hostility. In Portugal a powerful Holy Office lived off the wealth of its victims, and its primary target was Lisbon's New Christians.[144] João IV gave special protection to

---

[141] Smith, "Mercantile Class," pp. 101–105, 117–128; idem., "Old Christian Merchants," pp. 241–242, 253–254.

[142] See Sluiter, "Holandeses," pp. 190, 203–205; Boxer, *Portuguese Seaborne Empire*, pp. 336–337; idem., *Dutch in Brazil*, p. 19.

[143] Smith, "Old Christian Merchants," pp. 233–236, 240, 256; idem., "Mercantile Class," pp. 180–184, 280. The largest number of Old Christians who entered the ranks of Lisbon's merchants came from Oporto's province—Entre Minho e Douro. Most New Christian immigrants came from the Alentejo and Beira. A listing of the New Christians who contributed to the General Pardon (1629–1631), shows that relatively few were from ports like Viana and Oporto. See Smith, "Mercantile Class," pp. 19–22.

[144] The Inquisition's hostility to the new king and Portuguese independence is discussed in Godinho, "Restauração," pp. 319–320.

the New Christian merchants who invested in the Brazil Company: the Inquisition could not confiscate their property, even if they were arrested and convicted as Judaizers; and he defended the company's charter against the Holy Office and the nobles entrenched on the Overseas Council. Investment in the company was privileged because, as the king observed, the company "had reconquered Pernambuco without costing me a penny."[145]

After the death of João (1656), however, a weak regency was unable to control the Inquisition and its supporters. The company was stripped of its privileges, and during the 1670s New Christians faced a vicious barrage of arrests; many of the state's bankers were ruined.[146] Until the king's authority stabilized during the reign of Pedro II (1683–1706), powerful nobles rather than the king's ministers controlled the government.[147] Caught between the Holy Office and the nobility, Portugal's merchants were cut off from the councils of state. Only in the 1750s, after Pombal cowed these adversaries, did the realm's businessmen finally acquire political power.

The turmoil that plagued Portugal in the 1660s and 1670s was partly responsible for Brazil's less assertive royal government.[148] Salvador was without a bishop for 23 years (1649–1672) because the Holy See had refused to confirm ecclesiastical appointments.[149] Once its domestic position was consolidated, however, the crown took more initiative in Brazil. Pedro II set up new dioceses in Rio de Janeiro, Pernambuco, and Maranhão; crown-appointed judges were sent to preside over the most important town councils. After 1680 no Brazilian-born judges were appointed to Bahia's High Court for 38 years.[150] A more confident monarchy was less tolerant of colonial opposition: when Maranhão's câmara tangled with the Jesuits over Indian labor and expelled them (1684), the crown reinstated the Order and dealt harshly with the rebels—a similar event in the 1660s had not had such consequences.[151] In São Paulo the king tied the Paulistas and their bandeiras to the state's ambitious schemes; they received commissions as explorers and prospectors, and set up new colonies in the borderlands.

---

[145] Grant, "Mercantile Class," p. 173.

[146] Ibid., pp. 172–176; on the Inquisition, see pp. 190–260.

[147] Oliveira Marques, History of Portugal, vol. 1, pp. 331–333, 394.

[148] On this period, see Boxer, Salvador de Sá, pp. 333–392.

[149] Francis A. Dutra, "The Brazilian Hierarchy in the Seventeenth Century," Records of the American Catholic Historical Society 83 (1972), pp. 172–173.

[150] See Stuart B. Schwartz, Sovereignty and Society in Colonial Brazil. The High Court of Bahia and Its Judges, 1609–1751 (Berkeley, 1973), pp. 267–269.

[151] Mathias C. Kiemen, The Indian Policy of Portugal in the Amazon Region, 1614–1693 (Washington, D.C., 1954), pp. 79–154.

PORTUGUESE BRAZIL, 1660–1690:
SUGAR, SLAVES, AND TOBACCO

Portugal clung to its "milk cow," as the king bluntly called Brazil. To oversee colonial policy the crown created a specialized agency, the Overseas Council (1643). Bahia's High Court, disbanded by the Spaniards in 1626, was reestablished in 1652. As if to call attention to Brazil's preeminent position in the empire, the homeward-bound India fleets, lacking sufficient cargoes, now stopped at Salvador to load sugar and tobacco.[152] Maritime trade was closely tied to Brazilian exports and foreign markets. Sugar exports reached 1.4 million arrobas in 1645, rising to peaks of 2 million (64 million pounds) in the 1660s.[153] Tobacco exports to Portugal totaled 80,000 arrobas in 1666 and 128,000 by 1672, aside from what was shipped directly to African markets. Hides played a minor but growing role, and 15,000 to 20,000 cured skins were exported each year. Brazil's annual exports were worth 9 to 10 million cruzados.[154]

On occasion planters were active participants in the colony's trade. Some of Bahia's mill owners, for example, exported sugar on consignment to their Lisbon agents.[155] Salvador's merchants were not simply factors for Lisbon businessmen: the wealthiest owned their own ships, sent sugar to Lisbon on their own account, participated in the slave trade, and purchased Bahia's tax contracts. Compared to Lisbon, Salvador's businessmen faced fewer obstacles to their advancement; since there was no Inquisition in Brazil, it was easier to pass as an Old Christian. The most successful merchants were accepted into the Misericórdia, acquired land, and became part-time planters. Later they married into the best families, served as officers in the urban militia, and even became municipal councilors—by virtue of their new status as well-connected merchant-planters.[156]

Besides its exports, Brazil also sent direct subsidies to Portugal. The câmaras paid their share of the Dutch war indemnity and the infanta's English dowry, largely by taxing sugar. Salvador's câmara still owed a

[152] Boxer, *Portuguese Seaborne Empire*, pp. 219–220.

[153] Godinho, "Portugal, as frotas," p. 73; and Mauro, *Le Portugal*, p. 257.

[154] Godinho, "Portugal and Her Empire (1640–1670)," p. 385; Freitas, "Companhia Geral," p. 96.

[155] See Smith, "Mercantile Class," pp. 367–368.

[156] Ibid., pp. 297–325, 345–346, 381–402. Also see Rae Flory and David Grant Smith, "Bahian Merchants and Planters in the Seventeenth and Early Eighteenth Centuries," *Hispanic American Historical Review* **58** (1978), pp. 571–594. Virginia also had its merchant planters: see Edmund S. Morgan, *American Slavery American Freedom: The Ordeal of Colonial Virginia* (New York, 1975), pp. 223–225.

yearly sum of 90,000 cruzados in 1688, and did not completely pay off the debt until 1723.[157] Brazil also paid for the fleet system: colonists had to purchase foodstuffs at prices fixed by the company, and new levies on exports subsidized the costs of escort vessels. Opposition to these arrangements began almost as soon as they were put into effect. Salvador's câmara refused to pay the export duties pending a direct appeal to the crown. In Rio de Janeiro only captain de Sá's local connections prevented a similar action.[158] After some adjustments the recalcitrant town councils accepted the new taxes, but they intensified their opposition to the company's monopoly on foodstuffs. Prices soared and shortages occurred because the company's ships could not furnish enough grain, dried fish, and wine. So strong were the complaints from all quarters that the crown abolished the foodstuff monopoly in 1658.[159] The company's importance rapidly declined thereafter, but the fleet system continued.

The many taxes the crown levied on sugar made it more expensive at precisely the time Brazil no longer dominated production. During the 1660s the English and French sugar industries in the Caribbean had captured a share of the market. Consequently, prices for Brazilian sugar fell and production declined. An arroba of sugar sold for 3600 réis in 1659, 2400 réis in 1668, and only 1400 réis by 1688—a drop of 62% overall and 42% in 20 years (1668–1688).[160,161] Caribbean sugar glutted the market. The English West Indies exported about 17 million pounds of sugar in 1655 and 26 million pounds in 1669—still far below Brazil's peak capacity.[162] But West Indies' production hit 49 million pounds during the 1680s and surpassed Brazilian levels in the 1690s. The French sugar industry grew less rapidly; its Caribbean sugar colonies sent only 18 million pounds home in 1682, but production doubled over the next 20 years. Brazilian exports, by comparison, dropped 20%.[163] Although it was still an important producer, Brazil's harvests in the 1680s were worth roughly one-third their 1660s value, and expenses were to rise: between 1680 and 1700 slave prices doubled.[164] Brazilian planters now competed with the Caribbean

---

[157] Charles R. Boxer, *Portuguese Society in the Tropics: The Municipal Councils of Goa, Macao, Bahia, and Luanda, 1510–1800* (Madison, 1965), pp. 79–80.

[158] Boxer, *Salvador de Sá*, pp. 189–190.

[159] Freitas, "Campanhia Geral," pp. 95, 99–105.

[160] 400 réis = 1 cruzado.

[161] Godinho, "Portugal, as frotas," p. 74.

[162] Richard S. Dunn, *Sugar and Slaves* (New York, 1972), p. 203.

[163] The figures on English, French, and Brazilian sugar production are from Jacob M. Price, "The Map of Commerce, 1683–1721," New Cambridge Modern History, ed. J. S. Bromley. (London, 1970), vol. 6, *The Rise of Great Britain and Russia 1688–1715/25* p. 583.

[164] See Schwartz, "Free Labor in a Slave Economy," p. 194.

for equipment, slaves, and markets. Between 1676 and 1700 English and French sugar planters purchased 300,000 slaves compared to Brazil's 175,000.[165]

The fall in sugar prices was not confined to Brazil. English prices slid from £2 per hundredweight in 1660 to 16 shillings in the 1680s—a drop of 60%—while slave costs doubled.[166] Nevertheless, the Caribbean industry continued to expand while Brazilian production declined. Part of the explanation rests in the contrasting organization of the two industries. In Brazil cane growing and refining developed as separate enterprises during a period of high prices. Parceled out into relatively small plots, the land supported a class of modest growers whose holdings averaged about 15 acres and rarely exceeded 50. Largescale production in which mill owners directly combined planting and refining appeared in the 1670s, but the small growers were displaced only gradually. In 1680 sharecroppers still held one-half the land belonging to the Sergipe mill.[167] The Caribbean industry, however, expanded while prices fell; it adapted to market forces by rapidly consolidating land ownership and by concentrating refining and planting into a single enterprise. In Barbados (1680), 175 planters owned over 46,000 acres of land and 20,000 slaves.[168] Vertically integrated into huge sugar factories, the Caribbean industry enjoyed economies of scale the Brazilian system precluded.

Caribbean sugar had another advantage: large, protected markets in the mother countries. Portugal's small population consumed only a fraction of Brazil's sugar; the great stocks that remained on hand had to be exported. Domestic markets in England and France, however, absorbed a much larger share of the sugar the Caribbean colonies produced. To protect the home market, England and France used high protective tariffs to exclude Brazilian sugar. Colbert's colonial policy securely attached the French sugar colonies to the mother country. Parliament's Navigation Acts tied the English sugar industry to English ships, merchants, and markets. Consequently, Anglo-Portuguese trade declined during the 1670s.[169]

Brazilian planters faced a shrinking market not only because England and France had their own sugar colonies but because the Dutch now

---

[165] Philip D. Curtin, *The Atlantic Slave Trade* (Madison, 1969), p. 119.

[166] Dunn, *Sugar and Slaves*, pp. 205, 237.

[167] Schwartz, "Free Labor in a Slave Economy" p. 195; on the size of plots, see pp. 162–163.

[168] Dunn, *Sugar and Slaves*, p. 96.

[169] See Richard Sheridan, *Sugar and Slavery: An Economic History of the British West Indies 1623–1775* (Baltimore, 1973), pp. 41–53; and W. J. Eccles, *France in America* (New York, 1972), pp. 60–65.

bought Caribbean exports. The English reexported about one-third of their sugar to Amsterdam (1670–1700), where it competed successfully with its over-taxed Brazilian rival.[170] As early as the 1620s, taxes accounted for 30% of Brazilian sugar prices and new imposts kept appearing. English taxes were substantially lower. During 1668–1669, planters sold their crop for £180,000, paying customs duties in England of only £18,000, or 10%; the duties on reexported sugar were then rebated. Thus, English sugar had a definite advantage in Amsterdam.[171] For England, sugar represented only one of many growing trades that the state taxed—it could afford to subsidize exports. Portugal, however, relied heavily on sugar for its revenues; it could not afford the luxuries of long-run economics. To make their exports more competitive, Salvador's câmara argued persuasively for tax relief, but none was forthcoming.[172] Tied to a peripheral state that relied on foreign merchants for marketing, the fortunes of Brazil's sugar industry now fluctuated with Caribbean production.

Amsterdam was Europe's great tobacco mart; Dutch manufacturers mixed a variety of tobaccos to produce moderately priced blends. Brazil, though far outdistanced by the Chesapeake, was the second largest tobacco producer; exports to Portugal reached 2.5 million pounds in 1666 and about 4 million pounds in 1672.[173] But Chesapeake production captured the Amsterdam market. Rising from 1.5 million pounds in the 1630s, exports rose to 15 million pounds during 1668–1669 and doubled that by 1700.[174] Although tobacco faced a stiff import tax set at fivepence a pound in 1685, which was double the selling price in Virginia, England reexported most of it and rebated the duties.[175] In the 1660s Chesapeake tobacco was cheaper and of higher quality than Brazilian tobacco.[176]

Brazil's tobacco, like its sugar, faced marketing and price competition in Amsterdam; tobacco prices fell 65% in 20 years, from 200 réis a roll (1668) to 70 (1688).[177] Nevertheless, Bahian production increased, and so did the price of the tobacco contracts. Although exports still went to

---

[170] Wilson, *England's Apprenticeship*, p. 169.

[171] In addition, sugar exported from Barbados was taxed a 4.5% duty collected in the colony. See Dunn, *Sugar and Slaves*, pp. 205–206.

[172] The câmara's complaint (1687) and its proposed remedy is reprinted in Boxer, *Portuguese Society*, pp. 186–188; also, see Smith, "Mercantile Class," pp. 312–313.

[173] Godinho, "Portugal and Her Empire (1640–1670)," p. 385.

[174] Jacob M. Price, "The Economic Growth of the Chesapeake and the European Market, 1697–1775," *Journal of Economic History* **24** (1964), p. 497.

[175] Morgan, *American Slavery, American Freedom*, p. 197. The problems falling prices for exports caused in Brazil had strong parallels in Virginia; also see pp. 180–211.

[176] Price, "Economic Growth of the Chesapeake," p. 499.

[177] Godinho, "Portugal, as frotas," p. 75.

Lisbon and Amsterdam, Bahian tobacco, "better twisted and more sugared" found new markets in West Africa.[178] Between 1681 and 1710 Salvador's merchants sent 368 tobacco-laden ships to the Mina Coast; they either exchanged tobacco for slaves or sold their cargoes to Dutch, English, and French traders.[179] Some of Bahia's cane growers met the sugar crisis by growing more tobacco. But larger tobacco exports only partially compensated for lost sugar markets. The sugar business was a prestigious, agroindustrial enterprise; it required more expensive equipment and more credit than tobacco farming. To many sugar planters, tobacco seemed a vulgar, second-rate alternative.[180] Furthermore, other valuable trades declined, aggravating the empire's economic ills.

Sugar, slaves, and illegal trade with the Spanish Indies had promoted Portugal's commercial prosperity. But as each trade contracted, so did Portugal's business. By rebelling against Spain, the Portuguese lost their special status in Spanish America; they now faced the Inquisition, confiscation of their property, and expulsion.[181] Backed by Platine ranchers, Spain kept Portuguese traders out of Buenos Aires, thus halting the illegal flow of silver to Brazil. In the 1680s, to revive the contraband trade, Portugal set up a rival post at Colônia do Sacramento across the river from Buenos Aires; this strategy provoked a long and bitter contest in the borderlands.[182]

Portugal had recovered Angola, but the Dutch kept the factories they seized in Guiné, and the fortress of São Jorge da Mina. In West Africa the WIC developed trades in gold, ivory, and slaves. As slavers they outdid the Portuguese, since with the loss of Brazil, the slave trade became the WIC's chief enterprise.[183] After 1640 Spain refused to sign slave contracts (asientos) with Portuguese merchants and the lucrative business fell to the Dutch. From their bases in the Caribbean-like island Curaçao, the Dutch carried slaves to Mexico and Tierra Firme, as well as to the English and French sugar islands. The slave trade became a highly competitive venture as the English and French set up rival African companies to

---

[178] Boxer, *Portuguese Seaborne Empire*, pp. 170–171. On the price of the tobacco contracts, see Armado de Castro, "Tabaco," *Dicionário*, vol. 6, p. 106.

[179] Pierre Verger, *Bahia and the West African Trade 1549–1851* (Ibadan, 1964), p. 11.

[180] Schwartz, *Sovereignty and Society*, p. 244.

[181] See Lynch, *Spain under the Hapsburgs*, vol. 2, pp. 111–113; Hoberman, "Merchants in Mexico City," pp. 494–500; and Liebman, "Great Conspiracy," pp. 18–31.

[182] See Mario Rodríguez, "Dom Pedro of Braganza and Colônia do Sacramento, 1680–1705," *Hispanic American Historical Review* 38 (1958), pp. 179–208.

[183] See Cornelis C. Goslinga, *The Dutch in the Caribbean and on the Wild Coast 1580–1680* (Gainesville, 1971), pp. 339–370.

undercut the Dutch.[184] Portugal watched its Atlantic trade recede as stronger states moved in on the slave traffic, sold contraband in the Spanish Indies, and glutted Amsterdam with sugar and tobacco.

LUSO-BRAZILIAN TRADE: CONCLUSION

Compared to the Brazil trade, which was still impressive in the 1680s, Spain's American decline in trade began earlier, lasted longer, and was more severe. Between 1616–1620 and 1646–1650, the number of ships that sailed with the Spanish fleets fell from a total of 867 to 366; tonnage dropped 60%.[185] Meanwhile, the silver sent back to Spain on the king's account declined from a total of 4.3 million pesos to 1.6 million.[186] The fleet system continued, but it was no longer an annual affair: between 1650 and 1700, only 19 fleets arrived in Panama.[187] Although less silver reached Spain and trade diminished, it was not because America's mining industry had collapsed. Total bullion production in the 1670s was comparable to levels reached in the 1580s, a period of high trade volume and large silver exports.[188] Spanish America still had its silver, but the crown spent more on administration and defense: between 1651 and 1739, 80% of Lima's treasury receipts, or 155 million pesos. In Mexico, despite the problems miners faced, revenues held steady, but as in Peru, expenditures rose.[189]

The collapse of Spain's transatlantic trade reflected America's growing self-sufficiency. Spanish America had its own olive groves, vineyards, wheat farms, and sugar mills; it no longer needed Spain's agricultural exports. And contraband trade, especially in the Caribbean, reduced dependence on the fleet system for European merchandise. Spain's colonists retained more silver for their own use. They built ships, traded in regional commodities, invested in illegal trades, and developed their agriculture, ranching, and textile industries. Hispanic America was the

---

[184] See Charles Woolsey Cole, *Colbert and a Century of French Mercantilism*, 2 vols. (New York, 1939), vol. 2, pp. 1–56; and K. G. Davies, *The Royal African Company* (1957: New York, 1975).

[185] Lynch, *Spain under the Hapsburgs*, vol. 2, p. 184.

[186] Hamilton, *American Treasure*, p. 34.

[187] L. A. Clayton, "Trade and Navigation in the Seventeenth-Century Viceroyalty of Peru," *Journal of Latin American Studies* 7 (1975), p. 4.

[188] D. A. Brading and Harry E. Cross, "Colonial Silver Mining: Mexico and Peru," *Hispanic American Historical Review* 52 (1972), p. 579.

[189] Lynch, *Spain under the Hapsburgs*, vol. 2, pp. 212, 223–224.

most diversified and self-sufficient region in the New World, it was not Spain's commercial satellite. Colonists traded with each other more than they did with Spain. Still, Spain maintained the most extensive bureaucracy in the Americas. Spiritual and political bonds, held in place by the clergy and royal officials, not trade, bound America to Spain.[190]

While Spanish America diversified its economy, export agriculture shaped the character of English America. The Navigation Acts made the colonies a protected market for English goods; English ports were the required entrepôt for enumerated colonial exports. Even New England indirectly depended on sugar, since it provisioned the Caribbean colonies. By 1700 English America had become a very successful commercial enterprise, largely because England could market colonial exports such as sugar and tobacco while supplying the colonies with manufactured goods.[191] Unlike Spain, which spent its treasure on administration, England did not maintain a large colonial bureaucracy. Instead, local institutions, like the town, Puritan congregations, county courts and assemblies, supervised colonial society. Trade rather than a bureaucracy linked England to America, and England had the naval strength, marketing organization, industry, and capital to protect its commercial system.

How different was Brazil, where the export economy still depended on imported provisions and foreign marketing. Although Portugal could supply foodstuffs to Brazil, it had to import merchandise both for domestic use and as reexports. Brazil was caught in a double-dependency. Portuguese merchants purchased the sugar crop and shipped it to Lisbon. But once in Lisbon, the fortunes of Brazil's sugar passed out of Portuguese hands. Chesapeake tobacco, by contrast, was reexported from London to Amsterdam on English account. English merchants hired Dutch factors in Amsterdam to sell tobacco on commission.[192] But when it came to Brazil's trade, the Dutch and English used the Portuguese as commission agents. Brazil was a colony of Portugal, but Portugal was itself a colony of foreign merchants who set up their firms in Lisbon.

---

[190] America's growing self-sufficiency is stressed in Lynch, Spain under the Hapsburgs, vol. 2, 194–228; Clayton, "Trade and Navigation," pp. 1–21; Hoberman, "Merchants in Mexico City," pp. 479–503; Richard Boyer, "Mexico in the Seventeenth Century: Transition of a Colonial Society," Hispanic American Historical Review 57 (1977), pp. 455–478; and P. J. Bakewell, Silver Mining and Society in Colonial Mexico, Zacatecas 1546–1700 (Cambridge, Eng., 1971), 221–236. That self-sufficiency was also mixed with depression is argued by J. I. Israel, "Mexico and the 'General Crisis' of the Seventeenth Century," Past and Present, 63 (1974), pp. 33–57.

[191] See Ralph Davis, "English Foreign Trade, 1660–1700," Economic History Review 7 (1954), pp. 150–163, idem., "English Foreign Trade, 1700–1774," Economic History Review 15 (1962), pp. 285–198; and Wilson, England's Apprenticeship, 160–205.

[192] Price, "Economic Growth of the Chesapeake," pp. 500–501.

IV

Brazil: The Golden Age, 1690 – 1750

RECESSION AND RECOVERY

The taxes collected on sugar, tobacco, and slaves propped up Portugal's agrarian economy and made independence viable, but state income shrank as sugar exports contracted and prices fell in response to Caribbean competition. Receipts were only 4 million cruzados in 1681, which was below levels reached in the early years of the century.[1] Portugal now faced mounting deficits with Dutch and English suppliers who drained its scarce specie. In 1675 one-third of Portugal's imports had to be paid for with silver, which was particularly difficult to obtain[2] since Peruvian silver production was dropping in the 1670s and 1680s; consequently, less was reaching Spain and even less was trickling to Portugal.[3] In addition, Spain

---

[1] A. H. de Oliveira Marques, *History of Portugal*, 2 vols. (New York, 1972), vol. 1, p. 392.

[2] Vitorino Magalhães Godinho, "Portugal and Her Empire, 1680–1720." In *The Rise of Great Britain and Russia 1688–1725*, The New Cambridge Modern History, vol. 6, ed. J. S. Bromley (London, 1970), p. 511.

[3] On Peruvian silver production see D. A. Brading and Harry E. Cross, "Colonial Silver Mining: Mexico and Peru," *Hispanic American Historical Review* 52 (1972), pp. 545–579.

blocked the Platine contraband trade that had funneled Potosi's silver into the Luso-Brazilian economy. Brazilian planters, in turn, were hard-pressed by their Portuguese creditors. Salvador's câmara warned Lisbon that Portuguese firms were ruining Bahia's economy by requiring their Brazilian debtors to pay in cash or bills of exchange rather than in sugar.[4] In 1690 Salvador remitted over 80,000 cruzados to Oporto alone.[5] Brazil, like the mother country, faced a liquidity crisis. The problem, argued the Council of State, was how to reduce the kingdom's large trade deficit and stop the silver drain, "caused by foreigners who send three times more than they buy in return."[6]

The government's remedy was a program of restricted consumption and import substitution: sumptuary laws prohibited the use and sale of the most expensive English, Dutch, and French textiles; the state sponsored textile production, ironworking, glassmaking, and silk manufacturing. Portugal's industrial program, however, never took root: inadequate domestic production spawned so many exceptions that import restrictions became meaningless.[7]

But the main reason Portugal abandoned its industrial workshops was because trade revived. Brazilian sugar gradually found new markets in the Mediterranean, especially in Spain and Italy.[8] Some planters converted their sugar into a variety of local brandies (*cachaça, aguardente, geribita*), which they sold to slave traders instead of refining sugar for export to Portugal. Furthermore, the Nine Years War (1688–1697), which embroiled most of America's colonial powers and disrupted seaborne trade, benefited the Portuguese, who remained neutral, by providing ample markets and high prices for sugar and tobacco.[9] But the sugar boom soon leveled off: production in 1710, a fairly good year, was about 1.3 million árrobas—a 35% decline from the 1660s.[10] Bahia, now Brazil's leading sugar captaincy, exported 14,500 chests, followed by Pernambuco with 12,300 chests and Rio de Janeiro with 10,220.[11] Exports varied considera-

---

[4] A. J. R. Russell-Wood, *Fidalgos and Philanthropists, the Santa Casa da Misericórdia of Bahia, 1550–1750* (Berkeley, 1968), p. 65.

[5] Charles R. Boxer, *The Golden Age of Brazil, 1695–1750: Growing Pains of a Colonial Society* (Berkeley, 1962), p. 28.

[6] Jorge Borges de Macedo, *Problemas de história da indústria Portuguesa no século XVIII* (Lisbon, 1963), p. 27.

[7] Ibid., pp. 21–40.

[8] Oliveira Marques, *History of Portugal*, vol. 1, p. 439.

[9] Godinho, "Portugal and Her Empire," p. 519.

[10] Peak exports were about 2 million arrobas. See Frédéric Mauro, *Le Portugal et l'Atlantic au XVIIe siècle 1570–1670* (Paris, 1960), p. 257.

[11] Figures for 1710, an approximate date, are from André João Antonil, *Cultura e opulencia do Brasil por suas drogas e minas*, Translated into French by Andreé Mansuy (1711: Paris, 1968), pp. 281–282. A chest contained about 35 arrobas of sugar.

bly thereafter; Bahia's rarely exceeded 12,000 to 13,000 chests.[12] By then the captaincy's tobacco was more profitable than its sugar. The price of the tobacco contract more than doubled between 1681 and 1716, rising from approximately 700,000 cruzados to almost 2 million.[13] Tobacco found markets in Catalonia, India, China, and Africa. Salvador's merchants, for example, sent some 216 tobacco-laden ships to the Costa da Mina (1701–1710) and returned with 83,700 slaves.[14] The king was a great slave trader, too. In 1696 the Cacheo Company, one-third of whose capital the crown had supplied, obtained the Spanish asiento.[15] Two years later one of its ships, after unloading slaves in Cartagena and Havana, returned to Lisbon with 400,000 *livres* in silver; other ships freighted hides, cochineal, cacao, and dyewoods.[16]

Portugal's recovery, however, was not based exclusively on colonial trade. Lisbon's and Oporto's olive oil exports reached 15,000 pipes (1 pipe = 126 gallons) in 1691.[17] Domestic wine exports, however, showed the most spectacular growth. In fact, the wine trade pulled Portugal into England's trading system. From negligible quantities in the 1670s, Portugal's wine shipments to England jumped to over 5000 tuns (1 tun = 252 gallons) a year in the 1690s and reached almost 8000 tuns annually during the next decade.[18] In return, British textiles, especially new, moderately priced draperies, flooded Lisbon. Trade with Portugal almost trebled in value: from an average of £276,000 (1697–1699) to £787,000 (1704–1706). But wine and olive oil could not pay for British manufactures. Portugal's trade deficit rose accordingly; from £140,000 annually (1697–1699) to £522,000 (1704–1706).[19] Fortunately, a growing share of British exports were earmarked for the Brazil fleets, and Brazil could now pay for its imports.

---

[12] Boxer, *Golden Age*, p. 150.

[13] Vitorino Magalhães Godinho, "Finanças públicas e estrutura do estado," in *Dicionário de história do Portugal*, Joel Serrão, ed., 6 vols. (Lisbon, 1975), vol. 3, p. 39; and Godinho, "Portugal and Her Empire," p. 536. Also see Roberto C. Simonsen, *História econômica do Brasil* (São Paulo, 1967), pp. 368–369. The value in réis of cruzados minted in gold and silver fluctuated; but as a money of account its value was constant: 400 réis = 1 cruzado. Since sums expressed in réis are large and bulky, most figures are converted to cruzados. During most of the eighteenth century, there were about 3600 réis to the pound sterling. See Simonsen, pp. 67, 75, 464.

[14] Ship totals are from Pierre Verger, *Bahia and the West African Trade 1549–1851* (Ibadan, 1964), p. 11; for slave estimates see Philip Curtin, *The Atlantic Slave Trade, A Census* (Madison, 1969), p. 207. According to Curtin, these figures may overstate the traffic by 18%, see pp. 207–210.

[15] Cacheo was the center of Portuguese authority along the coast of present-day Bissau.

[16] Godinho, "Portugal and Her Empire," p. 515.

[17] Ibid., p. 520.

[18] A. D. Francis, *The Wine Trade* (London, 1972), pp. 317–318.

[19] H. E. S. Fisher, *The Portugal Trade, A Study of Anglo-Portuguese Commerce 1700–1770* (London, 1971), pp. 242–243.

Around 1700 gold from Minas Gerais began to reach Portugal in significant quantities. Registered consignments stood at 514 kilos in 1699, 4400 kilos in 1703, and 14,500 in 1712.[20] For the next half-century, Brazil's gold held the key to Portugal's commercial prosperity, since bullion shipments to London made the exchange of wine for textiles possible.

Portugal's Atlantic trading system staged a remarkable comeback. Income from taxes collected on maritime trade went up 84% between 1681 and 1716, from 1.7 million cruzados to 3.2 million. Total public receipts climbed from 4.2 million cruzados to 9.8 million, an increase of 134%.[21] The fifths, royalties collected on gold production, grossed more than 450,000 cruzados between 1700 and 1713.[22] No wonder the crown's manufacturing policy collapsed! Portugal again flourished as an entrepôt; prosperity returned to the treasury, to the realm's merchants, and to those members of the nobility who converted from cereals to vineyards. Manufacturing appeared superfluous; the great wine and olive growers replaced industrialists at Court.[23] The crown invested in the slave trade, not in textile workshops. Royal ships participated in the Brazil trade; the treasury farmed out the king's profitable monopolies. After a brief foray into the long-range task of developing its own industries, the state reverted to type: it taxed the wine, olive oil, and textiles that passed through its ports on the way to England and Brazil. But much as Portugal had been a way station for Brazilian sugar carried off to Amsterdam by Dutch merchants, British merchants now carried off Brazil's gold almost as quickly as it could be unloaded in Lisbon. The new cycle of prosperity did not alter Portugal's marginal status in its own commercial system; it remained an arbitrary point of distribution.

ENGLAND'S "PORTUGAL TRADE"

As West Indian competition drove Brazilian sugar from the English market, Brazilian trade, so promising in the 1660s, fell sharply in the 1670s and 1680s. The key to the trade's revival was the ability of the Portuguese to buy more English goods.[24] Most of England's wine came from France—15,435 pipes in 1678.[25] But France was a major commercial and political rival. By combining prohibition with excessive taxation,

---

[20] Godinho, "Portugal and Her Empire," p. 534.

[21] Ibid., p. 536; and Godinho, "Finanças públicas," p. 39.

[22] Boxer, Golden Age, p. 335. The total was 219,623,375 réis.

[23] Godinho, "Portugal and Her Empire," pp. 521–523, 536–539.

[24] Macedo, Problemas de história, pp. 42–58.

[25] Francis, Wine Trade, p. 92.

Parliament ruined the French wine trade in order to promote Portuguese imports. The Methuen Treaty (1703) gave legal status to a commercial quid pro quo already in effect for over a decade: the duty on English textiles was not to exceed 23% ad valorem; the tax on Portuguese wines was to be at least one-third less than the levy on French wines.[26] The privileges England obtained in 1654 were reaffirmed. While the wine trade helped rebuild Anglo-Portuguese trade, Brazil's gold financed the trade's extraordinary growth. When gold production declined in the 1760s, so did the volume of England's "Portugal trade."

The Dutch had once supplied the Portuguese market with northern goods, both for domestic consumption and for reexportation to Brazil and Africa. In the eighteenth century the provisioning of Portugal's Atlantic empire became a British specialty. Portugal bought twice as much from England as it purchased from the rest of Europe.[27] The value of British imports reached over £800,000 a year in the early 1720s, rarely slipped below £1 million between 1730–1760, and occasionally surpassed £1.5 million. (See Table IV.1.) During this period (1730–1760), the Luso-Brazilian market absorbed almost 20% of England's single most important group of exports, light woolen textiles; these constituted over 70%, by value, of all the goods England sent to Portugal.[28] After the principal woolen and worsted fabrics—bays, serges, perpetuanas—the grain trade was next in importance. England's agricultural revolution transformed productivity ratios: during the first 60 years of the eighteenth century, England became Europe's foremost grain exporter, surpassing all Baltic exporters combined.[29] Portugal, meanwhile, was chronically short of grain because the nobility preferred vineyards to wheat production. Portugal became a major market for English grain, purchasing about 20% of England's wheat exports.[30] Portuguese wines, in turn, dominated the English market. Their share of the market, which stood at 35% just prior to the Methuen Treaty, soon rose to 50%. Between 1741 and 1760 Portuguese wines held at least 70% of the English market.[31] By volume, exports rarely fell below 10,000 tuns; by value, the wine trade accounted

[26] Richard Lodge, "The English Factory at Lisbon," *Transactions of the Royal Historical Society* (Fourth Series), **16** (1933), pp. 213–221. The effects of the Methuen treaty on Portugal's economy are discussed in Sandro Sideri, *Trade and Power: Informal Colonialism in Anglo-Portuguese Relations* (Rotterdam, 1970), pp. 40–55.

[27] Fisher, *Portugal Trade*, p. 34.

[28] Ibid., pp. 126, 144.

[29] Jan de Vries, *The Economy of Expanding Europe in an Age of Crisis, 1600–1750* (New York, 1976), p. 81.

[30] Fisher, *Portugal Trade*, p. 127.

[31] Macedo, *Problemas de história*, p. 48; Francis, *Wine Trade*, p. 318.

TABLE IV.1
The Trade between England and Portugal, 1701–1770
(5-Year Annual Averages).

Years	Exports to Portugal (£000)	Imports from Portugal (£000)	Export surplus (£000)	The principal textiles exported: By value and as a percentage of total English exports to Portugal		Wine imports: By tuns, by value and as a percentage of total imports from Portugal		
				Value (£000)	Percentage	Tuns (000)	Value (000)	%
1701–1705	700	222	368	430	71	8.0	173	71
1706–1710	653	224	429	463	71	8.0	170	71
1711–1715	638	252	386	488	77	7.7	217	86
1716–1720	695	349	346	555	80	11.2	288	83
1721–1725	811	387	424	620	76	13.1	326	84
1726–1730	914	347	567	729	80	11.9	302	84
1731–1735	1024	326	698	744	73	11.5	287	88
1736–1740	1165	301	864	871	75	10.5	263	87
1741–1745	1115	428	687	822	79	13.1	367	86
1746–1750	1114	324	790	848	76	11.0	275	85
1751–1755	1098	272	826	799	73	9.2	230	85
1756–1760	1301	257	1044	1086	84	8.8	220	86
1761–1765	966	314	652	709	74	10.5	257	82
1766–1770	595	356	239	459	77	11.7	293	82

Source: Based on H.E.S. Fisher, *The Portugal Trade, A Study in Anglo-Portuguese Commerce 1700–1770* (London, 1971), appendix I, pp. 142–143, appendix III, p. 144, appendix V, p. 146. Used by permission.

for over 80% of Portugal's trade with England. Wine never paid for textiles and grain, however. (See Table IV-1.) Portugal—or more accurately, Portugal and Brazil, as the two economies were in fact inseparable—had huge yearly deficits that sometimes approached £1 million annually.

Underlying the immense volume of British imports was a flourishing reexport trade to Brazil. During the 1740s over 100 Portuguese ships left Lisbon each year with the Brazil fleets, bound for Recife, Salvador, Rio de Janeiro, and Belém.[32] Brazilian-based merchants funneled British goods into the slave trades and reshipped merchandise to Brazil's now thriving contraband base, Nova Colônia.[33] The Platine traffic in 1735 engaged

[32] Jorge Borges de Macedo, "Portugal e a economia 'Pombalina.' Temas e hipoteses," *Revista de História* No. 19 (1954), pp. 83–84.

[33] Besides brandy and sugar, the merchants of Salvador and Rio reshipped European and Asian textiles to Angola. See Herbert S. Klein, "The Portuguese Slave Trade from Angola in the Eighteenth Century," *Journal of Economic History* 32 (1972), pp. 909–910.

over 30 ships laden with manufactured goods that were exchanged for hides and Peruvian silver.[34] But it was surely Brazil's mounting gold production that sustained and solicited the great flood of British exports. Registered gold shipments to Lisbon reached a record 25,000 kilos in 1720, averaged around 11,000 in the 1730s, and between 1740–1755 only twice fell below 14,000 kilos.[35] Beginning in the 1730s, diamonds also joined the flow of precious minerals to Portugal. So great was the influx that their market value dropped by nearly two-thirds. To support prices the crown farmed out the diamond district to private contractors; their annual consignments were worth about 1 million cruzados in the 1740s.[36] Such figures, of course, do not reflect the entrenched contraband operations that stretched from the mines to Lisbon. Much of Brazil's gold escaped the mint, the treasury and the fleets—it did not escape the English. Although exporting bullion from Portugal was illegal, the business was practiced openly and was unofficially tolerated. Between 1730 and 1745 British warships and the biweekly packet boats carried off bullion worth £1 million annually, or about two-thirds of all the gold unloaded in Portugal.[37]

The bullion thus acquired represented more than simply the difference between imports and exports, because the English made profits on virtually every step that accompanied the exchange of merchandise. They ran the shipping business, carrying grain and textiles to Portugal and returning with cargoes of wine, olive oil, and dried fruits. Entrance and clearance traffic at Lisbon averaged almost 1000 English ships a year (1750–1755), 60% of the port's total traffic, and the Portuguese hired English ships for use in the Brazil trade.[38] Portuguese merchants did not market wine in England; they did not even control sales to shippers. Instead, English firms set up warehouses in the realm's great wine center, Oporto, and purchased wine directly from the growers; some Englishmen even owned vineyards.[39] Similarly, the British ran the wholesale trade in textiles. Rare indeed was the Portuguese merchant who made his purchases in London with his own capital. Instead, a chain of British credit followed the Portuguese who circulated textiles. Repayment on domestic sales in

[34] Boxer, *Golden Age*, p. 248.

[35] Godinho, "Portugal and Her Empire," pp. 534–535.

[36] Boxer, *Golden Age*, pp. 209–210, 220.

[37] Charles R. Boxer, "British Gold and British Traders in the First Half of the Eighteenth Century," *Hispanic American Historical Review* **49** (1969), p. 470. Estimates of the quantity of gold and diamonds shipped to Portugal can be found in Macedo, *Problemas de história*, p. 56. Fisher's estimates are more conservative; see *Portugal Trade*, pp. 22–23, 44–45.

[38] Macedo, "Portugal e a economia," pp. 95–99, appendices I and II.

[39] See Fisher, *Portugal Trade*, pp. 77–86, 132.

Portugal was normally deferred for 6 months; the Brazil trade tied up credit for as much as 2 to 3 years. Interest charges earned from 7 to 10% on goods sold in Lisbon, 15 to 17% "upon those they dispose of to the Shopkeepers of the Country,"[40] and from 25 to 35% in the Brazil trade. During the 1750s the credit debt Portuguese distributors owed British suppliers averaged £1.5 million a year.

In terms of shipping and organization, only the Brazil trade remained a Portuguese enterprise. Portugal refused to let the English set up factories in Brazil.[41] Nonetheless, British businessmen financed Luso-Brazilian merchants, even the peddlers who hawked their wares in the mining camps of Minas Gerais. As an English merchant in Lisbon noted (1710), "All their gold, sugars and tobaccos are the returns of our own manufactures, which our people give them upon credit . . . 'tis plain these people live by us, and cannot live without us."[42] However much the wine trade and mining reshaped the Luso-Brazilian economy, they did not alter the structural links that made Portugal so dependent on foreign capital, shipping, and industry. The most significant change was that the English in Lisbon had outdistanced Dutch and French competitors and gained the most from Portugal's recovery.

Portugal's underdevelopment fostered England's economic growth. Indeed, contemporaries thought that "England gained a greater Ballance from Portugal than from any other country whatsoever."[43] Only Amsterdam and Hamburg ranked above Lisbon as entrepôts for British exports. In fact, during the years 1710 to 1740, the demand that kept the British woolen industry booming came from Luso-Brazilian markets, whose customers took more goods than all of English America.[44] Indeed, the Luso-Brazilian economy met the requirements of British mercantilism more fully than did New England, whose exports—fish, cereals, and livestock—duplicated rather than complemented those of Great Britain.[45] Consequently, the New Englanders provisioned the French sugar colonies, a practice the mother country alternately approved, tolerated, and condemned.

---

[40] Ibid., p. 60. Also see pp. 37–38.

[41] Treaties allowed the British a few resident factors in Brazilian ports, but the crown jealously limited the concession. See Boxer, "British Gold and British Traders," pp. 462–464.

[42] Ibid., p. 459.

[43] Kenneth R. Maxwell, *Conflict and Conspiracies: Brazil and Portugal 1750–1808* (Cambridge, Eng., 1973), p. 7.

[44] Fisher, *Portugal Trade*, pp. 126–127; Elizabeth Boody Schumpeter, *English Overseas Trade Statistics 1697–1808* (Oxford, 1960), p. 17.

[45] See Curtis P. Nettels, "English Mercantilism and the Economic Development of the Thirteen Colonies," *Journal of Economic History* 12 (1952), pp. 105–114.

England's Portugal trade did not present such anomalies. Not only did it furnish valuable commodities and a favorable trade balance, but it supplied the gold that strengthened England's currency and credit. At the same time, Luso-Brazilians bought English goods and employed English shipping. Not that the Portuguese failed to skim off some of the profits for themselves; underdevelopment pays, at least for some. Luso-Brazilians, as independent traders or commission agents, cashed in on the flows of textiles and gold, sugar, hides, tobacco, and slaves. The Portuguese nobility benefited too. They were not only large producers of wine and olive oil on their own lands, but were also "great warehousemen for the export of produce received in payment for their seigneurial dues."[46] The Portuguese state, which lived by taxing trade, saw its revenues soar. Export duties on wine, for example, rose from 240 réis per tun (1678–1682) to 1270 réis (1732–1740), a 400% increase.[47] British textiles faced import taxes entering Lisbon, and again when leaving it as Brazilian-bound reexports—26% ad valorem.[48] The crown also taxed the prosperous mining industry.

This golden age of the Luso-Brazilian economy shored up Portugal's mercantile monarchy but did not transform its dependent character. Only in the 1750s, under the tutelage of the Marquis de Pombal, did Portugal try to escape Great Britain's economic dominance. Meanwhile prosperity simply reinforced the established socioeconomic order, particularly in Portugal. In Brazil the gold rush generated new sources of wealth that challenged Bahia's political preëminence and the primacy accorded its sugar and tobacco planters.

MINAS GERAIS: THE GOLD RUSH

Two currents of Brazilian expansion mingled and clashed in Minas Gerais. The Paulista bandeiras penetrated the region from São Paulo; and ranchers and squatters pushed into Minas Gerais from the São Francisco valley. During the economic crisis of the 1670s and 1680s, the bandeirantes, at the crown's behest, organized a series of prospecting expeditions.[49] The king's search for a Brazilian "El Dorado" was unsuccessful.

---

[46] Godinho, "Portugal and Her Empire," p. 538.

[47] Macedo, *Problemas de história*, p. 46.

[48] Dauril Alden, *Royal Government in Colonial Brazil, with Special Reference to the Administration of the Marquis of Lavradio, Viceroy, 1769–1779* (Berkeley, 1968), p. 388 n. 2.

[49] On the expeditions see Manoel Cardozo, "The Last Adventure of Fernão Dias Pais (1674–1681)," *Hispanic American Historical Review* 26 (1946), pp. 467–479; idem, "Dom

But the Paulistas, who had continued their excursions into the interior, discovered gold along the river beds in the 1690s. They blazed the trails that linked the mining zone to São Paulo, Rio de Janeiro, and the São Francisco valley. The supply routes from Rio and São Paulo were treacherous, winding through steep mountain passes and over largely uninhabited terrain. The São Francisco carved a wide, accessible highway, flanked by cattle ranches, into Minas Gerais; and its tributaries, like the Rio das Velhas, held rich deposits of alluvial gold. Consequently, the trails that converged on the river from Salvador and the northeastern sertão became, at first, the main arteries for the cattlemen, merchants, squatters, escaped slaves, and fortune-hunters who descended on the mining zone.

Whereas all of Brazil had labored to supply the plantations, the gold rush drained capital, merchandise, and labor from the coastal export zone. Backland ranchers diverted their herds to Minas Gerais; merchant houses in Rio and Salvador turned to the high profits that plentiful gold and the scarcity of goods created. They sent slaves and the best British textiles, along with provisions such as salt, flour, iron tools, wine, brandy, and tobacco.[50] Minas Gerais also attracted an unprecedented stream of immigrants from Portugal: during the first two decades of the eighteenth century, 40,000 to 60,000 men left northern Portugal, particularly the province of Minho, for Brazil.[51] André João Antonil, the famous chronicler who visited Minas Gerais in 1709, estimated that the region had 30,000 inhabitants engaged in prospecting, gold washing, and trade; in fact, business seemed brisker than in the ports.[52] Such quantities of goods and slaves reached the mines that labor costs and operating expenses rose for the mill owners and planters who could "no longer produce sugar and tobacco so abundantly as in times past."[53] Some Bahian cane growers even sold their slaves and equipment and left to seek their fortunes in the gold district. Salaried workers such as overseers, coppers, blacksmiths, bookkeepers, and ranch hands also joined the exodus, further dislocating wage and price structures. As a result, slaves took over skilled jobs, even that of sugar master.[54] Similar problems quickly developed in Rio de

Roderigo de Castel-Blanco and the Brazilian El Dorado, 1673-1682," *The Americas* 1 (1944), pp. 131-159.

[50] See Manoel Cardozo, "The Brazilian Gold Rush," *The Americas* 3 (1946), pp. 137-160; Antonil, *Cultura e opulencia*, pp. 366-386; and Boxer, *Golden Age*, pp. 30-60.

[51] Boxer, "British Gold and British Traders," p. 49.

[52] Antonil, *Cultura e opulencia*, p. 366.

[53] Ibid., p. 464.

[54] Stuart B. Schwartz, "Free Labor in a Slave Economy: The *Lavradores de Cana* of Colonial Brazil," in *Colonial Roots of Modern Brazil*, ed. Dauril Alden (Berkeley, 1973), pp. 196-197, 152 n. 10.

Janeiro. The governor advised the Overseas Council in 1702 that the city "was without the necessary stocks of meat and flour because the supplies went to Minas Gerais" and that shipping was delayed for lack of provisions.[55]

Complaints that gold mining had adverse effects on Brazil's economy troubled the Overseas Council. Convinced that the gold strikes were transitory it argued that "the best mines of Brazil are those of sugar and tobacco because these are stable and permanent."[56] To protect agriculture, the council tried to curb the indiscriminate rush to the backlands. In 1700 it restricted the sale of slaves there to an annual allotment of 200; the next year it closed the São Francisco trail to all persons and traffic except the cattle herds; departures for the mines from Rio de Janeiro now required a license from the governor. On every score the crown's policy failed. Royal officials connived with the region's suppliers. Bahia's governor-general, for example, overlooked the illegal slave trade at no small profit to himself. The governor of Rio de Janeiro, Álvaro da Silveira, complained that the laws were impossible to enforce, a condition his notorious business dealings had helped create.[57]

As the productivity of the gold fields became apparent, however, the Overseas Council changed its tune. As council member Francisco Dantas Pereira observed in 1708, "the wealth of Minas Gerais has given new life to the commerce of this Kingdom and to the colonies . . . the Fleets which today come from Brazil are richer than those of any other monarch in the world."[58] The crown soon ended the restrictions on trade and travel to the mines. Seeking new revenue sources, the crown now turned decisively to the interior for the first time in Brazilian history.

Because the bureaucracy was concentrated in the ports, the crown had little authority in the mining zone. Antonil complained that the region lacked "any kind of well-ordered government."[59] The only officials were roving superintendents who distributed allotments in the gold fields, collecting fees for their services. By law miners were required to bring their gold to Rio, where it was melted down, cast into bars, assayed, stamped, and a fifth deducted. If the authorities thought they could sit in Rio de Janeiro and collect the fifths as easily as they levied port taxes on sugar and tobacco exports, they were mistaken. Contemporaries calculated that 80% of Brazil's gold left the colony untaxed. One critic estimated that the fifths ought to yield 1 million cruzados a year, but the Rio

---

[55] Cardozo, "Brazilian Gold Rush," p. 145.
[56] Ibid., p. 149.
[57] Ibid., pp. 149–154.
[58] Ibid., pp. 159–160.
[59] Antonil, *Cultura e opulencia*, p. 368.

smelting house took in a meager 200,000 cruzados between January, 1708 and April, 1710.[60] To collect the fifths and tax the region's commerce, the crown had to intervene directly in the mining zone.

The bilingual Paulistas and their Tupí-speaking Indian slaves staked out the first claims in the mining zone. But a host of detested encroachers, both Brazilians and Portuguese, soon competed with them for allotments. Using their connections at Salvador and Rio, the newcomers, pejoratively dubbed *Emboabas* by the Paulistas, monopolized the sale of equipment and provisions, thereby reaping enormous profits.[61] Conflict between such distinct groups escalated into a battle for control of the principal mining centers (1708–1709), a battle the outnumbered Paulistas lost. Rio's governor, Dom Fernando Mascarenhas de Lencastre, rallied to the Paulistas' side, but the victorious Emboabas blocked the roads to the mining camps. His successor, António de Albuquerque, took a more conciliatory view, as did the Overseas Council. The crown recognized the fait accompli in Minas Gerais, and issued an amnesty that the Emboabas readily accepted. Manuel Nunes Viana, whom the Emboabas had chosen as acting governor, was forced to withdraw to his estates in the São Francisco valley. Albuquerque then toured the mining camps, and his authority was promptly acknowledged. The crown was now poised to assert the full range of its fiscal and institutional powers, and it lost little time in doing so.

António de Albuquerque became the first governor of a new captaincy-general that included both São Paulo and Minas Gerais—the first regional government created in almost a century.[62] To stabilize royal authority, the governor created municipal councils in the most important settlements—Ribeirão do Carmo, Vila Rica, Sabará—and supervised elections. To pay the fifths, the câmaras agreed to levy a head tax of 10 grams of gold on everyone working the mine fields, slaves included. Albuquerque frankly admitted that the gold tax would never equal its theoretical yield of 20% of total production. As he told the crown, "three parts of the fifths will be embezzled, whatever the precautions taken."[63] His skepticism reflected the dispersed character of Brazilian mining, for gold was deposited in river beds throughout the rugged highlands.

---

[60] Manoel Cardozo, "The Collection of Fifths in Brazil 1695–1709," *Hispanic American Historical Review* 20 (1940), pp. 375, 359–379.

[61] Manoel Cardozo, "The Guerra dos Emboabas, Civil War in Minas Gerais, 1708–1709," *Hispanic American Historical Review* 22 (1942), pp. 473–474, also see pp. 470–492.

[62] Formerly the sub-captaincy of São Vicente, subordinate to Rio de Janeiro.

[63] Boxer, *Golden Age*, p. 82, also see pp. 61–83. How the câmaras stabilized royal authority is also discussed by A. J. R. Russell-Wood, "Local Government in Portuguese America: A Study in Cultural Divergence," *Comparative Studies in Society and History* 16 (1974), pp. 194–197.

A more advanced technology and complex division of labor tapped the silver of Spanish America's subterranean mines. Because it was a concentrated industry, it was easier to tax.[64] How different was "mining" in Minas Gerais, where washing and panning for gold with the shallow, cone-shaped *bateia* was the favorite method of the region's itinerant prospectors! Particularly large strikes did lead to permanent settlements, however, and complex techniques were not uncommon. For example, miners and their slaves built elaborate dams to expose the river beds; on nearby banks and hills, they sunk shafts in the shallow layers of earth and shale.[65] Subterranean mining, however, was exceptional. Gold production remained high only because placer deposits were generously spread over a wide area; such a perverse mining ecology made regulation particularly difficult. As Antonil noted, miners moved from place to place "like the children of Israel in the desert."[66]

The procedures devised to collect the fifths never satisfied the crown, as the checkered history of the tax reveals. In 1713 a yearly quota of 30 arrobas of gold, guaranteed by the towns, replaced the head tax. The municipalities set up check points or *registros* to tax slaves, goods, and cattle in transit. Five years later, the crown reduced the câmaras' contribution to 25 arrobas, but took over the registros, renting them out to tax-farmers. Between 1714 and 1725 the towns sent 312 arrobas of gold, almost 10,000 pounds, to the royal exchequer.[67] Still, the state considered itself ill-used. During the same period, registered gold sent to Lisbon on private account exceeded 190,000 pounds; thus the state's cut came to about 5%, not the 20% it had designated.[68] Opposition from the miners prevented the crown from terminating the quota system. Finally, the king stationed two companies of Portuguese dragoons in the captaincy to bring his turbulent subjects to heel. Thus reinforced, the crown was determined to increase its receipts by taxing production. To collect the fifths directly, the Overseas Council ordered the new governor, the Count of Assumar (1717–1721), to set up smelteries in the mining towns. The

---

[64] On Spanish silver mining see Lewis Hanke, *The Imperial City of Potosi* (The Hague, 1956); J. P. Bakewell, *Silver Mining and Society in Colonial Mexico 1546–1700* (Cambridge, Eng., 1971); D. A. Brading, *Miners and Merchants in Bourbon Mexico 1763–1810* (Cambridge, Eng., 1971). In Zacatecas, Mexico's principal mining region, "the vast majority of silver produced passed the process of taxation, and was accounted" (Bakewell, pp. 184–185).

[65] Caio Prado, *The Colonial Background of Modern Brazil*, trans. Suzette Macedo (Berkeley, 1971), pp. 196–197; Boxer, *Golden Age*, pp. 38–39. Mawe visited the gold fields in the first decade of the nineteenth century and described some of the techniques used; see John Mawe, *Travels in the Interior of Brazil* (1812: London, 1822), pp. 108–110.

[66] Antonil, *Cultura e opulencia*, p. 370.

[67] Carnaxide, António de Sousa Pedroso, Visconde de, *O Brasil na administração Pombalina* (São Paulo, 1940), p. 244.

[68] The total was 87,900 kilograms: see Godinho, "Portugal and Her Empire," p. 534.

towns, led by Vila Rica, staged a series of armed riots that only the dragoons, with the aid of the governor, managed to quell. After pretending to agree to the insurgents' demands, Assumar treacherously attacked Vila Rica, seized the revolt's ringleader, Felipe dos Santos, and after a summary trial executed him on the garrote. Cautious in the face of such opposition, the crown temporarily retreated. But in 1725 a mint and smeltery opened in Vila Rica, and for the next decade the crown collected its own taxes.[69]

Even with its dragoons, governors, and judges, however, the royal government monitored but a fraction of the captaincy's gold production. With little risk or trouble, untaxed gold found its way into the ports via the secondary trails that led from the backlands. Merchants diverted contraband gold from Salvador and Rio de Janeiro into the slave trades, and gold fed the illicit traffic at Colônia. Homeward-bound East Indiamen, on one pretext or another, stopped at Salvador so their officers and crews could hawk Chinese silks, procelain, and Indian calicoes for gold. Since Oriental wares cost 40% more when imported from Lisbon, they found a ready market.[70] Even the annual Brazil fleets smuggled out gold "in barrels and chests and faggots of sugar."[71] Most notorious were the business companies formed exclusively to falsify the royal fifths. In 1730, informers exposed a clandestine mint and smeltery in the backlands that was operated by former crown employees. The gang's leader, Inacio de Sousa, hired the governor's secretary in Vila Rica as his chief agent. Evidently the racketeers had powerful Lisbon patrons since Sousa and his cronies, although caught red-handed, escaped imprisonment.[72]

Since the smelteries never met the government's expectations and were expensive to run, it gave up the regulatory battle and proposed another capitation tax. In 1735 the new levy was imposed on all slaves (whether employed in mining or not), on tradesmen, and on commercial establishments such as shops and taverns, according to size. Inhabitants who did not own slaves paid a head tax on themselves.[73] This method proved

---

[69] The description of fifth collection and its vicissitudes is based on Boxer, *Golden Age*, pp. 191–201.

[70] See Boxer, "British Gold and British Traders," pp. 460–461. Asian luxury goods had replaced spices as the chief cargoes; idem, "The Principal Ports of Call in the 'Carreira da India,' " *Luso-Brazilian Review* 8 (1971), pp. 18–22. A detailed study of the contraband trade with East Indiamen can be found in Amaral Lapa, *A Bahia e a Carreira da* Índia (São Paulo, 1968), pp. 229–252.

[71] Boxer, *Golden Age*, p. 201.

[72] Ibid., pp. 201–202.

[73] Carnaxide, *Administração Pombalina*, pp. 242–246. Also see Robert Allan White, "Fiscal Policy and Royal Sovereignty in Minas Gerais: The Capitation Tax of 1735," *The Americas* **34** (1977), pp. 207–229.

more profitable than previous levies, since the mining zone, like the coastal plantations, depended on slave labor. In 1736, for example, head taxes were collected on over 98,000 slaves.[74] Between 1736 and 1751 receipts averaged 125 arrobas of gold, about 1.6 million cruzados a year.[75] Mining was an expensive business when it involved an investment in machinery and slaves to divert streams and sink shafts into hillsides. It was a risky business, too, because flooding, drought, or a collapsed shaft could halt gold production. And whether or not a miner's investment paid off, he still had to pay the head tax on his slaves. Consequently, the tax actually discouraged large-scale mining ventures that gambled on long-run profits.[76] In 1734 the câmaras had jointly petitioned for a quota of 100 arrobas of gold in lieu of the head tax. Only in 1750 did the crown defer to its persistent colonists.

As a result of its experience with the captaincy's truculent gold miners, the crown took unprecedented steps in the 1740s to regulate diamond production. Only contractors and their licensed employees could extract the gems; independent prospecting was prohibited. The diamond district, a relatively confined, inhospitable region of Minas Gerais, became a special province administered by monopolists and policed by the dragoons. Between 1740 and 1752 the crown's privileged diamond farmers, including the Paulista, Felisberto Caldeira Brant, sent gems to Lisbon worth over 12 million cruzados and paid the crown 4.8 million for the privilege. Notwithstanding, illicit mining and illegal sales, often sponsored by the contractors, reached scandalous proportions. Indeed, Caldeira Brant ended up in jail.[77]

The provisioning of populous Minas Gerais was a vast enterprise whose supply lines reached from London and Lisbon to Salvador and Rio de Janeiro: in 1720, for example, 9753 fully packed mules entered the captaincy from Rio alone, and in the next year over 11,000 entered.[78] At checkpoints (registros) set up along the major trails, tolls were levied on incoming traffic: slaves, 3000 réis each; cattle, 1500 réis; horses and mules, 3000 réis. Receipts verified payment. Goods were divided into two classes:

---

[74] Boxer, Golden Age, p. 341.

[75] Total receipts were 8,437,477 oitavas, at 1500 réis per oitava: see Carnaxide, Administração Pombalina, p. 245.

[76] Francisco Adolfo de Varnhagen (Visconde de Porto Seguro), História geral do Brasil antes da sua separação e independência de Portugal, 3rd ed., 5 vols. (São Paulo, 1927–1936), vol. 4, pp. 136–137; and A. J. R. Russell-Wood, "The Impact of Gold Mining on the Institution of Slavery in Portuguese America," Journal of Economic History 37 (1977), pp. 61–64.

[77] Boxer, Golden Age, pp. 204–225.

[78] Cardozo, "Brazilian Gold Rush," p. 144.

wet (foodstuffs, wine, olive oil) and dry (agricultural implements, mining equipment, textiles, furnishings), and taxed according to their weight. In consequence, the bulky merchandise essential to the zone's economic life bore the brunt of taxation. A hundredweight of iron tools, worth from 4800 to 6000 réis when unloaded in Rio, was taxed 4500 réis; after adding transportation and marketing costs, it retailed for 14,000 réis in Minas Gerais. Similarly, an *alqueire* of salt (1.6 pecks) that cost 720 réis in Rio was taxed 750 réis, and finally sold for 3600 réis. At the same time, imported cloth and high-priced luxury textiles, since they were light in weight, virtually passed the customs tax free. A hundredweight of textiles, whether worth 100 *moedas* (1 *moeda* = 4800 réis) or double that amount, faced a fixed levy of 4500 réis, or less than 1%.[79] Regardless of the imposts charged, consumers picked up the tab, especially the miners, who paid high prices for equipment. Buying and selling rather than mining was the surest way to a fortune: such at least was the cynical opinion of Assumar.[80] He might also have recommended tax collecting, since that, too, was a growing and profitable business.

Generally, the crown did not collect taxes. Treasury officials (provedores) in the various captaincies farmed out Brazilian revenues to private contractors.[81] Purchasing a tax farm was a business investment; the buyer or syndicate expected to make a profit after covering the contract's sale price and collection costs. After the fifths, the registros netted the most for the Minas exchequer. Francisco Gomes Ribeiro, a resident of Rio de Janeiro, purchased the 3-year toll contract (1740–1742) along the Rio and Bahia roads for 84 arrobas of gold a year. The four triennial contracts negotiated between 1751 and 1764 were worth 6 million cruzados.[82] Purchasers of such contracts, besides employing factors, bookkeepers, and a host of assistants, depended on the help of military officers, judges, and treasury officials. Indeed, the crown ordered its bureaucrats to zealously assist the tax-farmers lest they default on their obligations. The dragoons assigned to Minas Gerais, for example, policed the registros and periodically changed their location to reduce fraud. Rake-offs (*propinas*) facilitated conscientious attention to duty. The farmer of the tolls paid these fees to a long list of bureaucrats connected with the administration of his contract (1750): 1200 drams of gold to the governor; 800 drams to the provedor; 200 drams each to the crown judge

---

[79] Myriam Ellis, "Contribuição ao estudo do abastecimento das zonas mineradoras do Brasil no século XVIII," *Revista de História*, no. 36 (1958), pp. 448, 460–461.

[80] Cardozo, "Brazilian Gold Rush," p. 145.

[81] Alden, *Royal Government*, pp. 308–309.

[82] Ellis, "Contribuição ao estudo," pp. 447, 452.

(ouvidor) and the scrivener of the exchequer; 50 drams each to the bookkeeper, the bailiff, and the clerk.[83]

Proceeds from the fifths and registros ended up in Lisbon, but the tithes levied on agriculture, ranching, workshops, and businesses defrayed the cost of local administration, including the cost of the dragoons. Between 1736 and 1750, the Minas tithe contracts brought in about 250,000 cruzados annually.[84]

Tax collection provoked opposition to royal authority, but it also produced strong partisans who had a vested interest in the profits it generated. Royal officials, army officers, contractors and their factors—many of them Brazilian-born—all benefited. Since the contract system joined important segments of the colonial oligarchy to the local bureaucracy and the crown, it reduced resistance to taxation. In the 1760s Mineiro businessmen ran the treasury and held all the contracts. Entrenched in the municipal councils, whose tasks and patronage expanded, the crown's tax collectors could hardly be distinguished from the local elite.[85]

SLAVES AND FREEDMEN

The social status of the extended families that ran the export economy rested on their untainted white lineage and advantageous marriage alliances.[86] Class distinctions were difficult to maintain in the turbulent society spawned by the gold rush. Antonil, for example, had few kind words for the mining camps, where "people of diverse races and social backgrounds mixed indiscriminately," and he disliked the lowborn upstarts who displayed their new wealth by wasting it "on gambling, frivolities, and mulatto concubines."[87] Many of the region's early governors charged that the "lowest and most ignorant class" had poured into the captaincy.[88] Particularly alarming was the prevalence of miscegena-

---

[83] Boxer, *Golden Age*, p. 350. Additional lists can be found in José João Teixeira Coelho, "Instrucção para o governo da capitania de Minas Gerais," *Revista do Instituto Histórico e Geográphico Brasileiro* 15 (Rio de Janeiro, 1852), pp. 265–269.

[84] The figures are from Carnaxide, *Administração Pombalina*, p. 248. On the tithes see Manoel Cardozo, "Tithes in Colonial Minas Gerais," *Catholic Historical Review* 38 (1952), pp. 175–182; and Boxer, *Golden Age*, pp. 347–349.

[85] Maxwell, *Conflicts and Conspiracy*, pp. 61–70, 91. On the diverse functions of Vila Rica's câmara see Russell-Wood, "Local Government," pp. 192–231.

[86] These themes are discussed in two works by A. J. R. Russell-Wood, "Women and Society in Colonial Brazil," *Journal of Latin American Studies* 9 (1977), pp. 1–34; and *Fidalgos and Philanthropists*, pp. 173–200.

[87] Antonil, *Cultura e opulencia*, pp. 368, 462.

[88] Boxer, *Golden Age*, p. 164.

tion, a pattern the racial and sexual composition of the migrants reinforced.

Luso-Brazilian families carefully regulated the social conduct of white
females; single white women did not join the horde of unmarried adventurers that flocked to Minas Gerais. When suitable marriages could not be
arranged, Bahia's upper-class patriarchs sent their daughters to Salvador's
nunnery. Consigning women to convents also protected estates from
being subdivided as marriage dowries. Bahia's wealthy families produced
so many candidates for the religious life that new convents had to be built;
even then, surplus daughters had to be packed off to Portugal to take the
veil.[89] Since few white women ventured into the mining zone during the
early years, the sons of Portugal cohabited with dark skinned women,
both slave and free. Miscegenation also occurred in Bahia, of course, but
there the white elite jealously guarded the privileges their presumed racial
purity conferred: the Third Orders and the Misericórdia excluded appli-
cants of "dubious racial origin," and expelled members who married a
black or mulatto woman.[90] In disordered Minas Gerais, however, wealthy
miners successfully passed on their estates and status to their mulatto
offspring; some mulattoes even held seats on the municipal councils. This
practice received a stern rebuke from the king in 1726; he found it "un-
seemly that these posts should be held by people with such a defect."[91]
The crown's policy was to promote legitimate marriages between whites
and discourage cohabitation. If the "important residents and even others"
could be coaxed into marriage, then the children, benefiting from a
legitimate family experience, would be "more obedient."[92] Presumably, a
less defiant citizenry would emerge. Denying public office to mulattoes
was a way to reward white families. Nonetheless, the patriarchal extended
family existed only for a small minority, and Mineiros continued to be less
diligent enforcers of the color bar.[93] In 1748 Vila Rica's câmara justified

---

[89] Salvador had only one convent until 1733: Santa Clara do Desterro, founded in 1677.
By the 1740s the number stood at four. On the convent's role in Salvador's social and
economic life, see Susan A. Soeiro, "Women and Nuns in Colonial Bahia," *Hispanic
American Historical Review* 54 (1974), pp. 209–232. Also see Russell-Wood, *Fidalgos and
Philanthropists*, pp. 177–181.

[90] A. J. R. Russell-Wood, "Class, Creed and Color in Colonial Bahia: A Study in Racial
Prejudice," *Race* 9 (1967), p. 153, also pp. 148–154.

[91] A. J. R. Russell-Wood, "Colonial Brazil," in *Neither Slave Nor Free: The Freedmen of
African Descent in the Slave Societies of the New World*, eds. David W. Cohen and Jack P.
Green (Baltimore, 1972), p. 112.

[92] Donald Ramos, "Marriage and the Family in Colonial Vila Rica," *Hispanic American
Historical Review* 55 (1975), pp. 207–208.

[93] For a description of family structure in Vila Rica, see Donald Ramos, "Marriage and
the Family," pp. 200–225. Emilio Willems has stressed the differentiation of the Brazilian
family along class lines; see Willems' "The Structure of the Brazilian Family," *Social Forces*

mulatto appointments, because "effective enforcement of the law depends on good service and not the accident of birth," a sentiment Salvador's câmara did not share.[94] Although wealth more readily obscured
the "defect of color" in Minas Gerais, most mulattoes did not have
socially prominent fathers, and many black freedmen were former slaves
whose color wealth could not conceal.

Although upper-class Mineiro families became whiter as the century
progressed, this did not reverse the captaincy's less orthodox racial system. The prosperous mining economy offered new opportunities for
slaves to buy their freedom. This type of manumission was not uncommon in the coastal zone, both in the cities and on the plantations, but the
practice underwent considerable elaboration in Minas Gerais and was
adopted with greater frequency.[95] For example, miners who could not
afford the investment placer mining required, let their slaves roam the
countryside panning for gold.[96] They reported back weekly to hand over
their earnings. When a slave had thus paid off a sum agreed upon in
advance, the slaveowner surrendered his property rights. The transaction
was recorded in a notarized document, the *carta de alforria*, which was
registered in the local archives; the freed slave retained a copy as a
guarantee.[97] Slaves who learned trades (carpentry, masonry, metal work),
or those employed by shopkeepers and merchants, also had a good
chance to buy their freedom; and so did many of the female slaves who
sold prepared food in the mining camps and towns, keeping a percentage
of the profits. Owners also freed their slaves for faithful service, and
because of the bonds love, kinship, and godparentage created. Although
most slaves died in servitude, manumission was common enough to
alarm Governor Assumar (1717–1721); he feared the captaincy would soon
be populated by free blacks. To prevent this, he prohibited granting cartas
de alforria without his consent, a measure that could not be enforced,
and which the crown refused to sanction.[98]

Although some slaves were lucky or enterprising enough to obtain their

---

[31] (1953), pp. 339–345, and "On Portuguese Family Structures," *International Journal of
Comparative Sociology* 3 (1962), pp. 65–79.

[94] See Russell-Wood, "Colonial Brazil," p. 113.

[95] See Stuart B. Schwartz, "The Manumission of Slaves in Brazil: Bahia, 1684–1745,"
Hispanic American Historical Review 54 (1974), pp. 603–635. Schwartz suggests that even
agricultural slaves participated directly in the market economy and could accumulate
capital; see his article "Resistance and Accommodation in Eighteenth Century Brazil: The
Slaves' View of Slavery," *Hispanic American Historical Review* 57 (1977), pp. 69–81.

[96] Trenches had to be dug in diverted river beds so that slave gangs, supervised by
overseers, could pan for gold "in place."

[97] On the procedures involved, see Schwartz, "Manumission of Slaves," pp. 604–605,
622–628.

[98] See Russell-Wood, "Colonial Brazil," pp. 86–90, 95.

freedom, thousands of others escaped into the rugged countryside, forming self-sufficient, fortified villages (quilombos) in remote regions of the
captaincy. Gangs of fugitive slaves also operated closer to the mining
camps and ranches, where they could attack farms, travelers, and commercial traffic. To cope with the menace they posed to local security and
the slave system, the authorities hired armed bands, often composed of
black freedmen and half-breeds, as slave hunters. Led by bush-whacking
captains, they tracked down fugitives and destroyed quilombos, pushing
the renegades deep into the sertão.[99] In 1790 the interior of Bahia had a
well-protected settlement of 1000 maroons governed by their own king
and captains;[100] quilombos were still being formed and destroyed in the
nineteenth century.

The status of the colored freedmen fell far short of that reserved for
whites. Mixed racial ancestry was a serious impediment to officeholding,
even though exceptions were made. Freedmen could not bear arms or
dress above their station; criminal offenses incurred the harsh penalties
inflicted on slaves, not the milder treatment meted out to whites. Although slaves trained as artisans and shopkeepers often continued such
occupations when freed, white guilds rarely licensed colored artisans, and
few shopkeepers became merchants. By prohibiting their ownership of
slaves and shops, Governor Assumar tried to block the freedmen's economic advancement, and his successor, Dom Lourenço de Almeida
(1721–1732), expelled freedmen from the diamond district.[101] These measures were revoked, but the ambiguous standing of the freedman in a
slave society persisted. Only the religious brotherhoods and the militia
units, organized by race, offered some relief and protection from the
arbitrary and discriminatory forms justice assumed when applied to
freedmen. The white elite supported such associations because they
promoted moderation and stability.[102]

Many freed slaves ended up as marginal workers, drifting from casual
employment to vagrancy; still, the formation of Mineiro society accentuated a crucial social pattern—the emergence of a large class of colored
freedmen that would play an indispensable role in the region's economy.

---

[99] See Roger Bastide, "The Other Quilombos," in *Maroon Societies: Rebel Slave Communities in the Americas*, ed. Richard Price (New York, 1973), pp. 191–201.

[100] Russell-Wood, "Colonial Brazil," pp. 92–93.

[101] Ibid., pp. 100–101, 109–111. Such discriminatory practices were common elsewhere in
Brazil. On the situation in Bahia, see Russell-Wood, *Fidalgos and Philanthropists*, pp.
139–145, 183–184; and idem, "Class, Creed and Color," pp. 148–154.

[102] A. J. R. Russell-Wood, "Black and Mulatto Brotherhoods in Colonial Brazil: A Study
in Collective Behavior," *Hispanic American Historical Review* **54** (1974), pp. 567–602. On
the militia units see Russell-Wood, "Colonial Brazil," pp. 122–177.

They became shopkeepers, tavern owners, craftsmen, and artisans; served as barbers and midwives, and took jobs as overseers in agriculture, ranching, and mining. The gold rush reshaped Brazil, not only because it fostered expansion and created a new kind of economy, but because it changed the colony's racial composition. According to the census taken in 1786, Minas Gerais, with approximately 363,000 inhabitants, was Brazil's most populous captaincy; about 66,000 were listed as white, 174,000 as slaves, and 123,000 as colored freedmen, 34% of the total.[103] In Minas Gerais and other regions of the sertão the color bar had to be relaxed to accommodate wealthy men and women who could never have passed the blood test applied in Bahia. This "tolerance" did not extend to freed slaves, nor did it make slavery less harsh; but it did create a more flexible system of racial stratification. In the United States there was no mulatto "escape hatch," no middle ground between slave and free.[104]

BRAZILIAN EXPANSION

To revive the lucrative contraband trade in the Plata estuary, the Portuguese established Nova Colônia in 1680, provoking determined Spanish resistance. Spanish settlers expelled the intruders a few months later. Until 1716, when the Treaty of Utrecht returned the outpost to the Portuguese, the Spaniards either occupied or blockaded Colônia. Over the next two decades, however, the outpost flourished because of its agriculture, ranching, and smuggling. Small ships from Rio and English merchant vessels brought Brazilian products, textiles, and hardware to be exchanged for Spanish silver and hides; between 1726 and 1734 hide exports exceeded 400,000 cured skins annually.[105] Spain's tolerance of the Portuguese raid on its Platine trade reflected the enduring contradictions in the organization of Spanish commerce. Because Madrid prohibited regular trade between Buenos Aires and peninsular ports, the Platine region lacked markets for its exports and was chronically undersupplied with merchandise.[106] The commercial strangulation this policy imposed

---

[103] Cohen and Greene, *Neither Slave Nor Free*, Table A-4, p. 336. In 1790 the American South had 1.3 million whites, 657,000 slaves, and 32,000 freedmen who constituted .05% of the total population; see Table A-9, p. 339.

[104] See Carl N. Degler's study, *Neither Black Nor White: Slavery and Race Relations in Brazil and the United States* (New York, 1971). In some regions of Spanish America, slavery and race relations paralleled the situation in Minas Gerais; see William Frederick Sharp, *Slavery on the Spanish Frontier: The Colombian Chocó, 1680–1810* (Norman, Okla., 1976).

[105] Boxer, *Golden Age*, p. 248.

[106] Spain's Platine commercial policy, especially as regards the slave trade, is discussed in

created a paradise for smugglers and their accomplices, but Spain was reluctant to attack Portuguese Colônia and jeopardize its shaky peace with Great Britain, Portugal's closest ally. By the 1730s, however, English merchants and Portuguese settlers posed a threat to Hispanic America, and pushed the Spanish government into action.

At Utrecht Spain had to cede the contract (asiento) for supplying its colonies with slaves to the victorious English. Abusing their privileges, the English brought so much contraband that it further reduced Spain's moribund fleet system.[107] Attempts to reduce illicit trade by searching English vessels provoked an Anglo-Spanish naval war in 1739. But before the clash, Spain had already struck against Colônia. In 1736 the Spaniards devastated the colony's hinterland and besieged the fortress. Although a truce was reached restoring the status quo, the outpost never recovered its former prosperity. Spain's now implacable hostility was caused by a fundamental alteration in the borderlands. Madrid saw Colônia as the vanguard of a new Portuguese expansion that endangered the integrity of Spanish territory from the Amazon to the Plata.

Much as the Paulistas had initiated the settlement of Minas Gerais, their far-flung quest for gold opened the vast continental interior. A new form of organization, adapted to prospecting and the regions great river systems, replaced the large overland treks characteristic of the slave-hunting bandeiras. Small bands traveling in slender, elongated canoes followed the course of the Tietê-Paraná-Paraguay and its tributaries deep into the sertão. Such an expedition in 1719 discovered alluvial gold near Cuiabá, far to the west of Minas Gerais. So rich were these and other deposits that the gold "could be extracted from the ground as cream is skimmed from milk."[108] Once, digging no deeper than a half-meter yielded 400 arrobas of gold in a month.[109] There followed another gold rush, although it never rivaled the exodus into Minas Gerais. Supplying the new mining camps proved incomparably more difficult than in Minas Gerais. The overland journey from Rio to Minas took a few weeks, whereas the floating caravans that left São Paulo along the Tietê took 5 months to reach Cuiabá—the same time the voyage from Lisbon to Goa took. For over a decade (1725–1735) the hostile Paiaguá preyed on the

---

Elena F. S. de Studer, *La trata de negros en el Río de La Plata durante el siglo XVIII* (Buenos Aires, 1958). Also see John Lynch, *Spanish Colonial Administration, 1782–1810: The Intendant System in the Viceroyalty of the Rio de la Plata* (New York, 1969).

[107] See George H. Nelson, "Contraband Trade under the Asiento 1730–1739," *American Historical Review* 51 (1945), 55–67.

[108] Sérgio Buarque de Holanda, "The Monsoons," in *The Bandeirantes, the Historical Role of the Brazilian Pathfinders*, ed. Richard M. Morse (New York, 1965), p. 156.

[109] Ibid., pp. 37–38, 59–60.

convoys, destroying several. In 1740 the region's population scarcely exceeded 6000, including whites, slaves, and freedmen.[110] Yet from this nucleus, centered on the town of Cuiabá, radiated a series of viable settlements that bolstered Portugal's claim to the South American interior, although it lay far beyond the Tordesillas line.

The state had only reluctantly followed its errant prospectors into Minas Gerais, but it now embraced and promoted the gods of expansion. In 1720 the Overseas Council detached São Paulo from Minas Gerais. The governor of the new Paulista captaincy had instructions to encourage far-western settlement "lest the Spaniards occupy that district."[111] Within a decade the crown elevated primitive Cuiabá to a full-fledged town with its own câmara, and appointed a crown judge (ouvidor) and treasury officials. Even São Paulo's governor undertook the arduous journey to the mining camps. This unprecedented state activity was partially a response to the region's gold. New strikes occurred in Goiás (1725) and along the banks of the Guaporé in Mato Grosso (1734). The far west, however, produced only a small portion of Brazil's gold, and the surface deposits were quickly exhausted. The crown collected the fifths and taxed the convoys that entered the zone with meager results: the gold tax netted 15 arrobas at the most;[112] the registros set up along the major river routes to Cuiabá sold for a scant 2.5 arrobas of gold in the 1740s, and those that guarded the overland trail to Goiás, blazed in the 1730s, brought only 15 arrobas.[113] Given the great distances involved, it was almost impossible to prevent fraud. When the chests containing Cuiabá's fifths arrived in Lisbon in 1728, "though securely locked and with the official seals still unbroken," they contained lead, not gold.[114] The wealth of the far west proved to be, and still is, largely untapped.

Although it was gold that had lured the state into the sertão, Lisbon's objectives went beyond simply collecting the fifths. Viable settlements were essential to the crown's territorial ambition. The creation of towns and new political subdivisions, backed by bureaucratic appointments, were the stratagems the state used to consolidate its colonists' gains. By the 1740s two vectors of expansion had converged in the far west, delineating a series of natural boundaries. From Belém the Portuguese

---

[110] Boxer, *Golden Age*, pp. 257, 261–267.

[111] David M. Davidson, "How the Brazilian West Was Won: Freelance and State on the Mato Grosso Frontier, 1737–1752," in *Colonial Roots of Modern Brazil*, ed. Dauril Alden (Berkeley, 1973), p. 70.

[112] Boxer, *Golden Age*, p. 259; there were at least 2400 drams in an arroba; see Table of Weights, p. 356.

[113] Ellis, "Contribuição ao estudo," p. 447.

[114] Boxer, *Golden Age*, p. 259.

followed the Amazon to the Madeira, the Mamoré and the Guaporé, which formed a continuous tributary system that terminated in Mato Grosso near the mining camps and the headwaters of the Paraguay.[115] Indeed, the far west could be more easily supplied from Belém than from São Paulo. To reinforce its claims, the crown established two new captaincies in 1748: Mato Grosso, which included the town of Cuiabá, and Goiás. Mere artificial constructs, the captaincies anticipated rather than reflected actual settlement. The towns of Vila Boa (Goiás) and Cuiabá, designated prelacies in 1745, had no bishops until the 1780s.[116]

In the 1730s, during the bitter conflict over Colônia, Spain finally learned the extent of Brazil's westward march. Spanish missions near the upper reaches of the Paraguay (Chiquitos) and by the confluence of the Mamoré and Guaporé (Moxos) offered the only buffer against Portuguese penetration. In 1742 the Council of the Indies approved a plan to invade Cuiabá from Asunción, aided by the Jesuits and their Indian allies.[117] The plan was abandoned once negotiations over disputed boundaries began. Spain's primary objective was the security of the Plata estuary. The Treaty of Madrid (1750) recognized Brazil's new fluvial boundaries, and Portugal agreed to surrender Colônia.

The Brazilian frontier advanced by leaps and bounds rather than in gradual progressions. The result was a sparsely settled hinterland outside the sphere of the export economy, a region where subsistence agriculture and barter predominated. This "unsuccessful frontier" of itinerant squatters bred racial patterns, kinship structures, and modes of production that diverged sharply from the dominant culture shared by planters, merchants, bureaucrats, and bishops.[118] Still, Brazil had reached its modern boundaries by 1750, almost a century before English Americans were to discover manifest destiny. France, whose fur traders had explored the Mississippi and its tributaries, also claimed the North American interior, but such ambitions had to withstand the challenge of English settlers moving west. Along the great rivers of central South America, however,

---

[115] Davidson, "Brazilian West," pp. 62–106; idem, "Rivers and Empire: The Madeira Route and the Incorporation of the Brazilian Far West, 1737–1808," doctoral thesis, Yale University, 1970).

[116] Oliveira Marques, History of Portugal, vol. 1, p. 433.

[117] See Davidson, "Brazilian West," pp. 89–96.

[118] See Emilio Willems, "Social Change on the Latin American Frontier," in The Frontier: Comparative Studies, ed. David Harry Miller (Norman, Okla., 1977), pp. 259–273, and his "Social Differentiation in Colonial Brazil," Comparative Studies in Society and History 12 (1970), pp. 31–49. The Brazilian view of the frontier is discussed in Mary Lombardi, "The Frontier in Brazilian History: An Historiographical Essay," Pacific Historical Review 44 (1975), pp. 437–457. Also see Richard M. Morse, "Some Themes in Brazilian History," South Atlantic Quarterly 61 (1962), pp. 159–170.

only the Spanish Jesuits contested Portuguese sovereignty. Content with the more abundant resources of the Andean sierra and the pampas, Spanish colonists left the humid flood plains to the Brazilians.

CONTINUITY AND CHANGE: COMMERCE

Growing from a cluster of coastal settlements in 1670, Brazil embraced half a continent in 1750. Its population, estimated at about 300,000 in 1690, surpassed 1.5 million in 1776.[119] The Luso-Brazilian economy of the 1680s, with its contracting markets and ruinous trade deficit, was fully recovered by the 1720s and boomed until the 1760s, largely because Brazil's gold paid the bills. Due to its proximity and improved roads, Rio de Janeiro superseded Salvador as the main port serving Minas Gerais. Separate fleets now sailed directly to Brazil's chief ports. In 1749 22 ships from Rio arrived in Lisbon with more than 15.1 million cruzados in coins, gold dust, and bullion—3.5 million of which was earmarked for the royal treasury; 11.6 million on private account—as well as 34 pounds of diamonds, 45,000 hides, and 3000 chests of sugar. The 5 ships from Belém arrived in Lisbon with 48,000 arrobas of cacao and small quantities of sugar, coffee, and cloves; the fleet that stopped at Recife and Salvador returned with 13,000 chests of sugar, 150,000 hides, and 7000 quintals of brazilwood loaded aboard 39 ships.[120] There was no separate fleet for Salvador in 1749, but the previous year a convoy of 43 ships had carried back 16,000 chests of sugar—an exceptionally good harvest.[121] Bahia also sent tobacco, hides, and considerable quantities of gold—in 1742 2.3 million cruzados worth, 95% on private account.[122]

The Brazil fleets were richer than ever, as gold animated every branch of colonial trade. Since gold followed the path of merchandise and credit, most of it ended up in London. But on the way there, substantial

---

[119] Simonsen, *História econômica*, p. 271: and Dauril Alden, "The Population of Brazil in the Late Eighteenth Century: A Preliminary Study," *Hispanic American Historical Review* **43** (1963), p. 193.

[120] Boxer, *Golden Age*, pp. 351–353; the total combines private capital with the amounts carried by the flag ships on royal account. The amount in gold was about 13.8 million cruzados; the remainder was probably in silver and copper coins.

[121] Ibid., p. 304.

[122] Alden, *Royal Government*, p. 331; conversions are made at the rate of 400 réis to 1 cruzado; a mil-réis = 1000 réis. The total was 932,746 mil-réis. Between 1739 and 1763 1539 merchant vessels entered Lisbon from Brazilian ports: 22 ships a year from Salvador and 14 from Rio de Janeiro; see Eulália Maria Lahmeyer Lobo, "O comércio atlântico e a comunidade de mercadores no Rio de Janeiro e em Charleston no século XVIII," *Revista de História*, no. 101 (1975), pp. 61–62.

amounts were diverted. Because Brazil boomed, so did the business of those who rented the crown's lucrative commercial monopolies and tax farms, as well as those who traded in tobacco, sugar, salt, slaves, gold, and all the other assorted goods that were channeled to every corner of the empire.

The career of the Portuguese merchant, Manuel de Basto Viana (1695–1760), is a case in point. From his beginnings as a modest clerk, he made his fortune as a trader in Brazil, coming and going between Rio de Janeiro and the mines. His partner in Vila Rica during the 1720s was António Lopes da Silva, the son-in-law of Domingos Tomé da Costa, assayer of the mint. By the time Basto Viana returned to Portugal in 1730, he had extensive Brazilian business contacts that he used to considerable advantage. For example, Vitorino Vieira Guimarães, a Rio resident, was Basto Viana's guarantor for the Brazilian salt contract which Viana obtained in 1738 for 91,000 cruzados annually. Guimarães was a wheeler-dealer in his own right; in fact, he was later arrested for gold smuggling. Although Basto Viana stayed in Portugal, his business ventures were still linked to Brazil: in 1750 he bid 140,000 cruzados on the contract to supply Rio de Janeiro with tobacco.[123]

Basto Viana represents those merchants who received on-the-job training in Brazil, many of whom stayed there permanently. Others, like the prominent Lisbon merchant Francisco Pinheiro (1680–1749), never left Portugal. Pinheiro's trading activities extended to every region of Brazil, including Mato Grosso, as his correspondence with Brazilian-based agents testifies; his factors, who worked on commission, included important colonial traders and an array of relatives. Pinheiro shipped large quantities of butter, cheese, codfish, wheat, olive oil, and wines, bar iron and iron-made implements, and a wide variety of textiles. In return, his agents remitted colonial staples like sugar and hides, but primarily they sent back gold. Pinheiro also invested in local offices—two notarial posts in Minas Gerais, and the post of surveyor of ships in Rio de Janeiro: the beneficiaries remitted half their earnings.[124]

To the extent that a merchant like Pinheiro traded in British goods, his gold ended up on the Lisbon packet boats; but in the process at least some of the profits stayed in Brazil as commissions. Likewise, Basto Viana relied on Brazilian factors to administer his salt contract. Trade was usually a joint Luso-Brazilian enterprise, but not always. The notorious *commissários volantes* are a case in point. These peddlers bought their

---

[123] See Virginia Rau, *Estudos de história* (Lisbon, 1961), pp. 103–116.

[124] See Dauril Alden, "Vicissitudes of Trade in the Portuguese Atlantic During the First Half of the Eighteenth Century," *The Americas* 32 (1975), pp. 282–291.

stocks in Portugal and then swarmed into Brazil, hawking their wares and returning to Portugal with the profits. Since they bypassed regular channels, their competition cut into the Luso-Brazilian commission business; and, by concealing merchandise in their luggage, they also defrauded the customs. In 1755 the crown forbade such independent trade with Brazil, but peddlers still found ways to get their wares aboard ship.[125]

Tobacco

Gold was the lodestone of Luso-Brazilian economy, but sugar, tobacco, hides, and slaves continued to be essential. Unlike sugar, which had uncertain markets and depended on foreign merchants for European distribution, tobacco had dependable outlets and the disbursement was supervised by the Portuguese. Tobacco was produced on hundreds of plantations concentrated in the township of Cacheira in the Bahian Recôncavo. When sugar production dropped in the 1680s, tobacco planting expanded. By the 1730s tobacco rivaled Bahia's sugar exports.

Tobacco was a demanding crop. After being cured and twisted into cords, it was dipped in a thick syrup made from sweet-smelling herbs, ambergris, tobacco juice, port lard, and molasses to enhance its savor, moistness, and aroma. The cords were fashioned into rolls weighing about 8 arrobas each and then wrapped in moist, pliant hides to maintain the tobacco's quality during shipment.[126] In Antonil's day, Bahia ordinarily sent 50,000 hides a year to Portugal, but the tobacco industry used almost as many.[127] Tobacco's most popular form was snuff; it was also chewed and smoked in pipes.[128] Between 1700 and 1710 exports to Portugal averaged about 25,000 rolls. From 15,000 to 20,000 rolls were generally of lesser grades, weighing 3 arrobas, and were set aside for the Mina slave trade. About 3000 rolls went to Rio de Janiero, much of it for use in the city's slave trade with Angola.[129]

---

[125] Maxwell, *Conflicts and Conspiracies*, pp. 8, 20–21; and John Norman Kennedy, "Bahian Elites, 1750–1822," *Hispanic American Historical Review* 53 (1973), p. 422. In the 1770s the viceroy was still complaining about the comissarios volantes; see Lahmeyer Lobo, "Comercio no Rio de Janeiro," p. 79.

[126] Antonil, *Cultura e opulencia*, pp. 300–312. For an excellent account of the colonial tobacco industry see Catherine Lugar, "The Portuguese Tobacco Trade and Tobacco Growers of Bahia in the Late Colonial Period," in *Essays Concerning the Socioeconomic History of Brazil and Portuguese India*, eds., Dauril Alden and Warren Dean (Gainesville, Fla., 1977), pp. 26–69.

[127] Antonil, *Cultura e opulencia*, p. 480.

[128] Fernand Braudel, *Capitalism and Material Life 1400–1800*, trans. Miriam Kochan (New York, 1967), pp. 188–191.

[129] Antonil, *Cultura e opulencia*, pp. 325 n. 10, 326, 328; Boxer, *Golden Age*, pp. 151, 230.

In 1722 the tobacco contract sold for 1.8 million cruzados, making it the king's most lucrative monopoly.[130] The concession included the exclusive right to purchase tobacco in Bahia for export to Portugal, a monopoly on domestic sales, and control of reexports. In addition, specific branches, such as sales in Rio de Janeiro, were sold separately.[131] For its convenience and profit, the crown restricted tobacco planting in other captaincies. Investing in contracts was a profitable business for those Portuguese merchant-financiers who could afford them.[132] The crown ordered its bureaucrats in Bahia to help the buyers inspect and grade tobacco. The contractors purchased their stocks at a fixed price, but sold them at market prices. Between 1756 and 1759 about 6600 rolls were sold domestically in Portugal and 12,000 rolls were reexported. East Indiamen loaded tobacco for Goa and Macao, but most of it went to markets in Italy, Spain, and Hamburg.[133]

Since tobacco fetched higher prices in Lisbon than monopolists paid in Brazil, it was popular with smugglers. Homeward-bound East Indiamen stopped at Salvador so their officers and crewmen could exchange Asian goods for gold and tobacco. And the Brazil fleets, when they returned to Lisbon, were crammed with illicit tobacco. Inspectors found tobacco concealed in sugar chests, in barrels with false bottoms, and in double-seamed clothing; they found it stuffed in the ships' artillery, and even inside the hollow images of saints.[134]

The Slave Trade

The Dutch, by capturing the Portuguese fortress at São Jorge da Mina (Elmina) in 1637, gained control of the West African slave trade. Bahian merchants returned to the region during the 1680s. The Dutch allowed them to trade their tobacco at selected factories along the Dahomey coast, but they had to pay a tax of 10% of the tobacco they had brought from Brazil. Although the King of Dahomey let the Bahians set up their

---

Throughout the eighteenth century estimates of Bahian production continued to range between 25,000 and 30,000 rolls, but the number of arrobas per roll rose from 8 to 15 and even to 20 arrobas. See Lugar, "Portuguese Tobacco Trade," p. 48.

[130] Antonil, *Cultura e opulencia*, p. 332; Simonsen, *História econômica*, pp. 368–369.

[131] Antonil, *Cultura e opulencia*, n. 15, pp. 327–329.

[132] Maxwell, *Conflicts and Conspiracies*, pp. 25–26.

[133] Jorge Borges de Macedo, A *situação económica no tempo de Pombal: Alguns aspectos* (Oporto, 1951), document 8, p. 293. An average of 53,000 arrobas were sold domestically; 97,000 arrobas a year were exported. Also see Godinho, "Portugal and Her Empire," pp. 520, 536; and Antonil, *Cultura e opulencia*, pp. 325 n. 10, 334–335 n. 9.

[134] Antonil, *Cultura e opulencia*, pp. 338–340.

own factory at Whydah in the 1730s, the Bahians still paid off the Dutch.[135] The trade's staple was third-grade tobacco, considered unfit for export to Portugal, but liberally brushed with molasses and so highly esteemed on the Mina coast that it became an indispensable commodity.[136] The Dutch, who obtained their supply from the Bahians, much of it free of charge, became obliging hosts. Between October and August of 1728 21 ships entered Salvador from the Costa da Mina with 8923 slaves.[137] Besides tobacco, the Bahians exchanged sugar and brandy for slaves and ran a brisk illegal trade in gold—90 arrobas a year, according to the viceroy.[138,139] In return they also acquired alarming stocks of foreign merchandise. When Bahia's slave traders stopped at Elmina it wasn't just to pay their taxes.

The tobacco trade with the Costa da Mina provided competition to the contractors who exported tobacco to Portugal; consequently, Lisbon's monopolists and Bahia's slave traders were constantly at loggerheads over allocations. Although the crown tried various schemes to restrict the Mina traffic, it was too vital to Bahia's economy to be prohibited.[140] Between 1701 and 1750 the Mina trade brought 350,000 slaves to Salvador, destined for the captaincy's plantations and for resale in Minas Gerais and Pernambuco.[141] If, in the process, merchants smuggled in textiles and took out more tobacco than allowed, the trade still had its merits from Lisbon's point of view. Port taxes collected on slaves subsidized Salvador's garrison and paid upkeep on the city's fortifications.[142] (See Table IV.2.)

Between 1701 and 1770 Angola exported almost 700,000 slaves to Brazil, over half of these to Rio de Janeiro. Sales to the mining zone strengthened Rio's position as a slave entrepôt because the Mineiros paid in gold. The king's share of the profits came from taxes levied at the ports.

---

[135] On the Costa da Mina slave trade see Verger, West African Trade, pp. 5–22; idem, Flux e Reflux de la traite des nègres entre le golfe de Benin et Bahia de Todos os Santos du dix-septieme au dix-neuvieme siècle (Paris, The Hague, 1966); also see A. F. C. Ryder, "The Reestablishment of Portuguese Factories on the Costa da Mina to the Mid-Eighteenth Century," Journal of the Historical Society of Nigeria 1 (1958), pp. 157–181.

[136] Although reserved for Portugal, some of the finest grades were illegally channeled into the slave trade; see Verger, Flux et Reflux, p. 117.

[137] Ryder, "The Re-establishment of Portuguese Factories," p. 164.

[138] The captaincy-general of Bahia became a viceroyalty in 1720.

[139] Verger, West African Trade, p. 7; and Boxer, Golden Age, p. 306.

[140] Lugar, "Portuguese Tobacco Trade," pp. 36–41.

[141] Curtin, Atlantic Slave Trade, p. 207; note his reservations on these estimates, pp. 207–210. Also see Verger, Flux et Reflux, p. 664.

[142] See Boxer, Golden Age, p. 155; these duties were usually farmed, see Verger, Flux et Reflux, pp. 663–664.

Table IV.2
Estimated Slave Imports into Brazil, 1701–1801 (10-Year Totals).

Years	From Costa da Mina	From Angola	Total
1701–1710	83,700	70,000	153,700
1711–1720	83,700	77,100	160,800
1721–1730	79,200	73,600	152,800
1731–1740	56,800	155,700	212,500
1741–1750	55,000	119,400	174,400
1751–1760	45,900	131,400	177,300
1761–1770	38,700	132,300	171,000
1771–1780	29,800	152,300	182,100
1781–1790	24,200	168,500	192,700
1791–1800	53,600	178,500	232,100
Total	550,600	1,258,800	1,809,400

Sources: Philip D. Curtin, *The Atlantic Slave Trade: A Census* (Madison, 1969), p. 207; and Herbert S. Klein, *The Middle Passage* (Princeton, 1978), p. 27.

Brazilian ships and crews predominated in the trade between Rio and Luanda. Although Lisbon's merchants seldom participated directly, they supplied capital and merchandise through their Rio agents. Carioca merchants made profits as shippers, factors, and distributors.[143] Rio planters gained too, not only because the city's slave trade provided a dependable source of labor, but because they furnished sugar-cane brandy and assorted provisions essential to the traffic.[144]

To what extent did the empire's trade imply shared Luso-Brazilian ventures? The picture was mixed. The contracts for supplying Brazil with salt, for purchasing tobacco, or for whaling along the coast were usually sold to Lisbon entrepreneurs; still, colonial-based businessmen made profits as factors and subcontractors. The collecting of taxes at Brazil's ports was a local concession, and contracts went to each region's financiers.[145] The wealthiest merchants owned their own ships and traded with

---

[143] A Carioca was a resident of Rio de Janeiro.

[144] See Herbert S. Klein, *The Middle Passage. Comparative Studies in the Atlantic Slave Trade* (Princeton, N.J., 1978), pp. 23–50; and Boxer, *Portuguese Society in the Tropics: The Municipal Councils of Goa, Macao, Bahia and Luanda 1510–1800* (Madison, Wis., 1965), pp. 110–140. On colonial shipbuilding see Lahmeyer Lobo, "Comércio no Rio de Janeiro," p. 84; and Amaral Lapa, *Bahia e a Carreira da Índia*, pp. 51–81.

[145] For a list of some Brazilian contracts held by metropolitan financiers, see Maxwell, *Conflicts and Conspiracies*, p. 261. The tax concession on Bahian slave imports was let in the captaincy, see Verger, *Flux et Reflux*, p. 664. On the involvement of local entrepreneurs in revenue collection see Alden, *Royal Government*, pp. 307–311; Kennedy, "Bahian Elites," pp. 420–424; and Maxwell, *Conflicts and Conspiracies*, 61–70. A document on how Salvador's câmara leased the brandy contract in the 1670s is reprinted in Boxer, *Portuguese*

Lisbon on their own account, but most of the time transatlantic trade with Portugal relied on the credit Portuguese businessmen supplied, backed-up in turn by the English. Viceroy Lavradio (1769–1779) claimed that Carioca merchants were simply commission agents for Lisbon.[146] Although peddlers from Portugal (commissários volantes) provided competition that established merchants resented, distributing merchandise was mainly a Brazilian enterprise; so too, was the trade in regional specialties between captaincies. The slave trade, however, was the most important Brazilian-based venture. Since colonial staples paid for slaves, it was one of the few trades where resident investors controlled the capital and the profits. In 1784 the secretary of state, Melo e Castro, complained that Brazil had taken over African trade to the total exclusion of Portugal.[147]

Salvador's Merchants

Commercial prosperity swelled the ranks of Salvador's business community. Merchants based their careers on diverse activities, often engaged in simultaneously: the export–import trades with Lisbon and the Mina coast, tax farming, shipping, and money-lending. Salvador's merchants traded in ports of other captaincies, and they extended the credit that financed domestic distribution.[148]

By the eighteenth century the city's merchant-financiers had acquired a social standing on a par with that of the planter elite. Between 1700 and 1739 23% of those elected to seats on the town council were merchants. Likewise, they were admitted to the Misericórdia as *nobres* (the highest rank), sat on its governing board, and became its presidents. Such privileges did not extend to retailers engaged in the measuring, weighing, or selling of merchandise. But in Salvador's vibrant, urban milieu, today's shopkeeper could become tomorrow's businessman. André Marques and Domingos Lucas de Aguiar, Portuguese immigrants, married the

---

Society, pp. 183–184. On the whaling industry see Dauril Alden, "Yankee Sperm Whalers in Brazilian Waters, and the Decline of the Portuguese Whale Fishery (1773–1801)," *The Americas*, 20 (1964), pp. 267–288; and Myriam Ellis, *A baleia no Brasil Colonial* (São Paulo, 1969). The salt monopoly is discussed in Myriam Ellis, *O monopólio do sal no estado do Brasil 1631–1801* (São Paulo, 1955).

[146] Marques de Lavradio, *Relatório do Marquês de Lavradio, Vice-Rei do Brasil de 1769 a 1779, apresentato ao Vice-Rei de Vasconcelos e Sousa seu sucessor*, reprinted in Carnaxide, *Administração Pombalina*, pp. 305–306.

[147] Maxwell, *Conflicts and Conspiracies*, p. 77; Verger, *Flux et Reflux*, p. 117.

[148] Rae Flory and David Grant Smith, "Bahian Merchants and Planters in the Seventeenth and Early Eighteenth Centuries," *Hispanic American Historical Review* 58 (1978), pp. 578–582.

daughters of local artisans; they succeeded financially and changed their social status. The Misericórdia, which certified social status, accepted them as nobres, and in the 1740s Marques and Aguiar held the brotherhood's highest post.[149]

Most of the city's resident merchants were born in Portugal. A steady flow of nephews, clerks, and factors came to Salvador to handle business for their uncles or Lisbon employers. Place of birth did not become a major source of friction, because successful merchants, whatever their origin, often acquired land and settled down as part-time planters. They became officers in the urban militia regiments, married into the best families, inherited estates as dowries, and sent their daughters to Salvador's convents.[150]

In Bahia the marriage market, joint investments, godparentage, and officeholding created reciprocal social ties between the elite sectors of the society: the planters, merchants, bureaucrats, and the military corps.[151] Elsewhere, the bonds that fostered social integration did not always prevail. Rio's prosperity, for example, depended on its role as a market center for Minas Gerais. The selling of slaves, equipment, and textiles to the Mineiros provided merchants with careers independent of sugar exports. Consequently, the Carioca business community formed a distinct group whose interests diverged sharply from the planters.[152] In Pernambuco merchants and planters were antagonists. The captaincy gained little from the gold rush, and the crown, to keep Bahian contract prices high, discouraged tobacco production. In 1711 the animosity between debt-ridden planters and their creditors, primarily Portuguese merchants, almost provoked a full-scale civil war. The unique residential division that separated the factions—planters lived in Olinda, merchants in the neighboring port of Recife—intensified the rivalry. Although it was larger and more prosperous, Recife had no câmara; hence, local patronage was doled out by Olinda's municipal council, which specifically excluded merchants. The crown triggered hostilities when it granted

---

[149] Ibid., pp. 582–593; A. J. R. Russell-Wood, *Fidalgos and Philanthropists*, pp. 117–126; idem., "Mobilidade social na Bahia colonial," *Revista Brasileira de Estudos Políticos*, no. 27 (1969), pp. 175–193. Russell-Wood notes the degree of acceptability merchants had acquired by the 1740s; Smith and Flory have shown that the breakthrough occurred much earlier. Also see David Grant Smith, "The Mercantile Class of Portugal and Brazil in the Seventeenth Century: A Socio-Economic Study" (doctoral thesis, University of Texas, 1975), pp. 273–402.

[150] Between 1680 and 1740 over 80% of Salvador's resident merchants were born in Portugal; see Flory and Smith, "Bahian Merchants," pp. 572–578, 582–593. Also see Soeiro, "Women and Nuns," pp. 217–218.

[151] Kennedy, "Bahian Elites," pp. 416, 420–424.

[152] Lahmeyer Lobo, "Comércio no Rio de Janeiro," pp. 78–86.

Recife its own câmara, thereby diminishing Olinda's political clout.[153] Pernambuco's residential segregation was exceptional. In Bahia merchants became accepted members of the captaincy's elite without such rancor; but Salvador had the largest coterie of merchant-planters.

CONTINUITY AND CHANGE: ROYAL GOVERNMENT

Brazil's stake in the empire cannot be measured simply by counting merchants and ascertaining their place of birth: trade occurred within a larger fiscal and bureaucratic context, and Brazil's native sons could be found everywhere. Rocha Pita's *História da América Portuguesa*, compiled in the 1720s, already contained an impressive list of distinguished Brazilians: governors-general of Bahia; governors of Maranhão, Pernambuco, Rio de Janeiro, Angola, Cabo Verde, and São Tomé; capitães-mores of Brazil's sub-captaincies; officers in the militia; justices in the High Courts of Bahia, Goa, Oporto and Lisbon; overseas councilors; secretaries of state for Overseas Dominions; chancellors of the Royal Exchequer. As the eighteenth century progressed, the crown added to this list, both locally and elsewhere in the empire.[154]

Brazil's planters, merchants, miners, and lawyers owned an assortment of bureaucratic offices: not only clerking positions, but crucial posts in the treasury department and the mint. The superintendent of Bahia's treasury during the 1750s and 1760s was Manoel de Matos Pegado Serpa; his family held a proprietary interest in the office. The Pires clan owned several posts at mid-century, including that of Salvador's chief customs officer. Similarly, the Bandeira de Melo family kept positions in Paraiba's treasury for three generations.[155]

Officeholding was a business, particularly as regards the treasury, which farmed out local taxes. In the seventeenth century that meant primarily the tithe contracts; during the eighteenth century, the crown added substantially to its Brazilian revenue. Trade, both transatlantic and domestic, bore the brunt of new taxation. Between 1699 and 1715 the crown imposed a new import tax (10% ad valorem) on Brazil's major

---

[153] A full account can be found in Boxer, *Golden Age*, pp. 106–125.

[154] Sebastião da Rocha Pitta, *História da América Portuguesa, desde o anno de mil e quinhentos do seu descobrimento, até o de mil e setecentos e vinte e quatro* (Lisbon, 1730), pp. 659–662. Also see Manoel Cardozo, "Azeredo Coutinho and the Intellectual Ferment of His Times," in *Conflict and Continuity in Brazilian Society*, eds. Henry H. Keith and S. F. Edwards (Columbia, S.C., 1969), pp. 72–74.

[155] Alden, *Royal Government*, pp. 22 n. 80, 296 nn. 52, 54, also 294–298.

ports. Local levies were charged on slaves and luxury imports like wine, brandy, and sweet oils. Each tax defrayed a specific expenditure such as salaries, funds for military garrisons, and special donations (*donativos*) pried from the harried town councils.[156] The registros and the fifths tapped the wealth of Minas Gerais.

The provedor of each captaincy auctioned off the local tax farms. As contractors, administrators, and employees, some Brazilians made a profit on collection: Salvador's merchants, for example, invested heavily in the tax business.[157] In addition, the provedor purchased and disbursed supplies to the garrisons and forts. Fraud in this section of Bahia's treasury cost the crown 30,000 cruzados while Pegado Serpa was superintendent. The judges that investigated the embezzlements claimed that local officials "concealed books and papers . . . and declined to testify."[158] It was a lucrative, disorganized porkbarreling operation, in which officeholders, contractors, and suppliers all had their hands in the till.

As the crown created more captaincies and towns, it opened up new jobs for the magistracy. With only three captaincies-general in 1690, Brazil had seven by 1750: Pernambuco and its subcaptaincies (Ceará, Rio Grande do Norte, Paraíba, Alagoas), Bahia (Sergipe, Ilhéus, Pôrto Seguro), Rio de Janeiro (Espírito Santo, Rio Grande do Sul, Santa Catarina, Colônia), São Paulo, Mato Grosso, Goiás. Until 1772 Pará and Maranhão constituted a distinct region beyond the jurisdiction of Brazil's viceroy. Each captaincy had at least one circuit judge (ouvidor); populous Minas Gerais, Bahia, and Pernambuco had several. The ouvidor presided over the câmara established in the chief town of his district (*comarca*).[159] Organizing new towns was a way to court backland potentates because, as municipal councilors, their locally defined status received broader legitimacy and recognition. They paid a price, however, since the crown often sent a magistrate (juiz de fóra) to supervise the câmara's affairs.[160] By mid-century, judges selected from the ranks of Coimbra's professional magistracy had replaced the local juiz ordinário in many of Brazil's major towns.[161]

Admission to the judicial fraternity was not restricted to the

---

[156] Ibid., pp. 301–307.
[157] Kennedy, "Bahian Elites," p. 421; Flory and Smith, "Bahian Merchants," p. 579.
[158] Alden, *Royal Government*, pp. 22–23.
[159] The list of captaincies is from Eulália Maria Lahmeyer Lobo, *Processo administrativo Ibero-Americano* (Rio de Janeiro, 1962), pp. 501–502; on local government see pp. 525–528.
[160] See Boxer, *Golden Age*, pp. 147–150.
[161] This trend began in the 1690s; see Stuart B. Schwartz, *Sovereignty and Society in Colonial Brazil: The High Court of Bahia and Its Judges, 1609–1751* (Berkeley, 1973), pp. 257–258; and Alden, *Royal Government*, pp. 423–424.

Portuguese-born. Brazil's elite sent their sons to Coimbra for legal studies: between 1690 and 1760 over 1000 Brazilian students attended the university.[162] Some entered the magistracy, serving as ouvidores and juizes de fóra in both Portugal and Brazil. The Relação of Bahia had three Brazilian-born judges in 1752; when the crown set up an additional High Court in Rio de Janeiro (1751) it selected the Bahian, João Pacheco Pereira, formerly ouvidor of Vila Rica, as senior magistrate.[163] As the bureaucracy proliferated, Brazilians, through purchase and appointment, took over strategic posts at every level. Their influence was greater than numbers alone would indicate, since Portuguese governors and judges acquired wives and business partners in Brazil.

In Portugal, powerful secretaries preempted the old councils, creating a greater degree of centralization.[164] In Brazil, although the crown added captaincies, the bureaucracy's decentralized character changed little. The crown conferred the title of viceroy upon Brazil's governor-general, but his authority was not upgraded; when Lisbon expected the governors to comply with viceregal orders, it issued special instructions to that effect. The drift toward regional governments continued. The residência fell into disuse; Bahia's High Court only conducted an investigation in exceptional cases, and the new Carioca Relação curbed what remained of Bahia's judicial pretensions. Consolidation reinforced the pattern: either larger captaincies absorbed smaller ones, or they became subordinate units whose crown-appointed capitão-mór was subject to a specific governor. The viceroy had little jurisdiction outside Bahia.[165]

Each captaincy-general was a distinct patronage system run by shifting alliances between segments of the bureaucracy, local plutocrats, and the town councils. A governor could not dispense with local allies; to do so was to court disaster. The Rio câmara, for example, deposed its controversial governor, Vaca Monteiro, in 1732. This cantankerous official had fought with the Benedictines over ownership of the Ilha das Cobras, with the planters over law enforcement, and with the municipal council over its finances.[166] The colonial oligarchy rarely presented such a united front as the one that deposed Monteiro, and an astute governor usually picked

---

[162] Francisco Morais, "Estudantes na Universidade de Coimbra nascidos no Brasil," *Brasilia, Revista do Instituto de Estudos Brasileiros da Faculdade de Letras de Coimbra*, (supplement to vol. 4), (Coimbra, 1949), pp. 51–236.

[163] Schwartz, *Sovereignty and Society*, p. 394; and idem, "Magistracy and Society in Colonial Brasil," *Hispanic American Historical Review* 50 (1970), p. 729.

[164] Oliveira Marques, *History of Portugal*, vol. 1, p. 418.

[165] Alden, *Royal Government*, pp. 34–44; on the infrequency of the residência see p. 478 n. 27.

[166] Ibid., p. 426 n. 18.

his way through the family rivalries that made up local politics. Conversely, the bureaucracy was far from monolithic. The governors, who were often professional soldiers and nobles, vied with the upstart lawyers who composed the magistracy: Brazil's viceroy, the Marquis de Lavradio (1769–1779), caricatured judges as venal, incompetent, time-servers.[167] There was, in short, plenty of room to maneuver on both sides. Even Governor Assumar, who used the dragoons against the Mineiros, had to mix the carrot with the stick. Conditions in Minas Gerais soon reverted to type, and the dragoons became one more appendage in the local patronage system: by 1780 there were more Brazilian officers than Portuguese.[168]

In the vast, cattle-ranching sertão, where towns were few, the crown commissioned the territorial magnates to form militia units; or more precisely, their armed retainers became the militia units.[169] The governors had little control over the *coronéis* who ran the backlands. The Feitosas, coronéis in the Sertão dos Inhamuns (Ceará), wiped out the rival Monte clan before the governor could intervene. When the crown investigated in the 1730s, a full decade after the conflict, it fined the Feitosas 6 leagues of land as court costs. By then the Feitosas were back in the governor's good graces: they got 3 leagues back.[170]

CONTINUITY AND CHANGE

The gold rush reshaped Brazil's economy, altered its geography, enhanced the status of its merchants, blurred racial categories, and overturned Bahia's political primacy, but it did not transform the basic commercial and political structures that bound Brazil to Portugal. As vast as Brazil had become, Portugal did not change the essential character of colonial administration: the registros simply extended port taxes to the countryside, and the new captaincies duplicated previous arrangements. Lisbon had exchanged the Dutch for the English; it had not escaped its dependence upon foreign merchants. The volume and diversity of goods circulating through the ports had changed, but not the way they were circulated or taxed. In 1756 the British Board of Trade lamented that £100 of English goods shipped to Brazil were taxed £62 in duties: 26% when unloaded in Lisbon, 26% when cleared for Brazil, and 10% in colonial ports. If the goods were destined for Minas Gerais, they were also taxed at

---

[167] Lavradio, *Relatório*, pp. 297–298.

[168] Maxwell, *Conflicts and Conspiracies*, p. 102.

[169] See Boxer, *Golden Age*, pp. 306–308; Alden, *Royal Government*, pp. 443–446.

[170] Billy Jaynes Chandler, *The Feitosas and the Sertão dos Inhamuns: The History of a Family and a Community in Northeast Brazil 1700–1930* (Gainesville, 1972), pp. 6–45. Also see Luís de Aguiar Costa Pinto, *Lutas de famílias no Brasil* (São Paulo, 1949), pp. 146–173.

the registros.[171] In addition, the crown rented out its monopolies on tobacco, salt, brazilwood, and whaling. Portugal remained a mercantile monarchy.

Brazil's opulence was legendary; its exports were worth £2.5 million in 1710, £4 million in 1750, £5 million in 1760.[172] The crown reserved colonial trade for Luso-Brazilian merchants. The size, dependability, and specialization of the Brazil fleets was in sharp contrast to the disarray in Spanish commerce: between 1715 and 1736 only five fleets left for Portobello and small squadrons called irregularly at Veracruz. As the convoy system collapsed, a large share of the Spanish-American market fell to smugglers who used the Caribbean as a base. Spain had the most restrictive trading system in the Americas. Merchants who resided in the Indies could not take silver to Spain to make direct purchases; to obtain goods they had to go through the Spanish trading guilds in Cadiz and Seville that monopolized trade with the colonies. Consequently, American-based merchants cooperated with British smugglers to undercut the fleets.[173] Only in the 1760s and 1770s did the Bourbon reformers rebuild Spain's colonial trade.

Great Britain was the strongest commercial state. Between 1700 and 1770 over one-third of England's trade consisted of reexported colonial staples;[174] during the same period, the English colonies increased their purchases from Britain by 600%.[175] Unlike Portugal, however, England did not burden its trade with heavy taxes. The government argued that excessive taxation only encouraged smuggling and reduced the competitiveness of British goods and colonial reexports. Domestic property taxes and the excise on articles of popular consumption such as tobacco, tea, pepper, and spirits financed the state.[176]

How, then, did Portugal's overtaxed commercial network manage to survive, in fact, to thrive? There are several interdependent explanations. Portugal kept the English out of Brazil. Except for their contraband trade at Colônia, which the Portuguese resented, British merchants operated

---

[171] Alden, *Royal Government*, p. 389.

[172] Carnaxide, *Administração Pombalina*, p. 81.

[173] J. H. Parry, "The Development of the American Communities, 1: Latin America," in *The Old Regime 1713–1763*, The New Cambridge Modern History, vol. 7, ed. J. O. Lindsey (Cambridge, Eng., 1970), pp. 494–497; and Walter L. Dorn, *Competition for Empire 1740–1763* (1940: New York, 1963), pp. 124–125.

[174] Ralph Davis, "English Foreign Trade 1700–1774," *Economic History Review* 15 (1962), p. 291.

[175] Between 1701–1705 and 1766–1770, the value of England's exports to its continental colonies rose from an average of £259,000 to 1.8 million; see Schumpeter, *Trade Statistics*, p. 17.

[176] Charles H. Wilson, *England's Apprenticeship 1603–1763* (London, 1965), pp. 318–319.

out of the Lisbon Factory. Spain was unwilling to let England set up factories in Seville. Consequently, Englishmen undercut the fleets by trading directly with Spanish America, either as interlopers or under the guise of licensed slave traders. When Spain tried to halt the practice, England declared war. Smuggling, the predictable nemesis, plagued Portuguese commerce, too; but at least its agents were Luso-Brazilians sporting enough to use the Brazil fleets and the East Indiamen. Another reason for the survival of Portuguese commerce was that England protected Portugal's oceanic trade. British warships, for example, had escorted the Brazil fleets during the War of Spanish Succession (1702–1713).[177] Finally, Portugal had remained neutral while conflicts were embroiling America's colonial powers; as a result, its empire was not so burdened with defense expenditures. At such times Luso-Brazilian shipowners made extra profits, for the British hired their ships.[178] If war extended British commerce, peace preserved Portugal's.

In sum, Portugal had the right European ally, and Brazil had a source of labor and an outlet for its staples that was relatively immune from competition. Luso-Brazilian merchants, for example, ran the Angolan and Mina slave trades; Bahia's tobacco did not compete with the Chesapeake's less expensive product, which was sold to different markets. This was not true of sugar, however, and Lisbon was often glutted with it. The industry trudged along, partly because planters converted to sugar-based alcohols sold to slave traders; in addition, Anglo-French warfare, by disrupting Europe's sugar supply, provided sporadic relief.[179] Finally, Luso-Brazilian trade flourished because gold propped up the system. When the crown collected £68 for every £100 of English goods shipped to Brazil, it was colonial consumers, not British merchants, who picked up the tab. Gold was the key: it allowed Brazilians to pay the high prices the fiscal apparatus imposed. All along the line, gold fed the multiple transactions that radiated from London and Lisbon to Brazil's ports.

---

[177] On Portugal's role in the War of Spanish Succession, see A. D. Francis, *The Methuens and Portugal 1691–1708* (Cambridge, Eng., 1966).

[178] Fisher, *The Portugal Trade*, pp. 89–90.

[179] Ibid., p. 39. How war affected the French sugar colonies is discussed in Richard Pares, *War and Trade in the West Indies 1739–1763* (Oxford, 1936), pp. 326–393.

V

The Luso-Brazilian Empire, 1750—1821

THE LUSO-BRAZILIAN ECONOMY, 1750–1780: DEPENDENCY AND SELF-SUFFICIENCY

Brazilian miners and their slaves worked for the benefit of the British textile industry. British sailors could be observed along the Lisbon waterfront stowing away Brazil's gold, a graphic reminder of Portugal's tributary status in its own empire.[1] As suppliers, shippers, and wholesalers, British firms ran the textile, wine, and grain trades with Portugal; for this service they collected freight charges, brokerage, commission, and interest. "Few or rare are the Portuguese merchants in a condition to do business with their own funds, none with goods that are not foreign," complained one Portuguese critic; he charged that "all the commerce of Brazil is made on credit by foreign houses."[2] Such was the diagnosis of

[1] Charles R. Boxer, "British Gold and British Traders," *Hispanic American Historical Review* **49** (1969), pp. 465–470.
[2] Kenneth R. Maxwell, *Conflicts and Conspiracies: Brazil and Portugal 1750–1808* (Cambridge, Eng., 1973), p. 8.

Map 6 Colonial Brazil, 1780. The captaincies-general (and their subordinate captaincies) are Grão Pará (Rio Negro), Maranhão (Piauí), Pernambuco (Ceará, Rio Grande do Norte, Paráiba), Bahia (Segipe, Espirítu Santo), Rio de Janeiro (Santa Catarina, Rio Grande do Sul), São Paulo, Minas Gerais, Mato Grosso, and Goias.

Portugal's situation in 1750, an appraisal shared by the new king's chief minister of state, Sebastião José de Carvalho e Melo, the Marquis of Pombal. "Gold and silver are fictitious riches," he said, "the Negroes that work in the mines of Brazil must be clothed by England, by which the value of their produce becomes relative to the price of cloth."[3] What was the remedy? How could the new regime nationalize the Luso-Brazilian economy without attacking the commercial privileges that sustained the Anglo-Portuguese alliance?[4]

While he was a diplomat in London (1738–1744), Pombal studied England's commercial system, especially its trade with Portugal.[5] The crux of the problem was how to create merchant houses in Portugal with enough capital to compete with foreigners. England's "Portugal trade" was virtually a closed shop, but colonial trade offered greater flexibility. Run by Luso-Brazilians, albeit with British credit, the Brazil trade could be reorganized without directly violating the Methuen Treaty. Using the state's fiscal and institutional powers, Pombal promoted the interests of the empire's wealthy businessmen to give them an opportunity to amass capital and dispense with the British. Banning the commissários volantes from the Brazil trade fit this scheme perfectly. The commissários volantes were interlopers who bypassed regular channels and undermined the Luso-Brazilian commission business. Since commissions were a major source of capital, prohibiting the casual trader was intended to concentrate resources in the hands of more substantial merchants.[6]

Attacking peddlers was an oblique approach to the problem of capital accumulation, for it did not directly challenge British firms. In 1755, however, Pombal established a Board of Trade responsible for all commercial affairs. Membership was restricted to a select group of state-subsidized businessmen: by reserving lucrative concessions such as the tobacco farm and the salt monopoly for these merchant-financiers, the state guaranteed them a steady capital supply. The businessmen thus favored also controlled the trading companies and industries the state created. But Pombal moved cautiously; he could not afford a direct clash with British interests. The monopoly companies set up in the 1750s traded exclusively with Pará-Maranhão and Pernambuco, regions outside the

[3] Alan K. Manchester, *British Preëminence in Brazil, Its Rise and Decline* (Chapel Hill, 1933), p. 40.

[4] See Maxwell, "Pombal and the Nationalization of the Luso-Brazilian Economy," *Hispanic American Historical Review* 48 (1968), pp. 608–631; Sandro Sideri, *Trade and Power: Informal Colonialism in Anglo-Portuguese Relations* (Rotterdam, 1970), pp. 97–104.

[5] Dauril Alden, *Royal Government in Colonial Brazil, with Special Reference to the Marquis of Lavradio, Viceroy, 1769–1779* (Berkeley, 1968), pp. 7–13.

[6] See John Norman Kennedy, "Bahian Elites, 1750–1822," *Hispanic American Historical Review* 53 (1973), p. 422 n. 25.

main Brazilian markets for British reexports. Although the companies could purchase and export British textiles, they preferred to purchase domestic manufacturers; indeed, the Board of Trade owned silk factories in Lisbon. The companies' protected markets stimulated the silk factories to branch out into woolens and cottons. The Board of Trade, the companies, and the industrialists represented privileged interests tied to the state. Inácio Pedro Quintella, who invested heavily in both companies, profited from tobacco, tithe, and whaling concessions. José Francisco da Cruz, administrator of the Lisbon customs house, helped draw up the statutes for the Pará-Maranhão Company; he became its director in the 1760s. José Rodrigues Bandeira, the Board of Trade's first chairman, was linked to the textile factories and served on the board of the Pernambucan Company.[7]

The companies' and the state's active roles in the economy tackled root causes, the British realized. The Lisbon factory warned London that the formation of new trading monopolies would "change the circulation and channel of trade from the hands of British subjects to Portuguese, and consequently, we shall be deprived of the great advantage of our commission business and other profits that arise from the sale and purchase of our commodities."[8] For the moment, however, the threat seemed remote. Placing the Amazon and Pernambucan economies under company tutelage did not initially affect British exports. Britain's surplus on the Portugal trade averaged over £1 million a year between 1756 and 1761, the largest ever.[9] But when trade declined after 1764, the British blamed Pombal's economic policies; cowed by London's threats, Pombal scrapped plans to create new companies for the state's business partners. Still, the original companies remained, and they transformed the regional economies where they operated.

PARÁ AND MARANHÃO: MISSIONARIES AND COMPANIES

A dry zone of scrub and thorn forest separates the Northeast region from northern Brazil. The north, a tropical rain forest with constant

---

[7] These interrelationships are discussed in Jorge Borges de Macedo, A situação económica no tempo de Pombal: Alguns aspectos (Porto, 1951), pp. 137–144; and Maxwell, Conflicts and Conspiracies, pp. 25–26, 51–53, 75. A list of salt contractors can be found in Myriam Ellis, O monopólio do sal no estado do Brasil (1631–1801) (São Paulo, 1951), p. 201. How much the Pará-Maranhão Company depended on capital the tobacco monopolists supplied is discussed in Manuel Nunes Dias, Fomento e mercantilismo: A companhia geral do Grão Pará e Maranhão (1755–1778), 2 vols. (Belém, 1970), vol. 1, pp. 251–254, 259–261.

[8] Maxwell, Conflicts and Conspiracies, p. 34.

[9] H. E. S. Fisher, The Portugal Trade: A Study of Anglo Portuguese Commerce 1700–1770 (London, 1971), p. 143.

temperatures, is ecologically distinct from the rest of Portuguese America. Belém, located at the mouth of the Pará river, sits in the heart of the Amazon basin; São Luís do Maranhão, situated along the spacious bay of São Marcos, skirts the southern edge of this tropical zone. The Amazon region was administered as a separate colony between 1626 and 1772, outside the jurisdiction of Brazil's governor-general. Contrary sea currents and the prevailing winds made communication from the Amazon easier with Lisbon than with Recife or Salvador.

There were scarcely 1000 white Portuguese settlers in 1650, and the population of northern Brazil stood at a scant 2000 a half-century later.[10] The vital resource was Indian labor. Disputes over the distribution of native workers pitted the town councils against the state-supported Jesuits; on two occasions, in 1661 and 1684, the colonists expelled the missionaries.[11,12] During the 1660s, Portugal was still consolidating its independence; in the 1680s, however, the crown started to rein-in Brazil's truculent câmaras: the ringleaders of the 1684 revolt were apprehended and executed; the role of the religious orders was strengthened. The laws of 1686 placed Indian villages (aldeias) under the exclusive control of the missionaries; they alone had permission to live among the Indians. The villages provided a labor pool for the settlers, but access was carefully regulated. Whereas the crown recognized how much the economy depended on Indian workers, it also realized how quickly direct exploitation decimated the native population. The new laws tried to protect the Indian worker from the rapacious settler, while channeling labor to productive economic tasks. Half the males between the ages of 13 and 50 were eligible for service 6 months of each year. The governor, assisted by representatives from the town councils, the superior of the missions, and the village pastors, distributed workers. Wages had to be paid in two installments: half was due before the Indians left the village, and half when they returned. Although most villages had obligations towards the settlers, some were reserved for the labor requirements of the missionaries, the towns, and the state.[13]

The constraints this system imposed discouraged plantation agriculture. The salary advance needed to obtain workers hurt less affluent

---

[10] Charles R. Boxer, *The Golden Age of Brazil, 1695–1750: Growing Pains of a Colonial Society* (Berkeley, 1962), p. 275.

[11] The expulsion in 1661 involved both Maranhão annd Pará; the 1684 revolt was confined to Maranhão.

[12] See Mathias C. Kiemen, *The Indian Policy of Portugal in the Amazon Region, 1614–1693* (Washington, D.C., 1954), pp. 79–154.

[13] Ibid., pp. 158–163; Colin M. MacLachlan, "The Indian Labor Structure in the Portuguese Amazon, 1700–1800," in *Colonial Roots of Modern Brazil*, ed. Dauril Alden (Berkeley, 1973), pp. 206–208.

settlers, even though the câmaras and the governors kept wages artificially low. To recover their investment quickly, colonists hired Indians to forage the vast river system in their canoes, collecting the region's natural products.[14]

The demand for labor generally exceeded the supply. To expand the labor pool, the crown ordered its missionaries to locate new villages in places convenient for trade and commerce. Those wealthy colonists who could afford to finance Indian resettlement obtained a lifetime claim on the village's labor pool, but the missionaries still controlled the community's affairs. Illegal slave hunting was another way to corral native labor. Although the new laws curtailed the "just war" pretext for Indian slavery, private expeditions (resgates) sent to "purchase" Indians held captive by other tribes continued. Profiteering governors like Christovão da Costa Freire (1707–1718) used this ruse to license slave-hunting expeditions. Nonetheless, the state-backed mission system flourished as, caught between the slave raiders and the Jesuits, the Indians opted for the mission-run villages. By 1730 the Jesuits alone had settled over 20,000 Indians in 28 villages; over the next decade, the number doubled.[15]

The crown had expressed its support for christianizing Indians before, on numerous occasions, but rarely had intention and practice coincided. In this instance, however, the state had ample cause to support the religious orders. As the vanguard of Portuguese expansion in the Amazon, the mission system served the state's geopolitical objectives. The villages set up along the coast north of the Amazon (Ampará) created a buffer against French and Dutch penetration from the Guianas. Located along the upper reaches of the Amazon and its tributaries, and beyond Manaus, the missions blocked the Spanish Jesuits supplied from Quito; furthermore, the mission system spread south and west along the Madeira, converging with the adventurers from Mato Grosso, who had followed the Guaporé-Mamoré to its confluence with the Madeira. The security of this Amazon passage to the Brazilian far west became a vital tenet of imperial policy; the rivers formed a natural Luso-Spanish boundary, and provided easier access to the isolated, far-western mines.[16]

The crown encouraged and protected the mission business, but did not pay for it. At least one-fourth of the villages were located in remote areas outside the coastal labor system. To provision and finance new settlements, the Orders used the profits the mission economy produced. The

---

[14] MacLachlan, "Indian Labor Structure," pp. 204–206.

[15] Ibid., pp. 203–204; Boxer, Golden Age, pp. 284, 290–291.

[16] Kiemen, Indian Policy, pp. 166–180; David M. Davidson, "How the Brazilian West Was Won: Freelance and State on the Mato Grosso Frontier, 1737–1752," in Colonial Roots, pp. 91–115.

Jesuits were astute businessmen. Since particular Indian villages were set aside for their use, the Jesuits had a dependable, cheap labor force to work their numerous farms and ranches. Besides hides, their estates produced cacao, sugar, cotton, manioc, and beans, both for sale locally and for export. The Jesuits also sent Indian expeditions along the Amazon and its tributaries to harvest the spices of the forest—wild cacao, cinnamon, vanilla, sarsaparilla, and cassia.[17] From the state's point of view, the missions were of strategic importance, and they were self-supporting. But what about the settlers point of view?[18]

The colonists charged that the missions usurped the land, the labor supply, and the region's trade. The Jesuit critic, Silva Nunes, told the crown that the villages were more like warehouses than places of prayer; however, he did not mention that the expanding mission system hurt the slave-hunting business. Francisco Duarte dos Santos, the magistrate who investigated these accusations in the 1730s, dismissed them. He reported that many colonists of Belém, far from being impoverished, had sumptuous homes, plenty of Indians, and dressed extravagantly. Despite their complaints against the cumbersome labor laws, the local elite had managed to prosper; they owned ranches as well as sugar and cacao plantations, and they built up their labor force by financing resettlement or by investing in the resgates.[19]

When Pombal became minister of state in 1750, he appointed his brother, Francisco Xavier Mendonça Furtado, captain-general of Pará-Maranhão. The new governor soon concluded that the missions strangled the region's economic potential. The Amazon's marginal economy contributed the least to Luso-Brazilian trade and the cost of royal government had to be subsidized by Lisbon.[20] Mendonça Furtado blamed this meager performance on the commercial advantages the Jesuits enjoyed at the expense of the colonists and the royal treasury. The Jesuits, who were exempt from customs duties on goods shipped to and from Brazil, also refused to pay the tithe, despite the crown's repeated demands; their tax-free estates and easy access to labor created unfair competition that impoverished the settlers and hindered plantation agriculture.[21]

---

[17] Cacao, Pará's chief export, was both collected in the forest and produced on plantations.

[18] MacLachlan, "Indian Labor Structure," pp. 200–201; Nunes Dias, *Companhia geral*, pp. 178–194.

[19] Boxer, *Golden Age*, pp. 286–290; Dauril Alden, "Economic Aspects of the Expulsion of the Jesuits From Brazil: A Preliminary Report," in *Conflict and Continuity in Brazilian Society*, eds. Henry H. Keith and S. F. Edwards (Columbia, S. C., 1969), pp. 34–40.

[20] MacLachlan, "Indian Labor Structure," p. 405.

[21] Alden, "Economic Aspects," pp. 30–33, 42–56.

Had economic conditions changed so drastically since the 1730s? It is true that the small-pox epidemic that afflicted the villages in the 1740s reduced the labor supply and sharpened local opposition to the privileged mission economy.[22] But many of the practices denounced by Mendonça Furtado were sanctioned by the crown 20 years before; in fact, the state had since changed the rules in the settler's favor as capital accumulation by businessmen, not Jesuits, was now the objective. The state wanted an assimilated, salaried labor force, not protected communities that preserved Indian languages. In this context, Pombal saw the mission economy as an obstacle to economic development; moreover, he thought the Order was a dangerous competitor of questionable loyalty.

The Treaty of Madrid (1750) had ceded the territory of the seven Guaraní missions in southern Rio Grande do Sul to the Portuguese and required the Spanish Jesuits and their Indian charges to evacuate the area. The Guaraní Indians, however, refused to leave their homeland and had to be forcibly expelled. In the far west the Spanish Jesuits had to abandon their missions on the eastern bank of the Guaporé. As the decade progressed, however, both Spain and Portugal lost their enthusiasm for the treaty's provisions; most of the territorial adjustments never took place, and the situation in the borderlands reverted to the status quo ante. Pombal blamed the Guaraní resistance on the Jesuits, and he mistrusted their presence in the Upper Amazon and along the Guaporé. He saw the Order as a powerful, independent organization, rather than an ally of the state: its missions now appeared to jeopardize Portugal's hold on the river system that linked northern Brazil and Mato Grosso. Pombal urged his brother to use "every possible pretext to separate the Jesuits from the frontier, and to break all communication between them and the Spanish Jesuits."[23] The state intended to secure the interior with fortresses and garrisons, not missionaries.

The same year that Pombal set up the Board of Trade and attacked the commissários volantes, he founded the Pará-Maranhão Company (1755–1777). Its task was to stimulate the region's exports by supplying ample credit, dependable shipping, and stable markets.[24] Pombal hoped

---

[22] Boxer, *Golden Age*, p. 291.

[23] Maxwell, *Conflicts and Conspiracies*, p. 28, also, pp. 27–29; Luis Gonzaga Jaeger, "Many Were the Pretexts," in *The Expulsion of the Jesuits from Latin America*, ed. Magnus Mörner, (New York, 1965), pp. 118–122. Pombal's campaign against the Jesuits and the impact of secularization on Portugal's baroque culture is discussed in Manoel Cardozo, "The Modernization of Portugal and the Independence of Brazil," in *From Colony to Nation: Essays on the Independence of Brazil*, ed. A. J. R. Russell-Wood (Baltimore, 1975), pp. 190–203.

[24] Attempts to promote the region's exports and diversity agriculture did not originate with

that the company's businessmen would accumulate enough capital to "compete effectively with foreign credit in every sector of Luso-Brazilian commerce."[25] Simultaneously, he attacked the privileged mission economy by secularizing the villages in 1757. Although the religious orders could still minister to the Indians' spiritual needs, they lost all temporal authority, including any jurisdiction over the allotment of workers; instead, lay captains administered the villages.[26]

The Jesuits were outraged by Pombal's policies, and so were many merchants who found themselves excluded from trade by the company's monopoly. The Portuguese nobility was overtly hostile to Pombal and the upstart businessmen who now controlled the state.[27]

An attempt to assassinate the king (1758), presumably led by the Duke of Aveiro, gave Pombal the pretext he needed to crush his adversaries. The aristocratic conspirators were ruthlessly exterminated. Testimony also implicated the Jesuits, who were expelled from all Portuguese dominions in 1759, and their property confiscated by the state. The value of the Order's plantations and its real estate holdings in Salvador and Rio de Janeiro was about 2.5 million cruzados. In Pará and Maranhão the Jesuit exodus destroyed what remained of the mission economy. The company could now pursue economic development with neither opposition nor competition from the missionaries.[28]

The state's policies reshaped the economy of the Amazon, and the Pará-Maranhão Company was the chief architect of that transformation. Its capital, about 1 million cruzados in 1758, came almost exclusively from Portuguese subscribers. To attract investors, the crown ennobled many of the affluent businessmen who purchased stock. Far from being a blot on an aristocrat's escutcheon, financial speculation now opened the doors to the prestigious military orders. A board of directors, elected triennially by stockholders, ran the company, but officers had to be selected from among those wealthy investors whose shares were worth at least 10,000 cruzados. Between 1763 and 1777 the company paid divi-

---

Pombal, but the crown never supplied sufficient capital or adequate incentives. See Sue A. Gross, "Agricultural Promotion in the Amazon Basin, 1700–1750," *Agricultural History* 43 (1969), pp. 269–273.

[25] Maxwell, *Conflicts and Conspiracies*, p. 19.

[26] The Directorate is discussed in MacLachlan, "Indian Labor Structure," pp. 209–222; idem, "The Indian Directorate: Forced Acculturation in Portuguese America (1757–1799)," *The Americas* 28 (1972), pp. 357–387.

[27] Maxwell, *Conflicts and Conspiracies*, pp. 24, 28–31.

[28] Gonzaga Jaeger, "Many Were the Pretexts," pp. 125–127. Alden estimated the value of the Order's Brazilian real estate as 1000 *contos* (1 *conto* = 1 million réis). Conversions are made at the rate of 400 reis = 1 cruzado; see his comments in Alden, "Economic Aspects," pp. 26–30.

dends ranging from 8 to 11%, and during the same period, its capital tripled. The crown's largesse in the form of kickbacks, exemptions, and monopolies helped underwrite the company's ventures. The company had the exclusive right to carry goods between Portugal and northern Brazil, and its agents controlled wholesaling; only retail trade was left to local merchants. Supplying the region with African slaves was likewise a company business, and as a stimulus, the slave traffic was exempted from taxation and rakeoffs at the ports; supplies and equipment for the company's use passed through the customs house duty free. Backed up by favorable tariff manipulations, the company fostered those exports that had secure markets; it discouraged sugar production.[29]

Under the company's tutelage, the total value of Pará's exports rose from 438,000 cruzados (1756–1758) to more than 1.2 million (1775–1777). Although the region sent a variety of tropical products to Lisbon, cacao accounted for about 60% of the total. Pará's cacao exports averaged 35,600 arrobas between 1759 and 1761, and more than 66,000 between 1775 and 1777.[30] Indian labor was still vital, but the growth of exports depended on the plantation system and the slaves the company supplied—over 14,000 between 1757 and 1777.[31] To encourage investment, slaves were sold at cost plus a small charge for freight.[32]

Pará was one of the few regions in Brazil where the Indians survived. The division of labor consigned Africans to the plantations, whereas Indian villages furnished boatmen and collectors, especially for wild cacao.[33] As skilled navigators, the Indians were essential in an economy that depended on river transportation to collect spices, to circulate goods, and to provision the forts in the Upper Amazon. As flotillas of canoes converged and dispersed from Belém, many Indian workers abandoned their villages to become wage earners in the city. Eventually miscegenation produced a predominantly *mestizo* population. In the rural areas, an acculturated peasantry formed, combining subsistence farming with collecting.[34]

---

[29] See Nunes Dias, *Companhia geral*, vol. 1, pp. 207–254: dividends, p. 245; capital assets, p. 246; privileges of larger investors, pp. 211–216. On the ennoblement of businessmen, see Macedo, A *situação económica*, p. 151.

[30] Nunes Dias, *Companhia geral*, vol. 1, pp. 378, 381.

[31] Nunes Dias, *Companhia geral*, vol. 1, pp. 429, 361–362; idem, vol. 2, pp. 55–61.

[32] Charles R. Boxer, *The Portuguese Seaborne Empire: 1415–1825* (New York, 1969), pp. 192–193.

[33] Unlike Nunes Dias, MacLachlan emphasizes how much Pará's economy remained tied to collecting: see MacLachlan, "Indian Labor Structure," pp. 214–216; idem, "African Slave Trade and Economic Development in Amazonia, 1700–1800," in *Slavery and Race Relations in Latin America*, ed. Robert Brent Toplin (Westport, 1974), pp. 112–138.

[34] MacLachlan, "Indian Labor Structure," pp. 210–230; idem, "Forced Acculturation,"

The company's success in Pará depended on the captaincy's traditional export, cacao; in Maranhão, it fostered new crops such as cotton. England's demand for raw cotton made large-scale production feasible. By mixing fibers, British manufacturers could copy the popular calicoes imported from India, but they were short of raw materials.[35] In 1760 Maranhão sent its first cotton shipment to Lisbon; between 1768 and 1778 the captaincy's tax free cotton exports totaled over 300,000 arrobas, much of it destined for England.[36]

Chronically short of grain, Portugal depended on wheat imported from England and Pennsylvania, and on rice from South Carolina.[37] Wild yellow rice, which was easily produced and collected, grew in Maranhão; but the European market favored white rice, an arduous, labor-intensive crop. To promote the cultivation of the more popular variety, the crown prohibited the cultivation of yellow rice. Exports of white rice were minimal in the 1760s, but rose sharply thereafter. Between 1771 and 1778 Maranhão sent over 600,000 arrobas to Lisbon. To improve the quality of exports, the company set up husking mills in the captaincy. Since the crown hoped that Brazilian rice would alleviate the dearth of Portuguese grains, it subsidized production by extending customs exemptions to all rice produced in Brazil and marketed in Portugal; in 1777, reexports from Lisbon were similarly favored. By the 1780s Portugal no longer imported rice from abroad. The cotton and rice sent from São Luís was more valuable than Belém's cacao, and the fleets were larger: 15 vessels annually as opposed to Belém's 8 or 9.[38]

In addition to its commercial privileges in northern Brazil, the company monopolized the Guinean slave trade. The trade was channeled through Portuguese factories at Bissau and Cacheu, and used the Cape Verde Islands as an entrepôt. African slaves produced Maranhão's new

---

pp. 357–387; and Eric B. Ross, "The Evolution of the Amazon Peasantry," *Journal of Latin American Studies* 10 (1978) pp. 193–218. In general, see Charles Wagley, *Amazon Town: A Study of Man in the Tropics* (1953: London, 1976).

[35] See Charles H. Wilson, *England's Apprenticeship 1603–1763* (London, 1965), pp. 296–297.

[36] Nunes Dias, *Companhia geral*, vol. 1, pp. 430, 453.

[37] Fisher, *Portugal Trade*, pp. 64–76.

[38] The discussion of cotton and rice production is based on Nunes Dias, *Companhia geral*, vol. 1, pp. 397–458: rice exports, p. 430; mill construction, pp. 437–438, 440; tax exemptions, p. 451; and Dauril Alden, "Manoel Luis Vieira: An Entrepreneur in Rio de Janeiro During Brazil's Eighteenth-Century Agricultural Renaissance," *Hispanic American Historical Review* 39 (1959), p. 528. Portugal's self-sufficiency in rice is noted by Nunes Dias, *Companhia geral*, vol. 1, p. 451; and by Dauril Alden, *Royal Government*, p. 366. Regarding the comparative value of exports and the size of fleets, see Nunes Dias, *Companhia geral*, vol. 1, pp. 378, 390, 418–423, 426.

exports. Of the 10,600 slaves sold in Maranhão—at cost and duty-free so the settlers could afford them—over 9000 came from Guiné; the rest were brought from Angola.[39] Similarly, most of Pará's slaves came from the company's Guinean factories; if Pará took more, many were resold in the Upper Amazon and Mato Grosso.[40]

Aided by tax breaks, the company advanced cheap credit and provided dependable shipping; it created a new economy in northern Brazil that was directly linked to European markets. Prices for the region's products held steady or rose, making sustained growth possible.[41] The company became a vast credit and marketing agent: between 1770 and 1777 it shipped exports to Lisbon worth a total of 5.7 million cruzados, 56% from Maranhão.[42] In exchange, the company sold slaves, equipment, textiles, and provisions to the colonists. Its ships and the stocks stored in its warehouses were worth more than 3 million cruzados.[43] Portuguese businessmen, not the British, reaped the profits. The company reexported rice and cotton in its own ships to London, Amsterdam, Hamburg, Cadiz, and Marseille, where its factors took charge of marketing and purchased tools, lead, tin, and cloth on the company's behalf.[44] An expanding sector of Luso-Brazilian trade was thus sealed off from the British factory at Lisbon.

The Pernambucan Company (1759–1778), which had privileges similar to those of its companion corporation, revived the captaincy's sugar industry and diversified exports. Capital investment in mills, abundant slaves, and cheap credit helped boost sugar exports to 7000 chests annually in the 1760s and to 10,000 chests in the 1770s. Drawing on its capital of more than 3 million cruzados, the Pernambucan Company built more than 100 new sugar mills and, between 1760 and 1775, furnished 30,000 slaves from Angola. To allow Pernambuco to specialize in tobacco, the crown terminated Bahia's monopoly on exports. Backed by company subsidies and stable prices, Pernambucan planters produced over 20,000 arrobas of tobacco in the 1760s; between 1762 and 1775, 68,000 rolls of tobacco were diverted into the slave trade. Hide exports picked up too, because the crown removed customs duties to help the cattle ranchers

---

[39] On slave imports, see Nunes Dias, *Companhia geral*, vol. 1, pp. 468–469; tax breaks, pp. 460–461, 470–471.

[40] The Amazon river system now supplied Mato Grosso; see Nunes Dias, *Companhia geral*, vol. 1, 516–517.

[41] Vitorino Magalhães Godinho, *Prix et Monnaies au Portugal 1750–1850* (Paris, 1955), p. 74; Nunes Dias, *Companhia geral*, vol. 1, p. 267.

[42] Nunes Dias, *Companhia geral*, vol. 1, pp. 378, 411–423.

[43] Ibid., pp. 305, 536.

[44] Ibid., pp. 499–504.

hurt by Spanish competition. Cotton production began in the 1770s but did not become significant until the next decade. Corporate profits between 1759 and 1775 exceeded 2 million cruzados; the company paid dividends of 16%.[45]

Domestic Industries

Some company profits were diverted to the workshops the Board of Trade supervised because the directors of the state-fostered textile industry also ran the trading monopolies with Brazil. The Royal Silk Factory became a general manufactory that integrated both household and factory production; it distributed capital, furnished raw materials, and centralized marketing. The diverse activities it coordinated included the silk industry, and the production of a variety of woolen textiles, lace, cutlery, buttons, shoes, crockery, and metal tools. In addition to being exempt from customs duties and exported under company auspices, such goods had protected markets in Pernambuco, Pará, and Maranhão; the Pernambucan Company sent domestic manufactures worth 1.5 million cruzados to Brazil (1760–1777), almost exclusively from the silk factory.[46] The link between the companies and domestic enterprises was the lever Pombal hoped would dislodge the English; British merchants attacked the monopolies in their dispatches to London: the companies, they complained, preferred "their own country's produce, which consequently must find a sale when no other goods are in competition with them."[47]

British opposition solidified in the 1760s, whereas Pombal's room for maneuver shrank. Britain emerged from the Seven Years War (1756–1763) as Europe's foremost naval and commercial power. In 1762 a joint Franco-Spanish invasion shattered Portugal's neutrality; the war reemphasized how much Luso-Brazilian security rested on British support. In America the Spaniards retook Colônia and drove the Portuguese from strategic settlements in Rio Grande do Sul. The Peace of Paris (1763) restored Portugal's ravished Platine fortress, but not occupied Rio

---

[45] Most of these figures are from Miguel Diegues, Jr. "As companhias privilegiadas no comercio colonial," *Revista de História*, no. 3 (1950), pp. 331–337; also see Maxwell, *Conflicts and Conspiracies*, pp. 41–42; and Alden, *Royal Government*, p. 361 n. 28. Klein estimates that between 1761 and 1786 the company shipped 49,000 slaves to Brazil. See Herbert S. Klein, *The Middle Passage: Comparative Studies in the Atlantic Slave Trade* (Princeton, 1978), pp. 44–47.

[46] See Maxwell, *Conflicts and Conspiracies*, p. 261. On domestic manufacturing, see Macedo, *A situação económica*, pp. 243–245; idem, *Problemas de história da indústria Portuguesa no século XVIII* (Lisbon, 1963), pp. 152–153; and Maxwell, *Conflicts and Conspiracies*, pp. 51–53.

[47] Maxwell, *Conflicts and Conspiracies*, p. 52.

Grande; Pombal needed Britain's diplomatic support to secure its restoration.[48] A frontal attack on British interests was now too risky. Unable to create new companies, Pombal abolished the convoys to Rio and Salvador (1765); Luso-Brazilian ships now sailed at their own convenience. This allayed British suspicions, but Pombal hoped the new system would benefit Brazilian producers by reducing delays and cutting freight costs.[49] Over the next decade, however, gold production dropped and Luso-Brazilian trade faltered.

Gold was the vital core of the Brazil trade. Falling production registered quickly, reducing trade and state revenues. Receipts from the Minas gold tax, which had averaged over 100 arrobas of gold (1752–1762), dropped to 85 arrobas during the next decade, and, between 1774 and 1785, yielded only 68 arrobas a year.[50] Gold coinage minted in Portugal totaled 17.6 million cruzados between 1753 and 1757, but only 8.9 million between 1769 and 1773;[51] gold exports from Rio exceeded 15 million cruzados in 1749, but never passed the 8 million mark in the 1770s.[52] Portugal had less gold to cover foreign purchases, especially British textiles.

England's trade with Portugal, over £1 million annually in the 1750s, dropped 43% (1766–1770) and did not recover until the 1790s.[53] Although the contraction was due mainly to sagging gold output, Britain's shrinking grain reserves aggravated the downward spiral: grain shipments, which had accounted for 13% of Britain's exports to Portugal (1761–1765), virtually ceased.[54] In the past, much of the British merchandise that went to Rio de Janeiro had ended up in Colônia as contraband destined for Buenos Aires, but Spain's determined resistance reduced Colônia's role as an intermediary. Meanwhile, Spain strengthened the Argentine bureaucracy and altered the region's commercial organization. Buenos Aires became the capital of a new Platine viceroyalty that stretched into

[48] The shifting fortunes of Luso-Spanish conflict in the borderlands is described in Alden, *Royal Government*, pp. 86–246; idem, "The Undeclared War of 1773–1777: Climax of Luso-Spanish Platine Rivalry," *Hispanic American Historical Review* 41 (1961), pp. 55–74.

[49] Maxwell, *Conflicts and Conspiracies*, pp. 38–39.

[50] Carnaxide, António de Sousa Pedroso, Visconde de, *O Brasil na adninistragão Pombalina* (São Paulo, 1940), p. 246; Maxwell, *Conflicts and Conspiracies*, pp. 252–253.

[51] Macedo, *A situação econômica*, p. 167.

[52] Alden, *Royal Government*, pp. 328, 331; Boxer, *Golden Age*, p. 351. Alden's figures are given in mil-réis: 1000 réis = 2.5 cruzados. Overall, the total value of Brazil's gold exports fell from £4.8 million (1760) to £3 million (1777); see Eulália Maria Lahmeyer Lobo, "O comércio atlântico e a comunidade de mercadores no Rio de Janeiro e em Charleston no século XVII," *Revista de História*, no. 101 (1975), p. 67.

[53] Macedo, *Problemas de história*, pp. 188–190; Godinho, *Prix et Monnaies*, p. 254.

[54] Fisher, *Portugal Trade*, pp. 45, 145.

Upper Peru (1776), and the city was opened to direct trade with Spanish ports. Free trade ended the chronic dearth of goods; abundant Spanish shipping provided new outlets for Argentine hide exports. The special conditions that made contraband so profitable and difficult to prevent no longer prevailed.[55] British textiles earmarked for Platine markets had to be rerouted from Lisbon to Spanish ports.

In Brazil the gold crisis had its most direct effect in populous Minas Gerais. The registro revenues (1764–1771), an index of the captaincy's external trade, fell 46%; tithe revenues fell 20%.[56] By the 1770s the contractors owed the crown almost as much as they managed to collect.[57] Rio de Janeiro, a transit point for the mining zone, had a drop in customs receipts of 25%, which was a serious matter because the Carioca treasury was saddled with the thankless task of supplying Colônia and defending the borderlands. Contrary to his standing orders, Rio's viceroy, the Marquis de Lavradio (1769–1779), spent the crown's fifths to cover military expenditures.[58]

Higher sugar prices spurred Bahian exports during the Seven Years War, but peace brought lower sugar prices—a 30% drop on the Amsterdam exchange—and reduced exports.[59] Tobacco, however, fared better; prices increased 14% between 1756–1760 and 1774–1778, while total reexports from Portugal jumped from a total of 478,000 arrobas, to 877,000.[60] As noted previously, cacao, rice, and cotton helped diversify Brazilian exports while Portugal's production of wine and olive oil held steady. Agricultural exports could not replace gold, however. As gold production fell, the state tried to cut foreign imports and halt gold outflows. Recession, the hostile British factory, and diplomatic realities blocked further tampering with the Brazil trade. Still, a Portugal "reestablished and in control of its own affairs" remained a fundamental objective.[61] A series of disjointed measures of varying effectiveness char-

[55] See John Lynch, *Spanish Colonial Administration, 1782–1810: The Intendant System in the Viceroyalty of the Rio de la Plata* (New York, 1969).

[56] See the figures compiled in José João Teixeira Coelho, "Instrucção para o governo da capitania de Minas Gerais," *Revista do Instituto Histórico e Geográphico Brasileiro* 15 (Rio de Janeiro, 1852), pp. 403, 411; and Maxwell, *Conflicts and Conspiracies*, pp. 247–248.

[57] Maxwell, *Conflicts and Conspiracies*, p. 67. The sale price of the tithe contracts (1768–1786), the amounts paid and delinquent, can be found in Dom Oscar de Oliveira, *Os dízimos eclesiásticos do Brasil* (Belo Horizonte, 1974), pp. 200–201.

[58] Alden, *Royal Government*, pp. 317, 343–344. Also see Lahmeyer Lobo, "Comério no Rio de Janeiro," pp. 78–80.

[59] Maxwell, *Conflicts and Conspiracies*, p. 257; Roberto C. Simonsen, *História econômica do Brasil 1500–1820*, 5th ed. (São Paulo, 1967), graph ar d tables following p. 382.

[60] Godinho, *Prix et Monnaies*, p. 257; Macedo, *A situação económica*, document 8, p. 294.

[61] Maxwell, *Conflicts and Conspiracies*, p. 38.

acterized the Pombaline state during the recession years; the most significant measures pertained to domestic industry.

The reduced capacity to purchase foreign goods created a favorable climate for import substitution. The Board of Trade acquired the silk factory as a kind of sideline, subordinate to the companies; it now turned decisively, if haphazardly, to industrial development: 80% of the enterprises Pombal's Board sponsored were authorized after 1770.[62] Besides luxury goods like silks, hats, tapestries, chinaware, and chandeliers, the state emphasized textile production, especially cottons and woolens.

Before Britain mechanized its textile industry, which would create a quantum jump in output and a corresponding drop in prices, Portugal's cottage industry could still compete effectively. Drawing on the hinterland's skilled but cheap labor, the state combined central workshops with the putting-out system. In 1799 the factory workshops in and around Portalegre employed over 1300 spinners and weavers.[63] At Corvihã, another woolen center, production doubled.[64] Cotton textiles likewise advanced, but production gravitated to the ports, close to the seaborne supply of raw materials. Water-powered mills, often run by foreign experts, produced cottons of "great beauty, equal to those of England and France."[65] Textile workshops and other enterprises benefited from fixed prices, monopoly privileges, and tax exemptions, both for raw materials and finished products.[66] Cottons had a special, if fortuitous, advantage. The Methuen treaty had ceded specific privileges to English "woolens" only. In 1781, without violating the treaty, the government prohibited imported English cottons.[67]

Pombal's program was unsystematic, studded with failures, and largely based on traditional methods, yet it yielded important new industries and an entrenched Lisbon business elite. The part businessmen played in the affairs of state endured. Pombal reduced the Inquisition to a crown tribunal and ended legal descrimination against New Christians. Converts could now hold public office, attend Coimbra, and enter the magistracy.[68]

---

[62] Macedo, A situação económica, pp. 254–255.

[63] Macedo, Problemas de história, p. 149.

[64] Ibid., p. 201.

[65] Maxwell, Conflicts and Conspiracies, p. 56.

[66] See Macedo, A situação económica, p. 258, also see his list of industries promoted by the Board of Trade, along with the special exemptions granted, in document 7, following p. 292.

[67] Manchester, British Preëminence, pp. 45–56.

[68] On Pombal's industrial program, see Maxwell, Conflicts and Conspiracies, pp. 51–58; Macedo, A situação económica, pp. 254–260; idem, Problemas de história, 144–154, and A.

Brazilians to some extent also adopted import substitution. Minas Gerais, for example, had its own textile workshops, a fact deplored by Carioca merchants whose sales in the mining zone declined.[69] In Pará, spinning rough cotton cloth was a village industry, but mainly as a state enterprise to reduce military supply costs.[70] The Board of Trade, much as it helped domestic enterprises, did back a few Brazilian schemes: a leather factory in Rio de Janeiro, an iron foundry in São Paulo, the manufacture of rigging in Bahia, and rice processing.[71] In specific cases, Pombal's mercantilism was notably inconsistent—textile production was promoted in Pará, tolerated in Minas Gerais, and prohibited in Pernambuco—but the thrust was clear.[72] The plan for Portugal's recovery stressed, on the Brazilian side, diversified agriculture—a policy acceptable to Brazil's planters.

In northern Brazil and Pernambuco, the companies promoted cacao, rice, cotton, tobacco, and sugar. Elsewhere, the crown instructed its governors to exploit "hitherto neglected resources, particularly fibers, dyestuffs, and cereals, [and to] keep a sharp eye out for promising flora." In response came a "stream of reports, memorials, and samples of hundreds of plants and minerals."[73] The Marquis of Lavradio (1769–1779), Brazil's viceroy and a founding member of Rio's Scientific Society, was a particularly persistent advocate of new crops and techniques. He appointed the Dutch agronomist, João Hopman, a Brazilian resident of long standing, as inspector of new plantations and farms. Hopman experimented with coffee, cochineal, and guaxima—a native hemp substitute—and introduced mulberry trees for sericulture. In the southern captaincies, especially the Rio Grande settlements, Lavradio promoted dairy products and wheat cultivation. In the 1790s the region was Brazil's granary. The most dramatic and immediate successes, however, came with rice and indigo.[74]

The Carioca entrepreneur, Manoel Luís Vieira, built a rice-processing mill near Rio de Janeiro. Aided by a 10-year customs exemption and a

---

H. de Oliveira Marques, *History of Portugal*, 2 vols. (New York, 1972), vol. 1, pp. 383–384. On the status of New Christians, see Boxer, *Seaborne Empire*, pp. 270–271.

[69] Alden, *Royal Government*, pp. 383–385.

[70] MacLachlan, "Indian Labor Structure," p. 219.

[71] See Maxwell, *Conflicts and Conspiracies*, pp. 40–41; and Macedo, *A situação econômica*, document 7, following p. 292.

[72] Alden, *Royal Government*, pp. 382–387, 385 n. 116; and MacLachlan, "Indian Labor Structure," p. 219.

[73] Alden, "Manoel Luís Vieira," p. 523.

[74] See Alden, *Royal Government*, pp. 359–380; and Maxwell, *Conflicts and Conspiracies*, pp. 39–40.

monopoly on rice exports, Vieira could offer attractive prices to local farmers. Between 1768 and 1770 his mill handled over 200,000 arrobas of rice, much of it earmarked for colonial markets.[75] Indigo, a small shrub whose processed leaves yield a rich, blue dye, was essential to the domestic textile industry. The state urged its cultivation to reduce dependence on foreign imports, largely Guatemalan. With Lavradio's support, Manoel da Costa Cardozo, a wealthy Rio businessman, built an indigo factory on his estate. The viceroy forwarded samples to Pombal, who responded enthusiastically; he instructed the viceroy to purchase, at fixed prices, all the indigo the captaincy could produce. By the late 1770s Rio was shipping 144,000 pounds a year to Lisbon, much of it on consignment to domestic textile producers and some for reexport.[76]

Pombal's economic ventures reinforced the quid pro quo that buttressed Luso-Brazilian trade: Portugal produced a greater assortment of textiles, hardware, and consumer goods; Brazil had more diverse agricultural exports.

After the Peace of Paris (1763) both England and Spain reorganized their American empires. Taxation by Parliament, however, directly challenged the assembly's role in local politics, and from the colonial point of view, English liberties. In Spanish America the Bourbon reformers altered the empire's bureaucratic and fiscal structure at the expense of Creole officeholders.[77] Pombal, however, involved Brazilians in his administrative creations "with a deliberation bordering on infatuation."[78] In 1750 he terminated the controversial capitation tax in Minas Gerais. In its place he accepted the proposals of Vila Rica's câmara—despite the Overseas Council's objections. The towns agreed to collect the fifths at the foundries set up in each district (comarca); if the annual yield fell below 100 arrobas of gold, they were to make up the difference by imposing a head tax. The region's elite ran the foundry houses: Pombal directed the câmaras to select the intendants and fiscals from among "the most substantial property owners," subject only to the approval of the ouvidor.[79]

The state courted and protected its Brazilian businessmen. Salvador's merchants were pleased with the injunctions against the commissários volantes, and vigorously enforced the law. In 1752 miners owning at least

---

[75] Alden, "Manoel Luís Vieira," pp. 529–537.

[76] Dauril Alden, "The Growth and Decline of Indigo Production in Colonial Brazil: A Study in Comparative Economic History," *Journal of Economic History* **25** (1965), pp. 46–56.

[77] White Spanish Americans were called Creoles or Criollos; the term did not imply a mixed racial ancestry.

[78] Maxwell, *Conflicts and Conspiracies*, p. 64.

[79] Ibid., p. 13; Alden, *Royal Government*, p. 12.

30 slaves were exempted from foreclosure; the debt collection practices that had disrupted sugar production in Pernambuco were likewise forbidden. Pombal established inspection boards (1751) in the ports to guarantee the just prices and good quality of exports; besides crown appointees, the boards included merchants, mill owners, and tobacco planters.[80]

Inspection boards, crown monopolies, and high taxes led to disputes between the town councils and local officials, but Pombal did not challenge colonial interests directly. Indeed, he strengthened the role Brazil's elite played in the colony's fiscal administration.

In 1761 the crown placed Portugal's exchequer affairs in the hands of a newly created Royal Treasury; its jurisdiction extended to the customs house and farming state monopolies, matters previously supervised by the Counting House and the Overseas Council. José Francisco da Cruz, a director of the silk factory and the Pará-Maranhão Company, became the first treasurer-general. In Brazil locally constituted treasury boards run by professional businessmen replaced proprietary officeholders. Governors were instructed to nominate "prudent and wealthy men," especially the "most opulent merchants," who could bring "commercial expertise to the exercise of local affairs."[81] In Rio de Janeiro, Lavradio selected the merchant and indigo entrepreneur, Manoel da Costa Cardozo, as treasurer-general.[82] The local boards introduced double-entry bookkeeping, administered the customs house, and farmed out the tax concessions—for which they received the customary kickbacks.[83] Brazilians had long been entrenched in the colony's fiscal bureaucracy, but Pombal legitimized the practice and gave it an institutional base. It was one thing, however, to keep an eye on new agencies set up in Lisbon, quite another to monitor reforms in Brazil. In Salvador and Rio de Janeiro the High Courts and a bevy of bureaucrats hemmed in the treasury boards, but not in Minas Gerais; there the local board's untrammeled patronage powers pulled governors and magistrates into its orbit: it became a tool of the Minas elite rather than the state's collaborator.[84]

Military reorganization likewise stressed the mobilization of Brazilians,

---

[80] Maxwell, *Conflicts and Conspiracies*, p. 14; Alden, *Royal Government*, pp. 12, 45 n. 78, 306 n. 85; Kennedy, "Bahian Elites," p. 422; and Catherine Lugar, "The Portuguese Tobacco Trade and Tobacco Growers of Bahia in the Late Colonial Period," in *Essays Concerning the Socioeconomic History of Brazil and Portuguese India* (Gainesville, 1977), pp. 42–44.

[81] Maxwell, *Conflicts and Conspiracies*, p. 44.

[82] Alden, *Royal Government*, p. 315.

[83] Ibid., pp. 291–294, 310–311. A list of the fees collected by Vila Rica's treasury board can be found in Teixeira Coelho, "Instrucção," pp. 265–270.

[84] Teixeira Coelho notes some of the abuses, see "Instrucção," pp. 301–304.

a pattern dating back to the Dutch occupation. The colony's security became a major priority after the Seven Years War. Since Portugal lacked a navy and did not have the resources to support a large standing army, Brazil could not be defended without Brazilians. The Portuguese regiments stationed in the various captaincies were progressively "Brazilianized" so as to constitute, along with the *Reinóis*, "one army under the same rules, with identical discipline."[85,86] By the late eighteenth century 60% of the commissioned officers in Bahia's military regiments were Brazilian-born, many of them from career-oriented military families. Others, the sons of skilled artisans, retail merchants, and lesser bureaucrats, came up through the ranks; but they "sympathized with the interests of other elite sectors and emulated their values."[87] The lower ranks, complained a disgruntled governor, were full of "free blacks, mulattoes, and thieves."[88] The governor probably disliked the special militia regiments reserved for free blacks (the *Henriques*), and the *pardo* units composed of freedmen with mixed racial ancestry; both groups had a separate officer corps.[89,90]

Unless admitted to the regular army as officers, the white elite preferred service in the urban and rural units organized by the local *mestres de campo*, the latter-day coronéis. In the backlands, the militia units were actually private armies. But in the coastal captaincies, especially near cities like Salvador and Rio de Janeiro, the coronéis were supervised by the governor and, in some cases, by army officers. When Lavradio was viceroy, the eight coronéis who ran Rio's rural parishes were the largest sugar producers in their districts. Under the crown's authority they recruited the local militia, apprehended criminals and renegade slaves, collected statistics on crops and population, and kept the peace. Occasionally the viceroy rebuked the coronéis for despotic behavior, but as their proximity diminished, so did the governor's ability to check abuses.[91]

The Reaction against Pombal

Pombal allied the state to Brazilian interests in an unprecedented fashion. When his patron, José I (1750–1777), died, Pombal was forced

[85] Reinóis refers to metropolitan-born Portuguese living in Brazil.

[86] Maxwell, *Conflicts and Conspiracies*, pp. 42–44.

[87] Kennedy, "Bahian Elites," p. 430.

[88] Ibid., p. 429.

[89] The *Henriques* were named after Henrique Dias, a black guerilla leader who fought against the Dutch occupation of Pernambuco.

[90] Ibid., pp. 427–431, and n. 48. Also see F. W. O. Morton, "The Military and Society in Bahia, 1800–1821," *Journal of Latin American Studies* 7 (1975), pp. 250–263.

[91] Alden, *Royal Government*, pp. 443–446. Also see Morton, "Military and Society," pp. 263–278.

from office, not by disgruntled Brazilians, but by the enemies he had acquired in Lisbon. Under Pombal, new state agencies such as the Board of Trade and the centralized Royal Treasury usurped the authority of traditional bodies like the Overseas Council, thus alienating vital sectors of the bureaucracy. The old nobility, excluded from the minister's inner circle, its ranks diluted by ennobled businessmen, attacked Pombal's commercial creations, especially the companies; free traders added their support.[92] The charter of the Pará-Maranhão Company, up for renewal in 1777, was rejected by the Council of State; the antimonopoly memorialists, campaigning on "liberty of commerce and the competition of businessmen," carried the day.[93] Sugar planters and mill owners, in debt to the companies, joined the assault, and in 1778 the Pernambucan Company was terminated. The aging Marquis of Angeja, lacking in fiscal expertise, took over the Royal Treasury. The crown reduced the role played by the Board of Trade and cut its membership.

The old guard won a few skirmishes, but it did not win the battle. The great merchant-financiers Pombal had subsidized were entrenched in the country's fiscal apparatus, in its trade, and in its industry. They were too powerful and well-connected to be dislodged, and they were indispensable as industrial experts and as managers of Portugal's growing volume of colonial reexports. In Corvilhã and Portalegre the new regime handed over state-fostered industries, along with tax exemptions and monopoly privileges, to Pombal's industrialists. A new agency, the Factory Board, supervised what remained of state enterprises, and continued to promote, although it did not direct, new industries. The state's lucrative monopolies still went to the capital-rich oligarchy, but the contractors, no longer supervised by their peers, had greater expertise than the new appointees who ran the Royal Treasury. By leasing the tobacco, soap, salt, and whaling concessions for long periods at fixed prices, contractors reaped windfall profits.[94]

The reaction against the companies and the Board of Trade left the business oligarchy's economic base untouched. True, the companies had to liquidate their assets, but a shadow company composed of former factors, merchants, and shippers continued to operate.[95] The state

---

[92] Oliveira Marques, *History of Portugal*, vol. 1, pp. 397–398.

[93] Maxwell, *Conflicts and Conspiracies*, pp. 70–74. The struggle over the companies and the reaction against Pombal is also discussed in Nunes Dias, *Companhia geral*, vol. 2, pp. 127–216.

[94] Maxwell, *Conflicts and Conspiracies*, pp. 73–76; and Sideri, *Trade and Power*, pp. 104–107.

[95] Maxwell, *Conflicts and Conspiracies*, p. 74; Nunes Dias, *Companhia geral*, vol. 2, pp. 234, 217–248. In the 1780s, the companies were still engaged in the slave trade; see Klein, *Middle Passage*, pp. 44–47.

weakened the Board of Trade and reduced its managerial role; the Factory Board, however, provided a forum for industrial interests; within a decade it had doled out privileges to 263 new workshops. Still, the reaction did have a singularly significant consequence: it dismantled the joint focus Pombal's agencies had given to both domestic and colonial affairs. The Board of Trade's "flexible mercantilism" had embraced, on occasion, even colonial industries. Such catholicity was not repeated by the more parochial Factory Board. Free from the constraints a broader imperial vision imposed, it attacked Brazilian manufacturing.[96]

The pace and scope of Pombal's projects obscured the divergent tensions within the Luso-Brazilian system. The new regime's policies provoked opposition at a crucial moment, when the revolt of English America had created a changed atmosphere, ripe for mutual distrust and recriminations. Indeed, as the regime stabilized during the 1780s, it was alarmed by the degree of commercial freedom and local participation Brazilians had acquired. The new colonial secretary, Martinho de Melo e Castro, a man closely associated with industrialists, viewed Brazil from the Factory Board's perspective. He charged that while contraband trade flourished, the slave trade virtually excluded Lisbon merchants; moreover, Brazil's textile workshops were prejudicial both to the customs house and domestic industries, and threatened to make the colony "totally independent of the metropolis."[97] Minas Gerais was notably recalcitrant in this respect. Viceroy Lavradio reported that "private individuals had established workshops and looms on their estates, which produced cotton, linen and woolen goods."[98] To placate the Factory Board, Melo e Castro ordered that all textile workshops be "closed and abolished whenever they may be in Brazil."[99] How rigidly the measure was enforced in unclear, especially since there was a loophole: the manufacture of coarse cloth for slaves was still permitted. But notice had been served; a less accommodating regime ruled in Lisbon. Those who had helped cast Pombal's broader imperial vision had fallen.

THE MINAS CONSPIRACY

Pombal had drawn Brazilians into colonial administration, but to what extent did the Brazilian plutocracy bend to the state's objectives?

[96] Maxwell, Conflicts and Conspiracies, p. 75.

[97] Ibid., pp. 77–80.

[98] Marquês de Lavradio, "Relatório do Marquês de Lavradio, Vice-Rei do Brasil de 1769-a 1779, apresentato ao Vice-Rei Luis de Vasconcelos, seu sucessor," reprinted in Carnaxide, Administração Pombalina, pp. 308–309. Also see Alden, Royal Government, pp. 383–385.

[99] Maxwell, Conflicts and Conspiracies, pp. 79, 78–80.

Nowhere did the local elite so dominate a captaincy's fiscal structure as in Minas Gerais, and nowhere, in Melo e Castro's opinion, were the results more disastrous.[100]

Wealthy Mineiros, entrenched in the treasury board, the foundry houses, and the diamond district's bureaucracy, doled out the tithe contracts and the registros to their opulent clients; they collected the fifths and controlled the diamond business. The dragoons who policed the mining area and the registros had a large contingent of Mineiro-born officers. Even some of the judges assigned to the captaincy had strong Brazilian ties. Alvarenga Peixoto, ouvidor of São João d'El Rei, was also a local landowner and miner. The ouvidor of Vila Rica, Tomás Antônio Gonzaga (1782–1786), was the son of a Brazilian-born High Court judge. Pombal relied on patronage and strong government agencies to restrain the Portuguese businessmen he attracted to state service. But in landlocked Minas Gerais, a strong, interrelated core of locally-born officials co-opted a less extensive bureaucratic network, giving it a distinctly regional, as opposed to Portuguese, focus. Royal governors and judges, isolated from Portugal and the High Courts of Salvador and Rio, sided with their Minas-born colleagues. They had a vested interest in doing so, too; their contract rakeoffs far exceeded their salaries.[101]

Awarding tax contracts was big business in Brazil. Ideally the practice was advantageous to the state because it spared the crown the expense of collection. When contractors defaulted, however, the crown faced costly litigation.[102] In Minas Gerais, diminishing gold production magnified the system's deficiencies, and default became endemic. In 1786 the wealthy merchant-contractor, João Rodrigues de Macedo, who held the registro concession (1776–1781) and the tithe farm (1777–1783), was in arrears to the sum of nearly 2 million cruzados. The treasury board did not press its errant debtor because the governor, Ouvidor Peixoto, and local estate owners all owed substantial sums to the Macedo. To foreclose on Macedo would place their own fortunes in considerable jeopardy as the profits a contractor like Macedo made on his investments, besides financing his own speculations, provided an important source of capital for the local economy. As the region's chief banker and merchant, Macedo necessarily extended credit to miners, estate owners, army officers, royal officials,

---

[100] Unless otherwise indicated, this section is based on Maxwell, *Conflicts and Conspiracies*, pp. 61–70, 84–203. All direct citations are noted, as well as the location of specific information. Although I have supplemented Maxwell's account with other sources, the basic arguments are based on his research.

[101] Maxwell, *Conflicts and Conspiracies*, pp. 46, 61–70, 96.

[102] See Alden, *Royal Government*, pp. 307–311.

and even the local treasury.[103] This circulatory apparatus generated fraud and evasion at every turn. The kickback system provided a legal ruse for bribery and forced loans; placing merchants in charge of the registros made them responsible for taxing their own trade, and the tithe, evaded by the rich, fell on the poor. At the local level, charged an outraged ouvidor, "tithe collectors were simply hired thugs who ravaged the countryside."[104]

The treasury was not the only place where wheeler-dealers held sway. Pombal had abolished the contract system in the diamond district (1771), placing the region under the Royal Treasury's direct control. The officials responsible for its administration, however, were mostly Brazilian-born. Despite meticulous and comprehensive regulations, the district became a haven for contraband traders and professional diamond smugglers. A liberal distribution of permits, handed out to self-styled itinerant traders, circumvented strict entry rules. Many tavern owners, cobblers, and tailors acted as agents for the smugglers, purchasing illegal diamonds and selling untaxed merchandise. José da Silva de Oliveira Rolim, a parish priest and the son of the diamond treasurer, "busied himself with a bewildering range of subterfuges, from mining in prohibited areas to the illegal importation of slaves."[105] The dragoons, although paid to prevent racketeering, were not so vigilant when their officers had relatives in the district.[106]

Rings of racketeers and negligent contractors were certainly not strangers to the Brazilian scene. Under such circumstances any governor who tried to replace the "ins" with his own cronies was bound to create a hopeless imbroglio, and the new governor of Minas Gerais, Luís da Cunha Meneses (1783–1788), arrived in Vila Rica with an "entourage of venal sycophants and hangers-on."[107] He replaced Dom Roderigo José de Meneses (1780–1783), a governor who supported local industries and was on good terms with the local elite, especially João Rodrigues de Macedo.[108] Cunha Meneses immediately clashed with the treasury board

---

[103] Maxwell, *Conflicts and Conspiracies*, pp. 66–70.

[104] Teixeira Coelho, "Instrucção," p. 303; Caio Prado, Jr., *The Colonial Background of Modern Brazil*, trans. Suzette Macedo (Berkeley, 1971), pp. 377–378.

[105] Maxwell, *Conflicts and Conspiracies*, p. 66.

[106] Ibid., pp. 66–67; also see Boxer, *Golden Age*, pp. 204–225; and Prado, *Colonial Background*, pp. 208–212.

[107] Maxwell, *Conflicts and Conspiracies*, p. 99.

[108] D. Roderigo proposed the establishment of an iron foundry, which "although at first sight might appear to be opposed to the system of this captaincy, would be seen on further reflection to be a matter of great public utility." The Factory Board did not agree. See *op. cit.*, pp. 90, 98.

and Ouvidor Gonzaga over farming the registros. He overruled the board and installed his hand-picked candidates, armed the contractors with debt-collection powers that circumvented the courts, and denied fees to the magistrates. In retaliation poet-ouvidor Gonzaga penned the famous *Cartas Chilenas*, a scathing parody on the governor's high-handed tactics; this provided potent ammunition for the local troubadours, who carried the controversy into the taverns. The governor had recklessly assaulted the captaincy's carefully assembled modus vivendi: under the pretext of cleaning up the diamond district, he harassed blackmarket businessmen such as Oliveria Rolim, only to replace them with his grasping Portuguese henchmen; he denied Brazilian-born officers promotions in the dragoons, and his blatant disregard for a powerful *coronel* like José Álvares Marciel alienated the captaincy's distinguished, extended families. Such actions produced a stream of acrimonious memorials drafted by the town councils and local magistrates. As always, the resolution was left up to Lisbon; but in this case, the matter ended up in the lap of Melo e Castro, the new colonial secretary.[109]

The governor's schemes to redirect the special lines of patronage, credit, and profiteering that kept the Minas plutocracy in line provoked the unrest in the captaincy. Viewed as a contest between a corrupt governor and a threatened elite, it had much in common with other famous colonial conflicts. However, the American Revolution, the narrow domestic focus of the post-Pombaline regime, and the growing self-reliance of Brazil's elite created an explosive context for Luso-Brazilian politics.

During the 1780s Brazilian students formed a secret society at Coimbra, dedicated to independence. José Joaquim da Maia, one of its members and a native of Rio de Janeiro, met in France with Thomas Jefferson to discuss support for Brazil's inevitable revolt. A growing number of Brazilians, schooled in the Enlightenment both at reformed Coimbra and French universities like Montpellier, returned to join the colony's scientific societies, literary clubs, and exclusive social circles.[110]

---

[109] Ibid., pp. 99–106.

[110] In 1772 Pombal's reformers modernized Coimbra's curriculum. The new theology, emphasizing biblical studies, church history, and Socratic inquiry, replaced the Schoolmen with their numerous commentators and rote learning. The introduction of the natural philosophy of Galileo, Copernicus, Newton, and Descartes finally brought the seventeenth-century scientific revolution to Portugal. See Manoel Cardozo, "Azeredo Coutinho and the Intellectual Ferment of His Times," in *Conflict and Continuity in Brazilian Society*, Henry H. Kieth and S. F. Edwards, eds. (Columbia, South Carolina, 1969), pp. 79–81.

Between 1770 and 1790 over 400 Brazilians studied at Coimbra;[111] the urban-oriented Mineiros were particularly well represented: of the 46 Brazilians who graduated in 1786 and 1787, almost half were from Minas.[112] The captaincy also boasted the largest private libraries in Brazil, well-stocked with French volumes: Voltaire, Rousseau, Condillac, the Encyclopédie. The largest, most cosmopolitan collections were owned by the Vila Rica lawyer, poet, and erstwhile secretary to Minas governors, Claúdio Manuel da Costa; by the canon, Luís Viera; and by the wealthy landowner, José Resende da Costa; judges Peixoto and Gonzaga had smaller collections. All joined the intrigue against the crown; all, Gonzaga excepted, were Brazilian-born.[113]

The gradual withdrawal of the Minas economy from the characteristic import–export syndrome reinforced the political divergence Cunha Meneses had set in motion. The registro system imposed double taxation on the captaincy's imports, creating a tariff barrier that promoted import substitution. Carioca merchants and viceroy Lavradio had attributed the region's declining volume of imports to its notorious workshops. This ignored the reduced capacity to purchase that was due to shrinking gold reserves; it likewise ignored the region's growing self-sufficiency.

The populous, urban-centered captaincy generated a domestic market supplied by a special kind of rural estate. Most of Brazil's planters specialized in a single crop; by contrast, the diversified Minas *fazendas* often combined gold washings with maize, manioc, and bean fields; some had cattle ranches and sugar mills. The region's cotton was woven into fine textiles and gross cloth for slaves. The fazendas supplied internal markets and neighboring captaincies; for as the gold boom tapered off, increased local trade was a logical and necessary alternative. The coastal captaincies produced much of their own food, too, but new export crops like cotton and indigo strengthened commercial ties with Portugal. Minas

---

[111] Francisco Morais, "Estudantes na universidade de Coimbra nacidos no Brasil," *Brasilia, Revista do Instituto de Estudos Brasileiros da Faculdade de Letras de Coimbra* (supplement to vol. 4) (Coimbra, 1949), pp. 272–351. On the conspiracy at Coimbra, see Maxwell, *Conflicts and Conspiracies*, pp. 80–81; Prado, *Colonial Background*, p. 424; and Ernesto Ennes, "The Trial of the Ecclesiastics in the Inconfidência Mineira," *The Americas* 7 (1950) pp. 184–185.

[112] Maxwell, *Conflicts and Conspiracies*, p. 95.

[113] See E. Bradford Burns, "The Enlightenment in Two Colonial Brazilian Libraries," *Journal of the History of Ideas* 25 (1964), pp. 430–438; idem, "Concerning the Transmission and Dissemination of the Enlightenment in Brazil," in *The Ibero-American Enlightenment*, ed. A. Owen Aldridge (Urbana, 1971), pp. 256–281; Alexander Marchant, "Aspects of the Enlightenment in Brazil," in *Latin America and the Enlightenment*, ed. Arthur P. Whitaker (1942: Ithaca, 1961), pp. 95–118; Maxwell, *Conflicts and Conspiracies*, pp. 125–127.

Gerais was one of the few places where trade moved in a very different direction.[114]

The turmoil in Minas Gerais reached a momentary climax in 1786. A judge from Rio's High Court conducted a special investigation of conditions in the diamond district; Cunha Meneses was replaced; Gonzaga was kicked upstairs to Bahia's Relação. Meanwhile, the colonial secretary drew up instructions for the new governor, the Visconde de Barbacena. Melo e Castro concluded that the "perversity of the captaincy's inhabitants" was responsible for the fiscal disarray in Minas Gerais; he instructed Barbecena accordingly.[115]

In the 1780s receipts from the fifths dropped to about 58 arrobas of gold per year.[116] Previously the Minas treasury board had advised Lisbon that the 100-arroba quota was unrealistic, and cautioned against a head tax being imposed to make up the difference. Melo e Castro disagreed. By 1788 the unpaid fifths had reached the staggering sum of 538 arrobas, a fact the colonial secretary attributed to "the great relaxation of those whose charge was the inviolable observance of the law." Declarations that the mines were exhausted he dismissed as "subterfuge to disguise the abuses and the fraud practiced in the captaincy"; he ordered Barbacena to impose the head tax forthwith, and to insist on indemnification for the arrears outstanding.[117]

Regarding the scandalous debts owed by contractors, the secretary again indicted the treasury board, "which cared only for its own self-interest and those of its clients, with irreparable prejudice to the exchequer." Barbacena was to terminate the contract system and prosecute the treasury's debtors "of whatever quality they may be."[118] The Royal Treasury conducted its own investigation of the diamond district. It concluded that the "indolence, corruption, and malpractice of the administrators" had proceeded from the choice of men born in the country for these positions." The dragoons, the crown's police force, were guilty of "unlimited greed and arbitrary and violent behavior."[119]

In Melo e Castro's opinion, the Minas economy had acquired an alarming degree of self-sufficiency. Noting that the registros taxed imported merchandise heavily whereas locally produced goods were tax-

---

[114] Maxwell, *Conflicts and Conspiracies*, pp. 87–90. Prado also stresses the unique and superior character of Mineiro agriculture and ranching; see Prado, *Colonial Background*, pp. 174–175, 186–187, 227–231.

[115] Maxwell, *Conflicts and Conspiracies*, pp. 106–107, 109.

[116] Ibid., p. 253.

[117] Ibid., pp. 108–109.

[118] Ibid., p. 110.

[119] Ibid., p. 111.

exempt, the secretary instructed Barbacena and the viceroy to adjust rates to favor mining equipment, agricultural implements, and imported textiles, thus directing a blow against the Minas workshops.[120] A revision of the rates was indeed long overdue, but the secretary's object was to reinforce the region's dependency upon Portuguese exporters. Rather than permit iron foundries, as Minas governor José de Meneses had recommended, Melo e Castro lowered the prices of iron exports.

Barbacena's instructions spelled disaster for wealthy Mineiros. Not only did they reveal a distinct anti-Brazilian bias, but they were based on the erroneous assumption that complaints about exhausted mines were nothing more than a clever trick to defraud the exchequer, despite abundant evidence to the contrary. Debt collection, the imposition of the head tax, and the termination of tax farming threatened the captaincy's credit system. The harsh course Melo e Castro mapped out penalized everyone, not just racketeers, since the head tax fell on defrauders and honest men indifferently, and the credit operations of a contractor like Macedo had benefited estate owners and miners, not just venal officeholders. The colonial secretary accomplished that local jealousies usually prevented: he created a clear division between local interests and the state bureaucracy that competing social networks could not bridge. He succeeded in the wrong place at precisely the wrong time.

At the treasury board's first meeting (July, 1788), governor Barbacena adhered obdurately to the secretary's hard line. In December a tightly knit group of conspirators, broadly representative of the Minas oligarchy and the region's principal districts, decided to revolt. Although not activists, the opulent contractors João Rodrigues de Macedo and Joaquim Silvério dos Reis lent their support; indeed, the plotters met in Macedo's stately Vila Rica mansion. José Álvares Marciel, a recent Coimbra graduate and son of the powerful coronel who had tangled with Cunha Meneses, was part of the inner circle; before returning to Minas, he had discussed Brazilian independence with British merchants. The American Revolution served as a kind of prototype, and copies of the Articles of Confederation and several state constitutions circulated among the conspirators. The ex-magistrates Gonzaga and Peixoto—the latter heavily indebted to Macedo—along with Marciel and the poet-lawyer Cláudio Manuel da Costa, fashioned the revolt's ideological core.[121] Oliveira Rolim, the influential smuggler and moneylender, had connections in the

---

[120] Ibid., p. 109; Ernesto Ennes, "The Trial of the Ecclesiastics in the Inconfidencia Mineira," *The Americas* 7 (1950), pp. 186–190.

[121] Although he had been appointed to Bahia's High Court, Gonzaga delayed his departure.

diamond district. Under a sentence of banishment from Minas Gerais, he lived in hiding at the house of Domingos de Abreu Vieira, the aged tithe contractor. The commandant of the dragoons, Francisco de Andrade, had married into the Marciel family. His father-in-law, the clan's patriarch and a former contract administrator with substantial sums in default, stood to lose his estates if the crown foreclosed. Moreover, the crown's indictment against the dragoons and the proposed reforms threatened Andrade's command. His participation was crucial; without the dragoons the revolt could not succeed. The enigmatic Silva Xavier, the famous *tiradentes*, "neither oligarch nor artisan," was the only conspirator who lacked the high social esteem enjoyed by those privy to the revolt. A low-ranking officer in the dragoons, his part-time profession as "toothpuller" made him an ideal go-between.[122,123]

Whether Portuguese or Brazilian-born, the conspirators were drawn from among those directly threatened by Melo e Castro's instructions. As contractors, bondsmen to contractors, or as wealthy men dependent on the contract business, they had a vested interest in reversing Barbacena's fiscal coup. Economic self-interest was not the only basis for collective action, especially for the Brazilians. A strong sense of regional identity and the overlapping social bonds created by kinship, godparentage, marriage alliances, and business dealings strengthened group cohesiveness. For some, the American Revolution and the intellectual ferment of the times gave independence an ideal as well as a practical meaning.

Minas Gerais was not the only place that felt the heavy hand of Lisbon's new regime. In Rio de Janeiro, prices rose and shortages occurred because of the crackdown on contraband and local workshops. The viceroy's spies went hunting for looms and industrial equipment, which they seized and shipped back to Portugal. The Minas conspirators expected Carioca merchants, because they desired "freedom of commerce," to back the revolt for "their own self-interest."[124]

The imposition of the head tax was bound to ignite popular unrest. The conspirators, led by Silva Xavier, planned to incite a riot in Vila Rica. The dragoons, summoned to quell the disturbance, would instead join the

---

[122] The literal meaning of *tiradentes* is toothpuller.

[123] The conspirators, their motivations and interrelationships, are fully discussed in Maxwell, *Conflicts and Conspiracies*, pp. 115–140. This account is based on Maxwell's research. Also, see Ennes, "Trial of the Ecclesiastics," pp. 190–196; and Nícia Vilela Luz, "Inquietação revolucionária no sul: conjuração mineira," in *A época colonial: Administração, economia, sociedade, História geral da civilização brasileira*, ed. Sérgio Buarque de Holanda. 4 vols. (São Paulo, 1960) vol. 1 (2), pp. 394–405.

[124] Maxwell, *Conflicts and Conspiracies*, pp. 136–137; also, see Charles R. Boxer, *Some Literary Sources for the History of Brazil in the Eighteenth Century* (Oxford, 1967) p. 28.

revolt. Barbacena was to be assassinated and a republic proclaimed. Everything hinged on the head tax, the revolt's ominous clarion, but the alarm never sounded. The conspiracy remained words not deeds. Instead of imposing the tax in February (1789) as anticipated, Barbacena announced its suspension because of "the circumstances in the captaincy." At the time, the governor had no knowledge of the plot; however, he soon found out. This dramatic turn of events, the sense, in Gonzaga's words, that "the occasion had been lost," broke the ranks of the less stalwart revolutionaries.[125] The contractor, Joaquim Silvério dos Reis, had joined the revolt to excape his debts; he now turned informant for the same reason.

The fact that a revolt was hatched and bandied about for months without the governor's knowledge[126] was unlikely to enhance his reputation, particularly since it had come perilously close to realization. Under the circumstances, Barbacena tried to cover his own tracks. He juxtaposed events in his letters to the viceroy, claiming that the head-tax suspension was a clever move to win popular support and thwart rebellion. Meanwhile, he surreptitiously undermined the conspiracy's inner circle by trading-off patronage and promises of protection in return for defection from the conspiracy. In this way, the dragoons were quickly neutralized. The governor hoped he could dispose of the matter without involving his superiors and without embarrassment to himself. The situation could be handled, he wrote the viceroy, without judicial inquiry; the leaders could be moved from Minas Gerais "without great display, attributing the cause to some other crime or saying nothing at all."[127]

Viceroy Vasconcelos e Sousa, a High Court judge from Portugal, insisted on an official investigation. Despite Barbacena's equivocations, he quickly grasped how serious the case was. By now, however, Barbecena had fabricated an elaborate cover up, which the viceregal inquiry threatened to undo. True, he had arrested some of the principal culprits: judges Peixoto and Gonzaga; the lawyer, Claudio Manuel da Costa; and Oliveira Rolim; but those under the governor's protection—Álvares Marciel, Rodrigues de Macedo, and the aristocratic commandant of the dragoons, Freire de Andrade—were as significant as those apprehended. To counter the viceroy, Barbacena conducted his own investigation, in fact, his self-serving misrepresentations reached Lisbon first. In the end, it became politically impossible to protect Marciel and Andrade; but the

---

[125] Maxwell, *Conflicts and Conspiracies*, pp. 141–144, quotations from p. 142; Ennes, "Trial of the Ecclesiastics," pp. 193–194.

[126] Ernesto Ennes, "Trial of the Ecclesiastics," pp. 183–197.

[127] Maxwell, *Conflicts and Conspiracies*, p. 154.

wealthy contractor, Rodrigues de Macedo, was never arrested, never called as a witness, and never interrogated. The most damaging testimony against the contractor was the unnotarized confession of Claudio Manuel da Costa, but the lawyer, imprisoned in Macedo's mansion, committed suicide.[128]

The conspiracy failed to unleash a revolt; instead, it unleashed politics with a vengence, both in troubled Minas and in Lisbon. By the time a sentence was imposed in 1792, the case was entangled in the bureaucratic politics of the empire. The dispute between the viceroy and Barbacena over the merits of their respective investigations was further complicated by a third inquiry launched by the overseas secretary. Melo e Castro had a stake in the "facts" of the case too; his harsh instructions to Barbecena had alarmed the queen. She had insisted that the head tax be imposed "only if the people of Minas were in a condition to support the tax," and advised some kind of debt moratorium.[129] Yet, the queen's conciliatory tone was deliberately withheld from the Mineiros. Now it appeared that the secretary's actions provoked the rebellion—an interpretation Melo e Castro was anxious to avoid. Protégés of Pombal now held important ministerial portfolios. Luís Pinto, a former governor of Mato Grosso and an opponent of the narrow protectionist stance taken by the Factory Board, became foreign secretary in 1790. He immediately sent two Brazilians to study mining at Freiburg at the state's expense. Melo e Castro's view that abuses and malpractices caused the exchequer's declining gold revenues was publicly challenged in scientific papers presented to the prestigious Academy of Sciences in Lisbon. The most significant discourse was the work of D. Roderigo de Sousa Coutinho—Pombal's godson. The overseas secretary was thus hard-pressed by those who advocated a wider, Brazilian-centered imperial policy.[130]

Barbacena's duplicity deflected attention from contractors like Macedo; it also obscured the role fiscal policy played in the conspiracy. Melo e Castro conveniently attributed the plot to "disgruntled military officers, lawyers, and clerics." Such a conclusion reduced his own culpability and "clouded the relationship between his economic policy and the nationalist response"; it also blocked any fundamental reassessment of conditions in the captaincy.[131] For the moment, the hard-liners prevailed.

In April 1792 the chancellor of the court of inquiry delivered his

---

[128] Maxwell's account is a masterpiece of scholarship and detective work: see *Conflicts and Conspiracies*, pp. 141–176.

[129] Maxwell, *Conflicts and Conspiracies*, pp. 111–113.

[130] Ibid., pp. 177–180.

[131] Ibid., pp. 187–188.

verdict: all the principal conspirators were condemned to death. As prearranged with the queen, however, the death penalty was commuted to banishment—except for Silva Xavier. His low status made him an easy target for royal justice. The Minas plot was hatched before the French Revolution, but for those who "dealt with its consequences, France was foremost in their thoughts." Silva Xavier, "white, ambitious, propertyless . . . bore all the characteristics of the revolutionary man."[132] He recklessly claimed sole responsibility for the plot; his gory and terrifying execution served as a warning to those who defied the crown.

The "incredible multitude of libertine and scandalous books" found in Minas libraries heightened the parent state's paranoia. Melo e Castro was convinced that other plots existed inspired by the "pernicious French principles of liberty." In Rio de Janeiro the authorities were alarmed by the growing hostility of Brazilians who thought "they possessed more talents—and that the Portuguese took away riches due to the native-born."[133] In 1794 nervous officials descended on the Carioca Literary Society, arresting and imprisoning its members. In 1795, the year Melo e Castro died, the parent state was on a collision course with its colony. The collision never came. Over the next decade Pombal's followers dismantled the politics of confrontation. They were helped by Brazilians who had lost their early enthusiasm for republicanism. Liberty as espoused by a slaveowner like Thomas Jefferson fit Brazilian conditions; what liberty means to the *sans-culotte* or rebellious Haitian slaves did not.[134]

THE LUSO-BRAZILIAN ECONOMY, 1780–1810: EXPANSION AND ACCOMMODATION

As Minas estate owners found alternatives to gold exports, the captaincy's economy began to focus on local rather than external markets; the transition left a staggering debt. The Minas pattern was not repeated elsewhere.

Although tax farmers in Rio de Janeiro also defaulted, the exchequer's creditors far exceeded its debtors;[135] and in many regions of Brazil, the

---

[132] Ibid., pp. 190–192, 197–198, quotations are from pp. 189, 191–193. The queen's instructions on sentencing are reprinted in Ennes, "Trial of the Ecclesiastics," pp. 202–203.

[133] Maxwell, *Conflicts and Conspiracies*, pp. 190, 192, 203.

[134] Maxwell, *Conflicts and Conspiracies*, pp. 190; 192, 203; Burns, "Transmission and Dissemination," p. 273; and Américo Jacobina Lacombre, "A conjuração do Rio de Janeiro," in *Administração, economia, sociedade*, História geral, vol. 1 (2), pp. 406–410.

[135] Alden, *Royal Government*, p. 349. In 1781, the Minas treasury owed half of all debts due the crown: see Alden, *Royal Government*, pp. 507–508.

agricultural experimentation of the 1770s produced spectacular results: between 1780 and 1810 the value of Bahia's exports trebled.[136]

Mechanization so transformed cost and productivity ratios in Britain's textile business that cottage industries could not compete with factory organization. In the 1780s a series of innovations—the spinning jenny, the water frame, the mule—closed the technological gaps between the weaving and spinning sections of the British cotton industry; English industrialists turned decisively to cottons.[137] Along with the West Indies, Brazil became a vital source of raw cotton: between 1785 and 1789 British manufacturers purchased 13 million pounds of Brazilian cotton.[138] During the 1790s they purchased a total of 68 million pounds, which made up 23% of all Britain's cotton imports.[139] Pernambuco-Ceará and Maranhão were the chief cotton captaincies; together they produced 7.5 million pounds per year in the early 1790s, and joint exports doubled by the first decade of the nineteenth century.[140] Not all of Brazil's cotton went abroad. In 1796 Portugal retained 1.7 million pounds for its domestic workshops.[141]

Rice production, especially in Maranhão, also expanded, from 164,000 arrobas in 1783 to 313,000 arrobas in 1798, and an average of 260,000 arrobas between 1805 and 1811; prices more than doubled (1790–1810).[142] In 1796 Rio de Janeiro sent 176,000 arrobas of rice and 187,000 arrobas of indigo to Lisbon; only its sugar, brandy, and reexported hides were more

---

[136] Simonsen, História econômica, p. 364.

[137] Michael M. Edwards, The Growth of the British Cotton Trade 1780-1815 (New York, 1967), pp. 3-6.

[138] Cotton production in the United States lagged behind Brazil's until the turn of the century. See Michael M. Edwards, The Growth of the British Cotton Trade 1780-1815 (New York, 1967), pp. 84-85, 251.

[139] The estimates of Britain's cotton imports from Brazil combine the tables in Edwards, British Cotton Trade, p. 84; and Godinho, Prix et Monnaies, p. 263; the missing data for 1793 is added in as the decade's average. Total British imports during the 1790s were 295 million pounds; see Edwards, British Cotton Trade, p. 250.

[140] Between 1789 and 1791 Pernambucan imports to Great Britain totaled 90,124 bags of raw cotton weighing 140 pounds each, for a yearly average of 4.2 million pounds; imports from Maranhão totaled 42,000 bags weighing 200 pounds each, for an average of 2.8 million pounds; see Alden, Royal Government, p. 366 n. 54. During the next decade (1801-1810), Pernambucan exports jumped to 3.2 million kilos annually (7 million pounds); between 1805 and 1812 Maranhão exported an average of 226,898 arrobas (7.3 million pounds); see Luís Amaral, História geral da agricultura Brasileira, 2 vols. (São Paulo, 1958), vol. 2, pp. 21, 24, 35.

[141] Jorge Borges de Macedo, O bloqueio continental (Lisbon, 1962), p. 44. This estimate is the sum of imports for 1796 minus exports. The figure may be too high, since exports to France are not recorded. Nonetheless, the table implies that Portugal retained considerable quantities of cotton for domestic use.

[142] Amaral, História geral, vol. 2, pp. 77-78. Rice prices can be found in Godinho, Prix et Monnaies, pp. 74, 185.

valuable.[143] By the turn of the century, Pará's cacao exports often exceeded 100,000 arrobas, and it sent almost as much rice.[144]

Brazil's sugar industry limped along during the eighteenth century, a hostage to Caribbean competition and the fortunes of war; but market conditions in Europe improved during the 1790s. Domestic consumption cut into England's sugar reexports,[145] in Saint Dominque, Haiti, production collapsed after 1792 because of slave revolts and French military action. Brazil's sugar filled the gap: exports stood at 720,000 arrobas in 1783, topped 2 million arrobas in 1796, and reached 2.5 million in 1800—the best performance since the record levels of the seventeenth century.[146] It was a bull market, too, and Amsterdam prices trebled. Under the circumstances, noted the Bahian chronicler, Luís dos Santos Vilhena, "there is no one who does not wish to be a sugar planter."[147]

Brazil's great sugar and tobacco producer, Bahia, basked in its renewed prosperity. In 1798 its 747,000 arrobas of sugar and 380,000 arrobas of tobacco were worth 5.8 million cruzados, and helped produce a 1.5 million cruzado surplus with Portugal.[148] Furthermore, the vitality of Bahia's commerce did not rest exclusively on trade with Portugal. Between 1790 and 1815 some 550 ships carried the region's tobacco and sugar-cane brandy to the Costa da Mina. The fleets returned with over 112,000 slaves and great quantities of contraband merchandise.[149] This was hardly a new pattern, but the dimensions had doubled since the 1770s. The value of Bahia's African exports was 670,000 cruzados in 1804, and registered imports, mostly slaves, were worth twice as much.[150]

Portugal's Asian trade picked up substantially in the period 1783 to 1814, and Salvador and Rio de Janeiro shared in the revival. Asian-bound traders could now lade sugar and brandy in Brazilian ports, and in the

---

[143] Alden, *Royal Government*, p. 365; idem, "Growth and Decline of Indigo," p. 55. By the first decade of the nineteenth century, India was England's chief source of indigo and Rio's production plummeted; see Alden, "Growth and Decline of Indigo," pp. 55–60.

[144] Simonsen, *História econômica*, pp. 346–348.

[145] Consult the figures in Elizabeth Boody Schumpter, *English Overseas Trade Statistics 1697–1808* (Oxford, 1960), pp. 61–62.

[146] Macedo, *Problemas de história*, p. 199.

[147] Maxwell, *Conflicts and Conspiracies*, pp. 213, 257–258.

[148] Luís dos Santos Vilhena, *A Bahia no século XVII (Recopilação de notícias soterpolitanas e Brasílicas)*, 3 vols. (Salvador, 1969), vol. 1, p. 60.

[149] Pierre Verger, *Flux et Reflux de la traite des negres entre le golfe de Benin et Bahia de Todos os Santos de dix-septieme au dix-neuvieme siècle* (Paris, 1966), pp. 654–655, 664–665; Vilhena, *Bahia*, vol. 1, pp. 59, 61; and Philip D. Curtin, *The Atlantic Slave Trade: A Census* (Madison, 1969), p. 207.

[150] José Honório Rodriguez, *Brazil and Africa*, trans. Richard A. Mazzara and Sam Hileman (Berkeley, 1965), p. 34.

1790s restrictions were lifted on the direct exportation of tobacco. The result was a brisk legal trade between Asian and Brazil that bypassed Lisbon; in 1804 Bahia's Asian imports produced a deficit of more than 1 million cruzados. A favorable balance of trade with Portugal, however, helped pay for Salvador's African and Asian imports.[151]

Europe's demand for cotton, sugar, tobacco, rice, indigo, and hides kept Brazil's economy booming. The growth of the export sector depended on slave labor, and the viceregal capital was the principal port of call for the slave trade. In the 1790s 24 Carioca ships a year called at Angolan ports; they brought Rio's staples such as sugar, brandy, rice, and reexports from neighboring captaincies. Between 1795 and 1811 traders returned with over 160,000 slaves carried abroad 370 ships. By then Rio de Janeiro had displaced Salvador as Brazil's foremost port.[152]

In 1800 Brazil's population was about 2.3 million people; 67% lived in four captaincies: Minas Gerais (21%), Bahia (19%), Pernambuco (16%) and Rio de Janeiro (21%).[153] Although intercaptaincy trade was an old phenomenon Brazilians were now exchanging products on an unprecedented scale. The impetus came from the export economy. The Bahian planter Manuel Ferreira da Câmara boasted that he had not "planted a single foot of manioc in order not to fall into the absurdity of renouncing the best cultivation of the country for the worst."[154] While planters cashed in on high prices, cities like Salvador and Recife went short of food. Severe drought in the backlands (1791–1793) made the situation worse, since it reduced the Northeast's salted meat supply.[155] Fortunately the region found a new source of provisions in Brazil's southern-most captaincy, Rio Grande do Sul.

The Treaty of San Ildefonso (1777) had ended 15 years of intermittent fighting in the borderlands: Portugal ceded Colonia to Spain, but retained most of Rio Grande do Sul.[156] In the late 1790s Rio Grande sent 300,000 arrobas of salted meat a year to Bahia, as well as tallow, wheat, and cheese.[157] In 1800 more ships entered Salvador from Rio Grande than

---

[151] Ibid. 5, p. 34; and Charles R. Boxer, "The Principal Ports of Call of the 'Carreira da India,' " *Luso-Brazilian Review* 8 (1971), p. 25.

[152] Herbert S. Klein, *Middle Passage*, pp. 51–72. Also see Rudolph William Bauss, "Rio de Janeiro: The Rise of Late Colonial Brazil's Dominant Emporium, 1777–1808" (doctoral thesis, Tulane University, 1977), pp. 34–87, 276–315.

[153] Dauril Alden, "The Population of Brazil in the Late Eighteenth Century: A Preliminary Study," *Hispanic American Historical Review* 43 (1963), pp. 191, 195.

[154] Maxwell, *Conflicts and Conspiracies*, pp. 224–225.

[155] Prado, *Colonial Background*, pp. 187–190, 225; Vilhena, *Bahia*, vol. 1, p. 158.

[156] In the far west the treaty followed the boundary lines specified by the Treaty of Madrid (1750).

[157] Vilhena, *Bahia*, vol. 1, p. 61.

from Lisbon.[158] According to John Mawe, an Englishman who traveled through Brazil in the 1810s, Rio de Janeiro and Recife also took great quantities of dried beef, tallow, hides, and wheat from Rio Grande. He estimated that this coastal trade employed 100 small ships, some of which made two or three trips a year.[159] During the early nineteenth century the captaincy exported 600,000 arrobas of salted beef each year, 300,000 hides, sent 10,000 to 20,000 cattle to neighboring captaincies, and supplied Brazil with pack animals—30,000 mules and 4000 horses annually.[160]

Rio Grande was also Brazil's greatest wheat producer; exports rose from 35,000 bushels in 1805 to 110,000 bushels in 1813.[161] One reason planters could respond to high sugar prices with such reckless abandon was because of Rio Grande's food supply. The southern captaincy's growth was both a cause and a consequence of the export zone's rapid expansion. Except for hides, this reciprocity did not involve the metropolis.

Brazil's trade with Portugal flourished, but so did intercaptaincy trade and the Brazilian-based slave traffic. The direct links between Asia and Brazil bypassed Lisbon, and populous Minas Gerais no longer contributed so much to Luso-Brazilian trade. The captaincy still had gold, but in the 1790s annual production was only 250 arrobas, scarcely one-half that of former years.[162] The results contradicted mercantilist doctrines: almost every Brazilian port had favorable terms of trade with Portugal; between 1796 and 1807 Brazil drew a balance of payments surplus in 9 out of 12 years. The net gain exceeded 57 million cruzados.[163] To pay its debts, Portugal shipped bullion to its colony.

How independence would improve Brazil's trading position was unclear to contemporaries. Indeed, the economic gains of the 1790s helped reconcile Luso-Brazilian interests. Sugar planters were not usually free-trade advocates. The most likely partner in such an event, Great Britain, excluded foreign sugar from domestic markets. Apologists for the sugar industry, like the Brazilian-born bishop-economist Azeredo Coutinho, accepted Lisbon as the colony's sugar mart and exclusive supplier. Viewed as a sugar plantation, Brazil's interests were not necessarily opposed to those of Lisbon. "The more the price of sugar rises," noted the bishop, "the greater becomes our production and commerce." The

---

[158] Maxwell, *Conflicts and Conspiracies*, p. 214.

[159] John Mawe, *Travels in the Interior of Brazil* (1812: London, 1822), pp. 140, 443–446.

[160] Prado, *Colonial Background*, pp. 234–238, 297–298.

[161] Amaral, *História geral*, vol. 2, p. 79 (2.5 *alqueires* = 1 bushel).

[162] Simonsen, *História econômica*, p. 297.

[163] Godinho, *Prix et Monnaies*, p. 275; also see Maxwell, *Conflicts and Conspiracies*, pp. 213–216.

Luso-Brazilian economy "ought to be considered like a farm or single farmers. . . . the owner of many estates does not care which procures him more revenues, but only rates the collective revenues of the whole."[164]

Between 1789 and 1800 Portugal's foreign trade tripled; such success promoted an accommodation with Brazil's planters. Although rising domestic exports like wine and raw wool contributed to Portugal's enhanced trade, the great surge came from Brazil.[165] A period of high prices (1790–1810) for sugar, tobacco, rice, cotton, wine, and olive oil created a substantial advantage for the Luso-Brazilian periphery.[166] Portugal's European trade produced a surplus in 10 out of 12 years (1796–1807) for a net gain of 88 million cruzados.[167] Now gold flowed back to Portugal, some of it for reshipment to Brazil—a dramatic reversal of the dependency Pombal detested.[168]

Portugal's industries strengthened the new pattern. Between 1796 and 1802 30% of all the goods shipped to Brazil consisted of Portuguese manufactures, especially cotton cloth.[169] For the moment, the prohibition against foreign cottons protected the realm's workshops from Britain's emergent factory system. British textiles, either legally or as contraband, still went to Brazil. In 1792 Lord Macartney found Rio's shops "full of Manchester manufactures, and other English goods even to English prints,"[170] but Britain no longer clothed Brazil to the exclusion of Lisbon. In 1798 Salvador imported the largest share of its "factory merchandise" from Portugal.[171]

The exchange the Methuen Treaty protected no longer favored Britain. Its cotton cloth was excluded from Portugal along with Irish woolens and linens; for they were not "English" as the treaty required.[172] Initially, British trade with Portugal declined because of Brazil's recession, but now Portugal's workshops and stiff competition from Dutch and French

---

[164] Maxwell, *Conflicts and Conspiracies*, pp. 216, 225–226; also see E. Bradford Burns, "The Role of Azeredo Coutinho in the Enlightenment of Brazil," *Hispanic American Historical Review* 44 (1964), pp. 147–153.

[165] Macedo, *Problemas de história*, pp. 195–200, 202.

[166] On prices, see Godinho, *Prix et Monnaies*, olive oil, p. 179; wine, p. 183; rice, p. 185; cotton, p. 263; Maxwell, *Conflicts and Conspiracies*, sugar, pp. 257–258; Amaral, *História geral*, vol. 2, cotton, p. 20. A price index for Rio de Janeiro can be found in Harold B. Johnson, "A Preliminary Inquiry into Money, Prices, and Wages in Rio de Janeiro, 1763–1823," in *Colonial Roots*, pp. 268–283.

[167] Godinho, *Prix et Monnaies*, pp. 272–273.

[168] Maxwell, *Conflicts and Conspiracies*, pp. 181–182.

[169] Godinho, *Prix et Monnaies*, p. 274.

[170] Boxer, *Some Literary Sources*, p. 27.

[171] Vilhena, *Bahia*, vol. 1, p. 60.

[172] Manchester, *British Preëminence*, pp. 45–46.

woolens reduced Britain's share of the empire's textile business. The damage seemed permanent. Compared to the 1750s, Luso-Brazilian purchases had dropped 48% in the 1780s; at the same time England's share of Lisbon's commercial traffic fell from 56% to 20%.[173]

English cotton manufacturers, clamoring for new outlets, lobbied for a commercial agreement with France. The Eden Treaty (1786) reduced the tariff on French wines, and gave English cottons entrance to French markets. But Portugal's wine exports suffered little; the trade was well established, as was the taste for port wine. And Britain took more Brazilian products than ever: not only cotton, but rice, indigo and cacao.[174] So England continued to be Portugal's most important trading partner: in 1789, for example, England took 43% of all Luso-Brazilian exports.[175] The average annual value of England's purchases from Portugal rose from £359,000 (1781–1785) to £779,000 (1791–1795) and Portugal gained a considerable surplus on the exchange—over £570,000.[176]

The British, disenchanted with the Methuen Treaty, now preached reciprocity. They demanded favorable treatment for their cotton goods, a concession Lisbon viewed as "thoroughly calamitous," if granted.[177] The Eden Treaty showed that England was willing to abandon Portugal for better markets; but England and France were at war in 1793, in a herculean struggle that was to last over a decade. Both sides purchased enormous quantities of foodstuffs and raw materials in Portugal; England, however, gained the most from Portugal's neutrality.[178] The average value of its Luso-Brazilian imports in the years 1801 to 1805 increased to almost £1 million (1801–1805)—double what the French took.[179] England returned to the Portugal trade in a spectacular way, and it was determined to keep the Luso-Brazilian economy out of Napoleon's grasp.

The antagonistic stance of the post-Pombaline regime had narrowly avoided a major revolt in Brazil, and plots were not confined to Minas Gerais. During the 1780s Rio's merchants openly discussed free trade; the crown's response was a crackdown on contraband and a harsh assault on

---

[173] Schumpeter, English Overseas Trade Statistics, p. 17; Macedo, Problemas de história, p. 194.

[174] Manchester, British Preëminence, pp. 45–53; A. D. Francis, The Wine Trade (London, 1972), pp. 245–246; and W. O. Henderson, "The Anglo-French Commercial Treaty of 1786," Economic History Review 10 (1957), pp. 104–112.

[175] Portugal's exports totaled 18.8 million cruzados; England's share was 8 million. See the tables in Macedo, Bloqueio, p. 41; and idem, Problemas de história, p. 202.

[176] Godinho, Prix et Monnaies, p. 254.

[177] Maxwell, Conflicts and Conspiracies, pp. 182–185.

[178] Macedo, Bloqueio, pp. 26–30.

[179] Sideri, Trade and Power, pp. 234–235. To compare the value of French and English purchases in Portugal, see Macedo, Bloqueio, pp. 38, 41.

local workshops. The recovery of the 1790s, however, reinforced the mutual advantages of Luso-Brazilian trade. High prices made up for high taxes. Still, prosperity was not really an argument against independence, for Brazil was the empire's true economic center. Portugal was a distribution point, not a final destination for Brazil's exports, and Brazilians ran important trades that bypassed Lisbon. No, the boom led to a compromise because Pombal's disciples regained control over colonial policy.

In 1795 Luís Pinto, a man who was experienced in Brazilian affairs and a vocal adversary of Melo e Castro, became interim colonial secretary. The queen, no longer capable of exercising authority, was succeeded by her son, Dom João, as prince regent. In a statement of intent sent to Brazil's governors and town councils, Luís Pinto blamed "defects of policy" for the impasse in Luso-Brazilian affairs. He proposed relief for the mining industry, the establishment of iron foundries, and the abolition of the salt monopoly, thus notifying the colony's elite that the crown was ready to accommodate Brazilian interests. The prince regent appointed a permanent overseas secretary in 1796, Luís Pinto's friend, Dom Roderigo de Sousa Coutinho. The new secretary, Pombal's godson and a critic of Melo e Castro's unscientific approach to the mining industry, had strong ties to Brazil. He was related by marriage to a wealthy Mineiro family, and owned estates in the captaincy.[180]

Much as Pombal put businessmen to work for the state, D. Roderigo opened new channels to Brazilians. He asked them to reassess Brazil's economy, to propose industrial projects, and suggest reforms for the mining district. Directly solicited by the secretary, or forwarded on private initiative, Brazilian ideas flowed back across the Atlantic, helping to formulate colonial policy. Even the exiled José Álvares Marciel drew up a memorial on iron mining, which received a favorable reading. With state support, a task force of knowledgeable Brazilians collected information on salt deposits, conducted mineralogical and metallurgical studies, and searched for copper and saltpeter deposits. The objective was explicit: the creation of colonial industries. In 1798 D. Roderigo instructed the governor of Minas to set up an iron foundry at the exchequer's expense.

A wide-ranging *rapprochement* reduced the aura of mistrust unleashed by the conspiracy. The arrested members of Rio's Literary Society were finally released; Brazilians were appointed to high posts in Minas Gerais and elsewhere, including men tainted by the events of 1789. By the time D. Roderigo was promoted to the presidency of the Royal Treasury, he had drawn up, with the help of the Minas town councils, a comprehensive plan to reorganize the captaincy's fiscal structure. The crown's edict

[180] Maxwell, *Conflicts and Conspiracies*, pp. 179, 204–206.

of 1801, "in favor of the inhabitant of Brazil and the freedom of commerce," abolished the salt and whaling monopolies, encouraged mining, and provided for gunpowder and iron production. Luís Pinto, D. Roderigo, and their Luso-Brazilian supporters once again placed colonial policy on the context of larger, imperial objectives; they returned foursquare to Pombal's position.[181]

Lisbon's overtures and its careful use of patronage helped reverse Brazil's drift away from the crown, but Brazil's leaders had other reasons for reassessing the proposition that independence through revolution was advantageous. Both the French "reign of terror" and the successful slave rebellion in Saint Dominque, Haiti revealed unsavory aspects to revolution that the revolt of gentlemen farmers in English America obscured. In 1789 the possibility of a reaction from below did not occur to the Minas conspirators, but by 1800 such naïveté was unthinkable. That the lower ranks of Brazil's racially stratified society might be infected by "abominable Jacobin ideas" received alarming confirmation in Salvador.[182] In 1798 informers exposed a cadre of young mulatto artisans whose handwritten manifestos, addressed to the "Republican Bahian People," called for an end to the "detestable yoke of Portugal." The manifesto declared that "all citizens, especially mulattoes and blacks . . . are equal, there will be no differences, there will be liberty, equality, and fraternity."[183] Such a doctrine, expressed in a city like Salvador, where black and mulatto freedmen constituted 40% of the population and slaves another third, was a dangerous attack on the privileged white minority.[184] The principal culprits were executed; the harsh justice meted out to the mulatto conspirators, without the clemency shown in Minas Gerais, placed the crown squarely on the side of the captaincy's planters.

The stirrings of revolt in Salvador exposed the paradox underlying

---

[181] Ibid., pp. 208–212, 229–230; Burns, "Transmission and Dissemination," pp. 278–279. During the 1790s Brazilian ideas had an unprecedented impact on colonial policy, but the pattern of Brazilian influence on Portugal's intellectual life was already firmly established. See Manoel Cardozo, "Azeredo Coutinho and the Intellectual Ferment of His Times," in *Conflict and Continuity* (Columbia, S.C., 1969), pp. 72–74.

[182] Maxwell, *Conflicts and Conspiracies*, p. 223, also see pp. 216–223.

[183] On the "Conspiracy of the Tailors," see E. Bradford Burns, "The Intellectuals as Agents of Change and the Independence of Brazil, 1724–1822," in *Colony to Nation*, pp. 243–245; Arthur Cézar Ferreira Reis, "A inconfidência baiana," in *Administração, economia, sociedade*, História geral, vol. 1 (2), pp. 411–417; and Maxwell, *Conflicts and Conspiracies*, 216–229.

[184] In 1775 Salvador had a population of 19,656: 7943 colored freedmen (40%), 6692 slaves (34%), and 5021 whites (26%); see Herbert S. Klein, "Nineteenth Century Brazil," in *Neither Slave Nor Free: The Freedmen of African Descent in the Slave Societies of the New World*, eds. David W. Cohen and Jack P. Greene (Baltimore, 1972), p. 313.

Brazilian slavery. The colony had more slaves than any society in the Americas, and proportionately, more freedmen—about 30% of all Brazilians in 1800.[185] Free blacks and mulattoes had their own militia units and religious brotherhoods. As mechanics, artisans, barbers, petty traders, shopkeepers, small farmers, and transporters of every sort, they were indispensable to the colony's economy. On the other hand, freed slaves and their descendants had swelled the ranks of the unemployed. White Brazilians did not know how to accommodate the growing number of freedmen, and some segments of the elite questioned the desirability of slavery in a society where whites were already a minority.[186]

Contemporaries exaggerated the threat posed by the nonwhite "enemies of the nation." Brazil's blacks and mulattoes formed mutually hostile groups. The Brazilian-born slave, for example, "expressed contempt for those born in Africa, as did mulatto for black, and freedman for slave."[187] These internal socioethnic divisions, reinforced by the militia units and the religious brotherhoods, made collective action difficult; the brotherhoods had separate chapters for blacks and mulattoes, organized by place of birth and by tribal allegiance.[188] But Brazil's white citizens were uneasy. This uncertainty gave policy makers like D. Roderigo room for maneuver. As the Napoleonic wars escalated in Europe, Brazil's elite, wary of republicanism, feared a French invasion of Portugal. If Napoleon severed Luso-Brazilian political ties, could the elite control the reaction in Brazil? The removal of the court to Brazil offered an escape from such a dilemma. The disillusionment with revolution, the economic boom, and D. Roderigo's pro-Brazilian stance made the move eminently acceptable to wealthy Brazilians.

When planning for the contingency of a French invasion, D. Roderigo argued that Portugal was neither "the best nor the most essential part of the monarchy." If the prince regent had to choose between Portugal and

---

[185] Ibid., pp. 312–313; on the tense atmosphere in Bahia, see Prado, *Colonial Background*, pp. 427–428.

[186] The growing uneasiness over slavery and half-castes is discussed in Maxwell, *Conflicts and Conspiracies*, pp. 229–442; Burns, "Intellectuals of Brazil," pp. 237, 239–240; and Emilia Viotti da Costa, "The Political Emancipation of Brazil," in *Colony to Nation*, pp. 67–70. On the role freedmen played in the slave economy, see A. J. R. Russell-Wood, "Colonial Brazil," in *Neither Slave Nor Free*, pp. 98–130; Henry Koster, *Travels in Brazil*, ed. C. Harvey Gardiner (Carbondale, Ill., 1966), pp. 174–182. After independence, the status of free blacks and mulattoes became a major political issue; see Thomas Flory, "Race and Social Control in Independent Brazil," *Journal of Latin American Studies* 9 (1977), pp. 199–224.

[187] See A. J. R. Russell-Wood, "Black and Mulatto Brotherhoods in Colonial Brazil," *Hispanic American Historical Review* 54 (1974), p. 574.

[188] Russell-Wood, "Black and Mulatto Brotherhoods," p. 576.

Brazil, D. Roderigo strongly recommended that he choose Brazil. In 1801 the British minister declared that "in the case of an invasion the British envoy was authorized to recommend that the Court of Portugal embark for Brazil."[189] For the moment, such plans undermined Portuguese neutrality. In 1803 D. Roderigo was forced to resign; but by then he had assembled an impressive body of legislation and a more Brazilian-centered imperial view, which crossed the Atlantic with the court.[190]

The Peace of Tilsit ended Franco-Russian hostilities, and with his continental opponents neutralized, Napoleon attacked Britain, closing Europe's ports to British trade. Lisbon's strategic location and its status as a neutral port created a serious gap in Napoleon's "continental system." In August 1807 the Portuguese government received an ultimatum: declare war on England or face a French invasion. The choice, however invidious, was clear enough. War with England meant the ruin of trade and the loss of Brazil: under no circumstances would the English let the Brazil trade fall to the French. Failure to comply meant certain defeat. The Council of State, in emergency session, endorsed D. Roderigo's Brazil plan. A regency was left in charge of Lisbon. On November 30, 1807, the court, escorted by British warships, left Lisbon's harbor. Brazil's colonial history ended.[191]

The transfer of the court to Brazil was not an abberation from some larger American pattern. The event was consistent with the overall thrust of Luso-Brazilian policy, a policy that recognized Brazil's commercial primacy and England's naval supremacy. That a European crisis could force the monarchy to Brazil had been anticipated for a half-century.[192] The climax, startling as it appeared, produced a reasonable and not unexpected resolution. The denouement, however reluctant the prince regent's acquiescence, fit Brazilian conditions, and the English had a vested interest in its success. That the Spanish crown did not follow suit was not surprising; the Bourbon reformers were as hostile to Spanish-American Creoles as Pombal was indulgent toward Brazilians. In Bourbon Spain, the kind of hard line espoused by Melo e Castro was the rule, not the exception; and Spanish policy, tied to France, generated a different set of geopolitical problems.

When the prince regent arrived in the Bay of All Saints, Brazil's national history began, and the architects of Brazilian independence built

---

[189] Maxwell, *Conflicts and Conquests*, pp. 233–235.

[190] The quotations are from Maxwell, *Conflicts and Conspiracies*, pp. 211, 213, 234–235.

[191] See Alan K. Manchester, "The Transfer of the Court to Rio de Janeiro," in *Conflict and Continuity*, pp. 149–153.

[192] Oliveira Marques, *History of Portugal*, vol. 1, p. 427; Maxwell, *Conflicts and Conspiracies*, p. 233.

on the past in a way Spanish-American republicans could not. How that transition from colony to nation took place is an important chapter in the history of American state-formation. The brief sketch that follows examines the quixotic relationship of a transplanted Portuguese state to Brazilian independence.

THE MONARCHY IN BRAZIL, 1808–1831

The flotilla of merchant vessels and warships that left Lisbon brought the royal family and its numerous retainers, important members of the Council of State—including D. Roderigo, restored to the prince regent's favor—judges from Portugal's High Courts, ministers, military men, bishops, prominent noblemen, merchants, and businessmen—some 8000 in all. Hectic as the actual departure was, advance planning was evident. Along with the bureaucracy and the court came the royal library, comprehensive collections from the state archives, the contents of the treasury, and a printing press—all the necessary men and equipment required to recreate the Portuguese state in Brazil.[193]

Once in Salvador, the prince regent faced a commercial crisis. To prevent Portuguese vessels from falling to the French, an embargo had been placed on ships departing for Lisbon; consequently, the port was filled with ships, and warehouses were stocked full of sugar and tobacco. Lisbon and Oporto had been captured by the French and blockaded by the British, and could no longer receive Brazilian exports. Without trade, the Brazilian monarchy had no revenues. Decisive action was imperative. With the advice of Salvador's câmara, the governor, and other leading citizens, the prince regent issued the *carta regia* of January 28, 1808, abolishing the Portuguese monopoly on Brazil's trade. Ships of all friendly nations could now carry merchandise to Brazil and secure cargoes, and the crown's subjects could trade directly with foreign ports. Duties on goods imported from abroad were set at 24% ad valorem, except for British merchandise, which received special treatment. Exports were taxed at the rates then current in each captaincy. After the prince regent set up shop in Rio de Janeiro (March, 1808), a few modifications followed. To facilitate tax collection, foreign ships were restricted to Brazil's chief ports: Belém, São Luís, Recife, Salvador, and Rio de Janeiro, and they could not engage in intercoastal trade.[194]

The duration of the French occupation and the outcome of the war

---

[193] Manchester, "Transfer of the Court," pp. 154–163.
[194] Ibid., pp. 164–170.

were uncertain in 1808. Under the circumstances, the exchequer was the state's first priority, and revenues depended on the Brazilian economy. The court could no longer afford to protect theoretical Portuguese interests. Freedom of manufacturing and industry was declared in April and the bank of Brazil was founded in October. Portugal's Asian empire was now ruled from Rio de Janeiro; the city became a distribution center for Indian calicoes, spices, and Chinese porcelain sent directly from Goa and Macao.[195]

Free trade emancipated the Brazilian economy from its dependence on Lisbon, but politically Brazil was a colony of the crown's new headquarters, Rio de Janeiro, where a Portuguese state, not a Brazilian one, took root. The reconstituted Council of State remained the bastion of the titled nobility; the ministerial portfolios went to men, "who in experience, point of view, and loyalties were continental Portuguese."[196] To accommodate the swarm of exiled officeholders who streamed into the capital, new bureaucratic posts had to be created. Rio's bloated bureaucracy, compared to viceregal days, was partly a consequence of transferring old agencies to Brazil. The Royal Treasury and the Customs House had their Brazilian counterparts. But as local agencies became imperial in scope, their personnel doubled and tripled. The establishment of a superior High Court in Rio de Janeiro (Desembargo do Paço) made appeals to Portugal unnecessary; it also created jobs for displaced Portuguese magistrates.

Rio's sprawling bureaucracy reflected its special status as the imperial capital; elsewhere, the parent state added to but did not reorganize local administration. New comarcas, towns, and judicial tribunals swelled the ranks of the magistracy, who took up posts as ouvidores, juizes de fóra, and High Court judges. To handle the growing volume of Brazil's trade and collect the new import taxes, additional staff were required in each port. As always, there were appointments and promotions to be made in the militia and in the regular army units. Brazil finally had a central government: one which was run by the Portuguese and paid for by the Brazilians.[197]

Nineteenth-century Brazil did not become a series of separate republics. In part, this was because of the centralization imposed on the colony from Rio de Janeiro. The viceroy's powers outside his own bailiwick had been largely nominal, but the drift towards regional governments was now reversed, if only because the patronage system was run directly from

---

[195] Olga Pantaleão, "Aspectos do comércio dos domínios Portuguêses no período de 1808 a 1821," *Revista de História*, no. 41 (1960), pp. 91-104.

[196] Manchester, "Transfer of the Court," pp. 168-173.

[197] Alan K. Manchester, "The Growth of the Bureaucracy in Brazil, 1808-1821," *Journal of Latin American Studies* 4 (1972), pp. 77-83; idem, "Transfer of the Court," pp. 172-173.

Rio de Janeiro. The court's prolonged residence in Brazil (1808–1821) created an institutional base and a degree of legitimacy for the imperial capital that the viceregal heritage could not confer. In 1815 the prince regent elevated the status of Brazil to a kingdom; Rio de Janeiro now rivaled Lisbon.

The state apparatus provided a unifying force, but it also intensified competition for special privileges. Native sons resented the influx of Portuguese officeholders, because as customs officials, governors, and judges, the Portuguese could bestow favors on their clients. Outsiders were also difficult to control, and they knew little about the subleties of local politics. To placate disgruntled Brazilians, the crown lavishly distributed titles of nobility and testimonials, especially to the rural oligarchy. Still, the state's policies divided Brazilians into pro- and anti-Portuguese factions. Those captaincies whose elites had easy access to the spoils—Rio de Janeiro, São Paulo, Minas Gerais—remained in the crown's camp; the state consolidated its support in the central-south.[198]

The court redefined Brazil's economic status and upgraded its imperial stature, concentrating fiscal and judicial control in Rio's state agencies. Such innovations received a mixed reception, for the captaincy system and economic specialization had reinforced a strong sense of regionalism. In the Northeast, which was as removed from Rio de Janeiro as from Lisbon, the new order magnified the region's political subordination at the very moment free trade had released it from the interdependency of the Luso-Brazilian economy. This paradox was particularly sharp in Pernambuco, a captaincy that now purchased the bulk of its imports from Great Britain and sent its raw cotton directly to English markets.[199]

Between 1810 and 1815 Pernambuco's trade showed a substantial surplus, but Rio de Janeiro siphoned-off port taxes, dispatching in return a host of Portuguese officials, who "monopolized choice civil and military positions, and took the profits of the land."[200] Antagonism was rife, especially within the ranks of the urban officer corps. Inspired by their Spanish-American counterparts, the Pernambucan officers revolted. The governor and numerous Portuguese fled to Bahia. The 1817 rebellion was a momentary victory for disaffected Recife; widespread support from the powerful but cautious rural clans, however, never materialized. Since the court sanctioned their local autonomy, Brazil's powerful landowners

---

[198] Manchester, "Transfer of the Court," pp. 171–172; and Maria Odila Silva Dias, "The Establishment of the Royal Court in Brazil," in *Colony to Nation*, pp. 97, 102–130.

[199] Panteleão, *"Aspectos do comércio,"* pp. 100–101.

[200] Manuel de Oliveira Lima, *Dom João VI no Brasil*, 2 vols. (Rio de Janeiro, 1908), vol. 2, p. 790.

made unenthusiastic republicans. The rural clans sided with the crown, provoking a civil war in the countryside. By the time royal troops arrived, the rebels were bottled up in Olinda.[201]

The court's intrigues in the explosive politics of neighboring Spanish Republics magnified the split between regional interests in Brazil. Luso-Brazilian troops annexed the Banda Oriental, Uruguay in 1817, thus securing the north bank of the Plata estuary.[202] The gaucho cattlemen of Rio Grande do Sul and the Carioca merchants had an economic stake in the conquest; elsewhere, resentment against "heavy taxes and conscriptions [imposed by a war] contrary to their interests" intensified regional divisions and undermined loyalist support, especially in Pernambuco.[203] The prince regent forced his way into the explosive politics of the borderlands to further the dynastic ambitions of the House of Braganza. Similarly, the court's concessions to Great Britain, of singular importance to Brazil, reflected the short-term interests of an exiled monarchy.

The treaty of 1810 gave the English the privileges they had clamored for since the 1780s. Duties on all British goods, including cottons, were reduced to 15% ad valorem, which was slightly lower than the tax on Portuguese imports. The right of British merchants to reside in Brazil, denied for so long, was conferred, and they could engage in both wholesale and retail trade. The guarantees extended to British citizens by the treaty of 1654—freedom of religion, exemptions from the jurisdiction of Portuguese courts and police—were transferred to Brazil. In the words of the British ambassador, Lord Strangford, England secured "the Advantages She must ever derive from the Magnitude of Her Capitals, the more practiced Industry of Her Manufactures, and from the Great Extent of Her Navigation"; Britain had become "the Protector and Friend of Brazil."[204] For that friendship, Brazil paid in full. The old colonial system had kept the British out of Brazil. Now the merchants of Salvador and Rio de Janeiro faced an influx of competitors armed with their "Capitals." What the crown had granted with one hand, it now took away with the other. The freedom to manufacture was a worthless gesture when the greatest industrial nation in the world had preferential access to local markets. The treaty crushed the new workshops that had been set up since 1808.[205]

---

[201] Ibid., pp. 819–824, generally, see pp. 785–828. A powerful clan like the Feitosas, in the subordinate captaincy of Ceará, remained staunchly royalist; see Billy Jaynes Chandler, *The Feitosas and the Sertão dos Inhamuns: The History of a Family and a Community in Northeast Brazil 1700–1930* (Gainesville, 1972), p. 40.

[202] On the war in the Banda Oriental, see Manchester, *British Preëminence*, pp. 110–158.

[203] Oliveira Lima, *Dom João VI*, vol. 1, p. 330; idem, vol. 2, p. 785.

[204] Manchester, *British Preëminence*, p. 82.

[205] Ibid., pp. 81–91.

Portuguese merchants clung desperately to their shrinking trade with Brazil. The French had evacuated Lisbon in 1808, and the port was reopened. Although the French had counterattacked and were not defeated until 1811, Luso-Brazilian traders were back in business the next year, and trade picked up considerably after the war. Nonetheless, some trades, such as cotton, were irrevocably lost.[206] Compared with the period from 1800 to 1804, Luso-Brazilian trade was almost 70% less during the war years (1809–1813), and was still down 25% in the early post-war era (1815–1819).[207] To some extent Brazilian exporters returned to their Portuguese trading partners, but Luso-Brazilian merchants now had competitors, and Lisbon's position as an emporium was precarious. The crown no longer had a favorable balance of trade with its European customers.[208] Repeated French invasions destroyed domestic industries, and the commercial treaty of 1810, which also applied to Portugal, dismantled the protective edifice so painfully pieced together since 1750. Between the years 1796–1800 and 1815–1819 the value of Portugal's exported manufactures dropped 70%.[209] The crown tried to prop-up Luso-Brazilian trade by reducing taxes; without stronger protection, however, Portuguese shippers, exporters, and industrialists could not compete with the British. In 1821 Portuguese vessels accounted for only 30% of Brazil's transatlantic shipping.[210]

Concurrently, British merchants were busy replacing the Portuguese. The English were sellers and shippers, not buyers. England's exports to Brazil always exceeded its imports by a wide margin.[211] Britain was a good market for cotton, but not for sugar. Potentially, this was a serious handicap. To help the carrying trade, the British government let Brazilian reexports pass through its ports duty-free.[212] Given Portugal's reduced role in Brazil's trade, some British merchants, for example John Luccock, abandoned Lisbon for Rio de Janeiro. Luccock became a prominent retailer in the city, although it took him awhile to figure out the local market: "Let us have no drabs—we have no Quakers here," he wrote

---

[206] Macedo, *Bloqueio*, p. 44.

[207] The totals were 279 million cruzados (1800–1804), 90 million cruzados (1809–1813), and 214 million cruzados (1815–1819); see Godinho, *Prix et Monnaies*, p. 275.

[208] Ibid., p. 273.

[209] Macedo, *Problemas de história*, pp. 237–238.

[210] Simonsen, *História econômica*, p. 440. Balancing colonial and metropolitan interests without alienating British support was an impossible task; see Emília Viotti da Costa, "Political Emancipation," pp. 51–58.

[211] This pattern continued throughout the nineteenth century; see Richard Graham, *Britain and the Onset of Modernization in Brazil 1850–1914* (Cambridge, Eng., 1968), pp. 73–111.

[212] Manchester, *British Preëminence*, p. 81.

his agents.[213] In 1820 Brazil purchased over £2 million worth of British goods, primarily colorful, lightweight cottons; this was twice as much as the English sold in Spanish America, and only a third less than the United States absorbed. Brazil's exports to Britain, primarily cotton, did not cover the cost of imported English merchandise. In 1820 alone the deficit with England came to £700,000.

The 1810 treaty wedded Brazil's economy to British industry, placing new obstacles in the path of local merchants and small textile producers. Free trade, however, brought Brazil greater access to world markets, as well as cheaper imports, benefits that were not at all distasteful to Brazil's planters. But the treaty also struck a blow against the slave trade, directly challenging the planters.

Abolitionists had forced Parliament to abolish the English slave trade in 1807; terminating the practice elsewhere became an essential aspect of British diplomacy. The 1810 agreement restricted Brazilian slave trading to Portuguese colonies, a measure that threatened Bahia's longstanding and lucrative trade with the Costa da Mina. British cruisers seized 17 Bahian slave ships in 1811, an act that almost provoked rebellion against the prince regent. Although the British ultimately agreed to pay an indemnity, the prince regent ratified additional conventions that granted the right of search and seizure to the British.[214] The result was an illicit traffic British vigilance could not prevent, as the spectre of abolition only increased the demand for slaves. And the agreement reduced the prince regent's political support, particularly in the Northeast.[215]

What did the transplanted state gain from its concessions to England? The British guaranteed that they would preserve the Portuguese throne for the House of Braganza, and they were in a good position to do so, as occupied Portugal was virtually a British protectorate.[216] To Brazilian leaders the unpopular treaties, an imperial war in the Banda Oriental, and a bureaucracy catering to Portuguese officeholders posed a disturbing dilemma: How could Brazil's oligarchy control the state without resorting to revolution? Hipólito da Costa, a journalist, was adamant in his condemnation of the court's abuses and of the war, but was also an opponent of the Pernambucan revolt. The consequences of revolution were always "unpredictable and usually disasterous"; rebellion was "the

[213] Herbert Heaton, "A Merchant Adventurer in Brazil 1808–1818," *The Journal of Economic History* 6 (1946), pp. 1–23.

[214] Ibid., pp. 167–180.

[215] See Verger, *Flux et Reflux*, pp. 665–667; and Klein, *Middle Passage*, pp. 54–72.

[216] Oliveira Marques, *History of Portugal*, vol. 1, pp. 427–430.

worst method to improve the government of any country whatsoever."[217]
He advocated that reforms be implemented by the proper authorities, not
by rebels. Constitutionalism became the rallying cry of conservative
Brazilians disenchanted with absolutism. A national assembly with legislative powers could restrain royal authority without abandoning the his-
toric legitimacy that monarchy conferred on the central government;
constitutionalism provided an escape from the revolutionary dilemma, a
path between the old regime and the apparent disaster that republicanism
had inflicted upon Spanish America. In 1820, when uprisings in Lisbon
and Oporto forced the regency to convoke the long dormant Cortes, the
constitutionalist movement gained momentum; for the last time, the
theater of action shifted back to Lisbon.

When the queen had died in 1816 the prince regent became king of
Portugal and Brazil. To retain his right to the Portuguese succession,
however, he had to return to Lisbon as the Cortes demanded; pressured
by his courtiers and the Portuguese garrison stationed in Rio de Janeiro,
the king left Brazil in April, 1821. The crown prince, Dom Pedro, remained in Brazil as regent.

Theoretically Brazil was a kingdom on a par with Portugal. It possessed
an independent treasury, court system, and a bureaucracy managed by
Rio's state agencies. Was Brazil once again to be governed from Lisbon
and Rio de Janeiro's authority reduced?

The adjustments that Brazil's new status required of Portugal had
contributed to the 1820 revolt. The erosion of Luso-Brazilian trade was a
disaster for Portuguese shippers, exporters, and textile producers. The
liberal Cortes, despite its constitutionalism, was colonialist with respect to
Brazil. Although Brazilian deputies attended sessions, they could not
counter the attacks against their co-kingdom: the Cortes was determined
to shatter Rio's bureaucratic apparatus. The Cortes detached the provinces from Rio's jurisdiction, and ordered the dismantling of the central
treasury, the superior court, the board of trade, and the various tribunals
and governmental bodies established during Dom João's residency. By its
edict, Brazilians were excluded from political and military posts. Finally
the Cortes demanded Dom Pedro's immediate return to Portugal. The
Cortes intended to govern Brazil.[218]

---

[217] Jane Herrick, "The Reluctant Revolutionist: A Study of the Political Ideas of Hipólito
da Costa, 1774-1823," *The Americas* 7 (1950), pp. 176-177.

[218] See Alan K. Manchester, "The Paradoxical Pedro, First Emperor of Brazil," *Hispanic
American Historical Review* 12 (1932), pp. 179-180; C. H. Haring, *Empire in Brazil: A New
World Experiment with Monarchy* (1958: New York, 1968), pp. 11-15; George C. A.
Boehrer, "The Flight of the Brazilian Deputies from the Cortes Gerais of Lisbon, 1822,"

This dramatic reversal of the Cortes temporarily united Portuguese officeholders with Brazilian constitutionalists. The stake they both had in free trade and Brazil's political autonomy was too great to be easily surrendered. The spectre of slave revolts and the implications of republicanism in Brazil's racially stratified society made wealthy landowners staunch advocates of political stability. However, the uncertainty and disruption provoked by the Cortes posed a greater threat to established interests than did a break with Portugal. The upper classes—planters, businessmen, bureaucrats—endorsed independence because it was the safest way to preserve their authority. And they did so without challenging the monarchy, for the crown prince, Dom Pedro, had become the agent of independence.[219]

Supported by delegates from Rio de Janeiro, São Paulo, Minas Gerais, and Rio Grande do Sul, Dom Pedro defied the Cortes and refused to return to Portugal. In Rio de Janeiro the local militia forced the capitulation of the Portuguese garrison. A Brazilian assembly was convoked, and Dom Pedro toured São Paulo to build up support. Lisbon voided these actions and demanded the arrest of Pedro's seditious advisors; its orders reached the crown prince on September 7, 1822. Forthwith, he declared Brazil's independence. The hostility of the Cortes and the shrewd maneuvering of Brazilian leaders had prevailed.[220]

Independence had preserved the central government in Rio de Janeiro. Support for Dom Pedro predominated in those regions most likely to dominate the new state: Rio de Janeiro, São Paulo, and Minas Gerais. In the northern captaincies, Rio's pretentions were viewed as a potential threat to the local power structure, and enthusiasm was more cautious. Only after an improvised navy had forced Portuguese garrisons in the ports to withdraw, did the north recognize Dom Pedro as Emperor of Brazil.

Independence was no longer an issue in the vicissitudes of Brazilian politics. But the unresolved agenda was considerable. The 1820s and 1830s were turbulent decades—the character of the state, whose interests it should serve, what powers it should have, the balance between centralism and federalism, the rights of individual citizens—all these issues divided Brazilian politicians. Although he had convoked a national as-

---

Hispanic American Historical Review **40** (1960), pp. 497–503; and E. Bradford Burns, *A History of Brazil* (New York, 1970), pp. 107–110.

[219] Viotti da Costa, "Political Emancipation," pp. 67–70, 80–84; Silva Dias, "Royal Court," pp. 89, 100–101.

[220] Manchester, "Paradoxical Pedro," pp. 180–186; and Haring, *Empire in Brazil*, pp. 20–22.

sembly, Dom Pedro was a reluctant constitutionalist who clung to autocratic Portuguese advisors. To prevent the assembly from placing strong constitutional limits on monarchical government, Dom Pedro terminated its sessions and exiled its leaders. Brazil's first constitution (1824) was implemented by imperial decree. On his own authority, Dom Pedro renewed the commercial treaty of 1810 with Great Britain and agreed to abolish the slave trade as the price of British diplomatic recognition. Although he was Emperor of Brazil, he schemed to maintain his right to the Portuguese throne. Such actions alienated Brazilian constitutionalists. Not until the Brazilian party forced Dom Pedro's abdication in 1831 did the state actually become a Brazilian enterprise. Dom Pedro's young son, supervised by regents designated by the National Assembly, remained as heir apparent.[221]

The monarchy had helped forge Brazilian unity, but it did not prevent conflict between centralists and federalists, monarchists and republicans, the cities and the countryside, planters and merchants, liberals and conservatives. Such divisions occurred elsewhere in the Americas, and the control and organization of the state was usually the dominant issue. Even in the United States, that enlightened triumph of statecraft, the Union had to be preserved by force. In Brazil, after a decade of federalism and regional revolts, the National Assembly abruptly terminated the interregnum, initiating the long reign of Emperor Dom Pedro II and the Second Empire (1840–1889).[222] The throne became the means used by conservative centralists to preserve Brazilian unity and a strong state. By then, electoral politics had reshaped the state's organization. Nonetheless, the way the imperial order trained, selected, and appointed its bureaucrats, particularly its magistrates, consciously built on colonial

---

[221] See Burns, *History of Brazil*, pp. 105–132; Manchester, "Paradoxical Pedro," pp. 187–197; idem, *British Preëminence*, pp. 159–219; and Haring, *Empire in Brazil*, pp. 18–43. On British recognition, see Leslie Bethell, "The Emancipation of Brazil and the Abolition of the Brazilian Slave Trade: Anglo-Brazilian Relations, 1822–1826," *Journal of Latin American Studies* 1 (1969), pp. 115–147. While Dom Pedro was emperor the Brazilians were driven from the Banda Oriental and had to accept an independent buffer state (Uruguay) between the empire and Argentina.

[222] On the regional revolts of the 1830s, see the essays in *Dispersão e unidade*, História geral, vol. 2 (2); Haring, *Empire in Brazil*, pp. 44–62; Burns, A *History of Brazil*, pp. 120–124. Also, see Manoel Correia de Andrade, "The Social and Ethnic Significance of the War of the Cabanos," in *Protest and Resistance in Angola and Brazil*, ed. Ronald H. Chilcote (Berkeley, 1972), pp. 91–107; and Joseph L. Love, *Rio Grande do Sul and Brazilian Regionalism 1882–1930* (Stanford, 1971), pp. 13–15. A theoretical perspective is presented in Love, "An Approach to Regionalism," in *New Approaches to Latin American History*, eds. Richard Graham and Peter H. Smith (Austin, 1974).

precedents, and Rio de Janeiro continued to court the powerful rural clans.[223] Under the Empire, secessionist movements ended, and the onset of modernization began. A strong state took shape in Brazil sooner than in the Spanish American Republics, and this monarchical resolution endured for a half-century. But the rights of ordinary citizens were yet to be determined, and that struggle continues today.

---

[223] For example, see Thomas Flory, "Judicial Politics in Nineteenth-Century Brazil," *Hispanic American Historical Review* 55 (1975), pp. 664–692; and Eul-Soo Pang and Ron L. Seckinger, "The Mandarins of Imperial Brazil," *Comparative Studies in Society and History* 14 (1972), pp. 215–244.

VI

Imperial Reorganization after 1750: The Spanish Indies, English America, Brazil

Between 1750 and 1780 Spain, England, and Portugal reorganized their empires. The strategy each state adopted suggests how different their empires were. The Spanish Bourbons reasserted Madrid's control over a bureaucracy local interests had subverted. In English America, Parliament tried to impose new taxes, despite the opposition of colonial assemblies. And Portugal wanted to dislodge the English from the dominant role they played in Luso-Brazilian trade.

The bureaucracy of Spanish America, the assemblies of English America, and the export economy of Brazil provide touchstones for understanding crucial aspects in each region's development.

SPANISH AMERICA: THE BUREAUCRACY

As reconstructed from the viewpoint of the Council of the Indies, the Spanish bureaucracy dominates colonial history. In the seventeenth century, when lawyers indexed the Laws of the Indies, they had to sort their way through some 100,000 royal *cedulas*; the *Recopilación de Leyes*

205

(1681) reduced the code to four volumes and a modest 6500 entries.[1] The bureaucracy was adept at distributing royal cedulas, but less adept at enforcement; the breach between intention and performance was considerable. The bureaucracy points to the special character of Spanish America not because it was the state's all-powerful agent, but because of the unique problems it was intended to resolve.

The Conquest was the decisive event that separated Spanish America from other colonial ventures in the New World; it created an agenda for royal government that was not duplicated elsewhere. In two decades the king's American domain spread out from a foothold in the Caribbean to immense, populous territories on two continents. Against the contentious forces unleashed by Cortés and Pizarro, Spain held a uniform bureaucracy and a single faith. Only Spain carried out a spiritual conquest of the Americas.[2] In Brazil the Church never matched the zeal, influence, or wealth of Spanish America's clergy. In Massachusetts a Puritan's "plantation of religion" did not include Indians.

Spain assumed the administration of pre-Columbian economies and the responsibility for Indian salvation. The keys to Spanish America were Tenochtitlán and Cuzco, just as sugar was the key to Brazil, tobacco to Virginia, and religious dissent to New England; they opened very different doors to the future.

Compared to Mexico and Peru, colonization in Brazil and Virginia produced meager results. In 1570 Portuguese Brazil was still a series of struggling sugar plantations confined to enclaves in Pernambuco and Bahia; Indian labor had failed to provide a suitable work force. Englishmen starved in Virginia before they found a marketable commodity—tobacco—to prop-up the colony's faltering economy; only in the 1680s, as African labor began to replace indentured servants, did Virginia's planters manage to control the labor force to their satisfaction.[3] In Spanish America the conquest of a rich and diverse economic system run by a skilled and well-organized labor force dramatically resolved such problems. The Spaniards had only to reap the harvest and adjust the labor system to accommodate European-style enterprises: sugar, wheat,

---

[1] Charles Gibson, ed., *The Spanish Tradition in America* (New York, 1968), pp. 194–201.

[2] For example, see Lewis Hanke, *The Spanish Struggle for Justice in the Conquest of America* (Philadelphia, 1949); Robert Ricard, *The Spiritual Conquest of Mexico: An Essay on the Apostolate and the Evangelizing Methods of the Mendicant Orders in New Spain: 1523–1572*, trans. Lesley Byrd Simpson (1933: Berkeley, 1966); and John Leddy Phelan, *The Millennial Kingdom of the Franciscans in the New World* (Revised ed., Berkeley, 1970).

[3] Initial similarities are stressed in Richard R. Beeman, "Labor Forces and Race Relations: A Comparative View of the Colonization of Brazil and Virginia," *Political Science Quarterly* 86 (1971), pp. 609–636.

and vineyard cultivation, textile production, mining, and construction.[4] In regions where Indian labor was not so available, or native cultures less adaptable, Spanish expansion was retarded and colonization more difficult.[5]

How different Spain's New World would have been, if Cortés had encountered the Tupinambá instead of the Aztecs, if Pizarro had faced Powhathan instead of Atahualpa!

The wealth of the Spanish Indies went to those who controlled Indian labor, ran the mines, and circulated commodities. To get its share of the spoils, Spain had to intervene in the New World in a way that was largely irrelevant to the export economies that initially developed in Brazil, Virginia, and English Barbados. Sugar and tobacco were only valuable as exports sold in Europe, and they could be taxed when unloaded in the mother country's ports. In Spanish Mexico and the Andean sierra however, there were many ways for gold and silver to escape the royal coffers, and the conquistadors, who were now the masters of the Aztec and Inca empires, posed a direct challenge to the crown's authority. The Conquest drew the state bureaucracy into the vortex of Spanish-American history. How else could the crown tax disparate, relatively self-contained agricultural economies and monitor silver production? How else could it prevent the conquistadors from becoming too powerful, or protect the Indians from the kind of exploitation that had annihilated the peoples of the Caribbean?

To oversee American affairs, the crown imposed the bureaucratic structure of Castile on its new kingdoms. Tithes collected on the produce of Indian communities supported the clergy; taxes on silver production paid the salaries of Spain's university-trained judicial cadres.[6] The authority of viceroys, High Court magistrates, and crown-appointed corregi-

---

[4] For example, see William H. Dusenberry, "Woolen Manufacture in Sixteenth-Century New Spain," *The Americas* 4 (1947–1948), pp. 223–234; Woodrow Borah, *Silk Raising in Colonial Mexico* (Ibero-Americana 20) (Berkeley, 1943); idem, *New Spain's Century of Depression* (Ibero-Americana 35) (Berkeley, 1951); Robert C. Keith, *Conquest and Agrarian Change: The Emergence of the Hacienda System on the Peruvian Coast* (Cambridge, Mass., 1976); P. J. Bakewell, *Silver Mining and Society in Colonial Mexico, Zacatecas 1546–1700* (Cambridge, Eng., 1971); and John Howland Rowe, "The Incas Under Spanish Colonial Institutions," *Hispanic American Historical Review* 37 (1957), pp. 156–191.

[5] On the relationship between Indian culture and Spanish colonization, see Elman R. Service, "Indian-European Relations in Colonial Latin America," *American Anthropologist* 57 (1955), pp. 411–425; idem, "The *Encomienda* in Paraguay," *Hispanic American Historical Review* 31 (1951), pp. 230–252.

[6] See Woodrow Borah, "The Collection of Tithes in the Bishopric of Oaxaca During the Sixteenth Century," *Hispanic American Historical Review* 21 (1941), pp. 286–409. On the training of judges, see Richard L. Kagan, *Students and Society in Early Modern Spain* (Baltimore, 1974), pp. 77–158; idem, "Universities in Castile 1500–1700," *Past and Present* 49 (1970), pp. 44–71.

dores reduced the initial political significance of town councils and the broad mandates ceded to the first conquistadors.[7,8] The king refused to turn conquerors into hereditary officials, and launched an attack against the conquistadors' economic base, the *encomienda*.

The men who had risked their lives and fortunes to enlarge the king's American domains expected to be rewarded. In royal grants called *encomiendas*, the crown placed Indian communities in the hands of the conquistadors. The recipients (*encomenderos*) could draft labor from the communities for work in agriculture, construction, and mining. In return the encomenderos were responsible for the spiritual and temporal welfare of their Indian charges. By the 1530s, however, the contradiction of commissioning armed bands of Spaniards to conquer Indians and, at the same time, convert them, was all too apparent. To protect the Indians and curb the power of the encomenderos, the crown reorganized the labor system. The New Laws (1542) shifted the obligations of native communities assigned to encomenderos from labor services to an annual payment, often made in kind.[9] Since payments were adusted to the size of communities, the demographic decline that followed the Conquest reduced their value.

European diseases cut down the native labor force. Central Mexico's indigenous population fell from around 25 million in 1500 to about 2 million at the end of the century. Had the Indian civilizations retained their demographic strength, there would have been less room for Spaniards and their estates. As it was, neither the encomenderos nor the native nobility provided the kind of continuity initially envisioned. Although the surviving population was large enough to support Mexico's mining industry and provision the growing number of Spanish cities and towns, the future belonged to those enterprising men who secured title to vacated lands and built up productive estates. The economy still depended on the many tasks Indian workers performed, but the bureaucracy and Spanish employers organized the labor force in new ways. In the process, many encomenderos failed to make the transition from tribute collectors to estate owners.[10]

---

[7] The powers of a Spanish corregidor combined the functions of the Portuguese juiz de forá and the capitão-mór.

[8] A summary of this process can be found in Mario Góngora, *Studies in the Colonial History of Latin America* (Cambridge, Eng., 1975), pp. 67–126.

[9] On the importance of Spain's theological problems, see the essays by John H. Parry, Etenne Grisel, Robert L. Benson, John T. Noonan, Jr., and Lewis Hanke in *First Images of America: The Impact of the New World on the Old*, ed. Fredi Chiappelli, 2 vols. (Berkeley, 1976), vol. 1, pp. 287–304, 305–326, 327–334, 351–362, 363–390. On the New Laws, see Lesley Byrd Simpson, *The Encomienda in New Spain: The Beginnings of Spanish Mexico* (Berkeley, 1950), pp. 123–144.

[10] The population figures are from Woodrow Borah and Sherburne F. Cook, *The Aborigi-*

The social history of Mexico and Peru revolves around the shifting relationships between Spaniards and Indians, but the precise pattern— the interplay of competing labor systems; how, why, and to what extent native communities were pulled into the orbit of Spanish institutions, or conversely, escaped and retained a significant degree of autonomy— varied greatly from one region to another, even from one valley to the next.[11] The closer Indian communities were to Spanish urban centers the more likely it was that they had to specialize in the goods and services Spaniards valued. The Spaniards reorganized production, and the silver mines provided capital to set up a European-style economy.

The mining industry and the Indian communities were productive enough to support the bureaucracy, the clergy, and Spanish estate own- ers. Neither Brazil's sugar plantations, Virginia's tobacco farms, nor New England's towns provided such a broad base for replicating the social forms of the mother country. By the 1580s the Spanish crown had divided the Indies into 2 viceroyalties, 10 Audiencias, and hundreds of smaller administrative districts. Spanish America had 22 bishoprics, 11 convents, 119 monasteries, and 5 universities.[12] By 1600 over 300,000 Spaniards had migrated to the New World, where they established almost 200 towns with diverse economic functions. In the empire's town's, colonists, royal of- ficials, and the clergy reproduced a faithful version of Spain.[13]

---

nal Population of Central Mexico on the Eve of the Spanish Conquest (Ibero-Americana 45) (Berkeley, 1963), p. 88. On the shifting character of the labor system, see Charles Gibson, *The Aztecs Under Spanish Rule: A History of the Indians of the Valley of Mexico 1519–1810* (Stanford, 1964); idem, *Spain in America* (New York, 1966), pp. 48–67, 136–159; James Lockhart, "Encomienda and Hacienda: The Evolution of the Great Estate in The Spanish Indies," *Hispanic American Historical Review* 49 (1969), pp. 411–429; and Robert G. Keith, "Encomienda, Hacienda, and Corregimiento in Spanish America: A Structural Analysis," *Hispanic American Historical Review* 51 (1971), pp. 431–446.

[11] Compare Gibson, *Aztecs Under Spanish Rule*, with William B. Taylor, *Landlord and Peasant in Colonial Oaxaca* (Stanford, 1972); idem, "Landed Society in New Spain: A View from the South," *Hispanic American Historical Review* 54 (1974), pp. 387–413. On Peru, see Keith, *Conquest and Agrarian Change*; and Manuel Burga, *De la encomienda a la hacienda capitalista: El valle del Jequetepeque del siglo XVI al XX* (Lima, 1976). On the mixing of Spaniards and Indians in the cities, see John K. Chance, "The Urban Indian in Colonial Oaxaca," *American Ethnologist* 3 (1976), pp. 603–632. How different each region of Mexico was is stressed in the essays in Ida Altman and James Lockhart, eds., *Provinces of Early Mexico: Variants of Spanish American Regional Evolution* (Los Angeles, 1976).

[12] Jorge E. Hardoy and Carmen Aranovich, "Urban Scales and Functions in Spanish America Toward the Year 1600: First Conclusions," *Latin American Research Review* 5 (1970), pp. 67, 81–87.

[13] In 1600 Brazil had about 30,000 Portuguese colonists; the great Puritan migration (1620–1642) brought about 58,000 Englishmen to America. See Woodrow Borah, "The Mixing of Populations," in *First Images of America*, vol. 2, pp. 708–709. Also see Peter Boyd-Bowman, "Patterns of Spanish Emigration to the Indies Until 1600," *Hispanic Ameri-*

The epic of Spain in America commenced on a scale unknown anywhere else in the New World, and its first century reveals a movement and rhythm that places what happened in Spanish America beyond the reach of a simple categorization as colonization. By contrast, sixteenth-century Brazil had little in common with its Iberian neighbors. The few scattered Portuguese officials did not make a bureaucracy, a single bishop and some missionaries did not constitute an ecclesiastical hierarchy. But then, the problems each state faced in America diverged sharply.

The mansions, textiles, and crops Indian labor produced for Spanish estate owners did not benefit imperial trade, for Spanish-American agriculture was geared to domestic markets, not to exporting. To tax the local economy Spain had to send its bureaucrats to the Indies. Brazil, however, developed into a sugar plantation. In the 1530s, when Brazilian colonization began, Portugal had already diverted its bureaucratic energies to taxing trade and organizing the spice fleets. The king's factors in Africa and Asia channeled slaves and pepper back to Portugal. Brazil's sugar industry fit neatly into this scheme. The crown took its share of the colony's wealth, but it did not dispatch a corps of bureaucrats to obtain it. The king waited in Lisbon for sugar to be unloaded at the customs house. If sugar planters imported African slaves, Portuguese slave traders had to buy a license from the king. In one way or another, much of Brazil's wealth ended up in Lisbon. The Portuguese king did not need a Spanish-style bureaucracy.

The Spanish crown created an elaborate bureaucratic system that embraced both the city of God and the city of man. Wealth, status, and power implied alliances with the king's officials, for the bureaucracy balanced the fiscal concerns of the crown, the religious mission of the Church, and the economic interests of the colonists. Under the Spanish Hapsburgs, the colonial bureaucracy was a broker between local elites, the Indian communities, and the crown.[14] Even the collapse of Spain's trade with America did not weaken the ties between colonial society and the royal government.

Until the 1620s the great Spanish fleets that supplied the Indies and returned with cargoes of silver were the envy of other European states. During the periods 1616–1620 and 1646–1650, however, total tonnage on the voyage from Seville to the Indies dropped 60%.[15] At the same time,

---

can Historical Review 56 (1976), pp. 580–604; and Magnus Mörner, "Spanish Migration to the New World prior to 1810: A Report on the State of Research," in First Images of America, pp. 737–776. On Spanish society as a representation of the New World, see James Lockhart, Spanish Peru 1532–1560 (Madison, 1968).

[14] John Leddy Phelan, "Authority and Flexibility in the Spanish Imperial Bureaucracy," Administrative Science Quarterly 5 (1960), pp. 47–65.

[15] John Lynch, Spain Under the Hapsburgs, 2 vols. (Oxford, 1964–1969), vol. 2, p. 184.

the silver shipped back to Spain on the king's account fell from a total of 4.3 million pesos to 1.7 million; private consignments declined from 30 to 12 million pesos.[16] From 1650 to 1700, only 19 fleets reached Panama, the terminus for Spain's trade with Peru.[17] This collapse was due to Spanish America's growing self-sufficiency, contraband trade, and the mounting cost of royal government, rather than to a drop in silver production.

American bullion output continued to reach high levels; the problem was that less of it came back to Spain to finance trade. For example, between 1651 and 1739 the crown spent 80% of Lima's treasury receipts— 155 million pesos—on local administration and defense. Even more significant, Spanish America bought less from Spain. Now agriculturally self-sufficient, America did not need the grain, biscuits, wine, and olive oil that Spain exported. And domestic workshops in Mexico and Peru produced a wide assortment of textiles and other necessities. Thus, Spain's colonists retained a greater share of silver for their own use. They built ships, traded in regional commodities, developed agriculture, and invested their capital in mining, ranching, and textile workshops.[18] Finally, contraband trade siphoned off America's silver. Under the guise of slave traders, the Portuguese invaded the Spanish Indies via Buenos Aires, Cartagena, and Veracruz. From their bases in the Caribbean, Dutch and English traders competed with the Spanish fleets for the empire's markets.

By the eighteenth century the sporadic fleets leaving Cadiz were an

---

[16] Earl J. Hamilton, *American Treasure and the Price Revolution in Spain, 1501–1650* (1934: New York, 1965), p. 34.

[17] L. A. Clayton, "Trade and Navigation in the Seventeenth-Century Viceroyalty of Peru," *Journal of Latin American Studies* 7 (1975), p. 4.

[18] On silver production, see Bakewell, *Silver Mining and Society*, pp. 221–236, 259; D. A. Brading and Harry E. Cross, "Colonial Silver Mining: Mexico and Peru," *Hispanic American Historical Review* 52 (1972), pp. 545–579. Spain's Atlantic trade is analyzed in Pierre and Huguette Chaunu, *Séville et l'Atlantique (1504–1650)*, 8 vols. (Paris, 1955–1959); idem, "The Atlantic Economy and the World Economy," in *Essays in European Economic History 1500–1800*, ed. Peter Earle (Oxford, 1974), pp. 113–126; and Lynch, *Spain under the Hapsburgs*, vol. 1, pp. 147–166; idem, vol. 2, pp. 160–184. America's growing self-sufficiency is stressed by Lynch, ibid., vol. 2, pp. 194–224; Clayton, "Trade and Navigation," pp. 1–21; idem, "Local Initiative and Finance in Defense of the Viceroyalty of Peru: The Development of Self-Reliance," *Hispanic American Historical Review* 54 (1974), pp. 284–304; Richard Boyer, "Mexico in the Seventeenth Century: Transition of a Colonial Society," *Hispanic American Historical Review* 57 (1977), pp. 455–478; and Louisa Schell Hoberman, "Merchants in Seventeenth-Century Mexico City: A Preliminary Report," *Hispanic American Historical Review* 57 (1977), pp. 479–503. Self-sufficiency was mixed with depression in some sectors of the economy. Mexico's political conflicts (1620–1664) were linked to competition between Creole estate owners and bureaucrats over Indian labor. See Jonathan I. Israel, "Mexico and the 'General Crisis' of the Seventeenth Century," *Past and Present* 63 (1974), pp. 33–57.

indication that Spanish America had withdrawn from the Spanish trading system.[19] After 1700, Mexican silver production rose steadily, and Peruvian output started to climb in the 1730s.[20] Yet Spain's American trade did not make corresponding gains. Capital was diverted to the domestic economy, the bureaucracy, the Church, and contraband trades.[21]

Whereas Portugal and England could tax colonial staples unloaded in Lisbon and London, Spain's colonies did not send it any tropical product that compared to Chesapeake's tobacco or to Brazil's sugar. Venezuela, for example, sent more cacao to Mexico than to Spain.[22] Spanish estates, whether they produced sugar, tobacco, hides, wheat, wine, or olive oil, supplied only local and regional markets. The textile workshops of Quito and Lima sent their wares throughout the viceroyalty of Peru; industrial towns like Puebla and Queretaro supplied Mexican markets.[23] In 1750 Spanish America's economy was more diversified than that of either Brazil or English America—and this was precisely Spain's problem. The wealth of the New World did not come to Cadiz; it circulated in America.

Compared to Brazil and the English colonies, Spanish America was linked only in haphazard fashion to the Spanish economy. In 1750 the Brazil fleets were richer than ever; although they brought English goods, the ships were Portuguese and the trade was a Luso-Brazilian venture. That England's treasure came from foreign trade was the axiom of the realm's merchants.[24] The Navigation Acts, rather than instructions to

[19] Cadiz had replaced Seville as the main terminous for American trade.

[20] D. A. Brading, *Miners and Merchants in Bourbon Mexico 1763–1810* (Cambridge, Eng., 1971), pp. 129–158, 261–302; Brading and Cross, "Colonial Silver Mining," p. 578.

[21] On contraband trade, see Allan Christelow, "Economic Background of the Anglo-Spanish War of 1762," *Journal of Modern History* 18 (1946), pp. 22–36; idem, "Contraband Trade Between Jamaica and the Spanish Main, and the Free Port Act of 1766," *Hispanic American Historical Review* 22 (1942), pp. 309–343; Sergio Villalobos R., *Comercio y contrabando en el Río de la Plata y Chile 1700–1811* (Buenos Aires, 1965); and C. Earl Sanders, "Counter Contraband in Spanish America, Handicaps of the Governors in the Indies," *The Americas* 34 (1977), pp. 59–80.

[22] Roland Dennis Hussey, *The Caracas Company 1728–1784* (Oxford, 1934), pp. 91–121. Central America's indigo and Mexico's cochineal were the most important tropical exports. See Robert S. Smith, "Indigo Production and Trade in Colonial Guatemala," *Hispanic American Historical Review* 39 (1959), pp. 181–211. On cochineal, see Brian R. Hamnett, *Politics and Trade in Southern Mexico 1750–1821* (Cambridge, Eng., 1971), pp. 2–3, 24–40. Local textile industries also provided a domestic market for dyes.

[23] For example, see Jan Bazant, "Evolution of the Textile Industry in Puebla, 1544–1845," *Comparative Studies in Society and History* 7 (1964), pp. 56–69; John C. Super, "Querétaro Obrajes: Industry and Society in Provincial Mexico, 1600–1810," *Hispanic American Historical Review* 56 (1976), pp. 197–216; Brading, *Miners and Merchants*, pp. 17–18; and Fernando Silva Santisteban, *Los obrajes en el virreinato del Perú* (Lima, 1964).

[24] The classic text was Thomas Mun, *England's Treasure by Foreign Trade* (1664: London, 1933); also see Charles H. Wilson, "Trade, Society and the State," in *The Economy of*

royal governors, were the core of England's colonial policy. British merchants supplied the colonies with slaves and English manufactures; they
carried away Virginia's tobacco and the Caribbean's sugar. During the
years 1701–1705 and 1741–1745, the average value of England's colonial
trade summing both imports and exports, rose from £1.4 million to £3.4
million. During the same period, Spain's colonial trade never approached
the record levels set around 1600. Its outdated commercial monopoly
kept the colonies undersupplied. Foreign merchants bypassed Cadiz and
the fleets, carrying their wares directly to the Caribbean and Colônia. In
1761 a Spanish critic claimed that the illegal trade between Mexico and
British Jamaica was worth 6 million pesos a year.[25]

As the Indies withdrew from Spain's trading system, the crown relied
on the Church and the bureaucracy to maintain its authority. In 1750 an
accommodation between Spanish and colonial interests prevailed.[26] The
Janus-faced colonial bureaucracy paid homage to Spain while local entrepreneurs used the state's patronage system to their own advantage.
The Church had become a powerful economic institution dominated by
Creole interests. Everywhere, influential local groups had infiltrated the
bureaucracy; it was no longer the state's agent—or so it seemed to the
Bourbon reformers. To strengthen Spain, the Bourbon state had to
reconquer America; it began by cleaning up what it considered to be a
corrupt, inefficient bureaucracy. In so doing, it attacked the interests tied
to the old order. Pombal's program, on the other hand, jeopardized
British interests; in Brazil, he courted the colonial elite.

To José de Gálvez, visitor-general in Mexico (1765–1771) and Minister
of the Indies (1775–1778), Spain's weakness was a consequence of the way
colonial interests subverted the bureaucracy. Creole officeholders, tied in
multiple fashion to colonial society, did not make reliable bureaucrats.
Yet, Americans bought their way into the bureaucracy. They held crucial
positions in the treasury, and even dominated the most prestigious Audiencias.[27] Town councils and corporations, such as Mexico City's mer-

---

Expanding Europe in the Sixteenth and Seventeenth Centuries, The Cambridge Economic
History of Europe, vol. 4, eds. E. E. Rich and C. H. Wilson (Cambridge, Eng., 1967), pp.
487–550.

[25] Christelow, "Contraband Trade," p. 313. On England's trade with the colonies, see
Elizabeth Boody Schumpeter, *English Overseas Trade Statistics 1697–1808* (Oxford, 1960),
pp. 17–18.

[26] The character of the old Hapsburg regime is portrayed in John Leddy Phelan, *The
Kingdom of Quito in the Seventeenth Century: Bureaucratic Politics in the Spanish Empire*
(Madison, 1967); and Peter Marzahl, *Town in the Empire, Government, Politics, and Society
in Seventeenth-Century Popayán* (Austin, forthcoming).

[27] See Mark A. Burkholder and D. S. Chandler, *From Impotence to Authority: The
Spanish Crown and the American Audiencias, 1687–1808* (Columbia, Mo., 1977); idem,

chant guild, purchased the contracts for collecting sales taxes on domestic trade.[28] The corregidor, the crown's local representative, was really a businessman who owned his office; in Indian towns, with the support of merchant backers, he monopolized trade.[29] When Spaniards purchased the office they often hired Creoles to be their lieutenants, thus allying themselves with local families. On the provincial level, the Church was better organized than the state. But from the Bourbon perspective, the Church was no longer a dependable ally. In Mexico Creole clergy staffed the cathedral chapters, the universities, the monasteries, and the parishes; even the Jesuits were predominantly native sons. Besides supervising its great estates, the Church held permanent mortgages on much of the rural property in Mexico, and it was a major source of credit for the domestic economy.[30] The Brazilian Church never acquired such economic and political significance.

To make its empire more profitable, Spain had to reshape the bureaucracy. The Bourbon "revolution" focused on America, not Spain. Through removal, transfer, and new appointments, Peninsular judges gradually regained control over the Audiencias. A cadre of treasury officials, trained in Spain, took over the reorganized exchequer; tax farming was curtailed, and rates increased. The numerous corregimientos were collapsed into larger intendancies. To replace the corregidores and govern its new provinces efficiently, the crown appointed intendants, often military officers seasoned in Spain, and armed them with extensive authority. The traditional privileges of the Church came under attack, and the crown expelled the Jesuits. The preferred instrument for retaining American loyalty was the army rather than the clergy. By sponsoring more efficient government, the Bourbon state antagonized powerful corporate groups previously allied to the crown.[31]

"Creole Appointments and the Sale of Audiencia Positions in the Spanish Empire Under the Early Bourbons," *Journal of Latin American Studies* 4 (1972), pp. 187–206; and Leon G. Campbell, "A Colonial Establishment: Creole Domination of the Audiencia of Lima During the Late Eighteenth Century," *Hispanic American Historical Review* 52 (1972), pp. 1–25.

[28] For example, see Robert Sidney Smith, "Sales Taxes in New Spain, 1575–1770," *Hispanic American Historical Review* 28 (1948), pp. 2–37; and Miles Wortman, "Bourbon Reforms in Central America: 1750–1786," *The Americas* 32 (1975), pp. 222–226.

[29] On the commercial activities of the corregidores, see Brading, *Miners and Merchants*, pp. 47–50, 82–89; Hamnett, *Politics and Trade*, pp. 3–8, 41–55; Rowe, "Incas Under Spanish Colonial Institutions," pp. 161–179; and John R. Fisher, *Government and Society in Colonial Peru: The Intendant System 1784–1814* (London, 1970), pp. 1–29.

[30] See Brading, *Miners and Merchants*, pp. 91, 213–214, 217–218; Asunción Lavrin, "The Role of the Nunneries in the Economy of New Spain in the Eighteenth Century," *Hispanic American Historical Review* 46 (1966), pp. 371–393; and Michael P. Costeloe, *Church Wealth in Mexico* (Cambridge, Eng., 1967).

[31] Generally, see Brading, *Miners and Merchants*, pp. 33–92; and Hamnett, *Politics and*

Under Gálvez, Spanish imperial reform bore an unmistakable prejudice against Americans. The office of intendant went to a bureaucrat
tested for competence and loyalty in Spain. Creoles, said Gálvez, were
too bound by "ties of family and faction to provide disinterested, impartial
government."[32] While Gálvez was displacing Creole officeholders, Pombal was just as busy appointing Brazilians to the colony's treasury boards.
The question is not which approach was the best; the character of each
empire required different strategies. For Pombal, the problem was how to
create companies in Portugal that could compete with the British; purging
Brazil's bureaucracy was less germane. But in Spanish America, the role
the bureaucracy played had tremendous fiscal significance. Unless the
state could tax domestic production more effectively, America's wealth
would not reach Spain. When Gálvez set up a tobacco monopoly in
Mexico under the exchequer's management, the objective was to control
Mexican distribution, not to channel exports to Spain: the American
market was more profitable.[33] Between 1765 and 1782 revenues collected
in Mexico rose from 6 million to 19 million pesos. Higher taxes, efficient
collection, and new domestic monopolies paid off handsomely.[34]

Drawing more revenue to Spain was not just a matter of taxing local
production and the mining industry. Silver ended up in Cadiz only to the
extent that Spain exported sufficient merchandise to the colonies. The
fleet system, however, kept American markets undersupplied and prices
high, as departures were irregular and trade was confined to a few
privileged ports. The Cadiz monopoly, however, suited Mexico City's
great merchants; they bought out the Veracruz fleet with their silver, and
then hoarded the goods until market conditions were most favorable. The
fortunes they accumulated depended on scarcity and high profit margins.[35] Thus, restricted trade was a profitable business for the powerful

---

Trade, pp. 56–94. On the transformation of the Audiencias, see Burkholder and Chandler,
From Impotence to Authority, pp. 83–144; and Mark A. Burkholder, "From Creole to
Peninsular: The Transformation of the Audiencia of Lima," Hispanic American Historical
Review 52 (1972), pp. 395–415. The attack on the Church and the rise of the military is
discussed in Nancy M. Farriss, Crown and Clergy in Colonial Mexico 1759–1821 (London,
1968); and Lyle N. McAlister, The "Fuero Militar" in New Spain 1764–1800 (Gainesville,
1957).

[32] Brading, Miners and Merchants, p. 35.

[33] On the tobacco monopoly, see Herbert Ingram Priestley, José de Gálvez, Visitor-
General of New Spain (1765–1771) (Berkeley, 1916), pp. 142–155.

[34] Bourbon financial success was not limited to Mexico. See Fisher, Government and
Society, pp. 106–114; Wortman, "Bourbon Reforms in Central America," pp. 222–238; and
Herbert S. Klein, "Structures and Profitability of Royal Finance in the Viceroyalty of the
Río de la Plata in 1790," Hispanic American Historical Review 53 (1973), pp. 440–469.

[35] How Mexico City's merchants dominated the domestic economy is discussed in Brad-

merchant guilds in Cadiz, Lima, and Mexico City, but the reduced volume that resulted was prejudicial to the exchequer and to Spanish industries, which were cut off from direct access to American markets. Strengthening the Spanish economy meant restructuring colonial trade; it also meant dislodging the merchants who profited from the monopoly system.

Between 1765 and 1789 free trade was gradually extended throughout the empire. All Spain's major ports could now ship their goods directly to a growing list of American trading centers. Now Spain finally provided abundant, regular, and dependable shipping. In exchange for merchandise, Spanish America exported increasing quantities of indigo, cochineal, sugar, hides, and cotton. Free trade promoted exporting as the fleet system never had, and American markets were flooded with cheap Catalan textiles to the detriment of local industries. Because it was fundamentally different from monopolistic economics, free trade required a new kind of expertise. Mexico City's wealthy merchants, faced with aggressive competitors and reduced profit margins, diverted their capital to the mining industry, or bought out Creole estate owners.[36]

The Bourbon reforms did not cause the Spanish-American revolutions, but they did unleash reactions with complex local variations.[37] Since the economies in each region of the empire were diverse, so were the consequences of the crown's commercial program. Peruvian estate owners, for example, could not embrace exporting as did Guatemala's indigo producers and Cuba's sugar planters; prohibitive transportation costs cut Peru off from Spanish markets. Free trade, however, turned Buenos Aires into

---

ing, *Miners and Merchants*, pp. 95–128; and Hamnett, *Politics and Trade*, pp. 41–59, 95–120.

[36] Priestley, José de Gálvez, Visitor-General of New Spain, p. 385. On the varying effects of free trade, see Brading, *Miners and Merchants*, pp. 114–119; Hamnett, *Politics and Trade*, pp. 95–120; Franklin W. Knight, "Origins of Wealth and the Sugar Revolution in Cuba 1750–1850," *Hispanic American Historical Review* 57 (1977), pp. 231–253; Floyd S. Troy, "The Guatemalan Merchants, the Government and the *Provincianos* 1750–1800," *Hispanic American Historical Review* 41 (1961), pp. 90–110; Miles Wortman, "Government Revenue and Economic Trends in Central America, 1787–1819," *Hispanic American Historical Review* 55 (1975), pp. 251–286; John Lynch, *Spanish Colonial Administration 1782–1810: The Intendant System in the Viceroyalty of the Rio de la Plata* (New York, 1958), pp. 42–45, 121–122, 169; and Guillero Céspedes, "Lima y Buenos Aires: Repercusiones económicas y políticas de la creación del Vireinato del Plata," *Anuario de Estudios Americanos* 3 (1946), pp. 669–874. On the growth of the Spanish economy, see Jaime Vicens Vives, *Economic History of Spain*, pp. 471–604.

[37] The impact of the Bourbon reforms was by no means uniform. Compare Brading, *Miners and Merchants*, with Lynch, *Spanish Colonial Administration*; Troy, "The Guatemalan Merchants"; and Jacques Barbier, "Tradition and Reform in Bourbon Chile: Ambrosio O'Higgins and Public Finances," *The Americas* 34 (1978), pp. 381–399.

a flourishing port: Platine ranchers finally had a dependable outlet for their hides, and the city's merchants took over trade with Upper Peru—at Lima's expense. Under the monopoly system, Cadiz sent merchandise to Panama for distribution to Pacific ports. From Lima and Arica, goods had reached the sierra and finally trickled into Argentina. Free trade reversed the flow: Spanish exports now went directly to Buenos Aires for reshipment to Asunción, Córdoba, Tucumán, and Potosí.[38]

As it replaced Creole officeholders with Spanish bureaucrats, reorganized trade, curbed the privileges of the Church, and strengthened the military, the Bourbon state displaced old lines of influence and patronage. Such innovations often met with determined resistance. The crown's fiscal policies provoked tax revolts in a number of cities and serious rebellions in Colombia and Peru.[39] The loyalty of Creoles to the new order was uncertain; yet, fiscal reforms continued. The bureaucracy's role as mediator—the Hapsburg scheme—gave way to a less flexible conception of state and empire.[40]

By 1800 three decades of reform had disrupted virtually every sector of colonial society and seriously divided the bureaucracy. Traditional institutions such as the Audiencia, resisted innovations that challenged its authority. For example, the Audiencia undercut intendants by refusing to support them in local disputes, and it opposed the autonomy of the exchequer. The Spanish-American revolutions occurred in societies where comprehensive reforms produced shifting sources of power, wealth, and status. The intricate rearrangements this caused in the composition of the elite created a volatile social order.[41] When Napoleon usurped the Spanish throne, bureaucratic authority in America lost its moorings, and the empire collapsed.

---

[38] Susan Migden Socolow, "Economic Activities of the Porteño Merchants: The Viceregal Period," *Hispanic American Historical Review* 55 (1975), pp. 1–24.

[39] See Sergio Villalobos R., "Opposition to Imperial Taxation," in *The Origins of the Latin American Revolutions 1808–1826*, eds. R. A. Humphreys and John Lynch (New York, 1966), pp. 124–137; Lillian Estelle Fisher, *The Last Inca Revolt 1780–1783* (Norman, Okla., 1966); Leon G. Campbell, "The Army of Peru and the Túpac Amaru Revolt, 1780–1783," *Hispanic American Historical Review* 56 (1976), pp. 31–57; and John Leddy Phelan, *The People and the King: The Comunero Revolution in Columbia, 1781* (Madison, 1978).

[40] See John J. TePaske, "The Collapse of the Spanish Empire," *Lex et Scientia: The International Journal of Law and Science* 10 (1974), pp. 34–46.

[41] For example, see D. A. Brading, "Government and Elite in Late Colonial Mexico," *Hispanic American Historical Review* 53 (1973), pp. 389–414; Hamnett, *Politics and Trade*, pp. 95–147; Hugh Hamill, *The Hidalgo Revolt, Prelude to Mexican Independence* (Gainesville, 1966), pp. 18–52, 89–116; and John Lynch, *The Spanish American Revolutions, 1808–1826* (New York, 1973), pp. 1–36, 294–318.

Each region of Spanish America had its own kind of revolution, and independence produced a series of independent republics.[42] To view this as a fragmentation of the imperial order ignores the extent to which the bureaucracy masked the empire's diversity. Spanish America was an amalgam of different castes, elites, and economies, and free trade only accentuated the economic divergence.[43] Only the bureaucracy maintained the facade of a unified Spanish empire. By 1810, however, the Bourbon program had produced turbulent societies and a discredited government.

Desperate in-fighting, fueled by the divisions the reforms created, preceded independence. At stake was the control of a bureaucracy whose authority was precarious. The struggle could not be contained. Independence produced civil wars in the midst of revolution; the imperial bureaucracy was destroyed. Spanish Americans faced the difficult task of both dismantling and constructing governments. In Brazil and English America, independence preserved an established political order. But in Spanish American there was no assembly or exiled monarchy to oversee the transition from colony to nation. The centrifugal forces inherent in Spain's empire surfaced; a series of republics replaced the old regime.

ENGLISH AMERICA: THE ASSEMBLY

Iberian colonists did not go to America to escape their king or to find new ways to save their souls, for the basis of the state's authority was resolved before colonization commenced. In Spain and Portugal, the Cortes was unable to contest royal authority as successfully as did the House of Commons. Colonists in the Spanish Indies and Brazil did not question the role the Church played in their salvation. In Iberian America, the king's authority was reinforced by the Church. Post-Reformation England, however, spawned a multiplicity of contentious sects; in America English colonists made their own arrangements with God.

In the seventeenth century Englishmen assassinated their king and

---

[42] How different the revolutions were is discussed in Lynch, *The Spanish American Revolutions*; and Richard Graham, *Independence in Latin America: A Comparaitve Approach* (New York, 1972).

[43] On the mixing of populations, see John K. Chance, *Race and Class in Colonial Oaxaca* (Stanford, 1978); Magnus Mörner, *Race Mixture in the History of Latin America* (Boston, 1967); Eric R. Wolf, "The Mexican Bajío in the Eighteenth Century: An Analysis of Cultural Integration," *Middle American Research Institute Publications* 17 (1955), pp. 117–200; and Brading, *Miners and Merchants*, pp. 223–246.

exiled the royal family. American colonization occurred during England's century of revolution, a period of unprecedented social mobility, political conflict, and religious fervor. Puritan dissenters threatened the Anglican establishment; a new class of wealthy merchants and gentry defended the liberties of the House of Commons against a monarchy bent on expanding its authority and income. The Stuart kings did not have an Asian spice trade or American silver to help finance royal government. Frustrated in its battle to pry subsidies from a distrustful Parliament, the crown tried to impose taxes on its own authority; at stake was control of the state and the path to religious salvation.[44]

Locked in a battle at home, the crown had little time to worry about the constitutional implications of empire. Meanwhile dissident Puritans in Massachusetts had established a Godly Commonwealth where the king's authority was hardly recognized. Although Virginia had a royal governor, laymen ran the parish vestries, and the House of Burgesses rather than Anglican bishops took responsibility for the colony's ecclesiastical organization.[45] During the 1650s Cromwell and Parliament ruled without the king. Once the Stuart monarchy was restored however, the crown tried to establish stronger control over the colonies. To do so it had to challenge the authority already claimed by Puritan towns and local assemblies. In 1689 revolts in Massachusetts, New York, and Maryland thwarted the royal scheme to rule the colonies without the assembly.[46]

Authority in the Spanish Indies derived principally from holding a royal office or a position in the Church. In English America, however, the crown's bureaucrats did not run the colonies: aldermen, circuit judges, preachers, and assemblymen did. As the frontier expanded, the assemblies incorporated new townships and counties into the colonial political order.[47] The assembly's authority did not represent the crown's vision of empire; instead, it reflected the interests of those who ran the Godly Commonwealth and Virginia's tobacco economy. Even in Brazil's sertão,

---

[44] See Christopher Hill, *The Century of Revolution 1603–1714* (London, 1961); Lawrence Stone, "Social Mobility in England, 1500–1700." *Past and Present* **33** (1966), pp. 16–55; and Wilson, *England's Apprenticeship*, pp. 89–107.

[45] William H. Seiler, "The Anglican Parish in Virginia," in *Seventeenth Century America*, ed. James Morton Smith (Chapel Hill, 1959), pp. 119–142.

[46] See David S. Lovejoy, *The Glorious Revolution in America* (New York, 1972).

[47] For example, see Bailyn, *Origins of American Politics*, pp. 80–81; J. R. Pole, *Political Representation in England and the Origins of the American Republic* (London, 1966), pp. 33–148; Warren M. Billings, "The Growth of Political Institutions in Virginia, 1634–1676," *William and Mary Quarterly* **31** (1974), pp. 225–242; and B. Katherine Brown, "The Controversy Over the Franchise in Puritan Massachusetts, 1954–1974," *William and Mary Quarterly* **33** (1976), pp. 212–241.

powerful landowners could claim the loyalty of their retainers, but not the allegiance of an entire province.

If local institutions run by local men became the hallmark of English colonization, such "democracy" bore bitter fruit for the thousands of indentured servants lured to Virginia. Those who had become successful planters used their control of the assembly and the county courts to systematically defraud and overwork their servants. Before the 1670s opposition to the laws passed by Virginia's assembly did not come from the crown; it came from overtaxed, discontented freedmen who wanted to dislodge the oligarchy that monopolized local offices, speculated in land, levied taxes, and narrowed the franchise. Bacon's Rebellion, the most serious colonial conflict before the American Revolution, was the result of this discontent.[48] In Virginia there were no Franciscans or Jesuits to protect the Indians, no royal judges to run the labor system.

Only in New England did a dissident, alienated community set up a Godly Commonwealth to stand against the decadence of the king's court. They came to establish a "plantation of religion," not a "plantation of trade." The ordered, spiritual life of the Puritans was an intense, personal response to the social disorder that prevailed in England. To the Puritans the notion that unrestrained, economic self-interest produced the common good was heresy. They did not come searching for gold, new export crops, or social mobility. They sought to construct a society of ordered relationships, "the kind of society that God demanded of all his servants but that none had yet given him."[49]

New England was run by theologians, Virginia by planter capitalists. That two such disparate offshoots were children of the same parent reflects the potent forces unleashed by the English Reformation. How planters and Puritans ended up on the same side of the American Revolution reflects the common stake they had in defending the liberties of the assembly. Despite their religious and economic divisions, English Americans had built their political systems around the threat they thought royal government posed to local institutions.[50] In Virginia slavery stabilized the

---

[48] See Edmund S. Morgan, *American Slavery–American Freedom: The Ordeal of Colonial Virginia* (New York, 1975), pp. 215–270; and Bernard Bailyn, "Politics and Social Structure in Virginia," in *Seventeenth-Century America: Essays in Colonial History*, ed. James Morton Smith (Chapel Hill, 1959), pp. 90–115.

[49] Perry Miller, *Nature's Nation* (Cambridge, Mass., 1967), p. 33; Edmund S. Morgan, *The Puritan Dilemma: The Story of John Winthrop* (Boston, 1958), pp. 46–47; and Michael Walzer, "Puritanism as a Revolutionary Ideology," *History and Theory* 3 (1961), pp. 59–90; idem, *The Revolution of the Saints: A Study in the Origins of Radical Politics* (New York, 1971).

[50] In early New England even elected governors were suspect. See T. H. Breen, "Persis-

colony's explosive social order. During the 1680s planters turned to exploiting slaves rather than other Englishmen; the assembly made peace with the common planter, reducing taxes and enlarging the franchise.[51] Although colonial politics was often intensely factional, rivals fought to control, not disband, the Lower House. Once in power, the very men who attacked the assembly's alleged abuses became staunch supporters of its authority. By 1750 the assembly had a legitimacy in local society that no cabildo or câmara could match; its strength reached into New England's towns and Virginia's counties.[52] Politically ambitious men often preferred election to the assembly rather than an office in the crown's service.

Like Brazil, English America had an export economy. Navigation Acts made England the required depôt for many colonial exports and for all European goods shipped to the colonies.[53] The credit English and Scottish merchants extended to Virginia's planters, and their ability to market exports, kept the tobacco business booming. Tobacco exports to Great Britain climbed from an average of 57 million pounds a year (1740–1744) to 82 million (1760–1764).[54] Although Massachusetts and Pennsylvania

tent Localism: English Social Change and the Shaping of New England Institutions," *William and Mary Quarterly* 32 (1975), pp. 3–38.

[51] On the character of this accommodation, see Morgan, *American Slavery American Freedom*, pp. 338–387; and John C. Rainbolt, "The Alternation in the Relationship Between Leadership and Constituents in Virginia, 1660–1720," *William and Mary Quarterly* 27 (1970), pp. 411–434. In the 1760s, however, religious movements provided a new focus for those excluded from genteel society. Revolutionary leaders, such as Madison, quickly embraced religious toleration. See Rhys Issac, "Evangelical Revolt: The Nature of the Baptists' Challenge to the Traditional Order in Virginia, 1765 to 1775," *William and Mary Quarterly* 31 (1974), pp. 345–368.

[52] Although this was generally the case, some assemblies ignored and alienated their western constituencies. See John S. Bassett, "The Regulators of North Carolina (1765–1771)," *American Historical Association Annual Report*, (1894), pp. 140–212; and James P. Whittenburg, "Planters, Merchants, and Lawyers: Social Change and the Origins of the North Carolina Regulation," *William and Mary Quarterly* 34 (1977), pp. 215–238.

[53] On the content and enforcement of the Navigation Acts, see Charles M. Andrews, *England's Commercial and Colonial Policy*, The Colonial Period in American History, 4 vols. (1934–1938), vol. 4 (1938: New Haven, 1964); Lawrence A. Harper, *The English Navigation Laws* (New York, 1939); and Thomas C. Barrow, *Trade and Empire, The British Customs Service in America 1660–1775* (Cambridge, Mass., 1967). The debate over the burdens this system placed on colonial development is summarized in Roger L. Ransom, "British Policy and Colonial Growth: Some Implications of the Burdens of the Navigation Acts," *Journal of Economic History* 28 (1968), pp. 427–440.

[54] Jacob M. Price, *France and the Chesapeake: A History of the French Tobacco Monopoly, 1674–1791, and of Its Relationship to the British and American Tobacco Trades*, 2 vols. (Ann Arbor, 1973), vol. 2, pp. 843–844. On the character of the tobacco trade, also see Price, "The Economic Growth of the Chesapeake and the European Market, 1697–1775," *Journal of Economic History* 24 (1964), pp. 496–511; idem, "The Rise of Glasgow in the Chesapeake

sent few of their exports "home," they provisioned England's Caribbean sugar colonies with grain, lumber, meat, and fish. During the 1750s Caribbean demand provided the stimulus for rising export prices in the northern colonies. Although mainland ports in English America carried on brisk local exchanges, it was the export sector, rather than coastal trades, that sustained growth.[55] With the profits they made as planters, merchants, and farmers, colonists purchased a growing assortment of British goods: the value of Britain's export trade with the mainland colonies increased from an average of £738,000 (1741–1745) to £1.8 million (1761–1765).[56] During the middle decades of the eighteenth century, colonial trade was the principal dynamic element in England's industrial growth.[57] If England had a colonial problem in the 1760s, it did not stem from the way trade was organized: colonial commerce largely conformed to the mercantilistic axioms embodied in the Navigation Acts.[58] The problem with English America was its peculiar politics, in particular, its assemblies.

Portugal collected the bulk of its Brazilian revenues by taxing trade in Lisbon; Spain profited most from the taxes it levied directly in America. England's strategy was more like Portugal's than Spain's.[59] Since Britain

---

Tobacco Trade, 1707–1775," *William and Mary Quarterly* 11 (1954), pp. 179–199; idem, "The Tobacco Adventure to Russia: Enterprise, Politics, and Diplomacy in the Quest for a Northern Market for English Colonial Tobacco, 1676–1722," *Transactions of the American Philosophical Society* 51 (1961), pp. 5–110; and J. H. Soltow, "Scottish Traders in Virginia, 1750–1775," *Economic History Review* 12 (1959), pp. 83–98.

[55] See Marc Egnal, "The Economic Development of the Thirteen Continental Colonies, 1720–1775," *William and Mary Quarterly* 32 (1975), pp. 191–222. On the structure of colonial trade, see James F. Shepherd, "Commodity Exports from the British North American Colonies to Overseas Areas, 1768–1772: Magnitudes and Patterns of Trade," *Explorations in Economic History* 8 (1970), pp. 5–76; James F. Shepherd and Samuel H. Williamson, "The Coastal Trades of the British North American Colonies, 1768–1772," *Journal of Economic History* 32 (1972), pp. 783–810; and James F. Shepherd and Gary M. Walton, *Shipping, Maritime Trade, and the Economic Development of Colonial North America* (Cambridge, Eng., 1972).

[56] Schumpeter, *English Overseas Trade Statistics*, p. 17.

[57] Ralph Davis, "English Foreign Trade, 1700–1774," *Economic History Review* 15 (1962), pp. 289–290.

[58] Oliver M. Dickerson, *The Navigation Acts and the American Revolution* (1951: New York, 1963), pp. 63–91; and Harper, *English Navigation Laws*, pp. 253–274. French trade with the West Indies, although legal, was variously approved, tolerated, and opposed by British authorities. See Richard Pares, *War and Trade in the West Indies 1739–1763* (Oxford, 1936); and Dorothy Bourne Goebel, "The 'New England Trade' and the French West Indies, 1763–1774: A Study in Trade Policies," *William and Mary Quarterly* 20 (1963), pp. 331–372.

[59] One of England's advantages was its ability to tax a more commercialized domestic economy. For a discussion of the relationship between the state and the economy it taxes, see Gabriel Ardant, "Financial Policy and Economic Infrastructure of Modern States and

was the entrepôt for colonial trade, it made more sense to tax tobacco when unloaded in London or Glasgow than to attempt the task in America. If sold in England, tobacco was taxed again as an item of popular consumption.[60] To keep colonial staples competitive however, England rebated duties on sugar and tobacco reexported to foreign markets. Similarly, exported British merchandise was lightly taxed. America was valuable to England because it was a good customer and supplier, not because it was a good taxpayer. Except for tobacco marketed in Britain, Parliament usually avoided excessive taxation on the empire's commercial traffic; experience showed that high duties only encouraged smuggling.[61] Besides, the realm's merchants and the West Indian sugar lobby, both powerful in the House of Commons, argued for keeping duties low.[62] By the 1760s English land taxes and the excise on domestic necessities consumed at home far exceeded the state's revenues from duties on overseas trade.[63]

The duties the crown managed to collect in America did not even cover salaries for customs officials.[64] To pay royal officials such as the governor, the crown depended on taxes authorized by the assemblies and collected under local supervision; without Parliament's approval, the executive was powerless to tax the colonies.[65] Although governors were hard-pressed financially by recalcitrant assemblies, the crown was reluctant to invoke Parliament's intervention; it did not want the House of Commons scrutinizing its patronage system, for rewarding supporters with colonial posts was one way the executive kept Parliament in line. Except for matters of trade, powerful Whig ministers were determined to prevent

Nations," in *Formation of National States in Western Europe*, ed. Charles Tilly (Princeton, 1975), pp. 164–242.

[60] See Price, *France and the Chesapeake*, vol. 2, pp. 840–841.

[61] Charles H. Wilson, *England's Apprenticeship 1603–1763* (London, 1965), p. 319. A notable exception was the high tax on the tea imported by the British East India Company, which became a prime target for smugglers, both in England and in the colonies. See Hoh-cheung and Lorna M. Mui, "Smuggling and the British Tea Trade before 1784," *American Historical Review* 74 (1968), pp. 44–73; and Barrow, *Trade and Empire*, pp. 149–150. The stiff duty on the molasses trade between the French West Indies and New England was also evaded; see Gilman Ostander, "The Colonial Molasses Trade," *Agricultural History* 30 (1956), pp. 77–84.

[62] On merchants and customs duties, see William Kennedy, *English Taxation 1640–1799* (London, 1913), pp. 95–150. The influence of the sugar lobby is discussed in Richard B. Sheridan, *Sugar and Slavery, An Economic History of the British West Indies 1623–1775* (Baltimore, 1973), pp. 54–74.

[63] Wilson, *England's Apprenticeship*, pp. 313–320.

[64] Barrow, *Trade and Empire*, p. 74.

[65] For example, see Marvin L. Michael Kay, "The Payment of Provincial and Local Taxes in North Carolina, 1748–1771," *William and Mary Quarterly* 26 (1969), pp. 218–240.

opponents in the House of Commons from meddling in colonial affairs.[66] The Whig strategy was to pay for colonial administration with the taxes levied by each assembly. As ministers Walpole and Newcastle realized, tampering with this arrangement was likely to provoke a constitutional crisis in America.[67] In the colonies, the crown had to reckon with a well-organized opponent—the assembly.

England's victory in the Seven Years War (1757–1763) made the Whigs' fiscal system untenable. At the Peace of Paris (1757–1763) France ceded Quebec, the Great Lakes, and the Mississippi Valley to the English. Britain now had an expanded American empire that placed additional burdens on a debt-ridden treasury: the national debt, much of it acquired in defense of the American colonies, had climbed from £78 million in 1757 to £132 million.[68] To defray the cost of empire, the king's ministers, with Parliament's approval, tried to raise modest revenues in the colonies; the consequence was the American Revolution.

Resistance to taxation occurred everywhere in the Americas. The Bourbons had to quell the tax rebellions that their fiscal policies helped create; the fifths could not be collected in Minas Gerais without the dragoons. But the Bourbons, whose objective went far beyond the modest remedies Parliament proposed, succeeded, whereas the English government failed. The crucial difference was the structure of colonial politics.

Throughout the eighteenth century the embattled assembly held center stage in colonial politics; it resisted the evil designs, the threats to liberty and property, that a patronage-ridden executive apparently posed to the rights of Englishmen. To prevent influence and patronage from destroying liberty, the assemblies kept a firm grip on local taxation and expenditures. The Lower House insisted on nominating or appointing the officials who collected, held, and paid out provincial revenues; it fixed all fees by statute, thus preventing the governor and his council from setting

---

[66] See Bernard Bailyn, *The Origins of American Politics* (New York, 1967), pp. 28–29, 88–91; and Stanley Katz, *Newcastle's New York: Anglo-American Politics 1732–1753* (Cambridge, Mass., 1968).

[67] Sir Robert Walpole was First Minister from 1721 until 1742; for a brief summary of his colonial policy, see Jack P. Greene, ed., *Great Britain and the American Colonies 1606–1763* (Columbia, S. C., 1970), pp. xxxi–xli. The Board of Trade took a more aggressive stance, but its position was undercut by the rise of the Cabinet vis-a-vis the old Privy Council. While he was Secretary of State for the Southern Department (1724–1748), the Duke of Newcastle, rather than the Board of Trade, controlled colonial patronage. See Oliver M. Dickerson, *American Colonial Government 1696–1765: A Study of the British Board of Trade in Its Relation to the American Colonies: Political, Industrial, Administrative* (Cleveland, 1912). On Newcastle's attitudes toward colonial government, see Bernhard Knollenberg, *Origins of the American Revolution 1759–1766* (New York, 1961), pp. 21–24.

[68] Wilson, *England's Apprenticeship*, p. 313.

them by executive order. The governor could appoint judges, but only the Lower House could pay their salaries; it did so only on an annual basis and by name. Consequently, most governors had to select judges who had the support of the assembly. By using a variety of stratagems, the Lower House successfully curbed the crown's patronage powers.[69]

How and to what extent the Lower House gained ground at the expense of the governor and his council varied. But by the 1760s most of the assemblies exercised powers that far exceeded the mandate contained in the governors' instructions. The assemblies' control of the pursestrings checked the crown's inflated claims. A financially independent executive, supported by Parliament's willingness to tax Americans, would pose a mortal danger to the assembly's political role and to the interests it defended.[70] What Parliament viewed as an intelligent program to finance an expensive empire colonial leaders viewed as a conspiracy to destroy home rule. An executive that could levy and spend taxes at its own discretion could expand the crown's pernicious influence; its grasp would soon spread to the judiciary, the assembly, the county, and the town. Liberty would be extinguished—or so it appeared on the American side of the Atlantic.

Underlying the events that stretched from the Stamp Act to Lexington and Concord was a dilemma. How could the crown reorganize colonial administration except at the assembly's expense? Suppressing tax revolts is the state's business. But in this case, the assembly had become more legitimate than its rival, the royal executive. England's colonial problem

---

[69] On colonial ideology and the assembly's growing power, see Bailyn, *Origins of American Politics*; idem, *The Ideological Origins of the American Revolution* (Cambridge, Mass., 1967); Leonard Labaree, *Royal Government in America* (Princeton, 1930), pp. 172–419; Jack P. Greene, "The Role of the Lower House of Assembly in Eighteenth-Century Politics," *Journal of Southern History* 37 (1961), pp. 451–474; idem, *The Quest for Power: The Lower House of Assembly in the Southern Royal Colonies 1689–1776* (Chapel Hill, 1963); idem, "Political Mimesis: A Consideration of the Historical and Cultural Roots of Legislative Behavior in the British Colonies in the Eighteenth Century," *American Historical Review* 75 (1969), pp. 337–360; Pole, *Political Representation*, pp. 3–382; and J. G. A. Pocock, "Machiavelli, Harrington, and English Political Ideologies in the Eighteenth Century," *William and Mary Quarterly* 22 (1965), pp. 549–583. At times, the governor and his cronies did manage to control the assembly; see Jere R. Daniell, "Politics in New Hampshire Under Governor Benning Wentworth, 1741–1767," *William and Mary Quarterly* 23 (1966), pp. 76–105.

[70] How various tax schemes threatened colonial interests is discussed in Dickerson, *Navigation Acts*, pp. 161–300; Knollenberg, *Origins of the American Revolution*, pp. 131–171; Arthur M. Schlesinger, *The Colonial Merchant and the American Revolution 1763–1776* (1918: New York, 1939); Edmund S. Morgan and Helen M. Morgan, *The Stamp Act Crisis: Prologue to Revolution* (Chapel Hill, 1953); and Robert J. Chaffin, "The Townshend Acts of 1767," *William and Mary Quarterly* 27 (1970), pp. 90–121.

did not stem from the character of the empire's trade; instead, it proceeded from a political culture organized specifically to oppose executive authority.

In English America the revolution preserved the social order the assembly represented; the problem of authority was already resolved. For Spanish Americans, who should govern, and how, was at the heart of the rebellions; the revolutions were also civil wars. Although English America had loyalists who supported the crown, they lacked sufficient strength to seriously challenge independence; most of the time, colonists fought the crown rather than each other.[71] The assembly helped organize the revolution and created the Continental Congress; later, state constitutions provided a model for the Republic.[72] During the eighteenth century, the pattern of colonial dependency changed more completely in the United States than anywhere else in the Americas; backed by a strong state, industrialists could defend domestic industries. Westward expansion helped delay the conflict between planters, manufacturers, and small farmers; ample land, credit, and new markets provided resources each could exploit. In Spanish-American republics like Mexico, there was no unclaimed frontier: liberals and conservatives battled over how to reorganize the domestic economy.[73] The revolutions produced weak states whose resources were appropriated by foreign entrepreneurs: Cortés returned in the form of the British.

CONCLUSION

Brazil: The Export Economy

In 1600 Brazil was a sugar plantation. Exporting fit the crown's fiscal scheme, for the state was organized to tax trade; its allies in Brazil were the planters. Compared to royal government in Spanish America, Brazil's bureaucracy was skimpy. Except in the ports, bishops and bureaucrats were scarce. In the countryside, the crown simply commissioned powerful landowners to raise militia units. Minas Gerais and its gold mines did

---

[71] How the loyalists misjudged American politics is discussed in Bernard Bailyn, *The Ordeal of Thomas Hutchinson* (Cambridge, Mass., 1974). The loyalist challenge is analyzed in Robert McCluer Calhoon, *The Loyalists in Revolutionary America 1760–1781* (New York, 1973).

[72] See Gordon S. Wood, *The Creation of the American Republic, 1776–1787* (1969: New York, 1972).

[73] See John H. Coatsworth, "Obstacles to Economic Growth in Nineteenth-Century Mexico," *American Historical Review* 83 (1978), pp. 80–100.

draw the king's men into the interior. In the region's most important mining centers, however, the crown merely duplicated the kind of government established in the ports. Gold production only reinforced the import–export syndrome.[74]

Spanish America had turned to domestic markets long before inter-colonial trade became significant in Brazil or in England's mainland colonies.[75] In the 1770s Luso-Brazilian trade contracted when gold exports declined, suggesting how export-oriented the colonial economy was. By contrast, in the Spanish Indies, trade with Spain dropped sharply during the 1630s, before the fall in silver production. Thereafter, despite substantial bullion output, Spain's American trade did not recover until the Bourbon reforms.

Each imperialist nation had to counter the centrifugal forces colonization implied. Brazil's export economy tied the colony securely to Portugal. Economically, this system reached deep into the sertão, since ranchers supplied the plantations with dried meat, hides, and oxen. In the north, Pombal's companies tied Pará and Maranhão more effectively to the Portuguese economy; during the 1790s Rio Grande's beef and wheat exports helped feed Salvador and Recife—planters were too busy producing sugar, tobacco, and cotton to worry about provisioning the cities.

The Luso-Brazilian economy was a shared enterprise. The division between merchants and planters was bridged by men who had a stake in both enterprises, or who participated indirectly, because of the social bonds that often linked both groups. Brazil's planters necessarily had connections in the ports; their livelihood depended on transatlantic trade. English America also had its merchant-planters. In Charleston, South Carolina, as in Salvador, immigrant businessmen often ended their careers as local politicians and members of the planter elite.[76] In Spanish America, however, most estate owners supplied domestic markets; they were isolated from Atlantic trade—one factor, among many, that kept Creole landowners and Peninsular merchants apart.

The productivity of Brazil's mines and plantations depended upon slave labor. During the eighteenth century the slave trade became a Brazilian-

---

[74] See Caio Prado, Junior, *The Colonial Background of Modern Brazil*, trans. Suzette Macedo (Berkeley, 1971), pp. 141–147.

[75] See Woodrow Borah, *Early Trade and Navigation Between Mexico and Peru* (Ibero-Americana 38) (Berkeley, 1954); and Eduardo Arcila Farías, *Comercio entre Venezuela y México en los Siglos XVI y XVII* (México City, 1950).

[76] See Eulália Maria Lahmeyer Lobo, "O comércio atlântico e a comunidade de merca-dores no Rio de Janeiro e em Charleston no século XVIII," *Revista de História*, no. 101 (1975), pp. 92–96, 101.

centered enterprise run from Salvador and Rio de Janeiro. Brazil's exports—tobacco, sugar-cane brandy, and gold—paid for slaves. One reason why Portugal's over-taxed trading system survived was because Brazil had a dependable source of slaves, and profits from the slave traffic stayed within the Luso-Brazilian economy. Only in Brazil was the slave trade a colonial business. Spanish Americans had to purchase their slaves with silver, and from foreign suppliers.[77] The English slave trade was managed by English merchants operating out of British ports.[78]

Brazil's royal government rarely challenged entrenched colonial interests. The crown protected its planters and miners, exempting them from foreclosure. The bureaucracy's job was to collect port taxes and make sure exports got back to Portugal. Even when gold provided new revenues (1720–1750), the crown did not set up a bureaucracy on the Spanish model: no vice-royalties, High Courts, or bishoprics were added. The crown levied taxes, but local tax farmers ran the business. When the king sent judges to supervise the colony, Brazilian students went to Coimbra and came back as magistrates. Brazil's planters did not have assemblies, but they had their own militia units. Although the state church was weak, local brotherhoods organized religious life. Neither the crown's authority nor the institutional strength of the Church reached into the countryside. On the local level, rural clans formed alliances that stretched into the cities and involved the bureaucracy. Such networks protected powerful families; they did not provide a forum or an ideology for independence. Although the state's authority was segmented, so too was that of its potential adversaries.[79]

For Pombal, Portugal's colonial problem had little to do with Brazil: in the 1750s the Brazil fleets were richer than ever, and Luso-Brazilian trade was booming. But at the core of that prosperity was a simple exchange of Brazil's gold for England's textiles. The Portuguese were reduced to commission agents for English merchants who supplied goods on credit. The profits from Portugal's empire ended up in London. The problem was not how to change Brazil, but how to change Portugal. Pombal's reforms challenged the old order in Portugal, not Brazil's planters. By

---

[77] Between 1713 and 1750 the British held the Spanish *asiento*; later, the Bourbons replaced them with Spanish contractors. See Jaime Vicens Vives, *An Economic History of Spain*, trans. Frances M. López-Morillas (Princeton, 1969), pp. 543–544.

[78] See R. B. Sheridan, "The Commercial and Financial Organization of the British Slave Trade, 1750–1807," *Economic History Review* 11 (1958), pp. 249–263; Gilman M. Ostrander, "The Making of the Triangular Trade Myth," *William and Mary Quarterly* 30 (1973), pp. 635–644; and K. G. Davies, *The Royal African Company* (1957: New York, 1975).

[79] See Maria Odila Silva Dias, "The Establishment of the Royal Court in Brazil," in *From Colony to Nation: Essays on the Independence of Brazil*, ed. A. J. R. Russell-Wood (Baltimore, 1975), pp. 90, 99, 103.

subsidizing a small group of businessmen, Pombal created wealthy entrepreneurs with enough capital to finance important sectors of the
Luso-Brazilian economy. This privileged group profited from the state's
commercial monopolies, and ran state-fostered industries and trading companies. In the new governmental agencies Pombal set up, businessmen superseded the old nobility. Opposition was centered primarily
in Portugal, not Brazil.

Far from attacking Brazilian interests, the treasury boards Pombal
established in the captaincies bolstered the role influential planters, merchants, and miners played in the colonial economy. By the 1770s Mineiro
businessmen controlled the fiscal apparatus of the crown's wealthiest and
most populous captaincy; even the officer corps of the Minas dragoons
was dominated by native sons. The companies that monopolized trade
with Pará, Maranhão, and Pernambuco supplied slaves on easy terms to
local planters, and promoted new export crops such as rice and cotton.
Pombal's policies reinforced the planter class.

Although the British carried off most of Brazil's gold, the miners of
Minas Gerais could hardly be blamed. Portugal's workshops simply could
not supply Brazilian markets. To reduce the empire's dependence on
British textiles and other manufactured goods, the state and its businessmen had to promote competitive industries in Portugal. This strategy
did not require any basic shifts on the Brazilian side of the empire's
economy. If Brazil could be supplied with more Portuguese merchandise,
it was the English, not Brazil's planters, who stood to lose the most. A
more diversified colonial economy producing high-priced agricultural
exports would benefit Portugal's reexport business, but would also create
a thriving slave trade and wealthy planters.

The Luso-Brazilian economy was shackled with its share of monopolies
and taxes. How and where these levies were collected is instructive. The
state taxed Brazil's export economy by collecting customs duties in Lisbon. In Brazil the crown concentrated its treasury officials in the ports,
since everything of value in Brazil—sugar, tobacco, slaves, equipment for
the mills, foodstuffs, and textiles—passed through Recife, Salvador, and
Rio de Janeiro. The gold rush modified but did not reverse the port
system. To deduct the king's share of gold production and tax the captaincy's imports, royal officials followed the miners into the backlands of
Minas Gerais. Nonetheless, tax collection continued to be a business that
the crown shared with local entrepreneurs. The largest share of the state's
Brazilian revenues still came from customs duties levied in Lisbon and
from the tobacco monopoly.[80] Compared to Spanish America, where the

---

[80] Emilia Viotti da Costa, "The Political Emancipation of Brazil," in *From Colony to
Nation*, p. 75.

bureaucracy had to tax a diversified domestic economy, royal government in Brazil gravitated to the export zone; the crown left the sertão to
the ranchers and their armed retainers. It was overseas trade that the
crown taxed, more than the circulation of goods domestically. Pombal's
policies left this system undisturbed: aside from the treasury boards, the
most significant bureaucratic reforms consisted in transferring the title of
viceroy from Bahia to Rio de Janeiro, and setting up a new High Court in
the Carioca capital. The core of Brazil's economy was shifting from north
to south, and the crown followed suit.

The point of departure for Brazil's colonial history is its export
economy. As long as the Brazilian economy did not produce its own
version of import substitution, as long as Brazil could find new exports to
pay its bills, then dependency paid dividends on both sides of the Atlantic.
When this equation broke down, as in Minas Gerais, local and imperial
interests soon parted company. The way Pombal and his disciples diagnosed Portugal's situation presaged accommodation, not a collision
course. Portugal strengthened its position in the empire by challenging
the British rather than Brazilians. In Spanish and English America,
imperial reorganization directly attacked the colonial status quo.

During the 1780s Melo e Castro's anti-Brazilian stance threatened the
wealthy Mineiro plutocrats who ran the captaincy's economy. Such a
confrontation, however, was not the norm. Pombal's protégés returned;
their more Brazilian-centered view of the empire helped check a potentially explosive situation. They had plenty of help: during the 1790s the
export economy paid unprecedented dividends. The state's income rose,
and so did the profits of the empire's merchants, slave traders, and
planters. Dependent upon and outnumbered by their slaves, Brazil's
planters had good reasons to fear the kind of republicanism practiced in
France and Haiti. The interests that controlled Brazil's economy saw the
monarchy as a stabilizing force rather than an adversary. When the
prince regent arrived in Brazil in 1808, he did not find a colony in revolt.

Brazil became independent without a revolution, and it did not become
a series of republics.[81] Tied to exporting and the slave labor system,
Brazil's planters were cautious and conservative. Only when the Portuguese Cortes attacked free trade and adopted measures that threatened
the colony's political stability, only then did planters endorse independence. Fortunately, an exiled monarchy had created a legitimate imperial
center in Rio de Janeiro that could be taken over by Brazilians, or more
accurately, by powerful Paulista coffee planters.

---

[81] On the conservative character of Brazilian independence, see Viotti da Costa, "Political
Emancipation," pp. 43–88; idem., "José Bonifácio: mito e histórias," *Anais do Museo
Paulista* **21** (1967), pp. 279–350.

Brazil's Second Empire (1840–1889) was a more advanced version of the colonial export economy. From 1865 to 1880 the value of Brazil's exports always exceeded its imports.[82] State expenditures, banking, railroad construction, and credit were all tied to the export business. In the United States, cotton planters, industrialists, and small farmers created competing versions of society; in 1860 the federal system collapsed. In Brazil, however, exporting provided a unified focus for the state, the business elite, and the planters. Economic policy was less controversial, and there was no Brazilian civil war.

---

[82] Richard Graham, *Britain and the Onset of Modernization in Brazil 1850–1914* (Cambridge, Eng., 1972), pp. 31, 51–111.

Bibliography

Alcântara Machado, José de. "Life and Death of a Bandeirante." In *The Bandeirantes: The Historical Role of the Brazilian Pathfinders*, edited by Richard M. Morse. New York: Knopf, 1965, pp. 64–67.

Alden, Dauril, Ed. *Colonial Roots of Modern Brazil.* Berkeley: University of California Press, 1973.

Alden, Dauril. *Royal Government in Brazil, with Special Reference to the Administration of the Marquis of Lavradio, Viceroy, 1769–1779.* Berkeley: University of California Press, 1968.

Alden, Dauril. "Manoel Luís Vieira: An Entrepreneur in Rio de Janeiro during Brazil's Eighteenth-Century Agricultural Renaissance." *Hispanic American Historical Review* 39 (1959): 521–537.

Alden, Dauril. "The Marquis of Pombal and the American Revolution." *The Americas* 17 (1961): 369–382.

Alden, Dauril. "The Undeclared War of 1773–1777: Climax of Luso-Spanish Platine Rivalry." *Hispanic American Historical Review* 41 (1961): 55–74.

Alden, Dauril. "The Population of Brazil in the Late Eighteenth Century: A Preliminary Study." *Hispanic American Historical Review* 43 (1963): 173–205.

Alden, Dauril. "Yankee Sperm Whalers in Brazilian Waters, and the Decline of the Portuguese Whale Fishery (1773–1801)." *The Americas* 20 (1964): 267–288.

Alden, Dauril. "The Growth and Decline of Indigo Production in Colonial Brazil: A Study in Comparative Economic History." *Journal of Economic History* 25 (1965): 35–60.

Alden, Dauril. "Economic Aspects of the Expulsion of the Jesuits from Brazil: A Preliminary Report." In *Conflict and Continuity in Brazilian Society*, edited by Henry H. Keith and S. F. Edwards. Columbia: University of South Carolina Press, 1969.

Alden, Dauril. "Black Robes vs. White Settlers: The Struggle for the 'Freedom of the Indians' in Colonial Brazil. In *Attitudes of Colonial Powers Toward the American Indian*, edited by Howard Peckham and Charles Gibson. Salt Lake City: University of Utah Press, 1969.

Alden, Dauril. "Vicissitudes of Trade in the Portuguese Atlantic Empire during the First Half of the Eighteenth Century: A Review Article." *The Americas* **32** (1975): 282–291.

Aldridge, Owen A., Ed. *The Ibero-American Enlightenment*. Urbana: University of Illinois Press, 1971.

Altman, Ida, and Lockhart, James, Eds. *Provinces of Early Mexico: Variants of Spanish American Regional Evolution*. Los Angeles: UCLA Latin American Center Publications, 1976.

Amaral, Luís. *História geral da agricultural brasileira*. 2nd ed. 2 vols. São Paulo: Companhia Editora Nacional, 1958.

Amaral Nogueira, Jofre. "Escravatura: Angola." In *Dicionário de história de Portugal*, edited by Joel Serrão. 6 vols. Lisbon: Initiativas Editorias, 1975.

Andrews, Charles M. *The Colonial Period of American History*. 4 vols. New Haven: Yale University Press, 1934–1938.

Andrews, Kenneth R. *The Spanish Caribbean: Trade and Plunder 1530–1630*. New Haven: Yale University Press, 1978.

Antonil, André João. *Cultura e opulencia do Brasil por suas drogas e minas*. Translated into French by Andrée Mansuy. [1711] Paris: Institut des Hautes Études de L'Amerique Latine, 1968.

Arcila Farías, Eduardo. *Comercio entre Venezuela y México en los siglos XVI y XVII*. Mexico: Fondo de Cultura Económica, 1950.

Ardant, Gabriel. "Financial Policy and Economic Infrastructure of Modern States and Nations." In *The Formation of National States in Western Europe*, edited by Charles Tilly. Princeton: Princeton University Press, 1975, pp. 164–242.

Bailyn, Bernard, *The Ideological Origins of the American Revolution*. Cambridge, Mass.: Belknap Press, 1967.

Bailyn, Bernard. *The Origins of American Politics*. New York: Vintage Books, 1968.

Bailyn, Bernard. *The Ordeal of Thomas Hutchinson*. Cambridge, Mass: Belknap Press, 1974.

Bailyn, Bernard. "Political and Social Structures in Virginia." In *Seventeenth-Century America: Essays in Colonial History*, edited by James Morton Smith. Chapel Hill: University of North Carolina Press, 1959.

Bakewell, Peter. *Silver Mining and Society in Colonial Mexico, Zacatecas 1546–1700*. Cambridge, Eng.: At the University Press, 1971.

Barbier, Jacques. "Tradition and Reform in Bourbon Chile: Ambrosio O'Higgins and Public Finances." *The Americas* **34** (1978): 381–399.

Barbour, Violet. *Capitalism in Amsterdam in the 17th Century*. [1950] Ann Arbor: University of Michigan Press, 1966.

Barrow, Thomas C. *Trade and Empire: The British Customs Service in Colonial America 1660–1775*. Cambridge, Mass.: Harvard University Press, 1967.

Bassett, John S. "The Regulators of North Carolina (1765–1771)." *American Historical Association Report* (1894): 141–212.

Bastide, Roger. "The Other *Quilombos*." In *Maroon Societies: Rebel Slave Communities in the Americas*, edited by Richard Price. New York: Anchor, 1973, pp. 191–201.

Bauss, Rudolph William. "Rio de Janeiro: The rise of late colonial Brazil's dominant emporium, 1777–1808." Doctoral thesis, Tulane University, 1977.

Bazant, Jan. *Alienation of Church Wealth in Mexico: Social and Economic Aspects of the Liberal Revolution, 1856–1875.* Edited and translated by Michael P. Costeloe. Cambridge, Eng.: At the University Press, 1971.

Bazant, Jan. "Evolution of the Textile Industry of Puebla 1544–1845." *Comparative Studies in Society and History* 7 (1964): 56–69.

Beeman, Richard R. "Labor Forces and Race Relations: A Comparative View of the Colonization of Brazil and Virginia." *Political Science Quarterly* 86 (1971): 609–636.

Bell, Christopher. *Portugal and the Quest for the Indies.* New York: Harper & Row, 1974.

Bertelson, David. *The Lazy South.* New York: Oxford University Press, 1967.

Bethell, Leslie. "The Independence of Brazil and the Abolition of the Brazilian Slave Trade: Anglo-Brazilian Relations, 1822–1826." *Journal of Latin American Studies* 1 (1969): 115–147.

Billings, Warren M. "The Growth of Political Institutions in Virginia, 1634–1676." *William and Mary Quarterly* 32 (1974): 225–242.

Bindoff, S. T. "Economic Change: The Greatness of Antwerp." In *The Reformation, 1520–1559,* New Cambridge Modern History, vol. 2, edited by G. R. Elton. Cambridge, Eng.: At the University Press, 1958.

Boehrer, George C. A. "The Flight of the Brazilian Deputies from the Cortes Gerais of Lisbon, 1822." *Hispanic American Historical Review* 40 (1960): 497–512.

Bolton, Herbert Eugene. "The Epic of Greater America." In *Do the Americas Have a Common History? A Critique of the Bolton Theory,* edited by Lewis Hanke. New York: Knopf, 1964, pp. 67–100.

Borah, Woodrow W. *Silk Raising in Colonial Mexico.* Berkeley: University of California Press, 1943. (Ibero-Americana 20)

Borah, Woodrow W. *New Spain's Century of Depression.* Berkeley: University of California Press, 1951. (Ibero-Americana 35)

Borah, Woodrow W. *Early Trade and Navigation Between Mexico and Peru.* Berkeley: University of California Press, 1954. (Ibero-Americana 38)

Borah, Woodrow W. "The Collection of Tithes in the Bishopric of Oaxaca during the Sixteenth Century." *Hispanic American Historical Review* 21 (1941): 386–409.

Borah, Woodrow W. "The Mixing of Populations." In *First Images of America: The Impact of the New World on the Old,* vol. 2, edited by Fredi Chiappelli. 2 vols. Berkeley: University of California Press, 1976.

Borah, Woodrow W., and Cook, Sherburne F. *The Aboriginal Population of Central Mexico on the Eve of the Spanish Conquest.* Berkeley: University of California Press, 1963. (Ibero-Americana 45)

Bowser, Frederick P. *The African Slave Trade in Colonial Peru 1524–1650.* Stanford: Stanford University Press, 1974.

Boyd-Bowman, Peter. "Spanish Emigrants to the Indies, 1595–98: A Profile." In *First Images of America. The Impact of the New World on the Old,* vol. 2, edited by Fredi Chiappelli. 2 vols. Berkeley: University of California Press, 1976.

Boyd-Bowman, Peter. "Patterns of Spanish Emigration to the Indies until 1600." *Hispanic American Historical Review* 56 (1976): 580–604.

Boyer, Richard. "Mexico in the Seventeenth Century: Transition of a Colonial Society." *Hispanic American Historical Review* 57 (1977): 455–478.

Boxer, Charles R. *Salvador de Sá and the Struggle for Brazil and Angola 1602–1686.* [1952] New York: Greenwood Press, 1975.

Boxer, Charles R. *The Dutch in Brazil 1624–1654.* [1957] Hamden: Shoe String Press, 1973.

Boxer, Charles R. *The Golden Age of Brazil 1695–1750: Growing Pains of a Colonial Society.* Berkeley: University of California Press, 1962.

Boxer, Charles R. *The Dutch Seaborne Empire 1600–1800.* New York: Knopf, 1965.

Boxer, Charles R. *Portuguese Society in the Tropics: The Municipal Councils of Goa, Macao, Bahia, and Luanda, 1510–1800*. Madison: University of Wisconsin Press, 1965.

Boxer, Charles R. *Some Literary Sources for the History of Brazil in the Eighteenth Century*. New York: Oxford, University Press (Clarendon), 1967.

Boxer, Charles R. *The Portuguese Seaborne Empire 1415–1825*. New York: Knopf, 1969.

Boxer, Charles R. *Women in Iberian Expansion Overseas, 1415–1815: Some Facts, Fancies and Personalities*. New York, Oxford University Press, 1975.

Boxer, Charles R. "Padre António Vieira, S. J., and the Institution of the Brazil Company in 1649." *Hispanic American Historical Review* 29 (1949): 474–497.

Boxer, Charles R. "English Shipping in the Brazil Trade, 1640–1665." *Mariner's Mirror* 37 (1951): 197–230.

Boxer, Charles R. "British Gold and British Traders in the First Half of the Eighteenth Century." *Hispanic American Historical Review* 49 (1969): 454–472.

Boxer, Charles R. "Portugal's *Drang Nach Osten*: A Review Article." *American Historical Review* 75 (1970): 1684–1691.

Boxer, Charles R. "The Principal Ports of Call in the *Carreira da India*." *Luso-Brazilian Review* 8 (1971): 3–29.

Brading, D. A. *Miners and Merchants in Bourbon Mexico 1768–1810*. Cambridge, Eng.: At the University Press, 1971.

Brading, D. A. "Government and Elite in Late Colonial Mexico." *Hispanic American Historical Review* 53 (1973): 389–414.

Brading, D. A., and Cross, Harry E. "Colonial Silver Mining: Mexico and Peru." *Hispanic American Historical Review* 52 (1972): 545–579.

Braudel, Fernand. *The Mediterranean and the Mediterranean World in the Age of Philip II*. 2nd rev. ed. Translated by Siân Reynolds. 2 vols. [1966] New York: Harper Torchbooks, 1972–1973.

Braudel, Fernand. *Capitalism and Material Life 1400–1800*, translated by Miriam Kochan. [1967] New York, Harper Torchbooks, 1974.

Breen, T. H. "Persistent Localism: English Social Change and the Shaping of New England Institutions." *William and Mary Quarterly* 32 (1975): 3–28.

Bridenbaugh, Carl. *Vexed and Troubled Englishmen 1590–1642*. New York: Oxford University Press, 1968.

Brown, B. Katherine. "The Controversy Over the Franchise in Puritan Massachusetts, 1954–1974." *William and Mary Quarterly* 33 (1976): 212–241.

Buarque de Holanda, Sérgio, Ed. *História geral da civilação brasileira*. 3 tomes, 9 vols. São Paulo: Difusão Européia, 1960–1977.

Buarque de Holanda, Sérgio. "As Monções." In *A época colonial*, Historia geral da civilização brasileira, vol. 1 (1), edited by Sérgio Buarque de Holanda. São Paulo: Difusão Européia, 1960, pp. 307–321.

Burga, Manuel. *De la encomienda a la hacienda capitalista: El valle del Jequetepeque del siglo XVI al XX*. Lima: Instituto de Estudios Peruanos, 1976.

Burgin, Miron. *The Economic Aspects of Argentine Federalism, 1820–1852*. [1946] New York: Russell & Russell, 1971.

Burkholder, Mark A. "From Creole to *Peninsular*: The Transformation of the Audiencia of Lima." *Hispanic American Historical Review* 52 (1972): 395–415.

Burkholder, Mark, A., and Chandler, D. S. *From Impotence to Authority: The Spanish Crown and the American Audiencias, 1687–1808*. Columbia: University of Missouri Press, 1977.

Burkholder, Mark A., and Chandler, D. S. "Creole Appointments and the Sale of Audiencia Positions in the Spanish Empire under the Early Bourbons, 1701–1750." *Journal of Latin American Studies* 4 (1972): 187–206.

Burns, E. Bradford, Ed. *A Documentary History of Brazil*. New York: Knopf, 1966.

Burns, E. Bradford. *A History of Brazil*. New York: Columbia University Press, 1970.

Burns, E. Bradford. "The Role of Azeredo Coutinho in the Enlightenment of Brazil." *Hispanic American Historical Review* 44 (1964): 145–160.

Burns, E. Bradford. "The Enlightenment in Two Colonial Brazilian Libraries." *Journal of the History of Ideas* 25 (1964): 430–438.

Burns, E. Bradford. "Concerning the Transmission and Dissemination of the Enlightenment in Brazil." In *The Ibero-American Enlightenment*, edited by A. Owen Aldridge. Urbana: University of Illinois Press, 1971, pp. 256–281.

Burns, E. Bradford. "The Intellectuals as Agents of Change and the Independence of Brazil, 1724–1822." In *From Colony to Nation: Essays on the Independence of Brazil*, edited by A. J. R. Russell-Wood. Baltimore: Johns Hopkins University Press, 1975, pp. 211–246.

Butler, Ruth Lapham. "Thomé de Sousa, First Governor-General of Brazil, 1549–1553." *Mid-America* 24 (1942): 163–179.

Butler, Ruth Lapham. "Duarte da Costa, Second Governor-General of Brazil." *Mid-America* 25 (1943): 163–179.

Butler, Ruth Lapham. "Mem de Sá, Third Governor-General of Brazil, 1557–1572." *Mid-America* 26 (1944): 111–137.

Calhoon, Robert McCluer. *The Loyalist Challenge in Revolutionary America 1760–1781*. New York: Harcourt Brace Jovanovich, 1973.

Campbell, Leon G. "A Colonial Establishment: Creole Domination of the Audiencia of Lima During the Late Eighteenth Century." *Hispanic American Historical Review* 52 (1972): 1–25.

Campbell, Leon G. "The Army of Peru and the Túpac Amaru Revolt, 1780–1783." *Hispanic American Historical Review* 56 (1976): 31–57.

Canabrava, Alice P. *O comércio português no Rio da Prata, 1580–1640*. São Paulo: Universidade de São Paulo, 1944.

Cardozo, Manuel. "The Collection of Fifths in Brazil, 1695–1709." *Hispanic American Historical Review* 20 (1940): 359–379.

Cardozo, Manuel. "The *Guerra dos Emboabas*, Civil War in Minas Gerais, 1708–1709." *Hispanic American Historical Review* 22 (1942): 470–491.

Cardozo, Manuel. "Dom Rodrigo de Castel-Blanco and the Brazilian El Dorado, 1673–1682." *The Americas* 1 (1944): 131–159.

Cardozo, Manuel. "The Last Adventure of Fernão Dias Pais (1674–1681)." *Hispanic American Historical Review* 26 (1946): 467–479.

Cardozo, Manuel. "The Brazilian Gold Rush." *The Americas* 3 (1946): 137–160.

Cardozo, Manuel. "The Lay Brotherhoods of Colonial Bahia." *Catholic Historical Review* 33 (1947): 12–30.

Cardozo, Manuel. "Tithes in Colonial Minas Gerais." *Catholic Historical Review* 38 (1952): 175–182.

Cardozo, Manuel. "Azeredo Coutinho and the Intellectual Ferment of His Times." In *Conflict and Continuity in Brazilian Society*, edited by Henry H. Keith and S. F. Edwards. Columbia: University of South Carolina Press, 1969, pp. 148–183.

Cardozo, Manuel. "The Modernization of Portugal and the Independence of Brazil." In *From Colony to Nation: Essays on the Independence of Brazil*, edited by A. J. R. Russell-Wood. Baltimore: Johns Hopkins University Press, 1975, pp. 185–210.

Carnaxide, António de Sousa Pedroso, Visconde de. *O Brasil no administração Pombalina. (Economia e política externa)*. São Paulo: Companhia Editora Nacional, 1940.

Carreido da Costa, Francisco. "Açores." In *Dicionário de história de Portugal*, edited by Joel Serrão. 6 vols. Lisbon: Initiativas Editoriais, 1978.

Castillo Pintado, Alvaro. "Los juros de Castilla: Apogeo y fin de un instrumento de crédito." *Hispania. Revista Española de Historia* 23 (1963): 43–70.

Castro, Armando de. "Tabaco." In *Dicionário de história de Portugal*, edited by Joel Serrão. 6 vols. Lisbon: Initiativas Editoriais, 1978.

Céspedes, Guillermo. "Lima y Buenos Aires: Repercusiones económicas y políticas de la creación del Virreinato del Plata." *Anuario de Estudios Americanos* 3 (1946): 669–874.

Chaffin, Robert J. "The Townshend Act of 1767." *William and Mary Quarterly* 28 (1970): 90–121.

Chance, John K. *Race and Class in Colonial Oaxaca*. Stanford: Stanford University Press, 1978.

Chance, John K. "The Urban Indian in Colonial Oaxaca." *American Ethnologist* 3 (1976): 603–632.

Chandler, Billy Jaynes. *The Feitosas and the Sertão dos Inhamuns: The History of a Family and a Community in Northeast Brazil 1700–1930*. Gainsville: University of Florida Press, 1972.

Chaunu, Pierre, and Chaunu, Huguette. *Séville et l'Atlantique (1504–1650)*. 8 vols. Paris: Institute des Hautes Études de L'Amerique Latine, 1955–1959.

Chaunu, Pierre, and Chaunu, Huguette. "The Atlantic Economy and the World Economy." In *Essays in European Economic History*, edited by Peter Earl. New York and London: Oxford University Press (Clarendon), 1974, pp. 113–126.

Chevalier, François. *Land and Society in Colonial Mexico: The Great Hacienda*. Translated by Alvin Eustis. [1952] Berkeley: University of California Press, 1963.

Chiappelli, Fredi, Ed. *First Images of America: The Impact of the New World on the Old*. 2 vols. Berkeley: University of California Press, 1976.

Chilcote, Ronald H., Ed. *Protest and Resistance in Angola and Brazil*. Berkeley: University of California Press, 1972.

Christelow, Allan. "Contraband Trade Between Jamaica and the Spanish Main, and the Free Port Act of 1766." *Hispanic American Historical Review* 12 (1942): 309–343.

Christelow, Allan. "Economic Background of the Anglo-Spanish War of 1762." *Journal of Modern History* 18 (1946): 22–36.

Christian, William A., Jr. *Person and God in a Spanish Valley*. New York: Academic Press, 1972.

Christian, William A., Jr. "Popular devotions in sixteenth-century New Castile based on village reports to Philip II, 1575–1580." Unpublished manuscript, 1977.

Clayton, Lawrence A. "Local Initiative and Finance in Defense of the Viceroyalty of Peru: The Development of Self-Reliance." *Hispanic American Historical Review* 54 (1974): 284–304.

Clayton, Lawrence A. "Trade and Navigation in the Seventeenth-Century Viceroyalty of Peru." *Journal of Latin American Studies* 7 (1975): 1–21.

Coatsworth, John H. "Obstacles to Economic Growth in Nineteenth-Century Mexico." *American Historical Review* 83 (1978): 80–100.

Cohen, David W., and Greene, Jack P., Eds. *Neither Slave Nor Free: The Freedmen of African Descent in the Slave Societies of the New World*. Baltimore: Johns Hopkins University Press, 1972.

Cole, Charles Woolsey. *Colbert and a Century of French Mercantilism*. 2 vols. New York: Columbia University Press, 1939.

Coleman, D. C. "An Innovation and its Diffusion: the 'New Draperies.' " *Economic History Review* 22 (1969): 417–429.

Coornaert, E. L. J. "European Economic Institutions in the New World: The Chartered Companies." In *The Economy of Expanding Europe in the Sixteenth and Seventeenth Centuries*, Cambridge Economic History of Europe, edited by E. E. Rich and C. H. Wilson. Cambridge, Eng.: At the University Press, 1967, pp. 220–274.

Cordeiro Ferreira, Maria Emília. "India, casa da"; "Mina, casa da." In *Dicionário de história de Portugal*, edited by Joel Serrão. 6 vols. Lisbon: Iniciativas Editoriais, 1975.

Correia de Andrade, Manuel. "The Social and Ethnic Significance of the War of the Cabanos." In *Protest and Resistance in Angola and Brazil*, edited by Ronald H. Chilcote. Berkeley: University of California Press, 1972.

Cortesão, Jaime. "The Greatest Bandeira of the Greatest Bandeirante." In *The Bandeirantes: The Historical Role of the Brazilian Pathfinders*, edited by Richard M. Morse. New York: Knopf, 1965, pp. 100–113.

Costa Pinto, Luís Aguiar de. *Lutas de famílias no Brasil*. São Paulo: Companhia Editora Nacional, 1949.

Costeloe, Michael P. *Church Wealth in Mexico: A Study of the "Juzgado de Capellanías" in the Archbishopric of Mexico 1800–1856*. Cambridge, Eng.: At the University Press, 1967.

Cross, Harry E. "Commerce and Orthodoxy: A Spanish Response to Portuguese Commercial Penetration in the Viceroyalty of Peru, 1580–1640." *The Americas* 25 (1978): 151–167.

Curtin, Philip D. *The Atlantic Slave Trade: A Census*. Madison: University of Wisconsin Press, 1969.

Curtin, Philip D. *Economic Change in Precolonial Africa: Senegambia in the Era of the Slave Trade*. Madison: University of Wisconsin Press, 1975.

Da Chuna, Euclides. *Rebellion in the Backlands (Os Sertões)*. Translated by Samuel Putman. [1897] Chicago: Chicago University Press, 1944.

Daniell, Jere R. "Politics in New Hampshire under Governor Benning Wentworth. 1741–1767." *William and Mary Quarterly* 23 (1966): 76–105.

Davidson, Basil. *The African Slave Trade: Pre-Colonial History. 1450–1850*. Boston: Little, Brown & Co., 1961.

Davidson, David M. "Rivers and empire: The Madeira route and the incorporation of the Brazilian far west, 1737–1808." Doctoral thesis, Yale University, 1970.

Davidson, David M. "How the Brazilian West Was Won: Freelance and State on the Mato Grosso Frontier, 1737–1752." In *Colonial Roots of Modern Brazil*, edited by Dauril Alden. Berkeley: University of California Press, 1973.

Davies, Kenneth G. *The Royal African Company*. [1957] New York: Octagon Books, 1975.

Davis, Ralph. "English Foreign Trade, 1660–1700." *Economic History Review* 7 (1954): 150–163.

Davis, Ralph. "English Foreign Trade, 1700–1774." *Economic History Review* 15 (1962): 285–298.

Degler, Carl N. *Neither Black nor White: Slavery and Race Relations in Brazil and the United States*. New York: Macmillian, 1971.

Della Cava, Ralph. *Miracle at Joaseiro*. New York: Columbia University Press, 1970.

Della Cava, Ralph. "Brazilian Messianism and National Institutions: A Reappraisal of Canudos and Joaseiro." *Hispanic American Historical Review* 48 (1968): 402–420.

De Studer, Elena F. S. *La trata de Negros an el Río de La Plata durante el siglo XVIII*. Buenos Aires: Universidad de Buenos Aires, 1958.

De Vries, Jan. *The Economy of Europe in an Age of Crisis, 1600–1750*. Cambridge, Eng.: At the University Press, 1976.

Dickerson, Oliver M. *American Colonial Government 1696–1765: A Study of the British Board of Trade in Its Relation to the American Colonies, Political, Industrial, Administrative*. Cleveland: Arthur E. Clark Co., 1912.

Dickerson, Oliver M. *The Navigation Acts and the American Revolution.* [1951] New York: Barnes & Co., 1963.

Diégues Júnior, Miguel. "As companhias privilegiadas no comércio colonial." *Revista de História*, no. 3 (1950): 309–337.

Diffie, Bailey W. *Prelude to Empire: Portugal Overseas before Henry the Navigator.* Lincoln: University of Nebraska Press, 1960.

Diffie, Bailey W., and Winius, George D. *Foundations of the Portuguese Empire, 1415–1580.* Minneapolis: University of Minnesota Press, 1977.

Domínguez Ortiz, António. *Política y hacienda de Felipe IV.* Madrid: Editorial de Derecho Financiero, 1960.

Domínguez Ortiz, António. "Los caudales de Indias y la política exterior de Felipe IV." *Anuario de Estudios Americanos* 13 (1956): 311–383.

Domínguez Ortiz, António. "Guerra económica y comercio extranjero en el reinado de Felipe IV." *Hispania: Revista Española de Historia* 23 (1963): 71–110.

Dorn, Walter L. *Competition for Empire 1740–1763.* New York: Harper & Row, 1940.

Duncan, T. Bentley. *Atlantic Islands: Madeira, the Azores and the Cape Verdes in Seventeenth-Century Commerce and Navigation.* Chicago: University of Chicago Press, 1972.

Dunn, Richard S. *Sugar and Slaves: The Rise of the Planter Class in the English West Indies, 1624–1713.* New York: Norton Library, 1973.

Durkheim, Emile. *The Rules of Sociological Method.* Translated and edited by Sarah A. Solovay, John H. Miller, and George E. G. Catlin. [1938] New York: Free Press, 1966.

Dusenberry, William H. "Woolen Manufacturing in Sixteenth-Century New Spain." *The Americas* 4 (1947): 223–234.

Dutra, Francis A. "A New Look into Diogo Botelho's Stay in Pernambuco, 1602–1603." *Luso-Brazilian Review* (1967): 27–34.

Dutra, Francis A. "Matias de Albuquerque: A Seventeenth-Century *Capitão Mór* of Pernambuco and Governor-General of Brazil." Doctoral thesis, New York University, 1968.

Dutra, Francis A. "Membership in the Order of Christ in the Seventeenth Century: Its Rights, Privileges, and Obligations." *The Americas* 28 (1970): 3–25.

Dutra, Francis A. "The Brazilian Hierarchy in the Seventeenth Century." *Records of the Catholic Historical Society* 83 (1972): 171–186.

Dutra, Francis A. "Centralization vs Donatarial Privilege: Pernambuco, 1601–1630." In *Colonial Roots of Modern Brazil*, edited by Dauril Alden. Berkeley: University of California Press, 1973.

Eccles, W. J. *France in America.* New York: Harper Torchbooks. 1972.

Edel, Matthew. "The Brazilian Sugar Cycle of the Seventeenth Century and the Rise of West Indian Competition." *Caribbean Studies* 9 (1969): 24–44.

Edwards, Michael M. *The Growth of the British Cotton Trade 1780–1815.* Manchester: Manchester University Press, 1967.

Egnal, Marc. "The Economic Development of the Thirteen Continental Colonies, 1720–1775." *William and Mary Quarterly* 32 (1975): 191–222.

Eisenstadt, S. N. "Empires." In *International Encyclopedia of the Social Sciences*, Vol. 5, edited by David L. Sills. 17 vols. New York: Macmillian, 1968.

Elliott, John H. *The Revolt of the Catalans. A Study in the Decline of Spain (1598–1640).* Cambridge, Eng.: At the University Press, 1963.

Elliott, John H. *Imperial Spain 1469–1716.* New York: Mentor Books, 1966.

Elliott, John H. "The Spanish Peninsula 1598–1648." In *The Decline of Spain and the Thirty*

Years War 1609–59, New Cambridge Modern History, vol. 4, edited by J. P. Cooper, Cambridge, Eng.: At the University Press, 1970, pp. 435–473.

Ellis, Myriam. *O monopólio do sal no estado do Brasil (1631–1801)*. São Paulo: Universidade de São Paulo, 1955.

Ellis, Myriam. *A baleia no Brasil colonial*. São Paulo: Edições Melhoramentos, 1969.

Ellis, Myriam. "Contribuição au estudo do abastecimento das zonas mineradores do Brasil no século XVIII." *Revista de História*, no. 36 (1958): 429–467.

Ellis, Myriam. "As bandeiras na expansão geográfico do Brasil." In *A época colonial*, Historia geral da civilização brasileira, vol. 1 (1), edited by Sérgio Buarque de Holanda. São Paulo: Difusão Européia, 1960, pp. 273–296.

Ennes, Ernesto. "The Trial of the Ecclesiastics in the Inconfidência Mineira." *The Americas* 7 (1950): 183–213.

Ennes, Ernesto. "The Conquest of Palmares." *The Bandeirantes: The Historical Role of the Brazilian Pathfinders*, edited by Richard M. Morse. New York: Knopf, 1965.

Erikson, Kai T. *Wayward Puritans: A Study in the Sociology of Deviance*. New York: Wiley, 1966.

Farnell, J. E. "The Navigation Act of 1651, the First Dutch War, and the London Merchant Community." *Economic History Review* 16 (1964): 439–454.

Farriss, Nancy M. *Crown and Clergy in Colonial Mexico 1759–1821: The Crisis of Ecclesiastical Privilege*. London: Athlone Press, 1968.

Fernandes, Florestan. "Antecedentes indígenas: Organização social das tribos tupis." In *A época colonial*, História geral da civilização brasileira, vol. 1 (1), edited by Sérgio Buarque de Holanda. São Paulo: Difusão Européia, 1960, pp. 72–86.

Ferreira Reis, Arthur Cézar. "A inconfidência baiana." In *A época colonial*, Historia geral da civilização brasileira, vol. 1 (2), edited by Sérgio Buarque de Holanda. São Paulo: Difusão Européia, 1960, pp. 406–410.

Fischer, Wolfram, and Lundgreen, Peter. "The Recruitment and Training of Administrative and Technical Personnel." In *The Formation of National States in Western Europe*, edited by Charles Tilly. Princeton: Princeton University Press, 1975, pp. 456–561.

Fisher, H. E. S. *The Portugal Trade: A Study of Anglo-Portuguese Commerce 1700–1770*. London: Methuen, 1971.

Fisher, H. E. S. "Anglo-Portuguese Trade, 1700–1750." *Economic History Review* 16 (1963): 219–233.

Fisher, John R. *Government and Society in Colonial Peru: The Intendant System 1784–1814*. London: Athlone Press, 1970.

Fisher, John R. "Silver Production in the Viceroyalty of Peru, 1776–1824." *Hispanic American Historical Review* 55 (1975): 25–43.

Fisher, Lillian Estelle. *The Last Inca Revolt*. Norman: University of Oklahoma Press, 1966.

Florescano, Enrique, Ed. *Haciendas, latifundios y plantaciones en América Latina*. Mexico: Siglo Veintiuno, 1975.

Flory, Rae, and Smith, David Grant. "Bahian Merchants and Planters in the Seventeenth and Early Eighteenth Centuries." *Hispanic American Historical Review* 58 (1978): 571–594.

Flory, Thomas. "Judicial Politics in Nineteenth-Century Brazil." *Hispanic American Historical Review* 55 (1975): 664–692.

Flory, Thomas. "Race and Social Control in Independent Brazil." *Journal of Latin American Studies* 9 (1977): 199–224.

Floyd, Troy S. "The Guatemalan Merchants, the Government, and the Provincianos, 1750–1800." *Hispanic American Historical Review* 41 (1961): 90–110.

Francis, A. D. *The Methuens and Portugal, 1691–1708*. Cambridge, Eng.: At the University Press, 1966.

Francis, A. D. *The Wine Trade*. New York: Barnes & Nobel, 1973.

Frank, Andre Gunder. *Capitalism and Underdevelopment in Latin America: Historical Studies of Chile and Brazil*. New York, 1969.

Freitas, Gustavo de. "A companhia geral do comércio do Brasil (1649–1720): A instituição da companhia." *Revista de História*, no. 7 (1951): 85–111.

Freyre, Gilberto. *The Masters and the Slaves: A Study in the Development of Brazilian Civilization*. Translated by Samuel Putman. Revised ed. New York: Knopf, 1964.

Furtado, Celso. *The Economic Growth of Brazil: A Survey from Colonial to Modern Times*. Translated by Ricardo W. de Aguiar and Eric Charles Drysdale. Berkeley: University of California Press, 1963.

Furtado, Celso. *Economic Development of Latin America*. 2nd ed. Translated by Suzette Macedo. Cambridge, Eng.: At the University Press, 1976.

Gerhard, Peter. *A Guide to the Historical Geography of New Spain*. Cambridge, Eng.: At the University Press, 1972.

Geyl, Peter. *The Revolt of the Netherlands, 1555–1609*. London: Williams & Norgate, 1932.

Gibson, Charles, Ed. *The Spanish Tradition in America*. New York: Harper & Row, 1968.

Gibson, Charles. *The Aztecs Under Spanish Rule*. Stanford: Stanford University Press, 1964.

Gibson, Charles. *Spain in America*. New York: Harper Torchbooks, 1966.

Gibson, Charles. "Writings on Colonial Mexico." *Hispanic American Historical Review* **55** (1975): 287–323.

Glamann, Kristof. *Dutch-Asiatic Trade 1620–1740*. The Hague: Martinus Nijhoff, 1958.

Godinho, Vitorino Magalhães. *Prix et Monnaies au Portugal 1750–1850*. Paris: Librairie Armand Colin, 1955.

Godinho, Vitorino Magalhães. *Os descobrimentos e a economia mundial*. 2 vols. Lisbon: Editora Arcádia, 1963–1965.

Godinho, Vitorino Magalhães. "Portugal, as frotas do açúcar e as frotas do ouro (1670–1770)." *Revista de História*, no. 15 (1953): 69–88.

Godinho, Vitorino Magalhães. "Portugal and Her Empire." In *New Cambridge Modern History*, edited by F. L. Carsten, Cambridge, Eng.: At the University Press, 1961. Vol. 5, *The Ascendancy of France 1648–88*.

Godinho, Vitorino Magalhães. "Complexo histórico-geográfico," "Especiarias," "Financas públicas e estrutura do estado," "Restauraçâo," "Sociedade portuguesa." In *Dicionário de história de Portugal*, edited by Joel Serrão. 6 vols. Lisbon: Initiativas Editoriais, 1975.

Godinho, Vitorino Magalhães. "Portugal and Her Empire 1680–1720." In *The Rise of Great Britain and Russia 1688–1715/25*, New Cambridge Modern History, vol. 6, edited by J. S. Bromley. Cambridge, Eng.: At the University Press, 1970, pp. 509–540.

Goebel, Dorothy Burne. "The 'New England Trade' and the French West Indies, 1763–1774: A Study in Trade Policies." *William and Mary Quarterly* **20** (1963): 331–372.

Góngora, Mario. *Studies in the Colonial History of Spanish America*. Translated by Richard Southern. Cambridge, Eng.: At the University Press, 1975.

Gonzaga, Jaeger, Luis. "Many Were the Pretexts." In *The Expulsion of the Jesuits from Latin America*, edited by Magnus Mörner. New York: Knopf. 1965, pp. 117–127.

Goslinga, Cornelis Ch. *The Dutch in the Caribbean and on the Wild Coast 1580–1680*. Gainsville: University of Florida Press, 1971.

Graham, Richard. *Britain and the Onset of Modernization in Brazil 1850–1914*. Cambridge, Eng.: At the University Press, 1968.

Graham, Richard. *Independence in Latin America: A Comparative Approach*. New York: Knopf, 1974.

Graham, Richard, and Smith, Peter H., Eds. *New Approaches to Latin American History*. Austin: University of Texas Press, 1974.

Greene, Jack P., Ed. *Great Britain and the American Colonies, 1606–1763*. Columbia: University of South Carolina Press, 1970.

Greene, Jack P. *The Quest for Power: The Lower House of Assembly in the Southern Royal Colonies 1689–1776*. Chapel Hill: University of North Carolina Press, 1963.

Greene, Jack P. "The Role of the Lower House of Assembly in Eighteenth-Century Politics." *Journal of Southern History* 37 (1961): 451–474.

Greene, Jack P. "Political Mimesis: A Consideration of the Historical Roots of Legislative Behavior in the British Colonies in the Eighteenth Century." *American Historical Review* 75 (1969): 337–360.

Greenleaf, Richard E. "The Obraje in the Late Mexican Colony." *The Americas* 23 (1967): 227–250.

Griffiths, Gordon. "The Revolutionary Character of the Revolution in the Netherlands." *Comparative Studies in Society and History* 2 (1960): 452–472.

Gross, Sue A. "Agricultural Promotion in the Amazon Basin." *Agricultural History* 43 (1969): 269–276.

Hamill, Hugh M., Jr. *The Hidalgo Revolt, Prelude to Mexican Independence*. Gainesville: University of Florida Press, 1966.

Hamill, Hugh M., Jr. "Royalist Counterinsurgency in the Mexican War for Independence: The Lessons of 1811." *Hispanic American Historical Review* 53 (1973): 470–489.

Hamilton, Earl J. *American Treasure and the Price Revolution in Spain, 1501–1650*. [1934] New York: Octagon Books, 1965.

Hamnett, Brian. *Politics and Trade in Southern Mexico 1750–1825*. Cambridge, Eng.: At the University Press, 1971.

Hanke, Lewis, Ed. *Do the Americas Have a Common History? A Critique of the Bolton Theory*. New York: Knopf, 1964.

Hanke, Lewis. *The Spanish Struggle for Justice in the Conquest of America*. Philadelphia: University of Pennsylvania Press, 1949.

Hanke, Lewis. *The Imperial City of Potosí: An Unwritten Chapter in the History of Spanish America*. The Hague: Nijhoff, 1956.

Hanke, Lewis. "The Portuguese in Spanish America with Special Reference to the Villa Imperial de Potosí." *Revista de Historia de America*, no. 51 (1961):1–48.

Hardoy, Jorge E., and Aranovich, Carmen. "Urban Scales and Functions in Spanish America Toward the Year 1600: First Conclusions." *Latin American Research Review* 5 (1970): 57–91.

Haring, C. H. *Empire in Brazil. New World Experiment with Monarchy*. [1958] New York: Norton Library, 1968.

Harper, Lawrence A. *The English Navigation Laws*. New York: Columbia University Press, 1939.

Harrison, J. B. "Colonial Development and International Rivalries Outside Europe: Asia and Africa." In *The Counter Reformation and the Price Revolution 1559–1610*, New Cambridge Modern History, vol. 3, edited by R. B. Wernham. Cambridge, Eng.: At the University Press, 1968, pp. 507–558.

Hawke, David. *The Colonial Experience*. New York: Bobbs-Merrill, 1966.

Heaton, Herbert. "A Merchant Adventurer in Brazil 1808–1818." *Journal of Economic History* 6 (1946): 1–23.

Helmer, Marie. "Comércio e contrabando entre Bahia e Potosí no século XVI." *Revista de História*, no. 15 (1953): 195–212.

Hemming, John. *Red Gold: The Conquest of the Brazilian Indians*. Cambridge, Mass.: Harvard University Press, 1978.

Henderson, W. O. "The Anglo-French Commercial Treaty of 1786." *Economic History Review* **10** (1957): 104–112.

Herrick, Jane. "The Reluctant Revolutionist: A Study of the Political Ideas of Hipólito da Costa, 1744–1823." *The Americas* **7** (1950): 171–181.

Hicks, John. *A Theory of Economic History.* New York and London: Oxford University Press (Clarendon), 1969.

Hill, Christopher. *A Century of Revolution 1603–1714.* [1961] New York: Norton Library, 1966.

Hoberman, Louisa Schell. "Merchants in Seventeenth-Century Mexico City: A Preliminary Report." *Hispanic American Historical Review* **57** (1977): 479–503.

Hoh-Cheung, and Mui, Lorna. "Smuggling and the British Tea Trade Before 1784." *American Historical Review* **74** (1968): 44–73.

Humphreys, R. A., and Lynch, John, Eds. *The Origins of the Latin American Revolutions, 1808–1826.* New York: Knopf, 1965.

Hurstfield, J. "Social Structure, Office-Holding and Politics, Chiefly in Western Europe." In *The Counter Reformation and the Price Revolution 1559–1610*, New Cambridge Modern History, vol. 3, edited by R. B. Wernham. Cambridge, Eng.: At the University Press, 1968. pp. 126–148.

Hussey, Roland D. *The Caracas Company 1728–1784: A Study in the History of Spanish Monopolistic Trade.* Cambridge, Mass.: Harvard University Press, 1934.

Hussey, Roland D. "Spanish Reaction to Foreign Aggression in the Caribbean to about 1680." *Hispanic American Historical Review* **9** (1929): 286–302.

Hussey, Roland D. "The Spanish Empire Under Foreign Pressures, 1688–1715." In *The Rise of Great Britain and Russia 1688–1715/25.* New Cambridge Modern History, vol. 6, edited by J. S. Bromley. Cambridge, Eng.: At the University Press, 1970, pp. 348–380.

Isaac, Rhys. "Evangelical Revolt: The Nature of the Baptists' Challenge to the Traditional Order in Virginia, 1765 to 1775." *William and Mary Quarterly* **31** (1974): 345–368.

Israel, Jonathon I. "Mexico and the 'General Crisis' of the Seventeenth Century." *Past and Present* **63** (1974): 33–57.

Johnson, Harold B., Jr. "The Donatary Captaincy in Perspective: Portuguese Backgrounds to the Settlement of Brazil." *Hispanic American Historical Review* **52** (1972): 203–214.

Johnson, Harold B., Jr. "A Preliminary Inquiry into Money, Prices, and Wages in Rio de Janeiro, 1763–1823." In *Colonial Roots of Modern Brazil*, edited by Dauril Alden. Berkeley: University of California Press, 1973, pp. 231–283.

Kagan, Richard L. *Students and Society in Early Modern Spain.* Baltimore: Johns Hopkins University Press, 1974.

Kagan, Richard L. "Universities in Castile, 1500–1700." *Past and Present* **49** (1970): 44–71.

Katz, Stanley. *Newcastle's New York: Anglo-American Politics 1732–1753.* Cambridge, Mass.: Belknap Press, 1968.

Kay, Marvin L. Michael. "The Payment of Provincial and Local Taxes in North Carolina, 1748–1771." *William and Mary Quarterly* **26** (1969): 218–240.

Keith, Henry H., and Edwards, S. F., Eds. *Conflict and Continuity in Brazilian Society.* Columbia: University of South Carolina Press, 1969.

Keith, Robert G. *Conquest and Agrarian Change: The Emergence of the Hacienda System on the Peruvian Coast.* Cambridge, Mass.: Harvard University Press, 1976.

Keith, Robert G. "Encomienda, Hacienda and Corregimiento in Spanish America: A Structural Analysis." *Hispanic American Historical Review* **51** (1971): 431–446.

Kennedy, John Norman. "Bahian Elites, 1750–1822." *Hispanic American Historical Review* **53** (1973): 415–439.

Kennedy, William. *English Taxation 1640–1799.* London: G. Bell & Sons, 1913.

Kent, R. K. "Palmares: An African State in Brazil." *Journal of African History* **6** (1965): 161–175.

Kiemen, Mathias C. *The Indian Policy of Portugal in the Amazon Region, 1614–1693*. Washington, D.C.: Catholic University of American Press, 1954.

Kiernan, V. G. "State and Nation in Western Europe." *Past and Present* **31** (1965): 20–38.

Klein, Herbert S. *The Middle Passage: Comparative Studies in the Atlantic Slave Trade*. Princeton: Princeton University Press, 1978.

Klein, Herbert S. "The Trade in African Slaves to Rio de Janeiro, 1795–1811: Estimates of Mortality and Patterns of Voyages." *Journal of African History* **10** (1969): 533–549.

Klein, Herbert S. "The Portuguese Slave Trade from Angola in the Eighteenth Century." *Journal of Economic History* **32** (1972): 894–918.

Klein, Herbert S. "Nineteenth-Century Brazil." In *Neither Slave Nor Free: The Freedmen of African Descent in the Slave Societies of the New World*, edited by David W. Cohen and Jack P. Green. Baltimore: Johns Hopkins University Press, 1972, pp. 309–334.

Klein, Herbert S. "Structure and Profitability of Royal Finances in the Viceroyalty of the Rio de la Plata in 1790." *Hispanic American Historical Review* **53** (1973): 440–469.

Knollenberg, Bernhard. *Origin of the American Revolution: 1759–1776*. New York, 1961.

Koenigsberger, H. G. "The Empire of Charles V in Europe." In *The Reformation, 1520–1559*. New Cambridge Modern History. vol. 2, edited by G. R. Elton. Cambridge, Eng.: At the University Press, 1958, pp. 301–333.

Koster, Henry. *Travels in Brazil*. [1816] Carbondale: Southern Illinois University Press, 1966.

Labaree, Leonard W. *Royal Government in America: A Study of the British Colonial System before 1783*. New Haven: Yale University Press, 1930.

Lacombre, Américo Jocabina. "A conjuração do Rio de Janeiro." In *A época colonial*, História geral da civilização brasileira, vol. 1 (2), edited by Sérgio Buarque de Holanda. São Paulo: Difusão Euopéia, 1960, pp. 406–410.

Lahmeyer Lobo, Eulália Maria. *Processo adminstrativo Ibero-Americano: Aspectos socio-economicos periodo colonial*. Rio de Janeiro: Biblioteca de Exército Editora, 1962.

Lahmeyer Lobo, Eulália Maria. "O comércio atlântico e a comunidade de mercadores no Rio de Janeiro e em Charleston no século XVIII." *Revista de História*, no. 101 (1975): 49–106.

Lang, James. *Conquest and Commerce: Spain and England in the Americas*. New York: Academic Press, 1975.

Lapa, José Roberto do Amaral. *A Bahia e a Carreira da Índia*. São Paulo: Companhia Editora Nacional, 1968.

Lavradio, Marquês de. "Relatório do Marquês de Lavradio, Vice-Rei do Brasil de 1769 a 1779, apresentado au Vice-Rei Luís de Vasconcelos e Sousa seu sucessor." Reprinted in Carnaxide, *O Brasil na administração Pombalina*. São Paulo: Companhia Editora Nacional, 1940.

Lavrin, Asunción. "The Role of Nunneries in the Economy of New Spain in the Eighteenth Century." *Hispanic American Historical Review* **46** (1966): 371–393.

Lavrin, Asunción. "The Execution of the Law of *Consolidación* in New Spain: Economic Aims and Results." *Hispanic American Historical Review* **53** (1973): 27–49.

Liebman, Seymour B. "The Great Conspiracy in New Spain." *The Americas* **30** (1973): 18–31.

Lockhart, James. *Spanish Peru 1532–1560, A Colonial Society*. Madison: University of Wisconsin Press, 1968.

Lockhart, James. "Encomienda and Hacienda: The Evolution of the Great Estate in the Spanish Indies." *Hispanic American Historical Review* **49** (1969): 411–429.

Lockhart, James. "The Social History of Colonial Spanish America: Evolution and Poten-
tial." *Latin American Research Review* 7 (1972): 6–45.
Lodge, Richard. "The English Factory at Lisbon: Some Chapters in Its History." *Transac-
tions of the Royal Historical Society* 16 (1933): 211–247.
Lombardi, Mary. "The Frontier in Brazilian History: An Historiographical Essay." *Pacific
Historical Review* 44 (1975): 437–457.
Love, Joseph L. *Rio Grande do Sul and Brazilian Regionalism, 1882–1930*. Stanford:
Stanford University Press, 1971.
Love, Joseph L. "An Approach to Regionalism." In *New Approaches to Latin American
History*, edited by Richard Graham and Peter H. Smith. Austin: University of Texas
Press, 1974, pp. 137–155.
Lovejoy, David S. *The Glorious Revolution in America*. New York: Harper & Row, 1972.
Lugar, Catherine. "The Portuguese Tobacco Trade and Tobacco Growers of Bahia in the
Late Colonial Period." In *Essays Concerning the Socioeconomic History of Brazil and
Portuguese India*, edited by Dauril Alden and Warren Dean. Gainsville: University of
Florida Press, 1977.
Lynch, John. *Spanish Colonial Administration. 1782–1810: The Indendant System in the
Viceroyalty of the Río de la Plata*. [1958] New York: Greenwood Press, 1969.
Lynch, John. *Spain Under the Hapsburgs*. 2 vols. Oxford: Basil Blackwell, 1964–1969.
Lynch, John. *The Spanish-American Revolutions, 1808–1826*. New York: Norton & Co.,
1973.
McAlister, Lyle N. *The "Fuero Militar" in New Spain 1764–1800*. Gainesville: University of
Florida Press, 1957.
Macedo, Jorge Borges de. *A situação económica no tempo de Pombal: Alguns aspectos*.
Opôrto: Livraria Portugália, 1951.
Macedo, Jorge Borges de. *O bloqueio continental: Economia e guerra peninsular*. Lisbon:
Delfos, 1962.
Macedo, Jorge Borges de. *Problemas de história da indústria portuguesa no século XVIII*.
Lisbon: Associação Industrial Portuguesa, 1963.
Macedo, Jorge Borges de. "Portugal e a economia 'Pombalina.' Temas e hipóteses." *Revista
de História*, no. 19 (1954): 81–100.
Macedo, Jorge Borges de. "Burguesia," "Comércio externo: naidade moderna," "Indústria."
In *Dicionário de historia de Portugal*, edited by Joel Serrão. 6 vols. Lisbon: Iniativas
Editoriais, 1975.
MacLachlan, Colin M. "The Indian Directorate: Forced Acculturation in Portuguese
America (1757–1799)." *The Americas* 28 (1972): 357–385.
MacLachlan, Colin M. "The Indian Labor Structure in the Portuguese Amazon, 1700–
1800. In *Colonial Roots of Modern Brazil*, edited by Dauril Alden. Berkeley: University
of California Press, 1973, pp. 199–230.
MacLachlan, Collin M. "African Slave Trade and Economic Development in Amazonia,
1700–1800." In *Slavery and Race Relations in Latin America*, edited by Robert Brent
Toplin. Westport, Conn.: Greenwood Press, 1974, pp. 112–145.
Magalhães de Gandavo, Pero de. *The Histories of Brazil*. Translated by John B. Stetson, Jr.
[1922] Boston: Melford House, 1972.
Manchester, Alan K. *British Preëminence in Brazil: Its Rise and Decline: A Study in
European Expansion*. Chapel Hill: University of North Carolina Press, 1933.
Manchester, Alan K. "The Paradoxical Pedro, First Emperor of Brazil." *Hispanic American
Historical Review* 12 (1932): 176–197.
Manchester, Alan K. "The Transfer of the Portuguese Court to Rio de Janeiro." In *Conflict
and Continuity in Brazilian Society*, edited by Henry H. Keith and S. F. Edwards.
Columbia: University of South Carolina Press, 1969, pp. 148–183.

Manchester, Alan K. "The Growth of Bureaucracy in Brazil." *Journal of Latin American Studies* **4** (1972): 77–83.

Mansilla, Justo, and Maceta, Simón. "Atrocities of the Paulistas." In *The Bandeirantes: The Historical Role of the Brazilian Pathfinders*, edited by Richard M. Morse. New York: Knopf, 1965, pp. 81–91.

Marchant, Alexander. *From Barter to Slavery: The Economic Relations of Portuguese and Indians in the Settlement of Brazil, 1500–1580*. [1942] Gloucester: Peter Smith, 1966.

Marchant, Alexander. "Colonial Brazil as a Way Station for the Portuguese India Fleets." *Geographical Review* **31** (1941): 454–465.

Marchant, Alexander. "Feudal and Capitalistic Elements in the Portuguese Settlement of Brazil." *Hispanic American Historical Review* **22** (1942): 493–512.

Marchant, Alexander. "Aspects of the Enlightenment in Brazil." In *Latin America and the Enlightenment*, edited by Arthur P. Whitaker. 2nd ed. [1942] Ithaca: Cornell University Press, 1961, pp. 95–118.

Marzahl, Peter. *Town in the Empire: Government, Politics and Society in Seventeenth-Century Popayán*. Austin: University of Texas Press, forthcoming.

Marzahl, Peter. "Creoles and Government: The Cabildo of Popayán." *Hispanic American Historical Review* **54** (1974): 636–656.

Masefield, G. B., "Crops and Livestock." In The Economy of Expanding Europe in the Sixteenth and Seventeenth Centuries, Cambridge Economic History of Europe, vol. 4, edited by E. E. Rich and C. H. Wilson. Cambridge, Eng.: At the University Press, 1967.

Mauro, Frédéric. *Le Portugal et l'Atlantique au XVIIe siècle, 1570–1670*. Paris: S.E.V.P.E.N., 1960.

Mauro, Frédéric. *Nova história e nôvo mondo*. São Paulo: Editôra Perspectiva, 1969.

Mawe, John. *Travels in the Interior of Brazil, and a Particular Account of The Gold and Diamond Districts*. 2nd ed. [1812] London: Longman, 1822.

Maxwell, Kenneth. *Conflicts and Conspiracies: Brazil and Portugal 1750–1808*. Cambridge, Eng.: At the University Press, 1973.

Maxwell, Kenneth. "Pombal and the Nationalization of the Luso-Brazilian Economy." *Hispanic American Historical Review* **48** (1968): 608–631.

Maxwell, Kenneth. "The Generation of the 1790s and the Idea of Luso-Brazilian Empire." In *Colonial Roots of Modern Brazil*, edited by Dauril Alden. Berkeley: 1973, pp. 107–144.

Miller, Perry. *Errand Into The Wilderness*. [1956] New York: Harper Torchbooks, 1964.

Miller, Perry. *Nature's Nation*. Cambridge, Mass.: Belknap Press, 1967.

Mintz, Sidney W., and Wolf, Eric R. "An Analysis of Ritual Co-Parenthood (compadrazgo)." *Southwest Journal of Anthropology* **6** (1950): 341–368.

Mörner, Magnus, Ed. *The Expulsion of the Jesuits from Latin America*. New York: Knopf, 1965.

Mörner, Magnus. *The Political and Economic Activities of the Jesuits in the La Plata Region: The Hapsburg Era*. Stockholm: Victor Pettersons, 1953.

Mörner, Magnus. *Race Mixture in the History of Latin America*. Boston: Little, Brown & Co., 1967.

Mörner, Magnus. "Spanish Migration to the New World Prior to 1800: A Report on the State of Research." In *First Images of America: The Impact of the New World on the Old*, edited by Fredi Chiappelli, vol. 2. 2 vols. Berkeley: University of California Press, 1976, pp. 737–783.

Montenegro de Sousa Miguel, Carlos Frederico. "Escravatura." In *Dicionário de história de Portugal*, edited by Joel Serrão. 6 vols. Lisbon: Initiativas Editoriais, 1975.

Moore, John Preston. *The Cabildo in Peru Under the Hapsburgs*. Durham: Duke University Press, 1954.

Morais, Francisco. "Estudantes na Universidade de Coimbra nacidos no Brasil. *Brasilia, Revista do Instituto de Estudos Brasileiros da Faculdade de Letras de Coimbra.* [Supplement to vol. 4]. Coimbra: Faculdade de Letras, 1949.

Morgan, Edmund S. *The Puritan Dilemma: The Study of John Winthrop.* Boston: Little, Brown & Co., 1958.

Morgan, Edmund S. *American Slavery American Freedom: The Ordeal of Colonial Virginia.* New York: Norton, 1975.

Morgan, Edmund S., and Morgan, Helen M. *The Stamp Act Crisis Prologue to Revolution.* Chapel Hill: University of North Carolina Press, 1953.

Morse, Richard M., Ed. *The Banderantes: The Historical Role of the Brazilian Pathfinders.* New York: Knopf, 1965.

Morse, Richard M. "Some Themes in Brazilian History." *South Atlantic Quarterly* 61 (1962): 159–182.

Morse, Richard M. "Brazil's Urban Development: Colony and Empire." In *From Colony to Nation: Essays on the Independence of Brazil,* edited by A. J. R. Russell-Wood. Baltimore: Johns Hopkins University Press, 1975, pp. 155–184.

Morton, F. W. O. "The Military and Society in Bahia, 1800–1821." *Journal of Latin American Studies* 7 (1975): 249–269.

Mosk, Sanford. "Latin America and the World Economy, 1850–1914." *Inter-American Economic Affairs* 11 (1948): 53–82.

Mun, Thomas. *England's Treasure by Forraign Trade.* [1664] London: Basil Blackwell, 1933.

Neme, Mário. "A Bahia e o atlântico." *Anais do Museo Paulista* 17 (1963): 133–349.

Nettels, Curtis P. "British Mercantilism and the Economic Development of the Thirteen Colonies." *Journal of Economic History* 12 (1952): 105–114.

Nunes Dias, Manuel. *Fomento e mercantilismo: A Companhia Geral do Grão Pará e Maranhão (1755–1778).* 2 vols. Belém: Universidade Federal do Pará, 1970.

Oliveira, Dom Oscar de. *Os dízimos eclesiasticos do Brazil nos periodos da colônia e do império.* [1940] Belo Horizonte: Universidade de Minas Gerais, 1964.

Oliveira Lima, Manuel de. *Dom João VI no Brasil.* 2 vols. Rio de Janeiro. 1908.

Oliveria Marques, A. H. de. *History of Portugal.* 2 vols. New York: Columbia University Press, 1972.

Ostrander, Gilman M. "The Colonial Molasses Trade." *Agricultural History* 30 (1956): 77–84.

Ostrander, Gilman M. "The Making of the Triangular Trade Myth." *William and Mary Quarterly* 30 (1973): 634–644.

Pang, Eul-Soo, and Seckinger, Ron L. "The Mandarins of Imperial Brazil." *Comparative Studies in Society and History* 14 (1972): 215–244.

Pantaleão, Olga. *A penetração comercial de Inglaterra na America Espanhola de 1713 a 1783.* São Paulo: Universidade de São Paulo, 1946.

Pantaleão, Olga. "Aspectos do comércio dos dominios portuguêses no periodo de 1808 a 1821." *Revista de História,* no. 41 (1960): 91–104.

Pantaleão, Olga. "A presença inglesa." In *O Brasil monárquico,* História geral da civilização brasileira, vol. 2 (1), 2nd ed., edited by Sérgio Buarque de Holanda, São Paulo: Difusão Européia, 1965, pp. 64–99.

Pares, Richard. *War and Trade in the West Indies 1739–1763.* Oxford: Clarendon Press, 1936.

Parry, John H. *The Sale of Public Offices in the Spanish Indies Under the Hapsburgs.* Berkeley: University of California Press, 1953. (Ibero-American 37)

Parry, John H. "The Development of the American Communities: Latin America." In *The Old Regime 1713–63,* New Cambridge Modern History, vol. 7, edited by J. O. Lindsay. Cambridge, Eng.: At the University Press, 1957, pp. 487–499.

Payne, Stanley G. A History of Spain and Portugal. 2 vols. Madison: University of Wisconsin Press, 1973.

Peckham, Howard, and Gilson, Charles, Eds. Attitudes of Colonial Powers Toward the American Indian. Salt Lake City: University of Utah Press, 1969.

Pedreira, Pedro Tomás. "Os quilombos baianos." Revista Brasileira de Geografia 24 (1962): 79–93.

Phelan, John Leddy. The Kingdom of Quito in the Seventeenth Century. Bureaucratic Politics in the Spanish Empire. Madison: University of Wisconsin Press, 1967.

Phelan, John Leddy. The Millennial Kingdom of the Franciscans in the New World. 2nd ed., rev. Berkeley: University of California Press, 1970.

Phelan, John Leddy. The People and the King: The Comunero Revolution in Colombia, 1781. Madison: University of Wisconsin Press, 1978.

Pierson, Peter. Philip II of Spain. London: Thames and Hudson, 1975.

Pike, Ruth. "The Genoese in Seville and the Opening of the New World." Journal of Economic History 22 (1962): 348–378.

Plumb, John H. The Origins of Political Stability: England 1675–1725. Boston: Houghton Mifflin, 1967.

Pocock, J. G. A. "Machiavelli, Harrington, and English Political Ideologies in the Eighteenth Century." William and Mary Quarterly 22 (1965): 549–583.

Pole, Jack R. Political Representation in England and the Origins of the American Republic. London: Macmillan, 1966.

Poppino, Rollie E. "Cattle Industry in Colonial Brazil: Beginnings of the Industry, 1500–1654." Mid-America 31 (1949): 219–247.

Prado, Caio, Jr. The Colonial Background of Modern Brazil. Translated by Suzette Macedo. Berkeley: University of California Press, 1967.

Price, Jacob M. France and the Chesapeake: A History of the French Tobacco Monopoly, 1674–1791, and of Its Relationship to the British and American Tobacco Trades. 2 vols. Ann Arbor: University of Michigan Press, 1973.

Price, Jacob M. "The Rise of Glasgow in the Chesapeake Tobacco Trade, 1707–1775." William and Mary Quarterly 11 (1954): 179–199.

Price, Jacob M. "The Tobacco Adventure to Russia: Enterprise, Politics, and Diplomacy in the Quest for a Northern Market for English Colonial Tobacco, 1676–1722." Transactions of the American Philosophical Society 51 (1961): 3–120.

Price, Jacob, M. "The Economic Growth of the Chesapeake and the European Market, 1697–1775." Journal of Economic History 24 (1964): 496–511.

Price, Jacob M. "Economic Activity: The Map of Commerce, 1683–1721." In The Rise of Great Britain and Russia 1688–1715/25, New Cambridge Modern History, vol. 6, edited by J. S. Bromley. Cambridge, Eng.: At the University Press, 1970, pp. 334–374.

Price, Richard, Ed. Maroon Societies: Rebel Slave Communities in the Americas. New York: Anchor, 1973.

Priestley, Herbert Ingram. José de Gálvez, Visitor-General of New Spain (1765–1771). Berkeley: University of California Press, 1916.

Rainbolt, John C. "The Alteration in the Relationship between Leadership and Constituents in Virginia, 1660 to 1720." William and Mary Quarterly 27 (1970): 411–434.

Ramos, Donald. "Marriage and the Family in Colonial Vila Rica." Hispanic American Historical Review 55 (1975): 200–225.

Ranson, Roger L. "British Policies and Colonial Growth: Some Implications of the Burden from the Navigation Acts." Journal of Economic History 28 (1968): 427–435.

Rapp, Richard T. "The Unmaking of the Mediterranean Trade Hegemony: International Trade Rivalry and the Commercial Revolution." Journal of Economic History 35 (1975): 499–525.

Ratekin, Mervyn. "The Early Sugar Industry in Española." *Hispanic American Historical Review* 34 (1954): 1–19.

Rau, Virgínia. *Estudos de história económica*. Lisbon: Edições Ática, 1961.

Rau, Virgínia. *Estudos de história*. Lisbon: Editorial Verbo, 1968.

Rau, Virgínia. "Fortunas ultramarinos e a nobreze portuguesa no século XVII." *Revista Portuguesa de História* 8 (1959): 1–25.

Rau, Virgínia. "Feitores e feitorias, 'instumentos' do comércio internacional português no século XVI." *Broteria* 81 (1965): 458–478.

Rau, Virgínia, and Macedo, Jorge de. *O açúcar da Madeira nos fins do século XV: Problemas de produção e comércio*. Funchal: Junta-Geral do Distrito Autónomo do Funchal, 1962.

Ribero, René. "Relations of the Negro with Christianity in Portuguese America." *The Americas* 14 (1958): 454–484.

Ricard, Robert. *The Spiritual Conquest of Mexico: An Essay on the Apostolate and the Evangelizing Methods of the Mendicant Orders in New Spain: 1523–1572*. Translated by Lesley Byrd Simpson. [1933] Berkeley: University of California Press, 1966.

Ricard, Robert. "Comparison of Evangelization in Portuguese and Spanish America. *The Americas* 14 (1958): 444–453.

Rich, E. E. "Colonial Settlement and Its Labor Problem." In *The Economy of Expanding Europe in the Sixteenth and Seventeenth Centuries*, Cambridge Economic History of Europe, vol. 4, edited by E. E. Rich and C. H. Wilson. Cambridge, Eng.: At the University Press, 1967, pp. 302–373.

Rocha Pitta, Sebastião da. *História da America Portuguesa desde o anno de mil e quinhentos de seu descobrimento, até o de mil setecentos e vinte e quatro*. Lisbon, 1730.

Rodney, Walter. *A History of the Upper Guinea Coast 1545–1800*. Oxford: Clarendon Press, 1970.

Rodney, Walter. "Portuguese Attempts at Monopoly on the Upper Guinea Coast, 1580–1650." *Journal of African History* 6 (1965): 307–322.

Rodrigues, José Honório. *Brazil and Africa*. Translated by Richard A. Mazzara and Sam Hileman. Berkeley: University of California Press, 1965.

Rodríguez, Mario. "The Genesis of Economic Attitudes in the Río de la Plata." *Hispanic American Historical Review* 36 (1956): 171–189.

Rodríguez, Mario. "Dom Pedro of Braganza and Colônia do Sacramento, 1680–1705." *Hispanic American Historical Review* 38 (1958): 179–208.

Roorda, D. J. "The Ruling Classes in Holland in the Seventeenth Century." In *Britain and the Netherlands*, edited by J. S. Bromley and E. H. Kossman, vol. 2. Groningen: J. B. Wolters, 1964, pp. 109–132.

Ross, Eric B. "The Evolution of the Portuguese Peasantry." *Journal of Latin American Studies* 10 (1978): 193–218.

Rowe, John. "The Incas Under Spanish Colonial Institutions." *Hispanic American Historical Review* 37 (1957): 155–191.

Russell-Wood, A. J. R., Ed. *From Colony to Nation: Essays on the Independence of Brazil*. Baltimore: Johns Hopkins University Press, 1975.

Russell-Wood, A. J. R. *Fidalgos and Philanthropists: The Santa Casa da Misericórdia of Bahia, 1550–1755*. Berkeley: University of California Press, 1968.

Russell-Wood, A. J. R. "Class, Creed and Colour in Colonial Bahia: A Study in Prejudice." *Race* 9 (1967): 133–157.

Russell-Wood, A. J. R. "Mobilidade social na Bahia Colonial." *Revista Brasileira de Estudos Políticos*, no. 27 (1969): 175–193.

Russell-Wood, A. J. R. "Colonial Brazil." In *Neither Slave Nor Free: The Freedman of Africa*

Descent in the Slave Societies of the New World, edited by David W. Cohen and Jack P. Greene. Baltimore: Johns Hopkins University Press, 1972, pp. 84–133.

Russell-Wood, A. J. R. "Local Government in Portuguese America: A Study in Cultural Divergence." *Comparative Studies in Society and History* 16 (1974): 187–231.

Russell-Wood, A. J. R. "Black and Mulatto Brotherhoods in Colonial Brazil: A Study in Collective Behavior." *Hispanic American Historical Review* 54 (1974): 567–602.

Russell-Wood, A. J. R. "Women and Society in Colonial Brazil." *Journal of Latin American Studies* 9 (1977): 1–34.

Russell-Wood, A. J. R. "Technology and Society: The Impact of Gold Mining on the Institution of Slavery in Portuguese America. *Journal of Economic History* 37 (1977): 50–83.

Russell-Wood, A. J. R. "Iberian Expansion and the Issue of Black Slavery: Changing Portuguese Attitudes, 1440–1770." *American Historical Review* 83 (1978): 16–42.

Ryder, A. F. C. "The Re-establishment of Portuguese Factories on the Costa da Mina to the Mid-Eighteenth Century." *Journal of the Historical Society of Nigeria* 1 (1958): 157–183.

Sanders, G. Earl. "Counter-Contraband in Spanish America, Handicaps of the Governors in the Indies." *The Americas* 34 (1977): 59–80.

Schlesinger, Arthur M. *The Colonial Merchants and the American Revolution 1763–1776.* [1918] New York: Facsimile Library, 1939.

Schumpeter, Elizabeth Boody. *English Overseas Trade Statistics*. Oxford: Clarendon Press, 1960.

Schwartz, Stuart B. *Sovereignty and Society in Colonial Brazil. The High Court of Bahia and Its Judges, 1609–1751.* Berkeley: University of California Press, 1973.

Schwartz, Stuart B. "Luso-Spanish Relations in Hapsburg Brazil, 1580–1640." *The Americas* 25 (1968): 33–48.

Schwartz, Stuart B. "Cities of Empire: Mexico and Bahia in the Sixteenth Century." *Journal of Inter-American Studies* 11 (1969): 616–637.

Schwartz, Stuart B. "The Mocombo: Slave Resistance in Colonial Bahia." *Journal of Social History* 3 (1970): 313–333.

Schwartz, Stuart B. "Magistracy and Society in Colonial Brazil." *Hispanic American Historical Review* 50 (1970): pp. 715–730.

Schwartz, Stuart B. "Free Labor in a Slave Economy: *The Lavrades de Cana* of Colonial Bahia." In *Colonial Roots of Modern Brazil*, edited by Dauril Alden. Berkeley: University of California Press, 1973, pp. 147–197.

Schwartz, Stuart B. "The Manumission of Slaves in Colonial Brazil: Bahia, 1684–1745." *Hispanic American Historical Review* 54 (1974): 603–635.

Schwartz, Stuart B. "Elite Politics and the Growth of a Peasantry in Late Colonial Brazil." In *From Colony to Nation: Essays on the Independence of Brazil*, edited by A. J. R. Russell-Wood. Baltimore: Johns Hopkins University Press, 1975, pp. 133–154.

Schwartz, Stuart B. "Resistance and Accommodation in Eighteenth-Century Brazil: The Slave's View of Slavery." *Hispanic American Historical Review* 57 (1977): 69–81.

Schwartz, Stuart B. "Indian Labor and New World Plantations: European Demands and Indian Response in Northeastern Brazil." *American Historical Review* 83 (1978): 43–79.

Schwartz, Stuart B., and Barrett, Ward J. "Comparación entre dos economiás azucareras coloniales: Morelos, México y Bahía, Brasil." In *Haciendas, latifundios e plantaciones en América Latina*, edited by Enrique Florescano. México: Siglo Veintiuno, 1975, pp. 532–572.

Seiler, William H. "The Anglican Parish in Virginia." In *Seventeenth-Century America*.

Essays in Colonial History, edited by James Morton Smith. Chapel Hill: University of North Carolina Press, 1959, pp. 119–142.

Sérgio, António. *Breve interpretação da história de Portugal*. Lisbon: Sá da Costa, 1972.

Serrão, Joel. "Madeira." In *Dicionário de história de Portugal*, edited by Joel Serrão. 6 vols. Lisbon: Initiativas Editoriais, 1975.

Service, Elman R. "The *Encomienda* in Paraguay." *Hispanic American Historical Review* 31 (1951): 230–252.

Service, Elman R. "Indian-European Relations in Colonial Latin America." *American Anthropolitist* 57 (1955): 411–425.

Sharp, Frederick William. *Slavery on the Spanish Frontier: The Colombian Chocó, 1680–1810*. Norman: University of Oklahoma Press, 1976.

Shepherd, James F. "Commodity Exports from the British North American Colonies to Overseas Areas, 1768–1772: Magnitudes and Patterns of Trade." *Explorations in Economic History* 8 (1970): 5–76.

Shepherd, James F., and Walton, Gary M. *Shipping, Maritime Trade, and the Economic Development of Colonial North America*. Cambridge, Eng.: At the University Press, 1972.

Shepherd, James F., and Williamson, Samuel H. "The Coastal Trade of the British North American Colonies, 1768–1772." *Journal of Economic History* 32 (1972): 783–810.

Sheridan, Richard B. *Sugar and Slavery: An Economic History of the British West Indies 1623–1775*. Baltimore: Johns Hopkins University Press, 1973.

Sheridan, Richard B. "The Molasses Act and the Market Strategy of the British Sugar Planters." *Journal of Economic History* 17 (1957): 62–83.

Sheridan, Richard B. "The Commercial and Financial Organization of the British Slave Trade, 1750–1807." *Economic History Review* 11 (1958): 249–263.

Sheridan, Richard B. "Africa and the Caribbean in the Atlantic Slave Trade." *American Historical Review* 77 (1972): 15–35.

Sideri, Sandro. *Trade and Power: Informal Colonialism in Anglo-Portuguese Relations*. Rotterdam: Rotterdam University Press, 1970.

Silva Dias, Maria Odila. "The Establishment of the Royal Court in Brazil." In *From Colony to Nation: Essays on the Independence of Brazil*, edited by A. J. R. Russell-Wood. Baltimore: Johns Hopkins University Press, 1975, pp. 89–108.

Silva Rego, António da. *Portuguese Colonization in the Sixteenth Century: A Study of the Royal Ordinances*. Johannesburg: Witwatersrand University Press, 1959.

Silva Santisteban, Fernando. *Los obrajes en el virreinato del Peru*. Lima: Museo Nacional, 1964.

Simonsen, Roberto C. *História econômica do Brasil (1500–1820)*, 5th ed. São Paulo: Companhia Editora Nacional, 1967.

Simpson, Lesley Byrd. *The Encomienda in New Spain: The Beginnings of Spainish Mexico*. Berkeley: University of California Press, 1950.

Singlemann, Peter. "Political Structure and Social Banditry in Northeast Brazil." *Journal of Latin American Studies* 7 (1975): 59–83.

Sluiter, Engel. "Dutch Maritime Power and the Colonial Status Quo, 1585–1641." *Pacific Historical Review* 11 (1942): 29–41.

Sluiter, Engel. "Dutch–Spanish Rivalry in the Caribbean Area, 1594–1609." *Hispanic American Historical Review* 28 (1948): 165–196.

Sluiter, Engel. "Documents: Report on the State of Brazil, 1612, (Rezão do Estado do Brasil)." *Hispanic American Historical Review* 29 (1949): 518–562.

Sluiter, Engel. "Os holandeses no Brasil antes de 1621." *Revista do Instituto Arqueológico Histórico e Geográfico Pernambucano* 46 (1961): 187–207.

Smith, Abbot E. *Colonists in Bondage*. Chapel Hill: University of North Carolina Press, 1947.

Smith, David Grant. "Old Christian Merchants and the Foundation of the Brazil Company, 1649." *Hispanic American Historical Review* **54** (1974): 233–259.

Smith, David Grant. "The Mercantile Class of Portugal and Brazil in the Seventeenth Century: A Socio-Economic Study." Doctoral thesis, University of Texas at Austin, 1975.

Smith, James Morton, Ed. *Seventeenth-Century America: Essays in Colonial History*. Chapel Hill: University of North Carolina Press, 1959.

Smith, Robert S. "Sales Taxes in New Spain, 1557–1770." *Hispanic American Historical Review* **28** (1948): 2–37.

Smith, Robert S. "Indigo Production and Trade in Colonial Guatemala." *Hispanic American Historical Review* **39** (1959): 181–211.

Socolow, Susan Migden. "Economic Activities of the Porteño Merchants: The Viceregal Period." *Hispanic American Historical Review* **55** (1975): 1–24.

Soeiro, Susan A. "The Social and Economic Role of the Convent: Women and Nuns in Colonial Bahia, 1677–1800." *Hispanic American Historical Review* **54** (1974): 209–232.

Soltow, J. H. "Scottish Traders in Virginia, 1750–1775." *Economic History Review* **12** (1959): 83–98.

Steengaard, Niels. "European Shipping to Asia 1497–1700." *Scandinavian Economic History Review* **18** (1970): 1–11.

Stone, Lawrence. "Social Mobility in England, 1500–1700." *Past and Present* **33** (1966): 16–55.

Super, John C. "Querétaro Obrajes: Industry and Society in Provincial Mexico, 1600–1810." *Hispanic American Historical Review* **56** (1976): 197–216.

Swart, Koenraad W. *Sale of Offices in the Seventeenth Century*. Rotterdam: Martinus Nijhoff, 1949.

Taylor, William B. *Landlord and Peasant in Colonial Oaxaca*. Stanford: Stanford University Press, 1972.

Taylor, William B. "Landed Society in New Spain: A View from the South." *Hispanic American Historical Review* **54** (1974): 387–413.

Teixeira Coelho, José João. "Instrucção para o governo da capitania de Minas Gerais." *Revista do Instituto Histórico e Geográfico do Brasil* (3rd series) **15** (1852): 257–463.

Teixeira Vieira, Dorival. "Política financeira." In *A época colonial*, História geral da civilização brasileira, vol. 1 (2), edited by Sérgio Buarque de Holanda. São Paulo: Difusão Européia. 1960, pp. 340–351.

TePaske, John J. "The Collapse of the Spanish Empire." *Lex et Sciencia: The International Journal of Law and Science* **10** (1974): 34–46.

Thompson, I. A. A. *War and Government in Hapsburg Spain 1560–1620*. London: Athlone Press, 1976.

Tibesar, Antonine. "The Alternativa: A Study in Spanish–Creole Relations in Seventeenth-Century Peru." *The Americas* **11** (1955): 229–283.

Tilly, Charles. "Clio and Minerva." In *Theoretical Sociology*, edited by John C. McKinney and Edward A. Tiryakian. New York: Appleton-Century-Crofts, 1970, pp. 434–466.

Tilly, Charles. "Revolutions and Collective Violence." In *Macropolitical Theory*, Handbook of Political Science, vol. 3, edited by Fred I. Greenstein and Nelson Polsby. Reading, Mass.: Addison-Wesley, 1975, pp. 483–555.

Tilly, Charles. "Reflections on the History of European State-Making." In *The Formation of National States in Western Europe*, edited by Charles Tilly. Princeton: Princeton University Press, 1975, pp. 3–38.

Tilly, Charles. "Western State-Making and Theories of Political Transformation." In *The Formation of National States in Western Europe*, edited by Charles Tilly, pp. 601–638.

Toplin, Robert Brent, Ed. *Slavery and Race Relations in Latin America*. Westport, Conn.: Greenwood Press, 1974.

Van Hoboken, W. J. "The Dutch West India Company: The Political Background of its Rise and Decline." In *Britain and the Netherlands*, edited by J. S. Bromley and E. H. Kossman, vol. 1, London: Chatto & Windus, 1960, pp. 41–61.

Varnhagen, Francisco Adolfo de (Visconde de Porto Seguro). *História geral do Brasil antes da sua separação e independencia de Portugal*, 3rd ed. 5 vols. São Paulo, 1927–1936.

Verger, Pierre. *Bahia and the West Coast Trade (1549–1815)*. Ibadan: Ibadan University Press, 1964.

Verger, Pierre. *Flux et Reflux de la traite des negres entre le golfe de Benin et Bahia de Todos os Santos du dix-septième au dix-neuvième siècle*. Paris: Mouton, 1968.

Verlinden, Charles. *The Beginning of Modern Colonization*. Ithaca: Cornell University Press, 1970.

Vicens Vives, Jaime. *An Economic History of Spain*. Translated by Frances M. López-Morillas. Princeton: Princeton University Press, 1955.

Vilar, Pierre. "The Age of Don Quixote." In *Essays in European Economic History 1500–1800*, edited by Peter Earle. Oxford: Clarendon Press, 1974, pp. 100–112.

Vilela Luz, Nícia. "Inquietação revolutionaria no sul: conjuração mineira." In *A época colonial*, História geral da civilização brasileira, vol. 1 (2), edited by Sérgio Buarque de Holanda. São Paulo: Difusão Européia, 1960, pp. 394–405.

Vilhena, Luís dos Santos. *A Bahia no século XVIII (Recopilação de notícias soterpolitanas e brasilicas)*. Edited by Braz do Amaral. 3 vols. Salvador: Editora Itapuá, 1969.

Villalobos, R., Sergio. *Comercio y contrabondo en el Río de la Plata y Chile 1700–1811*. Buenos Aires: Editorial Universitaria de Buenos Aires, 1965.

Viotti da Costa, Emília. "José Bonifácio: mito e histórias." *Anais do Museu Paulista* **21** (1967): 279–350.

Viotti da Costa, Emília. "The Political Emancipation of Brazil." In *From Colony to Nation. Essays on the Independence of Brazil*, edited by A. J. R. Russell-Wood. Baltimore: Johns Hopkins University Press, 1975, pp. 43–88.

Vogt, John Leonard, Jr. "Portuguese Exploration in Brazil and the Feitoria System, 1500–1530: The First Economic Cycle of Brazilian History." Doctoral thesis, University of Virginia, 1967.

Wallerstein, Immanuel. *The Modern World System: Capitalist Agriculture and the Origins of the European World-Economy in the Sixteenth Century*. New York: Academic Press, 1974.

Walzer, Michael. *The Revolution of the Saints: A Study in the Origins of Radical Politics*. [1965] New York: Atheneum, 1971.

Walzer, Michael. "Puritanism as a Revolutionary Ideology." *History and Theory* **3** (1961): 59–90.

Whitaker, Arthur P. *Latin America and the Enlightenment*, 2nd ed. [1942] Ithaca: Cornell University Press, 1961.

White, Robert Allan. "Fiscal Policy and Royal Sovereignty in Minas Gerais: The Capitation Tax of 1735." *The Americas* **34** (1977): 207–229.

Wagley, Charles. *Amazon Town: A Study of Man in the Tropics*. [1953] New York: Oxford University Press, 1976.

Whittenburg, James P. "Planters, Merchants, and Lawyers: Social Change and the Origins of the North Carolina Regulation." *William and Mary Quarterly* **34** (1977): 215–238.

Willems, Emilio. *Latin American Culture: An Anthropological Synthesis*. New York: Harper & Row, 1975.

Willems, Emilio. "The Structure of the Brazilian Family." *Social Forces* 31 (1953): 339–345.

Willems, Emilio. "On Portuguese Family Structure." *International Journal of Comparative Sociology* 3 (1962): 65–79.

Willems, Emilio. "Social Differentiation in Colonial Brazil." *Comparative Studies in Society and History* 12 (1970): 31–49.

Willems, Emilio. "Social Change on the Latin American Frontier." In *The Frontier: Comparative Studies*, edited by David Harry Miller and James O. Steffen. Norman: University of Oklahoma Press, 1977, pp. 259–273.

Wilson, Charles H. *England's Apprenticeship 1603–1763*. London: Longman's, 1965.

Wilson, Charles H. "Cloth Production and International Competition in the Seventeenth Century." *Economic History Review* 13 (1960): 209–221.

Wilson, Charles H. "Trade, Society and the State." In *The Economy of Expanding Europe in the Sixteenth and Seventeenth Centuries*, Cambridge Economic History of Europe. vol. 4, edited by E. E. Rich and C. H. Wilson. Cambridge, Eng.: At the University Press, 1967, pp. 487–575.

Wolf, Eric R. "The Mexican Bajio in the Eighteenth Century: An Analysis of Cultural Integration." *Middle American Research Institute Publications* 17 (1955): 177–200.

Wolf, Eric R., and Hansen, Edward C. *The Human Condition in Latin America*. New York: Oxford University Press, 1972.

Wolf, Eric R. "*Caudillo* Politics: A Structural Analysis." *Comparative Studies in Society and History* 9 (1967): 168–179.

Wood, Gordon S. *The Creation of the Republic, 1775–1787*. [1969] New York: Norton Library, 1972.

Wortman, Miles. "Bourbon Reforms in Central America: 1750–1786." *The Americas* 32 (1975): 222–238.

Wortman, Miles. "Government Revenue and Economic Trends in Central America. 1787–1819." *Hispanic American Historical Review* 55 (1975): 215–286.

Index

257

Index

STUDIES IN SOCIAL DISCONTINUITY

Under the Consulting Editorship of:

CHARLES TILLY
University of Michigan

EDWARD SHORTER
University of Toronto

William A. Christian, Jr. Person and God in a Spanish Valley

Joel Samaha. Law and Order in Historical Perspective: The Case of Elizabethan Essex

John W. Cole and Eric R. Wolf. The Hidden Frontier: Ecology and Ethnicity in an Alpine Valley

Immanuel Wallerstein. The Modern World-System: Capitalist Agriculture and the Origins of the European World-Economy in the Sixteenth Century

John R. Gillis. Youth and History: Tradition and Change in European Age Relations 1770 – Present

D. E. H. Russell. Rebellion, Revolution, and Armed Force: A Comparative Study of Fifteen Countries with Special Emphasis on Cuba and South Africa

Kristian Hvidt. Flight to America: The Social Background of 300,000 Danish Emigrants

James Lang. Conquest and Commerce: Spain and England in the Americas

Stanley H. Brandes. Migration, Kinship, and Community: Tradition and Transition in a Spanish Village

Daniel Chirot. Social Change in a Peripheral Society: The Creation of a Balkan Colony

Jane Schneider and Peter Schneider. Culture and Political Economy in Western Sicily

Michael Schwartz. Radical Protest and Social Structure: The Southern Farmers' Alliance and Cotton Tenancy, 1880-1890

Ronald Demos Lee (Ed.). Population Patterns in the Past

David Levine. Family Formations in an Age of Nascent Capitalism

Dirk Hoerder. Crowd Action in Revolutionary Massachusetts, 1765-1780

66622